'*Wilding* describes the inspirational story of a pioneering rewilding experiment that is changing the way we look at Nature, the countryside and conservation. Beautifully written, it marks the moment when the task at hand can no longer be about slowing down the inexorable decline of wildlife, but to begin the job of restoration.'

Tony Juniper CBE

'Isabella Tree's riveting book captures the excitement of an immensely powerful new idea: that to save our beleaguered wildlife, we should move beyond conserving what remains – we should restore what we have lost. Fascinating in its detail and thrilling in its sense of possibilities, this is essential reading for anyone concerned with the future of the natural world in the demanding times to come.'

Michael McCarthy, author of
The Moth Snowstorm: Nature and Joy

'Charming, inspirational and thought-provoking. *Wilding* beautifully captures the magic and excitement of the Knepp rewilding project.'

Dave Goulson, author of *Bee Quest*

'A thrilling, inspiring and deeply moving story of a wildlife revolution on an ordinary English farm, *Wilding* shows us what we have lost and what we could regain if we change our relationship with the countryside.'   Patrick Barkham, author of *Badgerlands*

'Anyone with any interest in the land – from a window-box to a National Park – needs to read this book.'

Simon Barnes, author of *The Meaning of Birds*

'So often we read of the countryside in shock and so seldom to we learn of its recovery. Many talk about re-wilding, but few try it. This is a pioneering, wonderful book, blooming with humour, practicality, science and lessons learned; a story whose heart beats in the same neck of the woods as *Walden* and *A Sand County Almanac*. Read *Wilding* and restore your belief in the return of nature.'

Nicholas Crane, author of *The Making of the British Landscape*

'Courage, persistence, care, infinite attention to detail and to understanding, combined with a deeply impressive decision not to pre-ordain: these are the dazzling qualities of the great Knepp experiment. In centuries to come, it will be the great landmark, the moment when Charlie and Issy Burrell showed the world there was another way, not telling nature what to do, but daring to stand back and be amazed at the excitement, beauty and unlikeliness of what nature is and can be. *Wilding* is truly the most magnificent and inspiring book.'   Adam Nicolson, author of *The Seabird's Cry*

'I read *Wilding* at one go. It is both highly engaging and (equally important) very informative about a unique experiment in nature conservation, set in the context of the depressing decline in Britain's wildlife. Wilding the Knepp Estate is one of the most exciting wildlife conservation projects in the UK, and indeed in Europe. If we can bring back nature at this scale and pace just sixteen miles from Gatwick airport we can do it anywhere. I've seen it. It's truly wonderful, and it fills me with hope.'

Professor Sir John Lawton, President of
The Institution of Environmental Sciences,
Chair of the Royal Commission on Environmental
Pollution 2005–11 and author of the 2010 report
Making Space for Nature

'A compelling account of a brave and far-sighted venture. At a moment when the future of our countryside hangs in the balance, Isabella Tree helps us understand how we become locked in by our personal experience and perspectives. A riveting, gloriously written read which expands our imagination, and fuels our commitment to reversing the cataclysmic decline of virtually all species, other than our own.'   Helen Browning, Chief Executive, The Soil Association

'Brilliantly researched and scripted, this riveting and powerful book will revolutionise farming and nature conservation.'

Matthew Oates, National Specialist on Nature at
the National Trust and author of *In Pursuit of Butterflies*

WILDING

Also by Isabella Tree

The Bird Man:
A Biography of John Gould

Islands in the Clouds:
Travels in the Highlands of New Guinea

Sliced Iguana:
Travels in Mexico

The Living Goddess:
A Journey into the Heart of Kathmandu

ISABELLA TREE

WILDING

The return of nature to a British farm

PICADOR

First published 2018 by Picador
an imprint of Pan Macmillan
20 New Wharf Road, London N1 9RR
Associated companies throughout the world
www.panmacmillan.com

ISBN 978-1-5098-0509-9

10

A CIP catalogue record for this book is available from the British Library.

Map artwork by ML Design
Printed and bound by CPI Group (UK) Ltd, Croydon, CR0 4YY

Visit **www.picador.com** to read more about all our books
and to buy them. You will also find features, author interviews and
news of any author events, and you can sign up for e-newsletters
so that you're always first to hear about our new releases.

For Charlie
and our children,
Nancy and Ned

What would the world be, once bereft
Of wet and wildness? Let them be left,
O let them be left, wildness and wet;
Long live the weeds and the wilderness yet.

Gerard Manley Hopkins, 'Inversnaid', 1881

'You may expel Nature with a pitchfork but she will always
return'

Horace, *Epistles I*, 20 BC
(quoted by Jeeves to Wooster in
The Love that Purifies by P. G. Wodehouse, 1929)

The cowman who clears his range of wolves has not
learned to think like a mountain. Hence we have dustbowls
and rivers washing the future into the sea.

Aldo Leopold, *A Sand County Almanac*, 1949

Contents

Timeline xi

Map of the Knepp estate xix

Introduction *1*

1. Meeting a Remarkable Man under a Remarkable Tree *13*

2. At Odds with Everything *31*

3. The Serengeti Effect *43*

4. The Secret of Grazing Animals *56*

5. A World of Wood Pasture *72*

6. Wild Ponies, Pigs and Longhorn Cattle *97*

7. Creating a Mess *117*

8. Living with the Yellow Peril *137*

9. Painted Ladies and the Perfect Storm *150*

10. Purple Emperors *167*

11. Nightingales *184*

12. Turtle Doves *194*

13. Rewilding the River *209*

14. Bringing Back the Beaver *229*

15. Pasture-fed *246*

16. Rewilding the Soil *268*

17. The Value of Nature *291*

Appendix: Knepp Wildland Advisory Board 309
Sources 311
Bibliography 329
Acknowledgements 332
Index 337

Timeline

12th century William de Braose (1144–1211), lord of the Rape of Bramber, builds the motte and bailey keep, now known as Old Knepp Castle.

1206–15 King John visits Knepp on several occasions to hunt fallow deer and wild boar.

1573–1752 Knepp estate owned by the Caryll family, Sussex ironmasters.

1787 Sir Charles Raymond buys the Knepp estate and gives it to his daughter Sophia and son-in-law, William Burrell.

1809–12 Sir Charles Merrik Burrell commissions John Nash to design Knepp Castle with a park in the style of Humphry Repton.

1939–45 Knepp Castle, requisitioned by the War Office, becomes HQ of the Canadian Infantry and Armoured Divisions during the Second World War.

1941–43 Widespread clearance of scrub and ploughing of permanent pasture at Knepp, including the Repton park, as part of the Second World War's 'Dig for Victory' campaign.

1947 Clement Atlee's government passes the Agriculture Act guaranteeing fixed market prices for farm produce in the UK in perpetuity.

1973	The UK joins the EEC and converts to farming subsidies under the Common Agricultural Policy (CAP).
1987	The author's husband, Charlie Burrell, inherits Knepp Estate from his grandparents. The farm is already losing money.
1987–99	Intensification of the farm, including amalgamating dairies, improving infrastructure, and diversifying into ice-cream, yoghurt and sheep's milk, fails to deliver profits.
2000	Sale of dairy herds and farm machinery; arable put out to contract.
2001	Restoration of the Repton park, with funding from Countryside Stewardship.
2002	*February* – Introduction of fallow deer from Petworth House to the restored Repton park.
	December – Charlie sends the Department for Environment, Food and Rural Affairs (DEFRA) a 'letter of intent to establish a biodiverse wilderness area in the Low Weald of Sussex'.
2003	First visit by scientists from English Nature to consider rewilding at Knepp.
	June – Introduction of twenty Old English longhorns to the Repton park.
	June – CAP reform, based on decoupled aid, allows farmers to take land out of production while still receiving subsidies, thus allowing Knepp to come out of conventional farming.
2003–6	The Southern Block of the Knepp Estate is left fallow, beginning with the worst fields and leaving the most productive fields to last.

2003   *August* – Neighbouring farmers and landowners invited to 'A Wild Wood Day' at Knepp, in an attempt to encourage them to support and/or join the rewilding project.

November – Introduction of six Exmoor ponies to the Repton park.

2004   Countryside Stewardship funds extension of the park restoration to the 'Middle' and 'Northern Blocks'; boundary fences around the Middle and Northern Blocks erected.

July – Twenty-three old English longhorns introduced into the Northern Block.

December – Introduction of two Tamworth sows and eight piglets to the Middle Block.

2005   *July* – Duncan, an Exmoor colt, introduced to the Middle Block.

2006   *January* – 'An Holistic Management Plan for a naturalistic grazing project on the Knepp Castle Estate' drawn up for Natural England.

May – Inaugural meeting of Knepp Wildland Advisory Board.

2007   *Summer* – First turtle doves recorded at Knepp.

2008   The 1.5 mile River Adur restoration project at Knepp gets the go-ahead from the Environment Agency after eight years of consultations and feasibility studies.

February – Natural England scientists advise that Knepp is unlikely to receive backing for the foreseeable future.

June – Andrew Wood, founder of the Higher Level Stewardship agri-environment scheme, visits Knepp.

2009
Knepp receives notice of Higher Level Stewardship (HLS) funding for the whole estate (to start on 1 January 2010), so now the Southern Block, too, can be ring-fenced for free-roaming animals.

March – A 9 mile perimeter fence is built around the Southern Block.

March – First ravens nest at Knepp.

May – A mass migration of 11 million painted lady butterflies from Africa descends on Britain; at Knepp, tens of thousands are attracted by an outbreak of creeping thistle.

May – 53 longhorn cattle introduced into the Southern Block.

August – 23 Exmoor ponies introduced into the Southern Block.

September – 20 Tamworth pigs introduced into the Southern Block.

Scrapes created along 3 kilometres of River Adur tributary floodplains.

Five-year monitoring survey reveals astonishing wildlife successes, including breeding skylarks, woodlarks, jack snipe, ravens, redwings, fieldfares and lesser redpolls; thirteen out of the UK's seventeen bat species, and sixty invertebrate species of conservation importance including the rare purple emperor butterfly.

2010
February – Forty-two fallow deer introduced into the Southern Block.

July – Beaver Advisory Committee for England set up, with Charlie as Chair.

Sir John Lawton's review *Making Space for Nature* submitted to government, with recommendations for 'more, bigger, better and joined up' areas of nature in Britain.

2012   A survey by Imperial College London identifies thirty-four nightingale territories at Knepp (from none in 2002), making it one of the most significant sites in the UK for this critically endangered bird.

2013   *April* – Red deer introduced to the Middle and Southern Blocks.

State of Nature report charting the continued cataclysmic decline of British species.

400 species identified in three transects at Knepp over one recording weekend, including thirteen birds on the International Union for Conservation of Nature (IUCN) Red List and nineteen on the Amber List; and several extremely rare butterflies and plants.

Studies by Imperial College identify nineteen species of earthworm at Knepp, indicating a marked improvement in soil structure and function compared with neighbouring farms.

2014   'Knepp Wildland' campsite and safari business opens.

Summer – Eleven male turtle doves recorded; first sightings of short-eared and long-eared owls. Knepp now has all five UK species of owl.

2015   Charlie becomes Chair of Rewilding Britain.

March – Official release of beavers into the River Otter in Devon – the first reintroduction of an extinct mammal in England.

2015   *July* – Knepp is now the site of the UK's largest
                breeding population of purple emperor butterflies.

                Knepp receives People. Environment.
                Achievement. (PEA) Award for Nature.

                Knepp receives 2015 Innovative and Novel Project
                Award at the UK River Prize for the River Adur
                restoration project.

2015/2016   Dave Goulson of Sussex University records
                sixty-two species of bee and thirty species of wasp
                at Knepp, including seven bee and four wasp
                species of national conservation importance.

2017   *Summer* – Sixteen male turtle doves recorded;
                peregrine falcons nest in a Scots pine; a red-backed
                shrike sets up a territory at Knepp for several
                weeks.

                Knepp receives the Anders Wall Environment
                Award for contribution to creating a 'positive
                rural environment' in the European Union.

2018   *January* – Knepp Estate is singled out in DEFRA's
                25 Year Environment Plan as an outstanding
                example of 'landscape-scale restoration in
                recovering nature'.

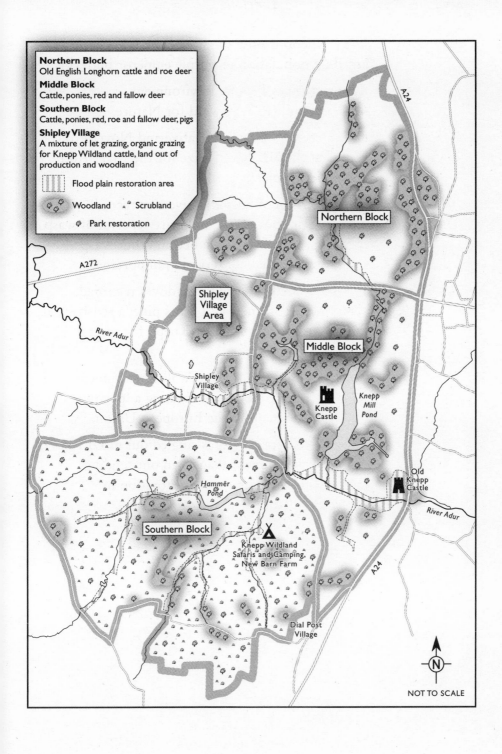

Northern Block
Old English Longhorn cattle and roe deer
Middle Block
Cattle, ponies, red and fallow deer
Southern Block
Cattle, ponies, red, roe and fallow deer, pigs
Shipley Village
A mixture of let grazing, organic grazing for Knepp Wildland cattle, land out of production and woodland

Flood plain restoration area

Woodland   Scrubland

Park restoration

Northern Block

A24

A272

Shipley Village Area

Middle Block

River Adur

Shipley Village

Knepp Castle

Knepp Mill Pond

Old Knepp Castle

Hammer Pond

River Adur

Southern Block

Knepp Wildland Safaris and Camping, New Barn Farm

A24

Dial Post Village

N

NOT TO SCALE

Introduction

'Flowers appear on the earth; the time of the singing of birds is come, and the voice of the Turtle is heard in our land.'

Song of Solomon 2:12

It's a still June day on Knepp Castle Estate in West Sussex. We can call it summer now. This is a moment we've been waiting for, not sure if we dare expect it. But there it is – from the thicket that was once a hedgerow, that unmistakable purring: soothing, inviting, softly melancholic. We tread quietly past an eruption of saplings of oak and alder, billowing with skirts of blackthorn, hawthorn, dog rose and bramble. The thrill of recognition is tinged with relief and, though neither of us tempts fate by expressing it, a hint of triumph. Our turtle doves have returned.

For my husband Charlie, their gentle burbling takes him back to the African bush, to his infancy running around on his parents' farm. This is where the doves have come from – their tiny flight muscles pumping 3,000 miles from deep in West Africa, from Mali, Niger and Senegal, across the epic landscapes of the Sahara Desert, the Atlas Mountains and the Gulf of Cadiz; over the Mediterranean, up the Iberian Peninsula, through France and across the English Channel. They mostly fly under the cover of darkness, covering between 300 and 450 miles every night at a maximum speed of 40 miles an hour, usually making landfall in England around May or early June. Like their fellow African migrant, the nightingale, they are famously timid. It is their call that tells us they are here. Like the cuckoo and the nightingale – who generally arrive here first – they have come to breed, to raise their young far from the predators and competitors of Africa and to take advantage of the long daylight feeding hours of the European summer.

For most people our age, born in the 1960s, who have grown up in the English countryside, turtle doves are the sound of summer. Their companionable crooning is lodged for ever, somewhere deep in my subconscious. But this nostalgia, I realize, is lost to generations younger than ours. In the 1960s there were an estimated 250,000 turtle doves in Britain. Today there are fewer than 5,000. At the present rate of decline, by 2050 there could be fewer than 50 pairs, and from there it would be a hair's breadth to extinction as a breeding species in Britain. Now, at Christmas, when we sing of the gifts my true love gave to me, few carollers have ever heard a turtle dove, let alone seen one. The significance of its name, derived from the lovely Latin *turtur* (nothing to do with the reptile; all to do with its seductive purring), is lost to us. The symbolism of 'turtles', their pair-bonding an allegory of marital tenderness and devotion, their mournful *turr-turr*-ing the song of love lost, the stuff of Chaucer, Shakespeare and Spenser, is vanishing into the kingdom of phoenixes and unicorns.

As its territory shrinks to the south-east corner of England, Sussex is one of the turtle's final redoubts. Even so, numbers for our county are reckoned to be at best 200 pairs. Trouble on the migration route is undoubtedly partly responsible: periodic droughts, changes in land use, the loss of roosting sites, increasing desertification and hunting in Africa – and the stupendous challenge of crossing the firing squads of the hunters of the Mediterranean. In Malta alone the slaughter claims 100,000 turtle doves every season. Around 800,000 a year are killed in Spain.

Yet these impacts, considerable though they are, are not

enough to explain the almost complete collapse of the population in Britain. In France, where hunters still shoot the birds on their return passage to Africa after the breeding season, numbers have decreased 40 per cent since 1989 – a significant loss, but nothing compared with ours, where, in recent times at least, we have opted not to shoot them. Across Europe, turtle-dove numbers have declined by a third over the past sixteen years to fewer than 6 million pairs – leading, in 2015, to a change in the bird's status on the International Union for Conservation of Nature (IUCN) Red List of Endangered Species from 'Least Concern' to 'Vulnerable', the start of a worrying downward slide.

But compared to the angle of European decline, the trajectory of the UK numbers is an almost vertical dive. The turtle dove's predicament in Britain is rooted in the almost complete transformation of our countryside – something that has come about in just fifty years. Changes in land use and, in particular, intensive farming have altered the landscape beyond anything our great-grandparents would recognize. These changes have taken place at all scales in the landscape, from the size of fields that now cover entire valleys and hills to the almost total disappearance of native flowers and grasses from farmland. Chemical fertilizers and weedkillers have eradicated common plants like fumitory and scarlet pimpernel, on whose tiny, energy-rich seeds the turtle doves feed; while the wholesale clearance of wasteland and scrub, the ploughing of wildflower meadows, and the draining and pollution of natural water courses and standing ponds has wiped out their habitat.

The same agricultural revolution has taken place on the Continent, but in Europe, it seems, there is enough wild land left – and in large enough areas – to slow the decline in turtle-dove numbers. But in lowland England what tiny fragments of nature remain, whether left by accident or by design, are like oases in a desert, disconnected from natural processes – the interactions and dynamism that drive the natural world. We lost more ancient woods – tens of thousands of them – in the forty years after the Second World War than in the previous four hundred. Between the beginning of the war and the 1990s we lost 75,000 miles of hedgerows. Up to 90 per cent of wetland has disappeared in England alone since the Industrial Revolution. 80 per cent of Britain's lowland heathland has been lost since 1800; a quarter of the acreage in the last fifty years. 97 per cent of our wildflower meadows have been lost since the war. This is a story of unremitting unification and simplification, reducing the landscape to a large-scale patchwork of ryegrass, oilseed rape and cereals, with scattered, undermanaged woods and remnant hedgerows the only remaining refuge for many species of wildflowers, insects and songbirds.

Underfunded and unprioritized, conservation measures have failed to hold ground against agricultural intensification and development. Ironically, England, which boasts one of the greatest traditions of recording its wildlife and has the largest membership of wildlife-protection organizations in Europe, has among the smallest amount of land nationally protected as nature reserves. Compared to 2.75 million hectares in France, England has only 94,400 hectares (364 square miles, less than 1 per cent of its land area) conserved for nature. Even Estonia manages over 258,000 hectares. Our tiny SSSIs (Sites of Special Scientific Interest), SACs (Special Areas of Conservation) and SPAs (Special Protection Areas designated under European legislation) are eroded, neglected and sometimes completely forgotten about. In many cases, their role is overruled by bigger priorities such as roads and building projects. All of England's ten National Parks contain large areas intensively grazed by sheep or managed as grouse moors. Unlike the American National Park model, sacrosanct areas of wilderness where nature is primary, ours are regarded primarily as 'cultural' landscapes for human recreation.

The transformation of our countryside has impacted not just on turtle doves but on birds in general. In 1966, according to the RSPB, there were 40 million more birds in the UK than there are today. Our skies have emptied. In 1970 we had 20 million pairs of what are known as 'farmland birds', such as quails, lapwings, grey partridges, corn buntings, linnets, yellowhammers, skylarks, tree sparrows and turtle doves – most of them songbirds that depend on insects for their chicks and copses or hedgerows for their nests. By 1990 we had lost half of them. By 2010 that number had halved again. It is hard to countenance figures of this magnitude. Reframing the statistics, putting them in another context, is helpful. Over those forty years, for example, our country has gained another 5 million people. So for every extra person living in the UK we have lost three pairs of what are now considered 'priority' farmland birds.

But what does this mean for us as a nation? Do we need to worry about the loss of these birds, lovely as they are? Certainly Charlie and I would be desperately sad if we or our children were never to hear a nightingale or a turtle dove on English soil again. But their loss represents something far more important than that. Familiar, conspicuous in our skies and in our landscape, birds are, in a very real sense, our canaries in the mine – casualties connected to far greater and less visible losses. Preceding them, and following in their wake, are all the other species – including the less glamorous forms of life like insects, plants, fungi, lichens, bacteria – that share their fate. As the American biologist E. O. Wilson explained just thirty years ago, life's diversity is dependent on a complex web of natural resources and inter-species relationships. In general, the more species living in an ecosystem, the higher its productivity and resilience. Such is the wonder of life. The greater the biodiversity, the greater the mass of living things an ecosystem can sustain. Reduce biodiversity, and biomass may decline exponentially; and the more vulnerable individual species collapse. In *The Song of the Dodo* (1996), David Quammen describes an ecosystem as being like a Persian carpet. Cut it into tiny squares, and you get not tiny carpets, but a lot of useless scraps of material fraying at the edges. Population crashes and extinctions are the signs of an ecosystem unravelling.

The ground-breaking 2013 *State of Nature* report, compiled

by scientists from twenty-five British wildlife organizations, reveals a bleak story for wildlife in the UK over the previous fifty years. The numbers of Britain's most endangered species have more than halved since the 1970s, with one in ten species overall threatened with extinction within our shores. The abundance of all wildlife has fallen dramatically. Insects and other invertebrates have been particularly badly hit, more than halving since 1970. Moths have declined 88 per cent, ground beetles 72 per cent and butterflies 76 per cent. Bees and other pollinating insects are in crisis. Our flora is also failing. Seed-bearing 'weed' species – upon which turtle doves and countless other birds depend – declined by 1 per cent every year during the twentieth century since the records began in the 1940s. According to the 2012 *Our Vanishing Flora* report, one plant species becomes extinct every other year in sixteen counties of the UK. And these are just the species that can be identified and monitored. Countless other insects, water plants, lichens, mosses and fungi are not even on the radar.

In 2016 a new *State of Nature* report, compiled by scientists from fifty conservation organizations, found some grounds for optimism. The numbers of certain species such as bats, including the greater horseshoe bat, have increased in recent years thanks to legal protection; the creation of new reed-beds has enabled the bittern to recover from just 11 booming males in 1997 to 156 in 2015. Some locally extinct species like the short-haired bumblebee and the large blue butterfly have been successfully reintroduced. Red kites have spread following successful introductions, and otters are making a comeback in many rivers. But the report offers a sober reminder of the longer historical context. 'Although these recoveries are certainly worth celebrating,' it says, 'we should remember that they have only brought species back to a fraction of their former level.'

Across the board, substantial losses continue. Between 2002 and 2013, more than half our species declined in numbers. This is not something we can assign conveniently to failures in the

1970s. In recent years, some of our best loved 'common' species like hedgehogs, water voles and dormice have become scarce. The government's own assessment, published in August 2016, found that a hundred and fifty of two hundred so-called 'priority' species are still falling in number across the country and we are in imminent danger of losing 10–15 per cent of our species overall.

It is tempting to assume that such declines are no different to the rest of the world. But they are different. Using the 'biodiversity intactness index' – a new system that measures the condition of a country's biodiversity – the updated 2016 *State of Nature* report discovered that the UK has lost significantly more biodiversity over the long term than the world average. Ranked twenty-ninth lowest out of 218 countries, we are among the most nature-depleted countries in the world.

Against this background of almost inconceivable loss the turtle doves' appearance at Knepp seems little short of a miracle. Our patch – 3,500 acres of former intensive arable and dairy farmland, just forty-four miles from central London – is bucking the trend. The turtle doves are here now because we have turned our land over to a pioneering rewilding experiment, the first of its kind in Britain. Their arrival has taken us and all those involved in the project completely by surprise.

We began to hear turtle doves, only ever recorded here in ones and twos, just a year or two after the project began – three in 2005, four in 2008, seven in 2013 and by 2014 we reckoned we had eleven singing males. In the summer of 2017 we counted sixteen. Occasionally, over the last couple of years, we've chanced upon a pair out in the open, sitting on telephone wires or on a dusty track, their pink breasts touched by the glow of evening, the tiny patch of zebra stripes on their necks a hint of Africa – a reminder that, just a few weeks earlier, these birds would have been flying over elephants. Their colonization of Knepp is one of the few reversals in the otherwise inexorable trend to national extinction; possibly the only optimistic sign for turtle doves on British soil.

But it's not just turtle doves that have found us. Other endangered British birds – migrants like nightingales, cuckoos, spotted flycatchers, fieldfares and hobbies, and residents like woodlarks, skylarks, lapwings, house sparrows, lesser spotted woodpeckers, yellowhammers and woodcock – have been recorded here in good numbers since the project began or are now breeding at Knepp. So too are ravens, red kites and sparrowhawks, lording it at the top of the food chain. Every season new species arrive. In 2015 the big excitement was long-eared owls and in 2016 we had our first pair of breeding peregrine falcons. Populations of common birds are rocketing, too, and occasional visitors like osprey, green sandpipers and little egrets are also on the rise.

And it's not just birds. Other rare creatures, solemnly declared 'UK Biodiversity Action Plan species' by the civil servants, are also back – Bechstein's and barbastelle bats, dormice, slow-worms, grass snakes and butterflies: purple emperor, brown hairstreak and white-letter hairstreak. The speed at which these events have happened has astonished observers, not least ourselves, particularly given the dire condition of our land before we made our first tentative steps into what we now call 'rewilding', back in 2001.

The key to Knepp's success, conservationists are beginning to realize, is its focus on 'self-willed ecological processes'. Rewilding is restoration by letting go, allowing nature to take the driving seat. In contrast, conventional conservation in Britain tends to be about targets and control, doing everything humanly possible to preserve the status quo, sometimes to maintain the overall look of a landscape or, more often, to micro-manage a particular habitat for the perceived benefit of several chosen species, or just a single, favoured one. In our nature-depleted world this strategy has played a crucial role. Without it, rare species and habitats would have simply disappeared off the face of the earth. Such nature reserves are our Noah's Arks – our natural seed banks and repositories of species. But they are also increasingly vulnerable. Biodiversity continues to decline in these costly and micro-managed oases, sometimes even threatening the very species these areas are designed to protect. Something drastic needs to happen, and happen soon, if we are to halt this decline, and perhaps even reverse it.

Knepp presents an alternative approach – a dynamic system that is self-sustaining and productive, as well as far cheaper to run. Such an approach can work in conjunction with conventional measures. It can be rolled out on land that on paper, at least, is of no conservation importance. It can add buffers to existing protected areas, as well as bridges and stepping stones between them, increasing the opportunities for species to migrate, adapt and survive in the face of climate change, habitat degradation and pollution.

Allowing natural processes to happen, and having no predetermined targets to meet, no species or numbers to dictate the plan, is a challenge to conventional thinking. It particularly unsettles scientists who like to test hypotheses, run computer models, tick boxes and fix goals. Rewilding – giving nature the space and opportunity to express itself – is largely a leap of faith. It involves surrendering all preconceptions, and simply sitting back and observing what happens. Rewilding Knepp is full of surprises, and the unexpected outcomes are changing what we thought we knew about some of our native species' behaviour and habitats – indeed it is changing the science of ecology. And it is also teaching us something about ourselves, and the hubris that has led us to our current predicament.

When we began rewilding the estate seventeen years ago we had no idea about the science or the controversies surrounding conservation. Charlie and I embarked on the project out of an amateurish love for wildlife and because we would have lost an impossible amount of money if we had continued to farm. We had no idea how influential and multi-faceted the project would become, attracting policy makers, farmers, landowners, conservation bodies and other land-management NGOs, both British and foreign. We had no idea Knepp would end up a focal point for today's most pressing problems: climate change, soil restoration, food quality and security, crop pollination, carbon sequestration, water resources and purification, flood mitigation, animal welfare and human health.

But what is happening here also seems to touch a deeper chord, something more visceral. In 2013 George Monbiot published a plea for a wilder Britain in his inspirational book *Feral*. The public response was extraordinary. He seemed to have attuned to a craving that people were feeling but hadn't yet voiced: the idea that we are missing something – some more fulfilling connection with nature in all its awe-inspiring, unfettered complexity; that we are living in a desert compared to our gloriously wild past.

Inspired by this public outpouring and desire for change, the charity Rewilding Britain was launched in 2015, with my husband Charlie as one of its trustees and then its chair. Its goals are ambitious. By 2030 it aims to have returned natural ecological processes and key species to 300,000 hectares of core land (1,158 square miles, equivalent to the size of Britain's golf courses, or roughly equivalent to a large county) and three marine areas, crucial for the restoration of our fisheries and marine wildlife. Over the next hundred years it hopes this will have extended to at least 1 million hectares, or 4.5 per cent of Great Britain's land and 30 per cent of our territorial waters, with at least one large rewilded area connecting both land and sea, descending from mountaintops to coastal waters. Its overall aim is not to rewild everywhere – prime agricultural land will naturally always be needed for food production and much land will still, of course, be required for housing and industry – but to restore parts of the British Isles to wild nature and to allow lost creatures, like the lynx and beaver, the burbot, eagle owl and Dalmatian pelican, and, in our remotest places, elk and wolf, to live here once more.

Knepp is but a small step on that road to a wilder, richer country. But it shows that rewilding can work, that it has multiple benefits for the land; that it can generate economic activity and employment; and that it can benefit both nature and us – and that all of this can happen astonishingly quickly. Perhaps most exciting of all, if it can happen here, on our depleted patch of land in the over-developed, densely populated south-east of England, it can happen anywhere – if only we have the will to give it a try.

1

Meeting a Remarkable Man under a Remarkable Tree

A single 400-year-old-oak . . . [is] a whole ecosystem of
such creatures for which ten thousand 200-year-old oaks
are no use at all.

Oliver Rackham, *Woodlands*, 2006

Ted Green came to a standstill under the canopy of the old
oak. He caressed the rippled bark with a weather-worn hand.
'You're a sight for sore eyes,' he said. As if in response a stirring
shuffled through the foliage above our heads and a smattering
of acorns thudded to the ground. Handing Charlie one end of
a 'Diameter at Breast Height' measure, Ted extended the tape
around the trunk and with a cry of delight read off 7m. Its girth
made it about 550 years old. Most likely, it had started life
during the Wars of the Roses, nearly three centuries before my
husband's family, the Burrells, had arrived at Knepp. It would
have germinated when 'Knap' was a thousand-acre deer park
owned by the Dukes of Norfolk, its acorns fodder – or
'pannage' – for wild boar and fallow deer. As a fine young tree
only a hundred years old, it would have welcomed the arrival
of the Carylls, Catholic ironmasters, owners of Knepp for over
a hundred and seventy years. In the mid-seventeenth century
it would have witnessed the Civil War, the assault on Knepp
by Parliamentary troops and counter-assaults by Royalists. It

had lived and breathed what we can only absorb from history books.

Looming over the approach to the nineteenth-century castle it has been known for as long as anyone can remember as the Knepp Oak. It would have been 350 years old when Charlie's ancestor Sir Charles Merrik Burrell, the 3rd baronet, commissioned the up-and-coming architect John Nash to build him a mansion house right next to it.

The Burrells have been associated with Sussex since the fifteenth century, first as farmers and vicars of Cuckfield, then as ironmasters in the seventeenth century. Knepp came into the Burrell family when William Burrell, a lawyer and Sussex historian, married an heiress, his second cousin, Sophia Raymond. Her father, Sir Charles Raymond, had bought Knepp in 1787, shortly after the Caryll dynasty had dissolved. Sir Charles gave the estate, then 1,600 acres, to his daughter, and the Raymond baronetcy to his son-in-law.

It was their son, Sir Charles Merrik Burrell (3rd Bt), who put down roots at Knepp. The new castle, designed by Nash in his new 'picturesque' Gothic style, would have crenellations and turrets and studded oak doors and stand on an 'elevated and beautiful' spot only 100 yards or so away from the great oak, overlooking the old 80 acre mill pond – then the largest body of water south of the River Thames.

Like all the Burrells who have lived here since, our fortunes have seemed somehow wedded to the fate of this tree. Horses and carriages, ponies and traps, steam ploughs, men heading off to two world wars, the first Bentley, Charlie's grandfather's Series One Land Rover, the first combine harvester would all have passed beneath its branches. It had witnessed marriage processions, funeral cortèges, bizarre twists of family fate. When our son was born in the autumn of 1996 – a prolific year for oak mast – we grew one of its acorns on in a jar and planted the sapling out for the future, a stone's throw from the original. We wondered how much longer the old tree could survive. Sometime in the early twentieth century it had begun to split down the middle and during the Second World War the Canadian army stationed at the castle had strapped it together with tank chains. By the late 1990s it seemed that its gigantic outstretched limbs were once again threatening to tear it apart. We were told of a man who would know what to do.

Ted stood back, assessing the bifurcating structure above us. His brow furrowed as he studied the chainsawed amputation of a lower limb. As it grows old a tree sometimes lowers its branches towards the ground, for stability, Ted explained, like an old man using a walking stick. To the modern eye this self-buttressing tendency is considered a weakness and the walking stick – the lowering branch – is generally removed. 'We have a fixed image of how a tree should look,' Ted said, 'like a child's drawing with a straight trunk and a pom-pom on top. We don't want to see anything else. We deny the tree its ability to grow old, to gain character, to be itself. It's like taking away my bus pass and giving me a facelift so I always look fifty.'

One of our longest-lived trees, the oak – so the saying goes – grows for 300 years, rests for another 300 years and spends the last 300 gracefully declining. But that mid-life period of 'standing still' is deceptive, Ted said. The tree may have reached its optimum mass but it is always shifting, balancing its weight, responding to its environment and the growth of vegetation around it – only at a pace that humans can barely register. Top-heavy and unable to find equilibrium, the Knepp Oak was struggling to hold itself together – an allegory, perhaps, of Knepp in the twentieth century.

Ted, at least, was optimistic about the tree. 'A bit of a haircut should do it – a little at a time over the next few years. If we can reduce the crown by 10 per cent – just a metre or two – that'll be enough to reduce the wind effect by around 70 per cent and prevent it wrenching itself down the middle. See, it's already beginning to drop this branch over here. In time, if you let that reach the ground, it'll have a lot more support.'

He looked thoughtfully up into the crown. 'This old soul could see another four centuries.'

For the past decade Ted Green, then in his sixties, had been custodian of the royal oaks in Windsor Great Park. One of the most distinguished tree experts in the country, and recently awarded the Royal Forestry Society's prestigious gold medal, he had, like the tree he was currently admiring, started out life on the other side of the fence. His father, captured in the war, had been killed when a US submarine torpedoed an unmarked Japanese ship carrying prisoners of war. The loss had devastated Ted, an only child, living with his mother on the borders of Silwood, Sunninghill and Windsor Great Parks in Berkshire. He turned feral, running wild in the woods and meadows. When Ted and his mother were evicted from their home they took over a hut from an abandoned military camp at Silwood. Ivy and honeysuckle wound around the inside walls and his mother slept in bed under an oilskin when it rained. A dab hand with a slingshot, Ted took to poaching rabbits and pheasants off the Crown Estates.

'I was a problem kid,' he said in his soft Berkshire burr. 'Running about on my own – that's how I made sense of the world. Nature taught me things: observation and patience. That's what saved me.'

Ted had arrived in academia sideways, thanks to a scientist he had met bird-watching. Posted as technician in plant pathology at Imperial College's new field station in Silwood Park, he was eventually given an honorary lectureship – only the second ever in the history of the college. His students, invariably, adored him. In the 1980s, after thirty-four years supporting research and teaching botany and biology, he left to become conservation consultant to the Crown Estates at Windsor. His life, it seemed, had come full circle.

As we wandered back along the drive towards the house Ted paused. 'Now those old trees,' he said, 'they're the ones we should be worrying about.' He was gazing out at the scattered oaks, once features of the nineteenth-century deer park, now stranded like lighthouses in a choppy sea of agriculture and currently presiding over a ley of shiny Italian ryegrass. It wasn't an exact science, identifying sickness in a tree, Ted said, more a matter of intuition, like sensing when a close friend is unwell. A healthy oak has the bloom of giant broccoli, with a dense, rounded crown, bursting with life. These trees, planted two centuries ago or more, sentinels of Humphry Repton's park setting for Nash's castellated mansion, were growing thin and stag-headed, losing their leafy abundance. Half the age of the Knepp Oak, they looked crumpled by comparison, like war-weary veterans. 'It's ploughing that's doing them in,' said Ted, 'and everything that comes with it.'

Like most of their landowning neighbours, the Burrells had responded with patriotic ardour to the government's cry to 'Dig for Victory' in the Second World War. Isolated, and with German U-boats torpedoing supply lines across the Atlantic, Britain's 50 million inhabitants faced starvation. As chairman of the West Sussex 'War Ag' (War Agricultural Executive Com-mittee), Charlie's great-grandfather Sir Merrik Burrell, then sixty-two, had been charged with impelling the county, most of which was under permanent pasture and made up of sub-sistence farms with small fields, horse-drawn machinery and little electricity between them, into intensive dairy and arable production. Sometimes, Sir Merrik admitted to the Royal Agri-cultural Society (of which he had recently been President), he had to 'lean quite hard' on farmers who were reluctant to put their pastures to the plough.

He had led by example, ploughing up those parts of his estate that for decades had been considered either sacrosanct or too costly and problematic to farm. Two huge tractors yoked with chains were sent into hundreds of hectares of scrub, rip-ping up gorse, hawthorn, sallow and dog rose, and levelling anthills. Easier to plough were the old water meadows, known locally as 'laggs', and the 350-acre Repton park around the house.

Timber was required for the war effort too, with carrot-and-stick incentives from the government – £60 for felling and grubbing out a mature oak, and a quota that every landowner

was required to fulfil. Sir Merrik felled the old trees along the
ancient droving road of Greenstreet and the great oaks of Big
Cockshalls, and clear-felled Jockey Copse. He spared – at least
– the oaks in the park around the castle, though to his dismay
he was forced to surrender the elm boards he was carefully
seasoning for the family's coffins.

The war utterly transformed West Sussex, like everywhere
in Britain. On Knepp's horizon, tides of wheat rolled over the
chalk grasslands of the South Downs – traditional grazing lands
since the Bronze Age, meadows of cowslips and orchids considered out of bounds even during the First World War, when
they supplied hay for military transport. Around the nearby
villages of Dial Post, Shipley and West Grinstead, woods were
felled and thousands of acres ditched and drained. At Knepp
and on neighbouring farms, farmers too old to go to war were
supported by an army of Land Girls, a national task force of
80,000 female volunteers and conscripts under the command of
Charlie's great-grandmother Trudie Denman, a pioneering
feminist. The Land Girls laboured up to a hundred hours a
week, mounting headlights onto tractors so they could plough
day and night. During the war they more than doubled the
acreage producing fodder for livestock and more than tripled
the acreage of fields under cereal.

'Dig for Victory' achieved what many had considered
impossible. In the years just before the war, Britain imported
nearly three-quarters of its food. Increased grain production
abroad – particularly in Russia and America – and cheap transport by steamship had pushed food prices to rock bottom.
Naturally enough, the acreage of arable land in Britain had
fallen to an all-time low – an effect of what we would today
refer to as 'globalization'. By the end of the war, arable land
in Britain, now subsidized by the government, had doubled to
20 million acres – from the smallest to the largest area ever in
just five years. An extra 10,000 square miles had been 'brought
under the plough', doubling Britain's output of wheat.

Whether or not Sir Merrik ever dreamed the park would

one day be restored to its original state, he must have given up hope by the time he died in 1957. After the war, Britain verged on bankruptcy. With little to export and little foreign currency to pay for imports, with much of Continental Europe starving, with dependants in her protectorates to feed, and her allies no longer coming to her aid, there was less food in Britain than during the war itself. Food rationing continued until 1954, a full nine years after VE-Day. And the result was a sea change in the nation's mentality. That memory of privation, stretching well into the 1950s, etched itself into the country's subconscious. Feeding ourselves became as much a matter of honour as it was of security. Never again, the government declared, would Britain allow herself to be threatened with starvation. Supported by subsidies, the country would remain in peak production. Fallow land came to be considered wasted land. As Charlie's aunt Penelope Greenwood, now in her eighties, describes it, 'We were all brought up to believe we would go to heaven if we made two blades of grass grow where one had grown before.' Knepp's park – indeed every conceivable inch of the estate – would remain dedicated to intensive agriculture.

Ted marched off across the ryegrass, clods of clay sticking to his walking boots, making a beeline for one of the old park oaks. We joined him on the tiny coracle of turf left unploughed directly around its trunk. 'This is the problem,' he said, leaning against the tree and staring at the tussocky ground beneath our feet. 'We never think of what's going on below ground. The tree we see is just the tip of the iceberg.'

An oak's roots spread way beyond the drip-line of the leaves, he told us, to a distance of up to two and a half times the radius of the crown. At Windsor recently, he had found roots from one of the veteran oaks extending a full fifty yards from the trunk. With oxygen available in soil only relatively close to the surface, the majority of a tree's roots are found in the top twelve inches and are therefore vulnerable to ploughing and compaction. Our dairy cows, weighing half a ton each, congregating en masse in the shade on a summer's day – a pastoral idyll, so we had thought – were doing the roots no favours, and the repeated ploughing and the traffic of heavy combines, power harrows and seed drills directly under the oaks and further into the field were constantly assailing their roots.

And the roots are just the beginning. A tree's life-support system extends further still, into a dark and invisible universe that microbiologists and mycologists are only just beginning to fathom: that of the mycorrhizae – fine, hair-like filaments of fungus that attach themselves to the roots and create a deep, intricate and vast underground network.

Mycorrhizae, from the Greek *mikas-riza* (literally 'fungus-root'), relate symbiotically to plants. The fine fungal filaments extend from the roots of plants to supply their hosts with water and essential nutrients. The plants, in return, provide the mycorrhizal fungi with carbohydrates they need for growth. At a hundredth of a millimetre in diameter – ten times finer than the finest root – these filaments, or 'hyphae', are invisible to the naked eye. A single filament may extend hundreds or thousands of times the length of one tree root. Mycorrhizal partnerships can be highly specific, Ted told us, associating only with an individual plant or species. They can also be generalist and promiscuous, creating vast community structures, known as common mycelial networks. These networks can be indefinitely huge, spanning – some believe – entire continents.

One of the most crucial processes of life on earth, mycorrhizae arose 500 million years ago, when primitive plants emerged from the oceans to experiment with terrestrial life. To colonize land, plants had to find a way of acquiring mineral nutrients, in particular scarce minerals like phosphate – an essential nutrient readily available in water but occurring in extremely low concentrations in soil. On its own, a plant's ability to extend its roots to explore for nutrients is limited. Partnerships with mycorrhizae expand that capability exponentially. 90–95 per cent of terrestrial plants in all ecosystems on every continent have mycorrhizal relationships. A single bluebell, for example, may be colonized by eleven or more species of mycorrhizal fungi, most of which have not yet been scientifically described. Without them, a bluebell, with its short, thick roots, growing in soils where phosphate is typically available at less than 1 part per 10 million, would die. The same is true for trees. One study in North America discovered over a hundred species of mycorrhizal fungi associated with a single tree. Using an arsenal of biochemicals unique to fungi, mycorrhizae can even mine rock, extracting minerals and bringing them into the plant food cycle.

Another key function of mycorrhizae is to act as an early warning system. Chemical signals transmitted by mycorrhizae from a plant under attack stimulate a defensive response in other plants in the vicinity, prompting them to raise levels of protective enzymes. By acting as a communications network – even between plants of different species – mycorrhizae alert plants and trees to the threat of pathogens, and to predation by insects and herbivores. They can even stimulate the release of chemicals from the tissues of a tree to attract predators for the particular pest assailing it. And they can alert trees to provide intensive care for ailing individuals or vulnerable offspring, supplying them with a boost of nutrients as though plugging them into an intravenous drip. As Canadian forest ecologist Suzanne Simard discovered in the late 1990s, and Peter Wohlleben describes in his remarkable book *The Hidden Life of Trees – what they feel, how they communicate* (2015), this underworld system of molecular signalling reveals a world where trees are responsive and sociable creatures, much more like us than we ever imagined.

The delicate mycorrhizae are, inevitably, destroyed by the churning blades of ploughs. They are also highly susceptible to agricultural chemicals, whether in fertilizers or pesticides. At low concentrations, phosphate is a nutrient that mycorrhizae convey to support life. When added to the land in large quantities as artificial fertilizer it becomes a pollutant, overwhelming natural biological systems and depressing the mycorrhizae's spore germination and viability. Nitrates, insecticides, herbicides and, of course, fungicides reduce mycorrhizal colonization of roots and inhibit the elongation of the hyphae, the fungal filaments. Even livestock dung, which is routinely loaded with anti-worming agents (avermectins) and, often, antibiotics, can leach into the soil and destroy mycorrhizae.

'So what we're seeing with these trees,' Ted explained, 'is most likely an effect of what's been happening to the soil. These trees have been cut off from their allies. They're stranded out there on their own.'

In the early twentieth century, a Prussian chemist, Fritz Haber, pioneered modern chemical fertilizers, by inventing a technique to draw nitrogen from the air and transform it into the plant-available nitrates that stimulate plant growth. A process that can take place only under intense heat and pressure, the manufacture of artificial nitrates requires huge inputs of fuel – generally, in today's world, gas. It can also generate the raw materials for explosives and before Haber's process became widely used in agriculture, it revolutionized the development of munitions in the Second World War.

After the war, switching manufacture from munitions to agricultural fertilizers was obvious and easy for industrialists. Tanks converted to tractors; poison gas to pesticides and herbicides. In the United States, where, far from the action in Europe, ten large-scale bomb-making factories remained unscathed after the war, nitrate production sky-rocketed, making the States the undisputed champion of artificial fertilizer, with a vested interest in driving up arable production in Britain and Europe.

Not everyone in Britain was sure that arable was the best way to continue after the war. A group of influential scientists led by Professor Sir George Stapledon, director of the grassland research station at Drayton, Stratford-upon-Avon, had recommended a return to food production based on grass – the country's richest and most reliable resource. The dash for arable crops in the early years of the war had been severely damaging to soil fertility and, in the closing years, the War Agricultural

Executive Committee had urged farmers to rotate their arable crops with leguminous nitrogen-fixating crops, such as clover, sainfoin and lucerne, and short-term pastures for livestock to allow the soil to recover. In Stapledon's view, this rotational system not only maintained soil fertility, it kept farmers self-sufficient by avoiding the need for chemical fertilizers and imported animal feeds. With low overheads farmers had no need to borrow money and build up debt. In periods of agricultural recession, mixed farming gave farmers greater resilience and stability. It was, he advised, the ultimate tool of food security.

Other celebrated farmers, like George Henderson, author of the bestselling *The Farming Ladder* (1944), also campaigned for a return to the traditional mixed-farming system. His farm in the Cotswolds had successfully weathered the agricultural depression of the 1930s and at the outset of the war had the highest outputs per acre in Britain. The Ministry of Agriculture had used it as a showcase farm, bussing people to the Cotswolds to learn from it. Maintaining the natural fertility of the soil, Henderson was convinced, was the key. 'If all of Britain was farmed this way,' he wrote, 'our country could easily feed a population of a hundred million people.'

Henderson was adamantly against continuing farm subsidies after the war. They would be disastrous for the country in the long run, he warned, removing all incentive, instinct and self-reliance for farmers, creating a culture of dependency and giving bureaucrats control over what farmers did with their land. However the National Farmers' Union disagreed and lobbied hard to retain subsidies. In 1947 Clement Atlee's government passed the Agriculture Act – drawn up by Professor John Raeburn, the agricultural economist behind the Dig for Victory campaign – guaranteeing fixed market prices for farm produce in perpetuity.

By the time Charlie's grandparents were running the Knepp estate, subsidies were already beginning to affect the choices farmers made. By the late 1960s the rising trend was for large, specialized farms, the majority of which focused solely on arable, with grass eliminated from the rotation altogether. Without the fertility-building benefits of grass, clover and livestock, chemical fertilizers and sprays were needed to grow decent crops, and it was the generous subsidies provided by the government that made these additional costs affordable for farmers. The idea of being able to fertilize the soil artificially seemed nothing short of a miracle and, together with improvements in technical efficiency, bigger and better machinery and the development of new varieties of crops, the era of industrialized agriculture – misleadingly named the 'Green Revolution' – was firing on all cylinders.

Trees had no place in this new scheme of things. Freestanding trees in the middle of fields were now an aggravation, disrupting the trajectory of farm machinery and taking up precious yards of viable land. Many farmers, if they did not remove them altogether lopped off the lower branches so they could plough right up to the trunk, as we did. Trees, particularly old trees, began to be seen as a potential source of disease and pests – a threat to crops. In an effort to maximize efficiencies and to accommodate bigger machines with broader turning requirements, fields were enlarged. Between 1946 and 1963, hedgerows were ripped out at the rate of 3,000 miles a year. By 1972, according to a report by the Countryside Commission, the rate of destruction had increased to 10,000 miles a year. Included in these hedgerows were thousands upon thousands of trees that, down the centuries, had been allowed to grow out and above the hedgerow for fodder, fuelwood, timber and shelter, the vast majority of them oaks.

To Ted, the loss of ancient open-grown oaks from Britain is an unacknowledged catastrophe. Britain's ancient Druids worshipped in groves of oaks, and our first kings adorned themselves with coronets of oak leaves. No tree, to his mind, is more closely entwined with our culture. A symbol of strength and survival, couples would marry under its branches, carry acorns in their pockets for good luck, decorate Yule logs of oak with mistletoe and holly at Christmas. Conspicuous in the landscape, oaks magnetized key moments in history. King John held political 'parleys' under landmark trees such as the King John Oak at Woodend Park in Devon and the Parliament Oak in Nottinghamshire's Sherwood Forest, both still surviving after nearly a thousand years. In 1558 Queen Elizabeth I learnt of her succession to the throne as she sat under a great oak in the park at Hatfield House. 'Her' tree became a place of pilgrimage; its hollow bole, propped and fenced, was celebrated in Edwardian postcards. When, eventually, the old tree died, the present Queen Elizabeth planted a young oak to replace it. In 1651, after losing the Battle of Worcester, King Charles II hid from his Roundhead pursuers in an oak at Boscobel House before escaping into exile – a feat immortalized in pubs up and down the country. There can be few Britons who have not downed a pint in a Royal Oak. The day of the king's entry into London after his exile – 29 May 1660 – became a national holiday, still celebrated in some parts of the country as Oak Apple Day.

To the commoner the oak was both sustenance and livelihood: providing acorns for feeding pigs and making bread; bark for tanning leather; pollarded branches as tree fodder for livestock in winter and fuel for domestic fires; sawdust for smoking meat and fish; oak galls for making ink; and wood for charcoal and hence for smelting iron – especially here in the Weald where iron foundries abounded until the end of the sixteenth century. But the English oak, one of the hardest and most durable woods in the world, was most prized for its timber – as boards for flooring, support beams for houses and barns and most important of all, for an island nation, for ship-building.

'See that limb there,' said Ted, extending his arm to mirror an upwardly arching branch, 'split in two that makes a matching pair of timbers for the hull of a ship. And the genius of it was, you didn't have to kill the tree to do it. You could just take the limbs that suited what you needed them for.' The oak's very name in Latin, *Quercus robur*, resonates strength and until the middle of the nineteenth century shipbuilders relied almost entirely on oak, 'the wooden walls of Old England' carrying sailors around the globe, fuelling the expansion of the British Empire. The tree is saluted in the naming of eight HMS *Royal Oak* warships down the centuries, in the 'Hearts of Oak' march of the Royal Navy and even in a verse of 'Rule, Britannia'.

But beyond its historic associations, it is for biodiversity in the present day that Ted most bemoans its loss. 'You never see crowns like these in woods,' he said looking across at five or six trees, spaced generously apart, standing between us and the lake. 'Oaks need light and space.' Spreading horizontal limbs in all directions to make the most of the sun, an open-grown English oak has six times the leaf cover of woodland trees. 'That's 360 degrees of niches and cover for wildlife,' he said. It supports more life forms than any other native tree, including over 300 species and subspecies of lichens and a staggering number of invertebrate species, providing food for birds including treecreepers, nuthatches, pied flycatchers, great and lesser spotted woodpeckers and several species of tits which nest in the tree's holes and crevices, or in the spreading branches. Bats roost in old woodpecker holes, under loose bark and in the tiniest of cracks. Its acorns – millions over a lifetime – feed badgers and deer in the run-up to winter, as well as jays, rooks, wood pigeons, pheasants, ducks, squirrels and mice, which, in turn, attract birds of prey such as owls, kestrels, buzzards and sparrowhawks, which may also nest in oaks. The soft leaves – 700,000 produced by a mature oak every year – break down easily in autumn, forming a rich leaf mould on the ground – habitat for scores of fungi including many colourful milkcaps, boletes, brittlegills and truffles.

But it is when it begins to retract and hollow with age that the oak really comes into its own as an ecosystem. As the heartwood rots down, the slow release of nutrients gives the trunk a new lease of life. The droppings of bats and birds roosting inside the hollow tree provide additional fertilizer. Bat guano, indeed, contains levels of phosphate and nitrogen as high as the guano of seabirds. Fallen branches supply yet more nutrients to the roots.

Key to this recycling process are yet more fungi, this time visible and above ground – such as the edible and appropriately named chicken-of-the-woods and beefsteak fungus. Fungi, often maligned as the harbingers of death for trees, are more often decomposers of deadwood than they are parasites, explained Ted. Rather than causing a tree to die, they rid it of the useless burden of dead tissues, breaking them down and creating another reservoir of plant nutrients accessible to the roots. In the process they convert the tree into a hollow cylinder, creating a stronger, lighter structure that can withstand hurricane-force winds – as testified by the ancient hollow oaks in Windsor Great Park that survived the storm of 1987, while younger, solid trees blew down. It was the strength and resilience of the hollow oak that inspired the eighteenth-century civil engineer John Smeaton to revolutionize the design of the lighthouse.

'I don't believe it!' Ted said, barely able to contain his excitement. He had led us to an oak on the edge of the lake and was pointing at a woody excrescence like a camel's foot protruding from the trunk. Black on top, dark ginger underneath, *Phellinus robustus* is one of the rarest of the bracket fungi in the whole of Europe, a species dependent on veteran oaks. 'As far as we know, there are fewer than twenty trees in the UK with this fungus. The reason it's so rare is the lack of host trees left for it to colonize.'

Ted was now like a terrier onto a scent, peering around the base of the old trees and up into their branches, searching for biological treasure. *Phellinus robustus* was soon joined by *Podoscypha multizonata*, a fungus that looks like a brain, growing in the grass at the foot of a tree, a species associated with the roots of old oaks; *Ganoderma resinaceum*, a bracket fungus that looks like American pancakes high up on a branch; and *Buglossoporus quercinus*, another bracket like a fungal tiramisu – all of them rare not just in Britain but in the whole of Europe.

'Because these fungi are associated only with veteran trees they are important indicators of biological continuity,' said Ted. 'They tell us that old oaks have been in this landscape for hundreds, if not thousands, of years. The spores will have passed down generations of ancient oaks. Once an ancient oak dies, if there are no other veteran oaks nearby, the fungus dies too.'

Ted's discoveries gave our trees a perspective extending way beyond their years. We were looking at descendants of fungi that would have fruited on oaks in the thousand-acre Norman deer park, the setting for the original Knepp castle – the twelfth-century hunting lodge, now little more than a single ruined tower. Standing on its grassy mound above the River Adur, old Knepp Castle stares across the lake at its Nash successor down a vista of a thousand yards and nigh on nine hundred years. The fortified hunting lodge of 'Cnappe' had once belonged to King John, who stayed here a number of times, hunting deer and wild boar in a park distinguished by great acorn-bearing oaks. During the first War of the Barons, King John used 'heart of oak from Cnapp' to build engine towers to protect Dover Castle from Prince Louis of France. His son Henry III visited Knepp after it was restored to its original owners, the de Braose family, and sent fifteen does from the park as a gift to the Archbishop of Canterbury. Edward II stayed here in the early fourteenth century and King Richard II sixty years later. Sometime in the late sixteenth century the thousand-acre deer park fell into disrepair and the castle was eventually destroyed by Parliamentary troops to prevent its use as a military asset by the Royalist Cavaliers during the English Civil War. In 1729 the site was robbed for hardcore to build the Horsham–Steyning road, now the A24 dual carriageway that roars alongside it. But the tower, standing sentinel on its knoll in the heart of the estate, touched by sunlight, as it seems to be on even the dullest of days, is a reminder of the royal hunting forest – a near-mythical landscape that breathed life into generations of oaks at Knepp and provided the nursery for Repton's nineteenth-century park is revival.

'So here we are, with these extraordinary trees in our land-scape, beacons of continuity, surviving against all the odds, and we barely give them a nod. Every one of these oaks would have a plaque on it if it was standing in Germany or Holland,' Ted said.

That might be because Britain, impoverished of ancient oaks as it is, still has many more than most countries in Europe. Over the centuries, as wars ebbed and flowed across the Continent, invading armies and displaced peasants plundered trees for shelter and firewood. Old, hollow oaks were the easiest to axe and easiest to burn. The nobility, champions of blood sports and hunting, had afforded some protection for oaks as source of the acorns that would see their deer and wild boar through the winter. But the Napoleonic code of inheritance rang the death knell for aristocratic estates in France and many other European countries. By the turn of the nineteenth century most traditional deer parks on the Continent had been broken up, depriving old oaks of their last redoubts.

In England, centuries of peace, primogeniture and the continuation of medieval deer parks as a source of pleasure for the nobility – the context for their stately homes – underpinned our ancient oaks' survival. A study recently conducted by the Woodland Trust identified 118 oaks in England with girths greater than 9m, making them around nine hundred years old or more – the majority of them in parkland on aristocratic estates – compared to only 97 oaks of the same age recorded in the whole of the rest of Western Europe. There are oaks at Windsor, Ted said, that quite possibly pre-date the tenth century, when the kingdom of England came into being.

That day in 1999, when Ted visited, Charlie and I began to look at the oaks we woke up to every morning with creeping unease. They were no longer stalwart companions, trees that would last out our lifetime and those of our great-grandchildren but beleaguered refugees, their skeletal limbs semaphoring distress. The implications of what Ted was saying were both profound and shocking. These oaks, which should be in their prime, were ailing, possibly fatally, and their condition was down to us. Intensive farming had been taking its toll, and not simply on the trees themselves but the very earth in which they stood. The soil of the park that, under permanent pasture five decades ago, would have been full of vegetal chatter as mycorrhizae fired off messages between trees like a chemical circuit board, was now, in all probability, as silent as the grave.

2

At Odds with Everything

Until we understand what the land is, we are at odds with
everything we touch.

Wendell Berry,
The Art of the Commonplace: Agrarian Essays, 2002

I am at two with nature

Woody Allen, *Clown Prince of American Humor*, 1976

Ted's visit to Knepp in 1999 was, in hindsight, an epiphany. It
was the beginning for us of a new way of thinking; a spark that,
ultimately, triggered a sweeping chain reaction that continues to
this day. Our decision to protect the park oaks would, within a
matter of years, begin to change everything. And as with all
such pivotal moments the timing was key. Had Ted come a
decade earlier his warnings might well have fallen on deaf ears.
We would have listened to the impassioned tree man, an expert
in his field, with interest, perhaps even regret, and unswervingly
continued as we were. We would have been too engrossed in the
unrelenting challenges of improving the farm and making a success of the business – not least, of clearing our overdraft – to
give nature a second thought. In 1999, however, all that was
about to change. By the end of the century, we were close to
hitting the buffers; our arable and dairy business was in crisis.
Faced with the uncomfortable truth that all our efforts over the

past fifteen years had come to nothing, we were desperately searching for alternatives to the current regime of intensive farming.

For over half a century Knepp had, like farms up and down the country, been speeding along a trajectory of intensification. Charlie had taken over the estate from his grandmother in 1987, her death attributed – by those who knew her well – to the twin blows of the hurricane that levelled acres of Knepp forestry and the Black Monday stock-market crash that had, for her, levelled everything else. In his early twenties, fresh out of Cirencester Agricultural College and a child of the so-called Green Revolution, Charlie was convinced he could make a go of a business that, even with heavy subsidies, had been haemorrhaging money. He had attributed the failing enterprise to his grandparents' failing energy and their reluctance to modernize. For a young man, working in partnership with them for two years had been fraught with frustration. In their weekly meetings in the Estate Office questions about efficiency and profit margins had been habitually brushed aside as bad form. The farm accounts were a gentlemanly pretence, with income presented every month excluding any of the associated costs, such as the wages of the farm manager and employees, the costs of farm machinery, tied cottages, the maintenance of farm buildings, veterinary bills and the rest. Talk had dwelled, instead, on country shows and livestock bloodlines and accessibility for the Hunt.

As soon as Charlie took over, shortly after he and I got together, he began doing what every modern farmer is supposed to do: rationalize, intensify, diversify and, if possible, spread fixed costs over a larger area. Britain, having joined the Common Market in 1974, was now wedded to European subsidies, which had neatly dovetailed with Britain's own post-war policy. After the war, France, desperate to protect her 'green gold', as de Gaulle referred to the country's farms, had persuaded the other Western European countries to subscribe to a similar system of government intervention based on industrial-scale production, guaranteed prices and protectionism.

Improvements in technical efficiency increased outputs further still – beyond what anyone had imagined – and by the 1970s Europe's agricultural supply so outstripped demand that grain and butter mountains, and milk and wine lakes accumulated in colossal grain bins and refrigerated warehouses across the Continent. By the early 1980s the Common Market butter mountain alone had reached 1 million tonnes. With a superabundance of grain the principal problem for the new wave of European cereal growers was how to prevent prices falling through the floor. Fattening beef animals on grain had been common practice for decades. Now, there was added incentive to feed animals on grain all year round. And not just beef animals. Sheep and dairy cows, too, would now be drawn into the compulsion for factory farming. The term 'zero grazing' became part of the vernacular.

Small farmers, especially those on marginal land like ours, were increasingly finding it impossible to compete with the new, big industrialized farms. By 1989 there were only 392 farms in Sussex maintaining a dairy herd – down from 1,900 in the mid-1960s – and the number of dairy cattle had halved. Only smallholders canny enough to improve their bloodlines, modernize their milking parlours and eradicate their inefficiencies could hope to survive. From just over 7,250 farms in Sussex in 1965 there were, by the late 1980s, fewer than 4,500 and these were mostly much larger and focused on arable.

By the time we took over, the five farm tenants at Knepp were ready to throw in the towel. Taking the tenant farms back in hand, amalgamating the dairies and investing in bigger and better machinery and farm buildings would, we hoped, bring us the efficiencies we needed to make the home farm profitable. Selling his grandmother's old-breed Red Poll cattle – the epitome, so it seemed to him at the time, of his grandparents' hobby-farming approach – had been a defining moment for Charlie. Following the national trend he had bought Holsteins and Friesians – modern cows bred specifically for dairy that could produce 8,500 litres of milk a year compared to a Red

Poll's 6,500 – and set about modernizing the farm infrastructure. He upgraded the three remaining dairies to process the larger animals and volumes of milk, enlarged slurry lagoons, built silage clamps and cattle yards for over-wintering, improved roads and tracks and installed centralized automatic feeding systems and computers to monitor milk production in each of the three new parlours. Two men were given the sole task of feeding the cows all day, every day of every year.

In an effort to bring escalating milk production under control, Europe had introduced milk quotas in 1984 which capped the quantity of milk each farm could sell, and we needed to buy extra quota to cover the production of an additional 1.5 million litres a year. At 16p/litre this meant a total spend of £240,000. There were other costs involved in intensifying, too. Certainly, there were economies of scale in taking tenant farms in hand, like being able to use the same farm manager and machinery. But the working capital involved in cultivating an extra 900 hectares (2,240 acres) – more seed, more sprays, more fertilizer, more diesel – was considerable. Our silage crops alone – fast-growing and with up to three harvests a year – required huge inputs of fertilizer, the price of which rose year on year with, as we now know, an ever-increasing carbon cost in fossil fuel. The regimen for wheat and barley – less targeted than it is today – was even more intensive. In addition to regular doses of artificial fertilizer, the plants had to be sprayed with two fungicides as they emerged from the ground, and a plant-growth hormone to prevent them growing too tall and the fragile, etiolated stems snapping in the wind. As they grew, they were given another cocktail of fungicides and growth hormones, followed by a third in the most rapid stage of stem growth and a final dose as the grains began to develop. Then there were the highly specialized silage mowers and harvesters we had to hire in two or three times a year for every cut of silage.

But above all, it was the Sussex clay that persistently threw a spanner in the works. The soil of the low Weald – 320 metres of heavy clay over a bedrock of limestone – is infamous. People who live here know it as bone-jarring cement in summer, and unfathomable, sticky porridge at all other times of the year. Like the Inuit who are supposed to have an entire vocabulary for snow, the old Sussex dialect has over thirty words for mud. There's clodgy for a muddy field path after heavy rain; gawm – sticky, foul-smelling mud; gubber – black mud of rotting organic matter; ike – a muddy mess; pug – sticky yellow Wealdon clay; slab – the thickest type of mud; sleech – mud or river sediment used for manure; slob or slub – thick mud; slough – a muddy hole; slurry – diluted mud, saturated with so much water that it cannot drain; smeery – wet and sticky surface mud; stoach – to trample ground to mud, like cattle; stodge – thick, puddingy mud; stug – watery mud; and swank – a bog.

Until the advent of sealed roads most traffic avoided all this mud by travelling by boat, along rivers and canals down to the coast, and around to London by sea. There were barely any east–west thoroughfares in the county until the late eighteenth century, and droving roads to markets in the capital were only viable in the height of summer. Folktales immortalize the horrors of a Sussex lane – like the traveller who, picking his way along a bank beside one, spotted a hat sitting on the muddy surface. On stretching out to pick it up, he found beneath it the head of a local man, sunk to the eyebrows. The man, yanked out, thanked the traveller and asked for help to haul out the horse he'd been riding. 'But he must be dead under all that mud,' the traveller said. 'Oh no, he's alive right enough,' the man answered. 'I could hear him munching away at something. Must be the haywain that sank along here last week.'

The ability of Sussex folk to survive in these conditions led to some extravagant theories. The famous physician Dr John Burton, travelling through Sussex in the mid-eighteenth century, wondered if the apparent long-leggedness of the oxen, swine and women in Sussex was a result of 'the difficulty of pulling the feet out of so much mud, by the strength of the ankle, that the muscles get stretched and the legs lengthened.' Even today, farmers on the Grade 3 and 4 land of the Weald, regardless of the length of their legs, look to the loamy Grade 1 plains of Chichester with undisguised envy.

Sussex's clay hampered our machinery and our ability to compete with farms on better soils. Though, astonishingly, hedgerows could be removed on British farms without permission until 1997, enlarging the fields was not an option for us. The Victorian grid of ditches and underground drains that made farming Knepp possible at all was aligned to our small fields. The cost of installing entirely new, industrial-style drainage was beyond the realms of possibility. But the existing system was still costly to maintain. Clearing all the drains and ditches – just keeping them functioning – was three months' work for one man every year.

Small fields, inevitably, restricted the size of our farm machinery. Combines, rotavators, harrows and sprayers had to be able to turn nimbly in field corners and fit through our gateways: the efficiencies of the massive prairie-style machines of East Anglia were beyond us. In wet weather the clay hampered our ability to do anything. The weeks following harvest in September were a headlong rush to get the winter crops sown, all the ditches cleared and hedges cut before the rains set in and turned the land into a no-go zone. Spring crops were rarely an option. Nine times out of ten, tractors could not get onto the land by then.

Nonetheless, we had seemed to have been making headway. From 2.5 tonnes of wheat per acre in 1987 our yields had increased to an average of 2.75 in 1990. We had come a long way from the 1940s when Sir Merrik considered it a good crop if you could throw your hat and it didn't land on the ground. Occasionally, when the sun and the wind and the rain had all done the right thing, when we had sown and sprayed and harvested at the right time, when all the components of the algorithm miraculously coalesced, a field or two would even hit the 3-tonne mark, the yield routinely achieved on the loamy soils of Chichester. In 1996, when several fields produced 3.5 tonnes, and one a stunning 4 tonnes, we thought we might have cracked it. I took photos of Charlie with our one-and-a-half-year-old daughter, jubilant in mountains of wheat safely stashed in our grain silos, hands plunged to the armpits in the fat, dusty grains. Our dairy herds were performing like a dream, consistently rated in the top 25 per cent of the British Oil & Cake Mills (BOCM) dairy herd costings, with one of our herds, run by a remarkable dairyman from Cornwall, rated top in the country. It was difficult to conceive of any dairy performing better on our type of soil.

We had diversified, too. Charlie Burrell's Castle Dairy Luxury Ice-Cream, produced in a state-of-the-art factory we installed in one of our old Sussex barns, was, by 1990, flying out of freezers throughout the south-east and in pride of place in Fortnum & Mason's, Harrods Food Halls and West End theatres, and we were poised to go national. Skimmed milk left over from the ice-cream was made into Castle Dairy low-fat yoghurt in a range of exotic flavours. We had even tried our hand at milking sheep and producing sheep's cheese and old-fashioned junket.

Quite when we realized the farm was doomed to fail is hard to pinpoint now, almost two decades on. Most years our sights were fixed so hard on improvements, always hoping the next year would bring greater returns, that failure seemed unimaginable. Increases in yields invariably instilled optimism as long as one looked at them head on without a sideways glance at the costs or the competition. Determination deceived us. The complexity of the mixed-farming business – dairy, sheep-dairy, beef and a rotation of nine different arable crops – made it difficult to identify the profitability of each enterprise month-to-month and year-to-year, throwing a smokescreen over a yawning chasm of costs – unrelenting capital investments in farm machinery and infrastructure: a new combine needed, further improvements to buildings, and compliance with endless new regulations from the Ministry of Agriculture, Fisheries and Food and from the EU, plus the rising costs of farm labour. And then there was the wildly fluctuating rate of the green pound (until 1999 the exchange rate used to calculate the value of financial support within the EU's Common Agricultural Policy), which periodically screwed up everyone's calculations.

With the ice-cream business the prognosis was more clear-cut. In 1991 the surprise invasion of the UK by Häagen-Dazs, a brand invented by the $15 billion US company Grand Met (the Darth Vader of food conglomerates), had us laying down our light sabres in surrender. With a sexy $35 million advertising campaign and an aggressive strategy of installing free Häagen-Dazs-only display freezers in thousands of outlets (a practice since made illegal), we were blown out of the galaxy along with most of the UK's ice-cream makers.

But it wasn't just Häagen-Dazs. Even if Darth Vader hadn't blasted into our orbit, ice-cream was probably never going to save us. The margins were much smaller than our advisers had predicted. Häagen-Dazs itself took over a decade to see itself out of the red.

Ultimately it was farming itself that undermined us. After fifteen years we had made a cash surplus in only two. As the global market expanded, farmers across Europe were competing with cheap cereals from Asia, Russia, Australia and the Americas. We were worried, too, about huge fluctuations in the value of milk quota, in which we were now invested to the tune of 3.2 million litres. Every time the price per litre dropped by a penny we lost a fortune, and when the price dropped, so did the value of our cows. Yet there was no let-up in the cost of maintaining the dairies and farm buildings. We were worried, too, for the long-term future of arable. The days of huge, illogical European farm subsidies – comprising a staggering 57 per cent of the total EU budget – were surely numbered. Sooner or later, one had to imagine, subsidies would be phased out and without them we, like virtually all farmers on marginal land in the UK, would be making unsustainable losses and heading towards the oblivion of bankruptcy.

In long, weary meetings with our land agents Charlie had begun considering our long-term strategy. We had become increasingly aware that we were tiptoeing around a time bomb. The fateful detonation was triggered in 1999, a few months before Ted's visit, when our farm manager suggested amalgamating two of the dairies. His plan made logical sense – it was another way of rationalizing the farm and ironing out inefficiencies – but it would cost us a cool £1 million. Our overdraft was already £1.5 million. The proposal threw our position into stark relief: we couldn't afford any more 'improvements'. And without improvements our productivity would stagnate. We were caught in a trap. The farm was unsustainable and the figures were now shouting it out.

This was the prospect we were facing when Ted came to advise us on the Knepp Oak. We were, for the first time since we had taken over the estate, open to other options. Looking at the park trees with fresh eyes suggested a solution for 350 acres around the house, at least. In 1991 the European Community, increasingly concerned about the environmental impact of agriculture across Europe, had set up an agri-environment programme. It was a somewhat perverse strategy that, for the first time, created two opposing forces of European funding administered under one roof: incentives for all-out intensive agriculture on the one hand and incentives for reversing the effects of intensive agriculture on the other. Under the European agri-environment umbrella the UK government had established the Countryside Stewardship Scheme administered by the Ministry of Agriculture, Fisheries and Food with aims 'to improve the environmental values of farmland throughout England'. They were currently appealing for park-restoration projects. The timing was spot on and our submission to restore the Repton park received funding, to commence the following spring.

The only alternative for the rest of the land – as far as we could see – was to cut our overheads, give up dairying, sell all our farm equipment and put everything to arable under contract. The only problem was that neither of the two big farming contractors in the country would take us on. In the end,

Charlie's uncle Mark Burrell, already contract farming on our northern border, came to our rescue. In much the same position as us, he could still see advantages in spreading his overheads over a larger area and agreed to take on all our arable land.

The decision to give up in-hand farming, though, was a sombre moment. On 1 February 2000 Charlie called our farm manager, John Maidment, into the office where, beneath the black and white photos of prize cows and sixty years of Royal Show certificates, he broke the news. Acutely conscious of the farm's predicament, John was, nevertheless, devastated. After all the hard work, with respectable arable yields and outstanding milk production, he found it impossible not to believe that another solution was waiting out there somewhere. The farm workers were stunned. With those patient enough to listen, or blankly disbelieving, Charlie went through the figures. They left the office grimly shaking their heads, trying to take it in. It was a black day. Eleven men lost their jobs.

Over the next six months Charlie and John tried to sustain morale long enough for the farm to be dismantled. Our three dairy herds were dispersed – forty or so cows at a time, loaded up directly after the early milking so they could make it to their destinations at other ends of the country in time to be milked that evening. For the first time in its history Knepp was without livestock.

The wet and windy weather that set in on Sussex in mid-September, causing the first of the big floods along the south coast, did not let up on Thursday 28th, the day we sold our farm machinery. It was the beginning of the bleakest autumn in the UK since records began in 1766 and the clay underfoot felt as though it was pulling the world down with it. The local farming community turned out in force – some to take advantage of knockdown prices, others, tight-lipped, wondering, perhaps, what lessons our demise might hold for them. Along the length of West Drive, the sale paraded Knepp Estate's failed investments and evaporated energies and aspirations for all to see. In place of honour stood our state-of-the-art John Deere

Hill Master combine – purchased second-hand for £80,000 in 1998 – which had, on fine days in July and August, churned through wheat, beans, peas, barley, oats, oilseed rape and linseed while Bob Lack, the driver, eight foot up in the cabin, taught himself Thai over his headphones.

Alongside it, a phalanx of Massey Ferguson and John Deere tractors; followed by the harrow, the disc harrows, the power harrows and the maize drills; the subsoilers and valiant mole plough; soil- and moisture-testing equipment; crop sprayers, fertilizer distributors and spray tanks; grain augers and driers, conveyor belts and gallons of chemicals. There was the silage and hay machinery: mowers, hay rakes, balers and forklifts; grain and silage wagons, hay trailers; the impressive Manitou fore-end loader and the silage feeder. And then the hedge-cutters, the electric fencing equipment, the stockyard gates, all the small tools from sledgehammers and post-thumpers to spades and grain shovels. Dairy equipment too cumbersome to move such as the electronic, computerized parlours, milk tanks, feed hoppers, cubicles, slurry sprinkler and rubber mats for the cows to lie down on was sold at the dairies. But the Keenan feeders, muck-spreaders, muck-trailers and scrapers, cattle crushes and sheep hurdles, hay racks, mangers and drinking troughs, the Hippo slurry pump, standby generator, farm vans, quad bike and a shepherd's hut joined the last post on West Drive, trailing in their wake all the intimate paraphernalia of animal husbandry – ear-tagging pliers and hoof-paring knives, semen flasks and artificial-insemination guns, footbaths, rubber teats and calf-feeding buckets.

Even in the rain with a tough winter ahead for farming, it was hard to shake off the funereal atmosphere. The vindication of Charlie's decision, though, was not far off. Less than a year after closing the dairies, milk quota fell from a high of 26p/litre – the price at which we had fortuitously sold – to being virtually worthless. Had we stuck it out, the value of our cows would have plummeted, too. His timing was spot on. And the sale of our quota, cows and farm equipment had cleared our overdraft. We were spared the agonies, too, of the foot-and-mouth outbreak, a crisis that erupted in February 2001 and continued until January 2002, crippling the UK meat and dairy industry, and leading to the destruction of 10 million sheep and cows at the cost to the taxpayer of £8 billion. We had escaped disaster by the skin of our teeth. We were free.

3

The Serengeti Effect

One touch of nature makes the whole world kin

William Shakespeare, *Troilus & Cressida*, c. 1603

The summer of 2002 was a revelation. Every morning we woke up cradled in undulating prairie. From our windows industrial farming had vanished. No excavated soil, no machinery, no serried ranks of arable, no fences. Returning the park to permanent pasture was more than a lifeline for the oak trees: it was proving a tonic for us. The land, released from its cycle of drudgery, seemed to be breathing a sigh of relief. And as the land relaxed, so did we. This was a different feeling from the relief of giving up in-hand farming on the rest of the estate. Handing over the farm to a contractor had lifted much of the angst and responsibility from our shoulders but apart from removing our dairy cows from the fields it hadn't changed the landscape or the way we thought about Knepp. With contract farming we were still asking the same of our land – only at a further remove. We were silent witnesses to the same Sisyphean struggles, locked in the same gritted-teeth compact with the clay. With those labours gone within the sightline of the house, there was a deeper sense of release. Something gentler, more harmonious, seemed to be stirring into life. For the first time, the park restoration showed us, we were doing something *with* the land, rather than battling against it.

Most conspicuous of all was the ambient noise: the low-level surround-sound thrumming of insects – something we hadn't even known we'd been missing. We walked knee-deep through ox-eye daisies, bird's-foot trefoil, ragged robin, knapweed, red clover, lady's bedstraw, crested dog's tail and sweet vernal grass, kicking up clouds of butterflies – common blues, meadow browns, ringlets, marbled whites, small and Essex skippers – and grasshoppers, hoverflies and all sorts of bumblebees.

To us, unattuned, as yet, to the explosive reactions of nature, it seemed this fluttering, flopping, hopping, buzzing phenomenon was coming from nowhere – like Virgil's bees from the belly of a rotting ox. But the truth was perhaps even more miraculous. Somehow, nature had found us, homing in on our tiny patch of land from unseen distances, the moment these few acres had become hospitable again.

Most insects travel with ease, often aided by the wind or passive dispersal by other birds and animals; many are opportunists, compelled by an urge to go forth and multiply even when the odds are mightily stacked against them. A marbled white or dark green fritillary butterfly, for example, can flutter determinedly over considerable distances in search of new territory. The adventure, for most, will end in starvation, predation or accidental death. But, in the remote event she does find the habitat with the particular plant she is seeking, a female can lay hundreds of eggs which will hatch into caterpillars – if the weather is favourable – in a matter of days. Others will have colonized Knepp's rejuvenated park from patches of margins closer by – from the old sward around the castle ruin or the untouched bases of hedgerows, or from the verges of the A24. The generation of invertebrates that found us that summer would have been doubly blessed by the fact that, as brand-new habitat, habitual predators in the form of bats, birds and reptiles were uncommonly scarce. The result was an insect paradise.

It had been an unsettling process, preparing the park for its new lease of life. Finding a source of grass and wildflower seeds native to our soil had proved shockingly difficult. In the whole of Sussex there are, as I write in 2016, fewer than 870 acres of wildflower meadows left. Since the 1930s, 97 per cent of the UK's wildflower meadows – 7.5 million acres – have been lost, mostly ploughed up for arable, fast-growing agricultural grass and forestry. In the lowlands the total remaining is 26,000 acres; in all of the British uplands, it's a pitiable 2,223 acres. The Weald Meadows Initiative had discovered a tiny one-acre remnant of unploughed pasture sixteen miles to the north-east of us from which it had collected seeds. This handkerchief of native flora on land belonging to Charlie's cousin had most likely survived, a clearing amongst acres of plantation, as a stand for a pheasant shoot. Like most meadows in the UK it owed its existence not to targeted conservation or enlightened altruism but to accidents of fortune. At Knepp, we had two or three tiny scraps of wildflower meadow left, including an apron of sward that had never been ploughed because it was tucked inside the early nineteenth-century arboretum known as the Pleasure Grounds, a short walk from the house. In September devil's bit scabious turns it a sea of smoky blue. But none of these remnants were diverse enough to provide us with the full spectrum of native seeds.

To give the botanical gold dust we bought from the Weald Meadow Initiative a chance to establish we had first to sterilize the soil of undesirable competition. Most of the soil in the UK, on which our native flora has evolved, is naturally poor so our land had to be returned to its original 'unimproved' state. This meant reducing the levels of nitrates and phosphates that, for decades, had been added to the soil to drive the growth of our arable crops. It felt counterintuitive, somehow, like intensifying a sickness to achieve a cure. We were aware of shifting between opposing systems of value. We went about the task like farmers but, for the first time, we were thinking like conservationists.

So, in spring 2001, having received our funding for the park, we ploughed and rotavated the soil to a fine tilth. Three weeks later, we sprayed off the resulting growth with the herbicide glyphosate; then surface-harrowed and sprayed again in mid-August. That September we sprinkled on our precious Weald Meadow seed mix. The following summer, we cut the new growth for haylage – a sort of semi-dry silage, giving the seeds a chance to fall from their stalks onto the earth again to germinate; and then second-cut the areas that grew back well, topping the rest. In the third year we repeated the cuttings again.

Nitrogen disappears rapidly from the soil, either used up by the plants themselves or through evaporation and run-off – which is why arable land growing non-nitrogen-fixating crops is always so hungry for it. Phosphates, on the other hand, can stay in the soil for twenty to thirty years. Cropping aggressively, repeatedly carting the vegetation growth off the land, is the most effective way of reducing artificial phosphates in the soil. By the third year we reckoned we had tipped the balance of the soil back in favour of our native broadleaf flowering plants and grasses. They could now compete with the residual seedbank of commercial grasses.

The drop in levels of chemical fertilizers, alone, was beneficial for the park oaks and over the next few years we would see a gradual rejuvenation of their crowns. But we were too late to save one grand old oak by the edge of the lake. Standing at the base of a slope where it was particularly susceptible to chemical run-off, it gave up the ghost even as the wildflower meadow erupted around it. Under the old regime we would have taken the chainsaw to it without a thought. Directly in the sightline of the house, it was a blot on the landscape; to a farmer's eye, a beacon of uselessness and neglect. Ted, by now a regular visitor, adviser and friend, cast it in a different light. He pointed us to eighteenth-century paintings with dead trees in the landscape. In the early Romantic period, Queen Charlotte, wife of George III, he said, had imported dead standing trees into the park at Kew to give a sense of age and continuity. Even Humphry Repton appreciated declining trees in his landscapes: 'The man of science and of taste,' he wrote, 'will . . . discover the beauties in a tree which others would condemn for its decay.'

The Victorians, Ted said, had a lot to answer for. It's from

them we get our corseted obsession with tidying up. That's
when the rot set in – or, rather, was never allowed to set in.
Dead and dying trees are part of nature's recycling process,
stimulating biodiversity, but they are now conspicuously missing from our landscapes. We have become as intolerant of
natural processes of decline and decay, Ted said, as we are of
our own ageing and dying.

We made a vow to leave the dying tree to its own devices. It
was our first lesson in sitting on our hands and leaving Nature
in the driving seat. We watched as the oak began to die, first
with discomfort, then fascination, and, ultimately, something
close to affection. A different aesthetic was beginning to dawn.
The oak took on a beauty all its own; a kind of sculptural, meta-
physical grandeur. Death became a different kind of living. As
beetles and other saproxylic (dead wood eating) invertebrates
began to colonize the tree, another universe sprang to life.
Greater spotted woodpeckers engaged in an orgy of chipping,
hacking and drilling, seeking out juicy insect larvae. For inter-
minable intervals in summer a heron would position itself on a
lower limb, stock-still, angled at the water. Shortly after a
colony of short-tailed voles took up residence amongst the
rabbit warrens in the roots, we spotted a big red dog fox circ-
ling the trunk, trying his luck. In winter his tracks trailed back
and forth to the tree from undergrowth on the other side of the
lake, leaving a single tramline through the dusting of snow on
the ice. The barn owl box nailed to the tree years ago had never
been used, but now it attracted a pair of sparrowhawks. In the
summer, a glide-past by a sparrowhawk over the castle would
set the house martins chattering and wheeling around the turrets in panic. For a while sparrowhawks zeroed in on the bird
table by the kitchen. We'd be startled from our lunch by the
sparrowhawks in search of theirs: a thudding of blue tits against
the windowpanes as the hawk swooped in and snatched her
stunned quarry from the paving stones.

In this new mindset, we left fallen branches from the other
trees in the park lying on the ground – another natural process

of fertilization for the tree. As its crown retracts, whether through age or stress, its outer limbs die back and eventually fall to the ground, providing an energy boost to the roots. Drag them away, as we used to do, and the ageing tree is deprived of an important source of nutrients. 'It's ingenious if you think about it,' Ted said. 'Imagine if I could eat my own arm to keep me going.'

Some trees, like Scots pine and the cedars of Lebanon on our lawn, would regularly lose limbs in a high wind or a heavy fall of snow – again, a mechanism for providing supplementary feed to the root system during times of stress. In nature, Ted reminded us, there is no such thing as waste. Yet we'd been interrupting this cycle, clearing away branches with the same tut-tutting conscientiousness as we picked the children's clothes up off the bedroom floor. The shedding of leaves in autumn, likewise, ensures a slow release of nutrients through the winter. 'If you have the worms and other invertebrates in the soil to pull the fallen leaves underground to mulch them, it's amazing how fast the leaves disappear,' said Ted. I thought of the old aggravations of autumn, the time with an expensive petrol leaf-blower in the garden, and vowed, from now on, to appreciate nature's blessing of free fertilizer.

The park could not be a park without grazing animals. To replicate the Repton landscape – rolling expanses of 'lawne' punctuated by groves and mature free-standing trees – we needed herbivores to keep the grass down and prevent the succession of bramble and scrub. We were persuaded in favour of fallow deer, the traditional grazers of English parkland, having been advised that the larger native reds, spectacular though they are, and resident without fuss in parks like Richmond, Woburn and Badminton, have a reputation for being aggressive in the rut and might threaten people using the footpaths that crossed our land. We could have had sheep – the park had been grazed by Jacob sheep in the 1900s – but that would have involved a return to farming. As wild animals, fallow could look after themselves.

The area given over to the restoration – 370 acres (150 hectares) – matched that of the nineteenth-century park on the old estate maps, except with kinks in the boundary ironed out to reduce the cost of the modern 6 foot 2 inch high perimeter deer fence. Where possible, we hid the fence behind existing hedgerows or groves of trees. Following Repton's principles, we ring-fenced small areas of woodland inside the park – Spring Wood, the Rookery, Merrik Wood and Charlwood – where the deer could not create a browse-line. These copses, visually solid down to the ground, would give a mosaic feel to the landscape and draw the eye down vistas and into open spaces. By the end of 2001, we had pulled up all the remaining internal fences and gates, removed miles of barbed wire, excavated new cattle grids across the drives at the park's perimeter and restored the deer-proof ha-ha around the lawn at the back of the house. After an empty two years Knepp was ready for animals again and we needed to go only fifteen miles to find them.

The fallow deer on the nearby estate of Petworth are world-famous. The bloodline goes back at least five centuries. Henry VIII is said to have hunted them here. With nine hundred fallow deer Petworth has the largest herd in Britain and their antlers – palmated, wide and flat, unlike the branching points of red deer – weigh eight or nine pounds a pair and can span nearly three feet across. The effort required to support their massive heads gives them a stately, prepossessing air – fitting poise for their aristocratic backdrop.

Fallow, with the lovely Latin name *Dama dama*, are not considered to be native to the UK like red and roe deer, though they were here in the previous interglacial, 130,000 to 115,000 years ago. Other escaped exotics – sika, muntjac and Chinese water deer – colonized the British countryside in the nineteenth and early twentieth centuries but fallow have been around for much longer. Historically, the Normans are credited with introducing them into Britain but a recent find of 10,000 animal bones in store-rooms of the Roman villa in Fishbourne on the south coast, just twenty-five miles from Knepp, shows that fallow were living in southern England, and quite possibly at other Roman sites around Britain, in the first century AD. Some of the bones belong to elderly fallow – evidence that the animals were not so much food or quarry but symbols of prestige, as they have remained in deer parks to the present day. They were kept with other exotics in enclosures known as 'vivaria', prototype safari parks – testimony, in a Roman's eyes, to man's civilizing control over nature. Sometimes they were even trained, to the delight of an audience, to assemble for feeding at the sounding of a horn.

Genetic analysis indicates that these Roman fallow – from the western Mediterranean – went extinct in Britain following the collapse of the Roman Empire. The fallow brought in by the Normans in the eleventh century came from the eastern Mediterranean. The Knepp deer park – a thousand acres of open wood pasture surrounding the old castle, emparked within a wooden pale (a fence made of cleft oak stakes set into the ground and nailed to a rail) – must have been one of the first, established at the very beginning of the Norman craze for hunting. Within the park, fallow were hunted on horseback with dogs – the sport of noblemen. Venison was a dish for feasts and the honouring of guests, and a gift beyond price. The castle itself, more hunting keep than fortress, was built by William de Braose, a powerful Norman supporter of William the Conqueror and Baron of the Rape of Bramber, one of the Norman subdivisions of the county, lying between the rapes of Arundel and Lewes. His base was a proper fortified castle down river near the coast, but even so, 'Cnappe' was well protected, raised on a mound of earth or 'motte' overlooking the Adur and surrounded by deep ditches most likely filled with water. It might well have been intended as a retreat from Bramber Castle in the event of invasion or rebellion.

The origins of the name are as diverse as its spellings – from the Saxon 'cneop' for the crown of a hill, perhaps; or 'knappen' meaning to hold fast; 'knappe' for a knave or knight; or the French word 'nape' for the skin of a stag. Tales and romantic imaginings swirl around the crumbling ruin like mist from the lake. The ghost of a white hart, symbol of royalty, signaller of quests, is said to paw the ground on the motte, retrieving secrets from the past. A medieval gold ring, unearthed in the eighteenth century, engraved with a doe lying under an oak and, inside the band, the words 'Joye sans Fyn' (Joy without End), is thought to bring untold fortune to whoever possesses it.

Certainly it is for the joy of the hunt and the riches of venison that 'Knappe' gained a reputation in the thirteenth century when King John confiscated the land from one of de Braose's descendants, taking it as his own royal forest. The king would travel on horseback, covering distances difficult to achieve on Southern Rail today. Eight days in April 1206 see him at Canterbury on Monday, Dover and Romney on Tuesday and Wednesday, Battle on Thursday, Malling on Friday, Knepp on Saturday, Arundel on Sunday and Southampton on Monday. He kept 220 greyhounds at Knepp and hunted here at least four times – in 1208, 1209, 1211 and 1215. Over one Christmas his queen, Isabella, a keen huntswoman herself, stayed eleven days in the keep. In his absence, the deer at Knepp were a source of benefaction. He wrote numerous letters to his agent at 'Knappe' instructing him to send carcasses of venison to certain nobles and the royal courts, or to entertain favoured guests: 'We send you Michael de Puning, commanding you to permit him to take all the fat deer he can without the park at Cnapp [sic]; as well as by bow as by his dogs.' And not just for deer-hunting: 'We send you Wido the huntsman and his fellows to hunt in our forest at Cnappe with our boar hounds, for that they may take daily three or four boars.'

The passion for deer parks continued throughout the thirteenth century as the aristocratic culture of hunting and game-eating intensified. By the 1300s there were over three thousand fallow-stocked deer parks in England and by the fourteenth century deer parks covered roughly 2 per cent of the English landscape. It is this Norman strain of fallow that colonized our landscape as escapees when deer parks began to fall into disrepair in the fifteenth century. Knepp itself was disem-parked sometime in the sixteenth century, the deer simply released into the open countryside. 128,000 fallow deer now live wild in the UK.

But it was the emparked deer at Petworth we had in our sights. Apart from their impressive size and lineage they are accustomed to walkers and their dogs, vehicles on the drives, a park boundary and wide-open spaces with no cover. They wander the Capability Brown landscape in full view – something we hoped they would be content to do once they found themselves in the restored Repton landscape at Knepp. Getting them here, however, was not a walk in the park. Dressed in camouflage like SAS commandos one bitter February morning and marshalled by Dave Whitby, Petworth's Head Keeper, a group of twenty of us corralled two hundred panic-stricken animals down an old avenue. Too many to tranquillize, the only way was to catch them up conscious and kicking. With the deer entangled in our nets, we leapt out to immobilize them, slipping plastic cones over their faces to calm them and trussing the thrashing bodies, legs tucked carefully under, into knotted bundles. The bucks had their antlers sawn off (since the mature antler is dead bone this process is no more painful for the ani-mals than clipping our toenails is for us) before being loaded with the others into the back of the truck.

It took the fallow the best part of spring to fully recover from the trauma of their ignominious capture but by summer they had settled down and were wandering quietly through the landscape like herds of impala in the Serengeti. Rooks and jack-daws, quick to adopt the habit of African cattle egrets, rode on their backs, pecking at parasites. During the end of June and early July our first generation of fawns were born. We would stumble across them, a day or two old, hidden in the long grass, while their mothers grazed with the herd. At this vulnerable age, until strong enough to run with the adults, they have little scent, to avoid detection by predators. Fawns are programmed to stay stock-still whenever they sense danger close by, until their mother returns to feed them. It can be hours between visits. We began to walk carefully in fear of stepping on one. Their caramel coats are perfectly camouflaged in the summer grass. Often the first thing you see is a pair of dark, unblinking eyes.

The deer were far less timid at night and soon we were opening the front door to find a group of forty or more fallow milling around on the grass circle in front of the stone Dog of Alcibiades, the oblivious castle guardian. Twenty feet away from us, the fallow barely looked up from their grazing. Fifteen years on, it's still a wonder to stand in the dark on a still night, listening to their gentle, mewing reassurances and the soft sound of munching.

Within a year the fallow could recognize us and all the regular local walkers with trustworthy dogs, and their daytime flight distance reduced to around twenty-five yards for the bucks and seventy for the does in summer. As soon as they spotted an unfamiliar dog, however, they would bound away, bouncing on four legs – 'pronking' – in a defiant show of strength and agility.

Our powers of recognition were improving, too, as we familiarized ourselves with the four distinctive colourings: 'common' – the classic chestnut coat with white mottles pronounced in summer but darker and less spotted in winter; 'menil' – with very distinct spots continuing throughout the winter coat; 'melanistic' – very dark, almost black, with no spots; and 'leucistic', the rarest – white with no markings, leaving just the dark eyes and nose.

While the summer herds lulled us with visions of the African veldt, autumn brought drama. In October our first rut began and the mists wafting up from the lake were laced with the stench of testosterone. Deep, groaning belches – primordial and unnerving – rolled around us in the damp air, the gruff eructations pumped out day and night a surer sign to the does of a buck's physical fitness than even the size of his body or antlers.

In the Pleasure Grounds, clumps of hair and branches shredded by thrashing antlers lay scattered amongst the rotting leaves. Walking through the woods, a pheromonal whiff would suddenly kick into the nasal passages – like opening the door onto a locker room after a 1st XV rugby match, Charlie recalled. These were territorial markers where the bucks had been rubbing their facial scent glands on the trees. With seven major external scent glands – in the forehead, under the eyes, in the nose, in the feet, inside the foreskin and inside and outside the hind legs – deer are like cervine skunks, communicating with individuals from their own and other species through the raw complexities of smell. In the rut these pheromonal emissions reach peak intensity with even their salivary glands emitting a pungent stench.

As the days began to shorten, the bucks braced themselves for battle, posturing and strutting shoulder to shoulder in pairs, in a formulaic choreography known as 'parallel walking'. Sizing each other up, they walked stiffly side by side, then, in a flash, turned and clashed together, locking antlers and wrestling, muscles straining, for minutes, until one of them cantered off, tired or intimidated.

The biggest bucks staked out a lekking site on the far side of the Pleasure Grounds, a site they still use. Pawing up the earth with their hooves, drenching themselves and the ground in urine, this is their gladiatorial arena, the battleground for possession of females; a case, sometimes, of live or die. With their blackened, urine-stained bellies, they roar like primeval beasts, stinking to the heavens, crazy with aggression and lust. These are different animals to the ones we have known all summer, the old boys grazing placidly on their own, the young bloods hanging out in a gang, all lads together. There is an edge to life – the call of sex, the desperate drive to perpetuate the genes. Every buck for himself. The does milling under the oak trees focus wisely on the business of loading up calories in preparation for winter. The bucks, on the other hand, will enter winter half-starved and exhausted. The weakest will die. Nature's culling of unnecessary mouths.

At first, before we grew accustomed to this cycle of life, it was disturbing to see the bucks at the end of the rut, great beasts brought to their knees, some so weary they had to rest their antlers lopsided on the ground, others hobbling like drunks after a backstreet brawl. The resilient revive, of course, but from time to time through the winter we would stumble on a buck that had obviously succumbed, its eyes already pecked out by the crows and magpies though its body was scarcely cold; robins jabbing away at holes in its hide to get at the layer of fat.

The addition of the fallow to the park had set something alight. We were returning to an older landscape, something that felt more alive. The land was in recovery. There was the Repton park of the nineteenth century, of course, once grazed by Jacob sheep and Red Poll cattle; but even more exciting, perhaps, were the echoes of medieval Cnappe – a vaguer, mistier time of kings and keeps, dykes and pale fences; with herds of fallow and wild boar for the chase, coursers and stalking horses, scenthounds and gazehounds, fewmets and spoor, harriers and hunting horns, bows and lances; a link to something wilder, more instinctive and visceral, to a time when nature was richer, deeper, all-enveloping. And perhaps deeper, still, to the parks of the Romans – to a vision of Arcadia where wild animals installed within the palings mimicked the untamed wilderness beyond the borders of civilization.

The deer park had launched us into the living landscapes of the past, allowing us to cut the Gordian knot of twentieth-century agriculture. But this was just the beginning. A visit to Holland was about to open up our horizons even further. We were poised on the threshold of a new way of thinking about our land and the animals that had governed it before human agriculture even appeared on the scene. It was an experience that would revolutionize our decisions about what to do with the rest of the land at Knepp.

4

The Secret of Grazing Animals

One swallow does not make a summer, but one skein of
geese, cleaving the murk of March thaw, is the Spring!

Aldo Leopold, *A Sand County Almanac*, 1948

Frans Vera's book *Forest History and Grazing Ecology* was
translated into English from the original Dutch in 2000, the year
we stopped in-hand farming. It sent ecologists and environmentalists all over Europe, but perhaps especially Britain, into a
spin. The reverberations washed over us, too – even where we
were standing, almost accidentally, with our toes in the water of
conservation. Ted Green and his colleague Jill Butler of the
Woodland Trust were brimming over with excitement. They
urged us to go and visit Vera's project, the Oostvaardersplassen
in the Netherlands. His theories, they said, blew open the possibilities of grazing animals in the landscape. What was
happening there could change the way we looked at the park at
Knepp. It could change the way we looked at nature.

And so we found ourselves standing with the tall, earnest,
grey-bearded Dutch ecologist one brisk May day, half an hour's
drive from Amsterdam, in the middle of one of the most
extraordinary and controversial nature reserves in the world.
The Oostvaardersplassen covers 23 square miles (6,000 hectares). It is part of the polder known as South Flevoland – 166
square miles (43,000 hectares) of land reclaimed from the IJssel,
a huge freshwater lake that had once been part of the Zuiderzee,

the Dutch bay that was reclaimed over the course of the twentieth century. The scene in front of us was almost incomprehensible: the flat, grassy landscape, as tightly cropped as Kenya's Maasai Mara, was populated by meandering herds of grazing animals: stocky, primeval-looking Konik ponies the height of a zebra with black legs and faces and mouse-grey coats, foals at foot; dark-coated Heck cattle with the sharp, curving horns of oxen; great gatherings of red deer. Through the binoculars we could see, on a raised mound, a knot of furry red fox cubs scrabbling over each other in excitement as their parent, brazen as a jackal, returned to the den with a goose in its jaws. As we approached a strip of open water, greylag geese tumbled down the banks with their young like a mini-crossing of wildebeest. Thirty thousand greylags – almost half the entire population of north-west Europe – now moult here every year. For sheer biomass Charlie and I had seen nothing like it this side of Botswana's Okavango Delta.

It was hard to imagine that, a few decades ago, this animated land was all under water. In 1989, only twenty-one years after being reclaimed, it was designated a Ramsar site, a wetland of international importance for nature. The biting wind carried with it the competitive cacophony of birds. From the reeds, the virtually subsonic 'boom' of bitterns – like a child blowing into a milk bottle – played the bass refrain in a symphonic chatter of reed warblers, penduline tits, bearded tits and the familiar *brekekekex-koax-koax* of marsh frogs. Lapwings displaying over the pools furled and unfurled like black and white handkerchiefs with piercing 'pee-wits'. Spoonbills wading in the shallows, head plumes ruffled by the wind, waggled their spoons back and forth through the water. Grey herons cast a steely eye from the banks. Great white egrets and little egrets, breeding here after an absence from the Netherlands of almost a century, lumbered into the air. High above us, beyond the trilling skylarks, three white-tailed sea eagles, wings like barn doors, were being chivvied by a marsh harrier. The eagles – the fourth largest eagle in the world and, until the 1980s, all but extinct in Western Europe – had built their nest, a gigantic shaggy thing like an African hamerkop's nest, in the branches of a dead willow. These habitués of ragged coasts and remote, secluded islands were, in effect, breeding below sea level in one of the most densely populated areas of Europe. Their arrival had been a surprise to all except, perhaps, Frans Vera.

'When I said, in 1980, that I was hoping to attract white-tailed eagles to the Oostvaardersplassen, everyone said I was mad,' Frans explained. 'For a start, I was told they would never nest so close to huge human populations, and never in anything but giant oaks, beech or pine – never in willows. But that was simply because no one had ever observed them to do this. There hadn't been that opportunity for them. So the white-tailed eagle has become tied in our minds to a remote montane habitat with oaks and pines. And if we want to conserve for white-tailed eagles, that's what we are told to provide.

'But this is a circular argument. We've become trapped by our own observations. We forget, in a world completely trans-formed by man, that what we're looking at is not necessarily the environment wildlife prefer, but the depleted remnant that wildlife is having to cope with: what it has is not necessarily what it wants. Species may be surviving at the very limits of their range, clinging on in conditions that don't really suit them. Open up the box, allow natural processes to develop, give spe-cies a wider scope to express themselves, and you get a very different picture. This is what the Oostvaardersplassen is about. Minimal intervention. Letting nature reveal herself. And the result is an environment we know nothing about.'

Softly spoken and meticulously reasoned, there is nonethe-less an air of impassioned determination about Frans Vera. He has a message he feels people should hear. The key to the Oost-vaardersplassen's extraordinary dynamism, he says, is grazing animals.

'We realized something important early on in the establish-ment of the reserve,' said Frans. 'That there's a fundamental process we haven't accounted for in nature, something that doesn't often get a chance to express itself when humans are in control: the influence of animals. Animals are drivers of habitat creation, the impetus behind biodiversity. Without them, you have impoverished, static, monotonous habitats with declining species. It's the reason so many of our efforts at conservation are failing.'

The harbinger of this insight was a complete surprise. 'It was the greylag goose that showed us how this worked. No one imagined this bird would turn out to be a keystone species. The geese solved what we thought was an insurmountable problem.'

The South Flevoland polder had originally been designated for agriculture, explained Frans, with the wettest, low-lying area – now the Oostvaardersplassen – earmarked for industrial development. When the oil crisis and economic recession of 1973 put industrial plans on hold, nature grabbed its chance. A large shallow lake remained in the lowest part of the polder. Very quickly, marsh vegetation developed around the shallow water and an astonishing number of wetland birds, many of them rare, began descending on the area. In 1978, a biologist, Ernst Poorter, published an article about the wildlife appearing on the polder in the *Journal of the International Council for Bird Preservation* (later 'BirdLife International'). The article was picked up by Frans Vera, Fred Baerselman and other ecologists who, excited by the arrivals, began lobbying for the area to be protected. In 1986 the Oostvaardersplassen was officially designated a nature reserve.

There were challenges in managing it for nature, however. The natural progression of such shallow ponds and marsh – as we knew from our rapidly shrinking lake at Knepp – is to close over with reeds, silting up until it is colonized by willow and eventually disappears altogether. In most wetland reserves an inordinate amount of time and effort is spent preventing this happening by mowing and cutting back the reeds. But the area of reeds in the Oostvaardersplassen was simply too large to be hand-cut the traditional way and the soil's load-bearing capacity could not sustain heavy machinery.

'Without proper management we assumed this area would simply turn very quickly into woodland,' said Frans. 'There was nothing we could do but sit back and watch it happen.'

And then something remarkable occurred. Greylag geese discovered the marsh. They came in thousands from all over Europe, attracted by the scale of the area and its inaccessibility which made it the perfect sanctuary for the four to six weeks of their summer moult as they waited – sitting ducks, you might say – for their flight feathers to grow again. For the month or so they were laid up in the Oostvaardersplassen they consumed huge quantities of marsh plants and their rhizomes and, as a result, the marsh and its interconnecting ponds did not close.

'We discovered something: the grazing of the greylags was preventing the area becoming covered with trees. This was the astonishing thing: the geese were leading vegetation succession – not the other way round. But more than that, their grazing was adding to biodiversity. They were changing extensive reed beds into a more complex habitat of reeds and shallow water, and this was attracting more species than other wetland reserves in the Netherlands that were carefully managed by humans.

'So now we had another problem. We needed to make sure the greylags would continue using the marshland. We realized we needed to create grassland – their usual habitat – adjacent to the marsh; somewhere they could congregate before and after moulting to build up their fat deposits. The question was how? Could we put grazing animals into the dry areas of the polder that were nothing but reed beds and willow saplings and see if, on their own, they could create grassland? Could grazing animals prevent the succession of trees on dry land, just as the geese had done in the marsh? And if we left the grazing animals to their own devices, as we had with the geese, might they, too, generate something even more interesting and more valuable in terms of biodiversity? In effect, could we manage this land for nature not by costly human intervention, but using natural processes, with grazing animals as the drivers?'

This idea – that grazing animals could prevent spontaneous

forest succession and generate more complex and biodiverse habitats instead – was heretical. Until this point, only one form of natural process was recognized by most ecologists as a primary driving force of nature – that of vegetation succession. As any European farmer knows, if you leave a patch of land abandoned, it soon reverts to scrub and, eventually, tall trees. It is a state known as 'climax vegetation' – the destination which nature is supposedly endlessly struggling to reach. Before human impact – the prevailing theory goes – any land with the climate, soil and hydrology for trees to grow was covered with closed-canopy forest. In temperate zone Europe only the tops of mountains, the very steepest slopes and some raised bogs would have been devoid of tree cover. This notion, known in scientific circles as 'closed-canopy theory', has permeated popular culture and become the mythological baseline for our distant past. In Britain, it is said, before men began swinging stone axes at the woods, a squirrel could have run from John O'Groats to Land's End across the tops of trees. Closed-canopy woodland has become synonymous with nature, and people are seen as its destroyer: it was man who opened up the primeval forest, and man who, maintaining the landscape for agriculture and habitation ever since, prevents the trees from taking over again.

'But this theory of closed forest overlooks another force of nature altogether,' said Frans, 'one that works in opposition to vegetation succession: animal disturbance.'

The problem, he explains, is that we have forgotten about the megafauna that would have been roaming our landscape before we arrived on the scene: large herbivorous mammals like the aurochs (the wild ox), tarpan (the original wild horse of Europe), wisent (the European bison), elk (known in North America as moose), European beaver and the omnivorous wild boar. All, according to fossil bone records, re-colonized the lowlands of Central and Western Europe along with red deer and roe deer about 2,000 years after the end of the last ice age – around 12,000 years ago. Trees, on the other hand – according to the pollen records – appear only between 9,000 and 1,500 years

ago. So, oak, lime, ash, elm, field maple, beech and hornbeam –
the key species of what is claimed to have been the primordial
closed-canopy deciduous forest of Europe – arrived at least
3,000 years after the large herbivores. This is a very different
picture to the one that has rooted in our mythology. It flies in
the face of the received wisdom that closed-canopy forest is the
natural habitat of these large animals. It also suggests – another
heresy – that large herbivores played a part in, or at least did not
prevent, the generation of trees in our landscape.

All these large herbivores, along with their predators the
wolf, bear, wolverine and lynx, were dramatically affected by
the growing population of humans as they converted wildlands
into fields and managed – often coppiced – woods. Inevitably,
predators came into conflict with pastoralists, too. They were
particularly persecuted as sheep numbers grew with the rise of
the wool industry in Europe in the thirteenth century. Wild
herbivores, readily hunted for meat, also came to be regarded as
competition for the grazing areas needed for rising populations
of domesticated livestock. The aurochs was hunted to extinction; the last died in Poland in 1627. Wild tarpans – or feral
horses closely related to them – survived in East Prussia and
Poland until the eighteenth or nineteenth century. The last
specimen is said to have died in Moscow Zoo in 1887. The
European beaver, once numbering millions across Eurasia, was
hunted to near-extinction, with only 1,200 individuals in eight
relict populations by 1900. Elk were exterminated from the
whole of Western Europe, surviving only in small numbers in
the remote northeast – in Latvia, Estonia and Russia. All three
subspecies of the European bison were hunted to extinction in
the wild: *Bison bonasus hungarorum* from the Balkans died out
in the mid-1800s, the last wild *Bison bonasus bonasus* was shot
in Białowieża forest on the Poland–Belarus border in 1921, and
the last *Bison bonasus caucasicus* was shot, appropriately
enough, in the north-west Caucasus in 1927. The European
bison that survive today are descendants of a dozen animals
held in zoos across the Continent.

In the British Isles, where wild animals had nowhere to escape to, extinctions happened much earlier. Britain's last beaver was probably killed in Yorkshire in the eighteenth century; Britain's last wolf in the Scottish Highlands in the seventeenth. The last truly wild boar were killed on the orders of Henry III in the Forest of Dean in 1260. The lynx is thought to have disappeared as early as the ninth century – so long ago that most people are unaware it was ever a native animal. The aurochs was probably exterminated in Britain in the Bronze Age, along with brown bears and elk; while the latest fossil evidence for British wild horses is some 9,300 years old.

By the late nineteenth century, when an interest in nature conservation began to stir, most of Europe had become a completely altered, intensively managed human landscape with only a few of the original grazers and browsers surviving in remnants of their original range. Those that remained, like red and roe deer, were tolerated by man only in very low numbers, and in particular places like parks, because of the damage they did to crops and plantations of trees. They therefore had little or no impact on the succession of trees on any land left to its own devices. There was simply not the number or diversity of wild herbivores left to demonstrate how they might interact with and disrupt natural vegetation succession. In the absence of these animals, closed-canopy forest came to be seen as the natural state of the European landscape. Which led to a further flawed assumption: if climax vegetation was the primordial impulse of nature, then all Europe's indigenous large herbivores – including the extinct aurochs and tarpan – must, originally, have been forest-dwellers. However, it was clear that, in the agricultural setting, large numbers of domesticated grazing animals (including, ironically, cattle and horses descended from the aurochs and tarpan) did prevent the regeneration of trees. Therefore, it was argued, in order for the original closed-canopy forest to have existed in the first place, the numbers of Europe's indigenous herbivores must have been very low indeed. It is a circular argument that is still in wide currency

today amongst both foresters and ecologists, and has Frans
shaking his head in frustration. 'The problem is,' he says, 'we're
always working from the wrong baseline.'

Climax vegetation theory, originally propounded by the
American botanist and author of *Plant Succession*, Frederic
Clements, in 1916, and subsequently further developed by the
English botanist Sir Arthur Tansley, author of *The British
Islands and Their Vegetation* (1939), among others, throws up
a further powerful psychological barrier for conservationists
devising strategies for nature management. Closed-canopy
forest is demonstrably species-poor compared with managed
habitats like meadows, pasture, heaths and traditional farmland.

'What it looks like, if you subscribe to the closed-canopy
story,' says Frans, 'is that, in Europe – before we embarked on
the destructive practices of modern industrial farming – man
actually improved biodiversity because traditional farming and
forestry practices like haymaking, pollarding and coppicing
clearly sustain a much broader spectrum of habitats for wildlife
than closed-canopy woodland.' This is the prevailing wisdom
amongst ecologists like Heinz Ellenberg who, in *Vegetation
Ecology of Central Europe* (1986), argues that 'Central Europe
would have been a monotonous wooded landscape, if mankind
had not created the colourful mosaic of fields, heaths, hay lands
and pastures.'

'No self-respecting ecologist wants to see a return to dark,
monotonous, species-poor forest across the whole of Europe,'
Frans went on. 'This presents us with an enormous responsibility and workload. If man is the driver of biodiversity, then man
has to continue to manage nature intensively and at huge
expense. We simply cannot believe that nature is capable of
doing this on her own. But where would biodiversity have
come from in the first place, if not from nature? We forget that
nature has been around a lot longer than us.'

Where, then, did all these species so happy in meadows and
pastures, coppices and commons, live before we arrived with
our oxen and pitchforks, our billhooks, hay carts and flails?

Ecosystems on the continent of Africa provided an answer. It is in the place of man's origin that, historically (until the colonial annihilations of the last two hundred years or so), we have had least impact on the indigenous flora and fauna. Evolving along-side man, African animals had a chance to develop defensive strategies. Elsewhere in the world, however, the arrival of humans – by then highly developed, weapon-carrying and rapidly populous – had a transformative, often catastrophic impact on wildlife, particularly on megafauna. Ecologists like Frans in the Netherlands and others in Germany were inspired by studies coming out of the African savannah including *Serengeti: Dynamics of an Ecosystem* – the work of Michael Norton-Griffiths and Anthony Sinclair, published in 1979 – which was one of the first to show how the actions of grazing herbivores encourage numerous species of plants and animals.

'Africa gives us a useful paradigm,' Frans explained. 'It shows the vital role played by large numbers of naturally occurring grazing animals in an ecosystem – how they create and sustain species-rich grasslands. So why couldn't this have happened in Europe? Why suppose that grazing animals can have a dynamic and positive impact there, but not here?'

And so began the experiment to release free-roaming grazing animals into the Oostvaardersplassen. As in Africa, the animals would be left to their own devices, living in natural herds, with no supplementary feeding or other intervention. They would need to be old breeds, sturdy, with strong survival instincts, able to fend for themselves through the winter – basically, more like their ancestors than modern, highly selected animals. They would, in effect, be acting as proxies of Europe's missing megafauna. The extinct aurochs, a beast of over ten feet from nose to tail, was represented by Heck cattle – a breed designed in the early twentieth century by the brothers Heinz and Lutz Heck, who intended to rescue the aurochs from confusion with the wisent, or bison – the other large bovine of Holocene Europe. The Hecks' attempt to recover the traits of the aurochs through selective breeding gained notoriety when it was subsequently celebrated by the Nazis as a symbol of their racial ideology. Although the Heck brothers' methodology remains controversial, their experiment succeeded in securing recognition for the aurochs as the ancestor of modern cattle. Heck cattle carry the genes of more than eight old breeds including the Highland cattle of Scotland, Britain's White Park cattle and fighting bulls from Spain. Though still a good eight to twelve inches shorter than the massive aurochs of old, and, with a Heck bull typically weighing in at 1,300lb, at least 220lb lighter than a bull aurochs, they are, nevertheless, imposing animals. Konik ponies, a short, stocky breed with dun coats and a dorsal stripe, originally from the Biłgoraj region of Poland, were chosen for the Oostvaardersplassen experiment for their hardiness and their supposed phenotypical resemblance to the extinct tarpan. They, too, had been the subject of a 'breed-back' experiment, started by a Polish count in 1936. Roe deer were already naturally present in the Oostvaardersplassen in small numbers, and red deer were added to the mix.

'We wanted to introduce the kind of grazing variation you find in Africa and that would once have prevailed in Europe. Of course, this is an imperfect representation of all the animals that would have originally been here but there are still huge positives from bringing these species together. All these ungulates eat in different ways – they have very different mouths, different digestive systems, different behaviours and different preferences. Roe deer are browsers, for example – they feed on twigs, brambles and saplings; cattle and horses are primarily grazers, with some supplementary browsing; red deer graze in the growing season and browse and de-bark in winter when the grass gets tougher. They can even de-bark poisonous elder by neutralizing the cyanide in their stomachs – something cattle and horses cannot do.

'The ancestors of these animals would have had the same or very similar feeding strategies. They would have had the same gut flora and seed-carrying capacity – cows, for example, transport two hundred and thirty plant species in their gut, hair and hooves. These different species would have existed together in the past and we felt their combined grazing actions in the Oost-vaardersplassen would create and maintain open grassland with greater floral complexity.'

As late introductions from the Middle East, goats and sheep – descendants of the wild mouflon of Mesopotamia – do not belong to the suite of herbivores associated with the postglacial ecosystems of Western Europe so they were excluded from the mix. At first, the numbers of grazers introduced were very low – thirty-two Heck cattle in 1983; twenty Konik ponies in 1984; thirty-seven red deer, transported from Scotland and elsewhere, in 1992. The idea was to let the populations grow at will. Here, too, Africa provided inspiration.

'In Africa you have vast herds of ungulates grazing together in the landscape. There are predators, of course, but population density itself is not regulated by predation.'

The size of grazing herds is driven primarily by the amount of food available. In times of plenty, with good rains and lots of vegetation growth, populations explode. In seasons when there is less to eat – notably, for Africa, during the dry season and droughts – they fall. Under-nourished females will not ovulate. If they are in slightly better condition they may ovulate but not conceive. If they do conceive, they may abort or absorb the foetus. And if they get as far as the later stages of pregnancy, the mother will prioritize the foetus over herself, to such an extent that she may suffer toxaemia, often fatally. Older animals – males in particular – weaken and die. A decline in herbivores releases the pressure of grazing on the vegetation, allowing for a burst of growth when the conditions are right, which stimu-lates another population spurt.

'It's a natural cycle of fluctuations,' says Frans. 'Although the climatic conditions in temperate zone Europe are not as harsh as Africa, I see no reason why this could not have been a process that once worked here too. Our long winters have a similar impact as an African dry season; a severe winter is like a drought. Seasonal variations and longer cycles of pressures on vegetation are, in effect, nature's way of controlling populations.'

The animals introduced into the Oostvaardersplassen did, indeed, multiply, demonstrating a far higher carrying capacity for the land than anyone thought possible. Herd numbers have now levelled out at around 800 ponies and 160 cattle grazing the 2,400 hectares of dry polder, and 2,000 red deer grazing both the dry and marshy areas, having pushed out the roe deer. Meanwhile, overall, biodiversity has risen, with the Oostvaardersplassen – grazed all year round – supporting greater species complexity than seasonally grazed farmland.

The animals do not graze every part of the reserve with equal intensity, explained Frans. The areas that are under-grazed or not grazed at all during the growing seasons of spring and summer produce grass and flowering plants, which benefits mice and mouse-hunting birds like marsh harriers and buzzards. The grazed areas become a temporary home to the geese. Over the winter, areas that have been under-grazed during the growing season are eaten off and trampled, giving many plant species the opportunity to germinate here as well, resulting in a profusion of grasses and forbs in the spring. Over all, the winter die-off of animals removes pressure from the grazing for the coming spring. The fluctuation in animal numbers allows for spontaneous bursts of thorny vegetation, and occasional outbursts of willow – which adds another habitat for small mammals and songbirds, which in turn are prey for owls, goshawks and sparrowhawks living in willows in the marshy areas.

'So what we've shown in the Oostvaardersplassen is that a mix of herbivores, allowed to express themselves freely, without human control, stimulates a much greater variety of animal and plant species than can be found on the short grassland characteristic of seasonal farmland grazing.'

Water voles, rabbits, hares, stoats, weasels, polecats, foxes, grass snakes, toads, ground beetles, dung beetles, carrion beetles and butterflies have all found their way to the reserve and now reside in the Oostvaardersplassen in large numbers. In all, an amazing 250 bird species have been recorded.

But the annual die-off has proved controversial. Starving and dying cattle, ponies and deer are a common sight at the end of winter, something for which modern Europeans are emotionally unprepared. Frans has received death threats from hunters, farmers and animal-lovers. The Heck cattle's Nazi association has provoked vicious comparisons, with cartoons depicting Frans as an ecological Josef Mengele conducting experiments in a zoological concentration camp. But Frans is unrepentant.

'Yet again, our view of nature is being dictated by the conventions of human control. The baseline for the welfare of farm animals is being applied to animals living in the wild,' he says. 'The fact that animals in the Oostvaardersplassen have a free life in a natural environment – they are not cooped up in some factory farm; they aren't pushed around by humans every day; they have normal sex rather than artificial insemination; they have a natural herd structure allowing calves to stay with their mothers; they can graze and browse what they are designed to eat, not what is artificially concocted for them by the farming industry – none of this seems to matter. The fixation is solely on their death not the quality of their lives.

'In particular, people believe these deaths are numerous and "unnatural" because there is a fence around the reserve preventing the animals from migrating in search of food – but cyclical die-offs happen even in the migrating populations of Africa. And in places where animals cannot migrate – like the Ngorongoro Crater in Tanzania, which has the highest density of predators in Africa – the dynamic is the same. Starvation is the determining factor. It is a fundamental process of nature.'

Nevertheless, public outcry has forced a compromise on the non-interventionist principles of the Oostvaardersplassen and, now, animals deemed to be on their last legs are humanely shot. According to Dutch and European law, cattle and horse carcasses – even those of de-domesticated animals – cannot be left to decay, so they are carted off and incinerated. But roe and red deer, since they are categorized as 'wild', are allowed to remain, their bodies providing food for the foxes, rats, crows and birds of prey – including the white-tailed eagle. Ultimately every scrap of flesh, fur, sinew and bone collapses, digested by all the insects, carrion beetles, bacteria and fungi that have colonized the Oostvaardersplassen since the project began. Together, these decomposers perform the enriching function of drawing nutrients such as phosphorus, potassium, calcium, magnesium and nitrogen down into the soil.

Charlie and I looked out at this landscape, a miracle of on-going creation, and something clicked. If such a productive response to natural grazing could happen on land reclaimed from the sea – a blank slate, in effect, with a non-existent ter-restrial biodiversity baseline – then something like this could happen anywhere, even – perhaps – on land that has been impoverished and polluted through decades of intensive farm-ing. By showing a way to reverse our catastrophic declines, the Oostvaardersplassen could provide a model for Europe.

For Charlie, the imprint of Africa was deep in his bones. The first years of his life had been spent in Rhodesia where, in the years before independence, his father Raymond had grown tobacco and cotton. Africa clearly drew him back and we had travelled together on wildlife safaris in Kenya, Tanzania, Namibia, Botswana and South Africa. To Charlie, numbers of animals on this scale felt natural; the atmosphere of an uncon-strained landscape, second nature. Encountering such an ecosystem amidst the densely populated, heavily managed, agri-cultural lowlands of Europe, though, was eye-opening. It merged two entirely different experiences, two previously separate worlds. Wild nature had pushed its way into a place where, until now, we had thought it should not logically be. Charlie's mind was whirring. What would happen, he won-dered aloud on the journey home, if we allowed comparable natural processes free rein at Knepp? Could we roll out the idea of the Repton park restoration into the surrounding farmland, but do something much wilder, and self-sustaining? Could we use grazing animals to create habitats and restore wildlife across the whole estate? Could a free-willed conservation project be the answer we'd been waiting for?

5

A World of Wood Pasture

Conservation should be based on practical observation rather than unstable theory.

Oliver Rackham, *Woodlands*, 2006

Charlie's 2002 'letter of intent' addressed to English Nature, the government's advisory body for nature, funded by the Department for the Environment, Food and Rural Affairs, was forthright and full of optimism. It declared our intention to establish 'a biodiverse wilderness area in the Low Weald of Sussex'. What we envisaged, the letter explained, was a 'land management experiment' using a mix of free-roaming grazing animals to create opportunities for wildlife similar to those we had witnessed in the Oostvaardersplassen. We were seeking funding to ring-fence the entire 3,500 acres of the estate, take up all 200 miles of internal fencing, leaving only fences around houses and buildings, cattle-grid the public B roads that run through it and build a land bridge over the A272 so the animals could traverse the whole area. There might be minor problems, the letter admitted, with ear-tagging wild cattle, possible conflicts between dog-walkers and free-roaming animals, a proliferation of weeds and the public distaste for rotting carcasses, but it was hoped these would not be insurmountable.

The choice of animals, alone, may have given English Nature cause to swallow hard: red deer, fallow deer, Heck cattle and Exmoor ponies were perhaps challenging enough, but the three 'Bs' – wild boar, European beaver and European bison – were almost unmentionable. We were aiming high.

We were particularly hopeful about wild boar. One aspect of animal processes conspicuously lacking from the Oostvaardersplassen is that of the large scavenger. Foxes and birds rip away at carcasses on the Flevoland plains but even there, there are no wild boar – Europe's equivalent of Africa's bone-crunching hyena. The other vital ecological function of wild boar is to act like a plough, their rootling exposing bare soil for colonization by invertebrates and the germination of flowering plants and shrubs. The Dutch government would not countenance an introduction into the Oostvaardersplassen on the grounds that wild boar could break out of the project and spread disease amongst the country's intensive pig farms. Ironically, many conservationists believe the threat is the other way round – that intensive pig farms, hotbeds of virus cultivation, spread disease to wild populations. Frans was holding out hope that wild boar might find their own way to the Oostvaardersplassen as they were known to be only twenty-five kilometres away. But with no pig farmers in our area, we hoped that introducing wild boar at Knepp would be less contentious than in Holland. Wild boar became extinct in England at least three hundred years ago but in recent years escapees and releases from wild-boar farms have re-established wild populations. A large population near the coast in East Sussex provides Rye's annual Wild Boar Festival in October with 'wild boargers', 'boargignon' and other delicacies from the 'last of the summer swine'. There have been sightings of wild boar only a mile or so away from us, on the other side of the busy A24 – a barrier which so far seems to have limited their westward expansion.

We were particularly keen to leave carcasses on the land rather than carting them off to be incinerated – though this, owing to UK health and safety legislation similar to that in the rest of Europe, would require a special dispensation. The absence of carcasses in the landscape is another lost aspect of natural processes. As a consequence, populations of an entire

community of necrophagous insect species such as clown beetles and blowfly maggots, as well as fungi and bacteria, have
collapsed. The dead donkey fly, which gets its name from the
site of its last British sighting, used to lay its eggs on decaying
carcasses at the advanced skin-and-bone stage. It died out completely in Britain once carcasses were no longer left lying
around. While, admittedly, few people other than entomologists may mourn the loss of these creatures, allowing carcasses
to rot down on the land keeps nutrients in the food cycle
including phosphorus and calcium, both of which are vital, for
example, for the production of birds' eggs.

Beavers, in 2002, were still a long way off being accepted in
Britain. Well on the way to recovery in Europe, they have
already been spotted in the Oostvaardersplassen and are likely
soon to be breeding in the reserve. With mounting evidence in
Europe of their beneficial impacts on the environment, we were
hopeful that the British government would see the advantages
of returning this keystone species to England. Knepp, with its
lakes, ponds, ditches and a considerable amount of boggy land,
could, we felt, be just the place to start.

Bison are another grazer making a comeback from near
extinction in Europe; Frans and other European ecologists
identify it as another keystone species. There is an ongoing
debate about whether bison were ever present in Britain after
the last ice age. No bison bones have yet been found here. But
fossil evidence is notoriously difficult to come by. No fossil
bones of the wolf, for example, have ever been found in the
Netherlands though it was widespread there until only a few
centuries ago. The last wolf shot was killed in the southern
Netherlands in 1845, and the last one seen in the country was
in 1897. Indeed, fossil evidence is so rare that when it comes to
light it often explodes all previous theories. A single accidental
find of mammoth bones in 2009 in Condover in Shropshire
moved the presence of mammoths in Britain closer to the present day by 7,000 years, to only 14,000 years ago. Uncomfortable
though it may be for scientists – particularly, perhaps, for

palaeoecologists – who prefer to deal in certainties and tangible remains, absence of evidence is not evidence of absence. Moreover, bison bones have recently been discovered in Doggerland under the North Sea dating to the beginning of the Holocene (our current post-ice age epoch which began around 11,700 years ago), along with remains of other Holocene fauna such as the aurochs, wild boar, elk, beaver, roe and otter. Doggerland was the land bridge that connected Britain to Europe until rising seas separated us 8,200 years ago. It is inconceivable that, when we were still physically part of the Continent, animals tamely stopped at Calais.

In one particular respect, however, we knew our vision would have to be more constrained than that of the Oostvaard-ersplassen. On private land one-third the area of the Dutch reserve, and with houses and gardens and people going about their daily lives in the middle of it, we couldn't leave animals to starve. While we felt it essential for the experiment that the grazing herds interact with their environment as naturally as possible, with minimum human intervention and no supplementary feeding, the thought of watching animals dying from our windows was unconscionable, and the authorities would, in any case, never allow it. The headquarters of the Royal Society for the Prevention of Cruelty to Animals is in Southwater, a neighbouring village. Knepp's size and location – as well as our own sensitivities – would impose limitations of their own. We proposed that once the herds had grown in number we would cull the animals to a level at which they could remain healthy and well fed throughout the winter. If any animal became sick or had trouble, say, giving birth, we would intervene with veterinary attention. Selling the meat of the culled cattle, deer and boar would help, we hoped, to defray culling costs. The ponies would be rounded up annually and surplus animals sold.

Charlie's letter also explained that we intended the experiment to be for a twenty-five-year period, after which we would review the project and decide whether to continue 'rewilding' or revert to some other form of land management. We were unsure of the outcomes and needed the reassurance of reversibility. As private landowners we were also concerned about the finances. If English Nature – or anyone else – decided to fund us and then withdrew support later, and if there were no other available sources of funding for conservation in twenty-five years' time, we didn't want to lock the next generation into a scheme that could become a millstone round their necks. We wanted our children and grandchildren to be free to make their own decisions about the land according to the circumstances of their lifetimes – which might conceivably involve a return to agriculture if, for some currently unimaginable reason, farming on our clay was to become viable again.

The following year English Nature's senior woodland scientist came down to Knepp to investigate. Keith Kirby, a shy academic with a long, wispy, grey Charles Darwin beard, was, like most British ecologists, being buffeted by the backwash of the response to Vera's book. Intrigued, if also cautious, he was keen to see Vera's theories tested on British soil. Ultimately, though, he made clear that his department was in no position to award our plan funding. Neither, he said, was there likely to be the will amongst the powers-that-be at English Nature to rush into something as radical as what we were proposing. He talked of computer modelling, targets, safeguards, setting parameters for the number of animals and vegetation cover, and lots and lots of further research.

We took encouragement from the fact that English Nature hadn't laughed us out of court but the dry response was frustrating and, ultimately, we felt, the guarded approach was missing the point. The only way to test the impact of free-roaming grazing animals in a landscape was to put them into action. The whole purpose of a process-led project was to let nature lead the way, and this meant shelving preconceived ideas and removing as many limitations as possible. Targets and parameters made no sense. The experiment had to be open-ended, with no specific goal other than the broad expectation of restoring natural processes and improving biodiversity. We simply had no way of knowing what would happen because there were so many variables and nothing like this had been allowed to happen in the UK before. The idea of constructing a computer model to identify the outcomes of self-willed land seemed like trying to predict the lifetime achievements of an unborn child.

Keith's visit was the first of many and opened up a dialogue with civil servants that would continue in much the same vein for over five years. Time and again our hopes rose that English Nature would commit itself to support, only to be dashed by another bout of political indecision and scientific navel-gazing. Without funding, we simply could not afford to ring-fence our 3,500 acres – the prerequisite to launching our naturalistic grazing project. Uncertainties at English Nature were compounded by the periodic shake-ups, policy shifts and restructurings that are the bane of any government organization. In 2006, for example, the department was reshaped as Natural England, incorporating the Countryside Agency and the Rural Development Service. But at the root of Natural England's prevarication was the controversy that continued to rage around Vera's theories and the nature of the original 'wildwood': was Britain in the pre-Neolithic, Atlantic era, about 7,000 years ago, closed-canopy forest? Or was it a more open landscape, a mosaic of grassland, scrubland, groves and solitary trees, grazed by large numbers of herbivores? Correctly identifying Britain's ecological past was clearly fundamental to considering how conservation should proceed in the future and would determine English Nature's response to projects like ours.

To Vera's supporters, there is an obvious flaw at the heart of the closed-canopy argument. It is our old friend, the oak. Conspicuous in the open landscape, its limbs outstretched in sun salutation, the oak is standing proof that temperate zone Europe could not have been entirely closed forest.

We already know that oaks were plentiful in our landscape from the pollen record and from fossils in our ancient floodplains. As Oliver Rackham says: 'The logs and tree stumps preserved in peat commonly known as bog oaks are a valuable complement to the pollen record. They are only a minute and unrepresentative fraction of all the trees that grew in prehistory; they lived in unusual places and died violent and unusual deaths, being killed by a sudden rise in the water table . . . Nevertheless bog trees are not to be despised. They tell us, as no evidence can, exactly what grew where, and about the structure, as opposed to the composition, of certain kinds of wildwood.' The abundant associations of fauna and flora with the oak are, in themselves, evidence of deep historical ecology. Trees that are historically rare or widely dispersed rarely have the opportunity to build up so many associations. The oak's particular association with the jay, the bird upon which it depends for the dispersal and germination of its acorns, must have evolved over millennia. So this is not a tree that has simply proliferated in modern times. And its conspicuous presence in our ancient landscape provides an obvious challenge to the closed-canopy theory.

Like hazel and birch, both oak species of lowland Europe – the sessile (*Quercus petraea*) and the pedunculate (*Quercus robur*), like the Knepp Oak – require a substantial amount of direct light, at recruitment (the early growth stage), at least. Unlike beech, hornbeam, ash, lime, sycamore, silver fir, maple, alder, wych elm, smooth-leaved elm and other tree species native to Central and Western Europe, oaks cannot regenerate in closed-canopy conditions. For foresters and tree men like Ted Green this is stating the obvious. But it is surprising how this fact has been, and continues to be, overlooked by most closed-canopy theorists.

Those that are aware of the oak's demand for light claim it can germinate and grow into a mature tree in the open glades that are created when a large tree or a clutch of trees topple in the forest due to storms or old age. Vera refutes this. He points to forest reserves across Central and Western Europe – including the so-called 'primeval' forest of Białowieża in Poland – where there is no long-term recruitment of oak, even in clearings. The oaks are, essentially, dying out. That oaks exist in these reserves at all is either because they have been planted by foresters and deliberately protected from competition, in which case they are all of the same age and grow with long tall trunks – valuable as timber – with no large lateral branches and small crowns on top; or because they are ancient oaks with spreading lateral branches that have grown in the open and been subsequently engulfed by shade-tolerant trees. Ancient oaks with spreading limbs, Vera argues, clearly indicate that the forest was once wood pasture – a naturally occurring ecosystem driven and sustained by grazing ungulates. These open-grown oaks might originally have been solitary trees, grown from an acorn planted by a jay or wood mouse near a free-standing thorn bush, or part of a grove of oaks arising from numerous acorns planted by jays in the fringes of thorny scrub. The thorny scrub would have acted as nurseries for the oak saplings, protecting them from grazing animals without depriving them of light. When the grazing animals disappeared from this wood pasture landscape, the brakes would have been released on vegetation succession. Inevitably, shade-tolerant species would have won the day, culminating in closed-canopy forest, now 'forest reserves' – hallowed ground to conservationists and protected by law. The tallest oaks might take centuries to die, as the surrounding trees begin to overtop them and steal their light. But die they inevitably do.

We saw this ourselves, in Romania, several years into our project. We stumbled across the Breite Nature Reserve, near Sighişoara, on a trip with friends to look at wildflower meadows in the Carpathian mountains. This rare patch of ancient wood pasture, dotted with oaks – magnificent gnarled veterans, six or seven centuries old – had been abandoned when traditional shepherding went into decline fifty years ago. Without the impact of grazing animals a phalanx of hornbeam and beech was marching in. Those oaks that had already been enveloped by the shady pioneers were losing their crowns and dropping their limbs, drowning in slow motion in a vegetative sea. A few, overwhelmed, had already crashed to the forest floor.

While seedlings from old oaks like this, clinging on in their crepuscular coffin, may take root (sometimes in large numbers) in available clearings, they inevitably fail within a few years, outcompeted by shade-tolerant saplings. The same thing happens in Britain. Not far from us in Sussex, in the Mens Nature Reserve – a non-intervention zone, claimed to be one of Britain's last scraps of natural lowland closed-canopy forest – ecologists studying the site expected to see a significant recruitment of oaks after the 1987 hurricane, a one-in-300-year event that brought down numerous trees. They have been puzzled to observe no oak succession to date.

Fire, caused by lightning, is also commonly cited by closed-canopy theorists as another forest-opener that would have allowed oak saplings to regenerate in prehistoric Europe. But this argument doesn't catch light either, at least in temperate climes. It is hard to understand how fire ever gained credence as an agent of disturbance in our land of fog and rain. Anyone who has ever tried to start a fire using only the available material in a British woodland knows how reluctant it is to ignite, even in the height of summer. Bonfires on Guy Fawkes' Night would be damp squibs without litres of petrol. In contrast to the dry pine forests of the arid countries of southern Europe, Britain has no readily ignitable tree species, apart, perhaps, from Scots pine, and outbursts of lightning do not scramble the fire engines. Electric storms, when they do come, are almost always accompanied by rain. In the Second World War the renowned forester Herbert Edlin noted that even during the Battle of Britain, over a long, dry summer, not one incendiary bomb, capable of burning through concrete, started a fire in woodland. In Carpenters Wood, part of Bisham Woods in Berkshire, the crater where a plane full of explosives came down in 1944 is still visible, marked by a memorial to the airmen that died. The explosion was heard tens of miles away. But the surrounding trees, including beech, just a hundred yards from the crash site did not catch fire. Even during the great drought of 1976 – at the height of the fashion for burning stubble – no trees caught alight. Oliver Rackham, our undisputed expert on British woodland, is categorical: apart from pine-woods, the native woods of Britain will not generate a blaze. 'Broadleaved woodland', he says, 'burns like wet asbestos'.

Since closed-canopy theory, by definition, does not regard grazing animals as significant disturbers, what other factors, prior to man, could have opened up forests sufficiently to enable the oak to proliferate? Prolonged drought, floods or storms? Disease? Extreme weather events are, by definition, just that – exceedingly rare, and often local. Outbreaks of pathogens are even rarer than floods and droughts, generally occurring hundreds, if not thousands, of years apart. Like elm disease or ash die-back, they generally attack a single species at a time. Extreme events are not enough, on their own, to explain the evolution or the survival, let alone the dominance, of oak in our landscape.

So why has the closed-canopy argument gained such a foothold in the scientific community? Why is it proving so difficult to shift? The reason, perhaps, is partly psychological. The idea of a dark, all-encompassing forest has tremendous power over the imagination. It is the stuff of the German folk tales appropriated by the English-speaking world in the nineteenth century – Hansel and Gretel, Little Red Riding Hood and Snow White: fairy tales from the dark conifer forests of Eastern Europe. In Scandinavia, the primeval forests were inhabited by trolls and other frightening, enchanting, mystical creatures that were, invariably, extremely dangerous to man.

The no-go area Where the Wild Things Are has settled into our collective subconscious. With its Freudian overtones of power and penetration, of early man felling timber, conquering the frightful, slavering beasts, letting light into the darkness, opening up the land with his plough, sowing his seed in the virgin soil, this is a strongly anthropocentric story with its roots deep in the psyche. 'The face of the earth being originally covered with wood, except where water prevailed,' proclaimed Thomas Pownall to the Society of Antiquaries in London in

1770, 'the first human beings of it were Woodland-Men living on the fruits, fish and game of the forest.' It was followed almost unquestioningly by science into the twentieth century. Holocene Britain was, according to the archaeologist Sir Cyril Fox in 1943, 'an illimitable forest of damp oakwood, ash and thorn and bramble, largely untrodden. This forest was in a sense unbroken.'

In the modern world, the idea of ubiquitous primal forest – verdant, infinite, unfathomable, prolific – has become, for those yearning for re-enchantment or nostalgic for a richer, deeper kind of nature, the antithesis of the depleted, polluted, parcelled-up landscapes modernity has left us with. It is a vision that continues to be endorsed by science, and it seems the lion's share of responsibility for the endurance of this myth must be laid at the door of the palynologists – the pollen experts – who have carried closed-canopy theory into the twenty-first century.

Fossil pollen evidence provided 'proof' for early twentieth-century climax-vegetation proponents such as Arthur Tansley and Charles Moss, and has become the foundation on which modern Europeans have generated their picture of the past. The Swedish geologist Ernst Jakob Lennart von Post created the first pollen diagram in 1916. By examining grains of tree pollen preserved in layers in peat bogs and lake sediments he maintained it was possible to identify the kind of forest that would have existed in lowland Western and Central Europe from the end of the last ice age to modern times. Tree species such as oak, elm, lime, beech, hazel and hornbeam – all big pollen emitters – are highly represented in the pollen evidence, while the amount of pollen from non-arboreal species, such as grasses, flowers and most shrubs, is conspicuously low. There was no doubt among early twentieth-century scientists that what they were looking at was the record of closed forests. Subsequent plant geographers and forest researchers have picked up this baton without questioning the hypothesis, arguing only the finer points about the component species of the primeval forest and the precise timing of when it might have emerged in the post-glacial landscape.

But palynology suffers from serious blind spots. The kind of prehistoric wood-pasture landscape Vera visualizes, its ecology driven by primeval herds of grazing animals, features thick 'mantle and fringe vegetation' made up of light-demanding scrub species such as blackthorn, hawthorn, dog rose, common privet, dogwood, wild apple, wild pear, wild cherry and rowan. It is the kind of landscape that still exists in the grazed, naturalistic wood pastures of Romania, the western Jura in France, the Borkener Paradies in Germany, Slovenský Kras in Slovenia and the New Forest in England. But all these light-demanding scrub species are pollinated by insects and shed little or no pollen into the atmosphere. The pollen is often sticky and lumpy, intended to adhere to chosen insects, and not light and dust-like, designed to be blown across the landscape. From the palynological point of view such plants are virtually invisible. The absence of these species in the pollen spectrum does not prove that they were not there. Indeed, the very existence of these species today proves that they must have existed in the past, and poses the question – how did they survive into modern times if our world was originally closed forest?

Hazel, another shrub characteristic of open wood pasture, does produce pollen – in prolific amounts – and this is dispersed by wind. While it can survive in closed-canopy forest it needs direct sunlight to flower successfully and produce high quantities of pollen. Between 20 and 40 per cent of the total quantity of pollen found in large peat bogs and lakes and smaller collection basins throughout Central and Western Europe is hazel pollen. However – strikingly – the early palynologists consistently omitted hazel pollen from their diagrams on the basis that hazel, being a shrub, represents the understorey of the closed-canopy forest. It does not compete with taller trees and therefore, to them, its presence was a distraction, clouding the identification of arboreal forest species. Lennart von Post, the father of palynology, set the pattern in 1916: 'I have not included hazel pollen in the sum [of forest tree pollen] . . . This is because hazel occurs mostly as a shrub layer in mixed oak-forest, and forms only exceptionally a separate community competitive with other forest types.' As British botanist and palynologist Sir Harry Godwin explained in a paper on hazel pollen analysis for the *New Phytologist* in 1934: 'From the commencement of pollen analytic investigation it has been customary to count, in all but the most difficult samples a minimum number of 150 grains of pollen. Pollen of Corylus-Myrica [hazel and bog myrtle] type is not reckoned in this total.' While hazel pollen is no longer excluded from modern pollen diagrams, it is – following Lennart von Post's example – still considered exclusively in the category of arboreal pollen. No one seems to consider high pollen percentages of hazel as an indicator of a more open landscape. This anomalous practice is, in Vera's view, tantamount to shutting one's eyes and sticking one's fingers in one's ears. Like the oak, hazel pollen is a key indicator – not of closed-canopy forest, but of mantle vegetation in open wood pasture.

One of the most frequent arguments cited by palynologists as proof that there was little or no open grassland in the prehistoric landscape is low levels of grass pollen in the fossil record. There could be an obvious reason for this. A large number of grazing animals would eat the grass before it flowers, just as they do in the Serengeti, where – according to Tony Sinclair – grasses flower only sporadically when, for one reason or another, the grazing impact declines temporarily. But there are physical factors, too, that might have influenced the amount of grass pollen falling into the collection basins of lakes and peat bogs. Mantle and fringe vegetation – the dense, thorny scrub characteristic of wood pasture – acts as a wind break. It is made up of the same species with which we have, for centuries, laid hedges in our landscape both as an impenetrable barrier for animals and as protection from wind and snow. In the complex structure of wood pasture, where areas of open grassland are dotted with groves and free-standing trees, and fringed and interspersed with clumps of thorny scrub, wind is diverted and interrupted, making it far less effective as a disperser, particularly for pollen lying low to the ground. There are pockets of stillness, here, even on the windiest of days. These barriers are at their most effective from mid-summer onwards, when all the trees and shrubs of the mantle and fringe vegetation are in leaf – the season in which grasses and herbs tend to flower. Low levels of grass pollen in the sediments may be explained by both the grazing of animals and the pollen being trapped in thick, thorny, low-lying fringe vegetation.

Higher above ground, protruding from these thorny nurseries, and flowering before any of the other shrubs or trees come into leaf, hazel shrubs have a greater chance of dispersal. Their pollen is picked up by rising air currents in the open spaces and blown over great distances – explaining, perhaps, why hazel is so well represented in the collection basins of regional pollen rain.

Finally, Vera argues, palynologists are wrong to assume that a high proportion of tree pollen found in sediments necessarily indicates a high proportion of trees. Shade-tolerant trees, such as lime (which is pollinated by wind as well as insects), produce far more pollen when they are free-standing than when living in closed-canopy conditions. Out in the sunlight, with room to spread, they develop an expansive crown – much like the oak – which opens up much lower down on the trunk and flowers profusely. Towering above the scrub and grassland their pollen is easily transported by air currents and moved over long distances. Consequently, Vera argues, in a park-like landscape of a certain area, a smaller number of trees may emit an equal or even larger amount of pollen into the atmosphere than a closed forest of the same area. In addition, he points out, 'the modern pollen spectra of park-like landscapes grazed by large herbivores reveal striking similarities, in terms of species diversity and relative representation, to the pollen spectra of prehistoric times, which are interpreted as being of a closed forest.'

But it is not only Vera who sees the primal landscape of

Europe as more open and diverse. Other scientists, in the UK, have recently been approaching the same conclusion from other directions. Dr Keith Alexander, an independent specialist in saproxylic beetles, has been battling with palaeo-entomologists who cite sub-fossil – or partly fossilized – saproxylic beetles as evidence of closed-canopy forest. Lumping all tree-associated beetle species together under one category 'wood and trees', including a number of beetles that are not associated with trees at all, palaeo-ecologist Dr Chris Sandom and his colleagues at the University of Sussex claim these beetles indicate 'mostly closed or semi-closed woodlands, or closer to the former' in the early Holocene. Alexander argues that they suggest precisely the opposite. Saproxylic species such as *Dryophthorus corticalis* and one of the commonest beetles of the Early Holocene, *Prostomis mandibularis*, for example, are highly specific and require large-girth tree trunks containing volumes of decayed heart-wood. Closed-canopy conditions do not produce such trees. The beetles found in the very same peat deposits which yield the oak and hazel pollen, Alexander claims, point instead to open-grown trees.

Keith Alexander's position is reinforced by the Invertebrate Species and habitats Information System (with the unfortunate acronym ISIS) – a new analysis of the habitat associations of modern invertebrate fauna recently developed by Natural England. ISIS translates any species list into distinct groups based on their 'ecological assemblage types' – communities of different species occupying the same geographical area. Alexander has fed Chris Sandom's data for different palaeo-ecological time-periods into ISIS to provide an objective overview. For the early Holocene it shows 28 per cent of the subfossil (not fully fossilized) beetle fauna were grassland and scrub species; 13 per cent arboreal; and 47 per cent wood decay. In the late Holocene, 44 per cent were grassland and scrub species; 11 per cent arboreal; and 34 per cent wood decay. The composition shows very low levels of shade-demanding species – so while trees are well represented, shade is clearly scarce. The Late Holocene records therefore indicate increased open grassland and scrub, as well as the presence of early successional mosaic vegetation – the kind of pioneer species that colonize bare ground and that would be expected as humans re-colonized the land and agriculture developed. For both the Early and Late Holocene, predominant open-wood pasture is consistent with the data; closed-canopy forest is not.

A similar picture emerges from the fossil evidence of chalk grassland snails. In the late 1990s, just as Vera was completing his thesis, environmental archaeologist and conchologist Dr Mike Allen, Lecturer at Oxford University and Research Fellow at Bournemouth University, began questioning the prevailing archaeological belief that the chalk grasslands around Stonehenge, Avebury, Dorchester and Cranborne Chase in Wessex were blanketed in postglacial woodland. The sub-fossil snail record, Allen realized, pointed, instead, to a landscape of open grassland with open-grown fruiting trees and shrubs. It is his work that has informed the stunning visual displays depicting the evolution of the chalk landscape in the new museum at Stonehenge. Herds of grazing and browsing animals kept these savannahs open, providing habitat for the snails; and it was this open landscape supporting a huge biomass of animals that attracted the early human populations to the area.

The lichenologist Dr Francis Rose, former Lecturer at King's College London, agonized over closed-canopy theory from the 1970s until his death in 2006. His work was largely concerned with epiphyte forest lichens and for thirty years he studied them, in particular in the New Forest. He noticed that very few species of lichen – or, indeed, mosses or liverworts – could be found within dense stands of trees. Almost all require light and are found on either open-grown trees or trees along rides and the edges of glades. He also observed species of moss and Arctic alpine plants that had survived on common land in Denmark in habitat typical of the last glacial period, or Devensian era (i.e. before trees returned to our landscape as the climate warmed). The fact that this common land was still grazed by horses convinced Rose of the role of herbivores in keeping areas open of tree cover. Similar Devensian-era habitats in Norfolk, he noted, were vanishing with the abandonment of traditional grazing, and small fen plants like northern bog sedge and butterwort, and various species of orchid and subarctic type bryophytes were disappearing with them. He wrote enthusiastically to Vera after reading his 'landmark' book in 2000: 'It covers in a masterly way all of the points that have made so many of us very doubtful about the "classic" hypothesis, namely that the temperate forests were very dense closed canopy in pre-history.'

One of the most persistent sources of confusion in the whole closed-canopy/open-wood pasture debate stems from the loose definition of the word 'forest'. It is a word, as Oliver Rackham puts it, that 'has been much abused in its history' and its indiscriminate use today continues to cloud our vision of how our landscape looked. 'To the medievals', he states, 'a Forest was a place of deer, not a place of trees. If a Forest happened to be wooded it formed part of the wood-pasture tradition.' And it is this medieval wood-pasture tradition – a landscape of 'the commons', of wild, open-grown trees, scrub and pasture, grazed by domesticated animals – that is, in Frans Vera's view, the closest modern analogue to the original European wilderness.

The medieval Latin term 'forestis' – from which we get 'forest', the French 'forêt' and the Germans 'Forst' – first appears in the seventh century as a legal concept in the deeds of donation of Merovingian and Frankish kings. It relates to uncultivated, uninhabited wilderness and is most likely derived from the Latin 'foris' or 'foras' referring to areas 'outside' the civilized domain of settlement and tilled fields. It applied to wilderness in general and to wild trees, shrubs, wild animals, water and fish in particular. Under the *ius forestis* all these 'wild' provisions belonged to the king. Land that had not been tilled or scythed had no ownership. The king held prestigious rights over these unowned lands to hunt wild boar, red and roe deer, tarpan, aurochs and bison. He also held the right of 'bannum', and could grant hunting rights to his favourites amongst the nobility, and permission to commoners to forage, graze their animals, keep bees and take timber and firewood from the 'forestis'. He appointed 'forestarii' to regulate these grants, to punish those who exceeded the allocations and to extract payment for these privileges in the form of a quota of the harvest and/or servitude.

This 'forestis' was anything but closed-canopy woodland. All the indigenous wild animals that were hunted here (apart, perhaps, from roe deer) require, in varying degrees, pasture for grazing as well as shrubs for browsing and cover. Hunting on horseback – the sport of kings – is, itself, impossible to imagine in the modern definition of a forest as a mass of dense, uninterrupted trees.

In time, as populations of large wild animals approached extinction through hunting, domestic herds began to replace them. Kings granted commoners rights of 'pannage', allowing them – in return for payment – to release domesticated pigs into the forest in the autumn to fatten on acorns and fallen fruit. This was a landscape characterized by light-demanding wild pear, apple and cherry trees, and the king of the forest – the open-grown oak. Our word 'acre' – related to 'aecer', the Old English for acorn – originally denoted an area with oak trees. Someone who had the right to 'acker' pigs – to fatten them on acorns – was called an 'ackerman' or, in German, 'Ackerbürger'. Forest grazing rights for cattle were also granted in what, today, seem remarkably high numbers, even taking into consideration their smaller size compared to modern breeds. In 1664, in the French royal forest of Fontainebleau, 6,367 pigs and 10,381 cows were pastured on 14,000 hectares – an area that was still providing large numbers of deer for the royal hunt. While commoners were granted rights to collect firewood and tree fodder in the forest, regulations were routinely issued to restrict the extraction of the thorny scrub upon which the regeneration of trees depended.

The earliest use of the now archaic word 'wald' was to refer to the leaves of a tree that could be used as fodder for animals. Later it was used in relation to the uncultivated land where such trees grew and became synonymous with the word 'forest'. We get from it 'wold' in place names such as Southwold and the Cotswolds, and our own Sussex 'Weald'. In medieval times no distinction was made between 'wood' and 'pasture'. The 'wald' was both, and more: it was a system characterized by a mosaic of shrubs, groves of trees, thorny scrub, big, free-standing trees and grassland; valued for being naturally rich in resources and a vital source of food for livestock. A tree – or 'wood' – was considered an integral part of all the other vegetation in which it stood. Its leaves and branches were conceptually no different from grassland since they were animal fodder, too.

In eighteenth-century Britain, the changing demand for timber led, for the first time, to the artificial development of continuous stands of mature trees. Increasingly, the concepts 'woodland' and 'pasture' become separated. But it was only in the nineteenth century that the terms became mutually exclusive. A German, Heinrich von Cotta, founder of the Royal Saxon Academy of Forestry, pioneered the concept of modern forestry – practices that soon swept across Europe. In man-made plantations thorny scrub became a hindrance; and without thorny scrub to protect the young saplings, grazing and browsing animals caused devastation. At all costs, livestock and wild ungulates such as deer now had to be kept out of the plantations using ditches and fences around the boundary. Soon the role of thorny scrub in the regeneration of trees was forgotten altogether. Without it, trees – as dictated by modern forestry – could never naturally regenerate in the presence of grazing animals. With animals and thorny scrub out of the picture, 'natural regeneration' was redefined as 'simply the germination of the seeds which fall from mature trees'. The 'forest' had become a place of trees; 'pasture', a place of grassland without trees. The dynamic between wood and pasture was lost. Wood pasture came to be seen as degraded closed-canopy forest – a landscape that had been opened up by the axe of man, and was kept open by grazing animals. Now, when ancient and medieval texts describe a place as 'forest' the modern reader visualizes a closed canopy, when in reality it was anything but. 'Historians of modern forestry', says Oliver Rackham, 'often fall into the trap of assuming that it is the successor of the medieval Forest system, but the two have little in common but the name.'

Given the evidence, much of it common sense to anyone with practical knowledge of trees, it is hard to see why other scientists have felt so provoked by 'the Vera theory'. But the world of academia is a strange, sometimes counterproductive and often sluggish place. Where one might expect it to be open and responsive to new thinking, it can be oddly conservative and resistant to radical ideas. It tends to favour theories that grow organically, from the root-stock of previous theories. Papers, judged by peer review, are duty-bound to acknowledge earlier publications on the subject, whether in agreement or disagreement, and are generally discouraged from rejecting out-right what has gone before. A theory as radical as Vera's does not sit easily in this milieu. By redefining the baseline on which studies and professional careers had rested for the best part of a century, Vera's work, described by British ecologists as a 'challenge to orthodox thinking' and an attempt to 'demolish fundamental scientific assumptions' was, in effect, whipping out the rug from under the scientific establishment, and the assumptions of palynology in particular. It was clear it was going to take time for the academics to recalibrate and acknow-ledge mistakes, let alone embrace an entirely different paradigm. As the old saying goes: 'Science advances, one funeral at a time.'

A few months after visiting Knepp in 2003, Keith Kirby started the ball rolling by initiating what he hoped would be a rigorous debate to clear the air. While there was some interest amongst British government agencies in the ideas of rewilding and creating 'near natural areas', he explained, there needed to be broad scientific agreement before English Nature could approach DEFRA at a senior policy level to back the project at Knepp. In an effort to achieve some sort of consensus he there-fore invited scientists and conservationists to contribute to an e-discussion on natural grazing, and commissioned 'a review of the evidence for Vera's hypothesis as applied to British conditions.' In an information note about the research project, entitled 'Fresh Woods and Pastures New', he described its aims:

> Recently Frans Vera, a Dutch ecologist, has challenged ideas of what the natural forest was like: he proposes that the wildwood that once covered much of western Europe including Britain, may actually have been rather open, not unlike wood-pastures in fact. There is little doubt that the role of large animals such as the (now extinct) wild ox in shaping forests has been under-estimated, but whether much of Britain would really have been open parkland is debatable.
>
> Irrespective, however, of what the former landscape was like, the work of Vera and his colleagues has shown that rich mixed landscapes can be created and maintained now on a big scale by using free-ranging cattle and other large herbivores. The 5000 ha [sic] reserve at Oostvaarder-splassen is a show-case example of this.
>
> Could such an approach be appropriate for British conditions? That is what we want to find out.

It was surprising to us that our scientists regarded British ecological conditions as likely to be significantly different from those in Europe, considering that we shared the same evolutionary history and had only been separated from the Continent for 8,200 years – a blink of the evolutionary eye. We also felt that, despite the scientific controversy, the British response was excessively cautious. The Dutch, with a higher population density and far less land to play with, were willing to give rewilding a try. But our considerably smaller project at Knepp had fallen into a bog of feasibility studies, esoteric definitions and health and safety fears. Simply letting land go, leaving things to nature, was going to be far more challenging to the British authorities than we had ever imagined. The British attitude to nature seemed to have become defined by our insularity, by a narrowing of the field of vision.

While as private landowners there was nothing stopping us going ahead with rewilding the land without external support, we needed funding from government, or elsewhere – principally to cover the cost of erecting deer fences around our boundaries. In an email sent on 24 November 2004, Keith spelt out English Nature's position on Knepp: 'The advice to date from our agricultural policy specialists is that there would be little point in putting up big, novel ideas without a) having a sound scientific base for what is being proposed and b) evidence that the potential practical problems have been considered.' In sum, 'English Nature is unlikely to be a major funder of management schemes on the ground.'

Meanwhile, however, and much to our relief, our plans for Knepp had been gaining a momentum of their own. In 2003, we were awarded additional funding from the Countryside Stewardship Scheme – the government agri-environment programme behind the restoration of the Repton park. The estate was now divided, post fields, into three distinct areas separated by roads. We refer to them – somewhat unimaginatively – as the Northern, Middle and Southern Blocks. The Northern Block makes up the land north of the A272; the Middle Block includes the castle, the Repton park, the old castle and the River Adur; the Southern Block, the remaining land south of Swallows Lane. The area to the west of the Middle Block, comprising little pockets of land fragmented by lanes around the village of Shipley, remains outside the fenced areas but still, notionally at least, within the project.

Our new Countryside Stewardship Scheme agreement allowed us to incorporate the whole of the Middle Block – 280 hectares (700 acres) – and the Northern Block in the park restoration. Charlie's cousin Anthony Burrell, our neighbour, added 75 hectares (185 acres) of his land to the project in the Northern Block, making this area 235 hectares (580 acres) in total. We were now able to move the deer fence to the outer perimeter of the Middle Block, swallowing up what had once been Swallows Farm; and erect a deer fence around the four-and-a-half-mile perimeter of the Northern Block, while removing another twelve miles of internal fences. Forsaking the expensive wild-flower mix we had used in the Repton park restoration, we sowed the areas of the Northern Block that were not already under permanent pasture with a standard Countryside Steward-ship mix of native grasses.

For the time being the two areas of the park restoration – the Middle and Northern Blocks – would have to remain separate. The land bridge we dreamed of over the A272, allow-ing passage of grazing animals, was considered too expensive to attract funding. Green bridges were pioneered in the Nether-lands, where sixty-two 'ecoducts' have been constructed since 1988. One of the earliest was the Terlet overpass near Arnhem, planted with trees, which, within six years, was being used by three species of deer, wild boar, red foxes, badgers, wood mice, common shrews and common voles. Another, the Groene Woud ecoduct, near Eindhoven, has a chain of small pools across it and access ramps for amphibians. In Sweden, over-passes are used with considerable success to reduce road accidents caused by elk and roe deer. The impact of busy roads on wildlife, not just in terms of roadkill but in the far more insidious effects of physical and genetic isolation, is almost completely overlooked in Britain, even today. We have only two green bridges of any significance in the UK – one over the A21 at Scotney Castle in Kent, in the High Weald Area of Natural Beauty; the other, spanning five lanes of the M11, built to overcome the fragmentation of Mile End Park in London. There is a long way to go before green bridges are seen as a desirable and necessary tool of conservation in Britain.

The inspiration behind the extension of the deer park harked back to the estate as it was depicted on the 'Crow map' of 1754. Crow's map, commissioned by John Wicker who bought the estate from the ironmaster Caryll family – owners of Knepp for almost two centuries – hangs in the castle hall. The outline of Knepp's boundary, across two sheets of undulat-ing vellum, looks like a mongrel sitting up, begging. The lake, in a wobbly 'L', flows through the middle like an alimentary canal. The estate boundary on the map is an odd shape, incorporating a bulbous excrescence to the north of what is now the A272 – the head and paws of the dog – suggesting it had been extended to include a remnant of the original medieval deer park belonging to the old castle. The Countryside Stewardship Scheme was happy to include this area under an older definition of park restoration. It was a thrilling thought to have the Normans re-colonizing the landscape of Humphry Repton but we knew we'd also been extraordinarily lucky. We'd been knocking on the door of DEFRA at a time when they had ample funds from Europe for arable reversion and were keen to enlarge projects already included in the Countryside Stewardship Scheme.

Not long afterwards, we received another unexpected shot in the arm – again, under the auspices of Europe – that allowed us to release the Southern Block from farming. In June 2003, EU farm ministers announced a fundamental reform of the Common Agricultural Policy based on 'decoupling' subsidies from agricultural production – a policy that would come into effect in May 2005. The outgoing system of subsidies had weighted arable crops as the most lucrative with the result that farmers like us had, for decades, been motivated to plant them on unsuitable land. Incentivized by subsidies, we had all specialized in producing crops that were globally falling in price as a consequence of over-supply. One of the aims of the EU reform was to give marginal farmers the chance to consider alternatives, whether in terms of other crops more suited to their land, or entirely different forms of land management. Surprisingly few British farmers took advantage of this change in policy. They stuck doggedly to what they knew. But for us it was a game-changing opportunity. We could take all our land out of intensive agriculture, effectively putting it all into 'set-aside' and letting it all go fallow, and continue to claim the new Single Farm Payment, as it was called. The payment would be based on an average of the subsidies we had received over our last three years of farming. The only stipulation was that the land remain in 'cultivatable condition' but even with the topping, ditch maintenance and hedge-cutting that would entail, we would be looking at banking over 80 per cent of our subsidy. It was a no-brainer. By 2003, farming our land, even through a contractor, was losing us money. While Charlie's uncle was shouldering the labour and machinery costs we were still having to pay for fuel, fertilizer, agrichemicals and seed – the prices of which continued to rise – and the cost of hiring him as the contractor. Meanwhile, arable prices were falling steeply. In 2004 the price of wheat fell to less than £68 per tonne from a high of £125 in 1994 when Rural Payments Agency records began. Charlie's uncle needed no persuasion to give up the contract for Knepp. He was rarely making a profit farming our land and would need to renegotiate the agreement if he were to continue. Within a few years he, too, would abandon contract farming and concentrate his efforts on raising beef. The subsidies that for decades had skewed land management decisions in favour of intensive farming at Knepp had now been decoupled from the growing of crops. We could allow the land to revert to type, releasing our soils from the plough. Suddenly we had the wherewithal to embark on a naturalistic grazing project under our own steam.

6

Wild Ponies, Pigs and Longhorn Cattle

We patronise the animals for their incompleteness, for their tragic fate of having taken form so far below ourselves. And therein we err, and greatly err. For the animal shall not be measured by man. In a world older and more complete than ours, they are more finished and complete, gifted with extensions of the senses we have lost or never attained, living by voices we shall never hear.

Henry Beston, *The Outermost House*, 1928

It was almost impossible to imagine other farmers and land-owners in the same predicament as us, on the same kind of land, not wanting to follow suit. Who wouldn't throw in the towel on farming, pocket the subsidies for arable reversion and seize the chance to restore their soils and recover some of our country-side's missing wildlife? Encouraged by his cousin's commitment of adding 75 hectares (185 acres) to the Northern Block, Charlie drew up a map with obvious potential for expanding the project much further – a rectangular 10,000-acre block around Knepp defined by main roads. On 6 August 2003 we invited other neighbouring farmers and landowners, fifty in all, to an afternoon of presentations followed by supper in the bothy in the park. Avoiding the contentious word 'rewilding' we called it 'A Wild Wood Day'. Hans Kampf, an environmental policy adviser to the Dutch government, drove over from Holland to present the evidence of the Oostvaardersplassen and explain Vera's theories about grazing animals and natural processes, Ted Green showed slides of wood-pasture ecosystems in Spain, Portugal, Romania and Britain's New Forest, and Tony Whitbread, CEO of the Sussex Wildlife Trust, talked about the enormous biological potential of creating something like this in Sussex.

We knew the idea was challenging but hoped there would be at least a flicker of interest from our audience and that, in time, this might ignite support for the project and perhaps even a desire to join forces. We had no idea how far off the mark this was. Hans's slides of fighting Konik stallions, avalanches of greylag geese and Dutch backpackers sidestepping maggoty carcasses were met with stony silence. When Charlie stood up to show how he envisaged the landscape of Knepp changing over the next few years, the tidy Sussex fields and manicured hedges devolving into rampant scrub and untrammelled wet-land, the room erupted into a dissident murmuring and shaking of heads. It wasn't simply that our neighbours (including some other members of the family) thought this wasn't right for them. Chatting to them afterwards, Charlie and I realized it was more visceral than that. It was an affront to the efforts of every self-respecting farmer, an immoral waste of land, an assault on Britishness itself.

As our neighbours drove away that August day in 2003, unpersuaded if not downright appalled, they might have passed the herd of old English longhorns we had introduced into the park two months earlier. On reflection we had decided against Heck cattle. Having seen them in action in the Oostvaarders-plassen we felt they had too much Spanish fighting bull in their blood for the parish of Shipley. Walkers on the footpath, par-ticularly with dogs, had to be safe. We needed a traditional breed with enough of its wild ancestor's genes to survive all year round outside but one that had been bred for docility and was receptive to handling. With a pang of regret Charlie realized that his grandmother's beloved herd of Red Polls that he had sold off sixteen years earlier would have been perfect for the job.

We stumbled on old English longhorns through a local rubble-moving contractor who kept a herd at Gatwick and had some to spare. Fourteen cows and heifers – with thick brown and white coats and a distinctive white line, or 'finching', down their backs – made an immediate impression on the park. With their dramatic horns, sometimes curving upwards like the Texan (no direct relation), sometimes swooping downwards and framing their faces, occasionally pointing quizzically in different directions, there is more than a hint of the aurochs about them. They trace their ancestry back to the oxen used as draft animals in the sixteenth and seventeenth centuries in the north of England. They were prized for their longevity, their ease of calving, the high butterfat content of their milk and their horns, transparent slivers of which used to be made into buttons, cutlery, lamps and drinking cups – the poor man's glass. The breed was improved for beef during the Industrial Revolution to supply growing urban populations but, like most traditional cattle, lost out in the modern farming race to short-horned or polled (hornless) specialists like Friesians and Holsteins for dairy, and fast-growing Charolais, Hereford and Aberdeen Angus for beef. It was rescued from oblivion by the Rare Breeds Survival Trust in 1980.

Like the fallow deer, the cattle took time to settle. They spent their first few weeks tracing the perimeter fence, testing their boundaries. Only then did they begin to explore the interior, wandering outside the house, investigating the lake and ponds, constantly on the move. Though freedom like this was new to them, they demonstrated behaviours that were surprising to us, having only seen cows previously in the limiting context of the farm. They weaved amongst the trees, rubbing themselves against trunks and low-lying branches, raising their heads above the fallow browse-line to strip off leaves and buds with their long, gluey tongues, foraging in the margins of ponds and streams, wading through the marsh. They seemed to love the sallow at the head of the lake and when the flies and midges were bothersome they would rub their horns against the branches, stripping off leaves and bark and smearing sap onto their faces as insect repellent. The sight was very different to our single age-group herds of Friesians and Holsteins, short-lived, under-stimulated, heads down in the featureless fields. Ours had been by no means a bad system of dairying by modern standards. Yet we realized now that we had lost the ability to see the whole animal. To us, cows had become, for the most part, uniform and functional – a sad conclusion to our species' long and close association with them. But then perhaps it was this very reduction in character, this restraining of natural expression, that had made it easier for us to process them through the impersonal systems dictated by intensive farming.

Most of the longhorns were pregnant when they arrived at Knepp and the first calves were born within a few weeks. As with the fallow, we found ourselves suddenly encountering new-borns lying up in a ditch or hedge. This was far more disconcerting than stumbling across a fawn. Not intervening, particularly during calving, felt entirely alien. We had to make a conscious effort not to interfere without cause, trusting in the innate expertise of the cows.

Shortly before she is due to calve, a cow leaves the herd to find a good birthing spot. In some cases, she'll remain loyal to this spot for the rest of her life. If she is not a creature of habit it can take hours, if not days, for us to find her calf to tag it – something we are required to do by law, like any farmer. Shortly after the birth a cow will often seek out a patch of nettles to eat, presumably to replenish her levels of iron. After suckling her new-born the new mother will return to the herd, commuting sometimes miles to her fellows and back again until her calf is strong enough, usually when it is two or three days old, to follow her. The calf's introduction to the herd is momentous. The cattle crowd around, lowing gently, sniffing at the new arrival one by one, imprinting its aroma, the sense of its being, on the collective. While the calves are still young, often one or two experienced matrons will guard them in a nursery while the herd moves on to feed.

It took about two years for the herd to settle into a recognizable pattern. We began to predict the places where they would lie up in the rain, cooling themselves off in summer, or sniffing out the early spring grass or tender young nettles shooting up amongst the brambles. By then a multi-generational structure including a growing number of bull calves was beginning to develop, and the dominant females were throwing their weight around. They had also chosen a leader – an older cow – as the decision-maker. This leading matriarch has galvanizing authority. The herd might be lazing in the sunshine or holed up in warm leaf litter in the woods when suddenly she will begin to bellow and lead off. Time for pastures new. As one, the herd rouses itself and lumbers on behind her, responding with dutiful mooing as she bellows them on, sometimes encouraging them into a brisk trot. Seeing the cattle crashing through the Pleasure Grounds on some unknown mission is reminiscent of the elephant march in *The Jungle Book* – except that, of course, Kipling's lead elephant, Colonel Hathi, should have been an old female battle-axe. Most herd animals – including elephants and deer – are governed by a matriarchy that out-yins the herd yang and keeps even boisterous young males in check. Almost all accidents on farms involving cattle and the public are caused by young, single-generational, usually single-sex, groups of animals penned together in a field, and often provoked by the sight of a dog. Deprived of the natural herd dynamics, steers or young heifers are like bored teenagers lacking parental control.

Once they had had time to settle it was clear we had no need to worry about our free-roaming longhorns and the footpaths. Despite their intimidating appearance (it is surprising how often people assume horns mean bulls) they barely raise an eyebrow at walkers and their dogs. Only if someone gets between a mother and her calf do the eyes begin to flicker and the head to lower. Centuries of domestication, of breeding out aggressive genes, have reduced the risk posed by their dramatic horns, but ultimately maternal instincts rule the day.

Allowing the herd to expand naturally meant that calves could be suckled until they were almost as big as their mothers. In nature, a cow will generally only start kicking her offspring away from her teats once her udders have begun to 'bag up', or swell with extra milk, in readiness for another birth. But even after the arrival of the new calf the family bond remains strong – complex relationships that, again, we were unused to seeing. I remembered agonizing nights, living in a house on the estate when Charlie's grandparents were still alive, listening to bellowing calves, newly separated from their mothers, in the cowshed next door. They had been allowed the benefit of their mothers' colostrum – the yellow cream, rich in antibodies, let down in the udder in the first few days after birth – but at three days had been separated into calf units where they were fed on powdered milk from an automated machine at regulated times of day. The bull calves would be taken to slaughter at the age of about eighteen to twenty weeks for 'white' veal, or twenty-two to thirty-five weeks for 'pink' veal; while the pick of the heifers would be grown on at Knepp to continue the dairy herd and the others sold off at the market. Back in the dairy, the mothers would call for their calves, sometimes for days, as they rejoined the treadmill of milk production for human consumption. A dairy cow's life is unrelenting. By five or six years old, having produced three to four calves and an average of 22 litres of milk every day for 365 days a year (we had one cow that, during peak lactation, gave us 75 litres a day), she is ready for the knacker's yard, her meat good for little more than dog food and meat pies. The toll on her health is unsurprising given that, in nature, the amount of milk she produces for her calf is 3–4 litres a day. One particular affliction of modern dairy cows is mastitis – a painful inflammation of the udder caused by bacterial infection. In a herd of a hundred cows in the UK there can be as many as seventy cases of mastitis every year.

In our naturalistic system, however, particularly while we were growing the herd, we could allow even the older barren cows to live on, culling them only when it became the humane thing to do. The oldest amongst them would reach the ripe old age of twenty-one.

In early March, before the arrival of spring grass, the long-horns' former owner paid us a visit, anxious to see how his cattle had weathered the winter without human intervention. The cows had lost a little weight – to be expected over winter – but browsing heavily on twigs and vegetation they were robust and healthy, and the summer calves were thriving. He simply couldn't believe we hadn't supplementary fed them. There had been no need for the vet and no calving problems, other than one accident – a calf, born beside the river, had fallen in and drowned. Our calving and health statistics were better than most conventional cattle farms.

The Exmoor ponies, six fillies, arrived in the park several months after the cattle, in November 2003. They had been gathered from Exmoor for market in the annual autumn round-up and been loaded up for transport for only the second time in their lives. As they galloped from the trailer, bucking their way back to freedom, we could see we were dealing with an animal way wilder than the longhorn. Another Dutchman, Joep van der Vlasakker, an expert in wild horses and conservation grazing, had advised us on the breed. To Joep's mind, Exmoors are amongst the oldest horses in Europe, closer genetically to the original tarpan than even Koniks. The Konik had been chosen for the Oostvaardersplassen back in 1984 principally because it was believed to be descended directly from the tarpan. Whether or not these claims are valid (Joep is dubious), he feels there is a strong genetic and ecological argument for using more than one breed in conservation grazing projects as a replacement for the extinct wild horse – Hucul horses in the Carpathians, for example; Norwegian Fjord ponies or Swedish Gotlandruss ponies in Northern Europe, Koniks in lowland Eastern Europe; and Exmoors in Western Europe.

There is little doubt about the Exmoor's credentials as an equine aboriginal. Fossil remains have been found in the area of Exmoor dating back to around 50,000 BC. Roman carvings in Somerset depict ponies phenotypically similar to Exmoors, and the Domesday Book records ponies on Exmoor in 1086. Whether Exmoors have been pure-bred since the ice age remains a subject of debate. The DNA evidence is inconclusive and there are stories of domesticated stallions over the centuries breaking out onto the moor to breed with wild Exmoor mares – one is said to have been an Arab, Katerfelto, who swam ashore after the wrecking of the Spanish Armada. Unlike the Konik, however, there has been little intentional breeding inter- ference of free-living Exmoors by man, other than to take stallions off the moor to promote hybrid vigour in domesti- cated stock.

What is evident is that the Exmoor's characteristics continue to dominate, even in cross-breeding. With its powerful build, stocky legs and small ears, its dark bay colouring with mealy 'pangaré' markings around the eyes, muzzle, flanks and under- belly, the Exmoor is the living image of the horses depicted in the Palaeolithic cave paintings of Lascaux in the Dordogne, dating back 17,300 years; and its bones and skeleton closely resemble fossil records of primitive equines such as the wild Alaskan horse.

Enduring and perfectly adapted to its rugged environment it is a miracle, nonetheless, that the Exmoor has survived into the present day. During the Second World War, when Exmoor became a military training ground, soldiers used the ponies for target practice. Others were rustled by locals for food. By the end of the war there were fewer than fifty left. Despite breeding programmes since, it remains on the UK Rare Breeds Survival Trust's endangered list, with fewer than 500 free-roaming indi- viduals on Exmoor, and just over 3,000 elsewhere in the UK and a handful of other countries. Globally, its predicament is 'critical', according to the Equus Survival Trust. Knepp had become a custodian of an animal rarer than the tiger.

In the eyes of the American writer and poet Alice Walker, horses make a landscape more beautiful. She was thinking of the wild mustangs and Appaloosas of America's rocky canyons and prairies, rather than quarter-horses in a Kentucky paddock. The Exmoors brought that frisson to Knepp – creating an atavistic bond with the landscape of our past. With their characteristic 'toad' eyes they seem to be looking at the world from the ice floes. They are evolved for the harshest of conditions, with deep chests, large hearts and lungs, broad backs, strong legs and hard hooves; big heads with small nostrils for breathing freezing air; strong jaws and long, deep-rooted teeth for macerating the toughest fibres; thick manes and long forelocks, and fanned, water-deflecting 'ice tails'. In winter, they grow an insulating woolly under-layer beneath an outer coating of long, water-resistant oily hair. Their eyelids are insulated with fatty pads to deflect rain and snow and, perhaps, to protect from the claws of the predators that would have once roamed the moors. They are spirited, defiant, inquisitive, with – one senses – an imperious contempt for human beings. To begin with, at least, their flight distance at Knepp was almost twice that of the longhorns.

One of our initial concerns was that, after the wilds of the moors, our lowland clay might be too soft for them, our grasses too rich. We worried about laminitis, a disease affecting all ungulates but particularly horses, whose single stomachs make them susceptible. Laminitis is caused by carbohydrate overload. If a horse is fed grain or clover in excess, it can accumulate sugars, starch and fructans, which ferment in the gut, killing off beneficial bacteria, increasing the acidity and permeability of the gut lining and producing a build-up of toxins in the bloodstream. This results in body-wide inflammation, particularly in the feet where swelling tissues have no place to expand without structural injury. It is the dread of every horse-lover yet, paradoxically, it is most often caused by indulgent over-feeding. In severe cases it can require aggressive treatment or even euthanasia.

The following year, during the spring flush of new grass, Mark, our stable manager who had taken on custody of the Exmoors, spotted the telltale signs of laminitis in one of the fillies. Deploying his impressive horse-whispering skills he caught her up and installed her in the old paddock next to the house where, for four weeks – to the curiosity of her sisters who rubbed noses with her over the fence – she was fed nothing but small amounts of hay. Gradually the symptoms subsided and she was released again onto the rougher summer grass. The disease had been caught in time. The following spring we watched the Exmoors anxiously and when one began to show signs of inflammation, erring on the side of caution, Mark caught them all up and put them on strict rations in the paddock for ten days before releasing them again. We were worried this would be the pattern but the following year, none of them showed signs of the condition. With declining artificial nitrogen in our soil, the sugars and fructans in the grass had finally dropped to levels that the ponies could metabolize.

Once we were confident the Exmoors would do well at Knepp we set about building a herd. Enter Duncan, in July 2005 – a semi-domesticated pure-bred Exmoor colt, a fine specimen who had been taken off the moor at a year old and halter-broken so he could be shown as a future stallion. Though never ridden he was accustomed to being handled, washed, brushed and led around a ring. His introduction to Knepp was not his finest hour. The ponies were calmly grazing in front of the house, casting shadows in the evening sun, when Duncan arrived. As he trotted up to befriend them the six mares turned on him in unison and, snorting with affront, belted him with their back legs. Whinnying with shock he took cover behind us as the thug misses pawed the ground, baying for blood.

We had chosen a semi-domesticated colt because we thought he would be easier to handle as a stallion. Now we worried he wouldn't be tough enough for the job. Mark was sanguine. 'Let them settle down,' he said, and we walked purposefully away, leaving Duncan to his fate. Sure enough, the following morning, there was Duncan, shell-shocked and still acting a little furtively, but in with the girls. We watched the group grazing in front of the lake and let out a cheer as the valiant little colt began to cover them.

Eleven months later – the average gestation of an Exmoor – it was still virtually impossible to tell if any of the mares with their naturally rotund bellies was pregnant. We had almost given up hope when, one freezing, rain-swept day in October, our first foal was born, out in the open, just yards from the main drive. More than the fawns, or even the calves, this little colt standing and collapsing on his shaky legs, shielded by his mother in the driving rain, marked a milestone, bringing rewilding to life. In December another colt was born, and a filly the following April, swelling the global population of free-living Exmoors.

However, as Duncan grew bolder his temperament was becoming a problem. Natural Exmoor curiosity combined with an over-familiarity with humans gave him a brazen disregard for boundaries. He staked out his territory with a dunging spot directly outside the Estate Office where our accountant parked her car, positioning himself – it seemed – as king of the castle. Every day Mark would shovel away the dung heap steaming with pheromonal urine, only to find the beginnings of another territorial mound in the same spot the following morning. One day Duncan strolled into the entrance hall of the office, giving Charlie's PA a near heart-attack as his head appeared at the reception window.

But it was Duncan's behaviour towards riders in the park that caused us most concern. Though the wild Exmoor mares and their offspring were curious, they tended to keep a healthy flight distance from humans and their horses. Duncan would charge up and challenge. He would gallop onto the practice polo field in front of the house, straight through the spectators, to investigate his strange cousins chasing a ball. The chukka would end up, more often than not, in a game to evict Duncan from the pitch. His semi-domestication was proving a liability for rewilding, and in July 2007 he was sent away to a new home with 'Exmoor' Paul – a friend of Mark's who had a small domesticated herd of his own. A year later we received a photo of Duncan, trotting through his show classes, good as gold, with a child on board, looking for all the world like a Thelwell cartoon. His days in the twilight zone between wild and tame were over.

The Exmoor mares' dominion over the park had been rocked, in December 2004, by the arrival of our two Tamworth sows and their eight piglets. The Dangerous Wild Animals Act, prohibiting the release of wild boar into the British country-side, had forced a compromise on our original plan. Enacted in 1976 to prevent releases of dangerous and exotic pets such as pumas, boa constrictors, venomous reptiles, spiders and scorpions – for which there had been a craze in the late 1960s and early 1970s – the Act had, in 1984, been amended to include wild boar, despite their being acknowledged as a native species that had once been widespread in Britain.

The contradiction has led to a bizarre anomaly in the status of wild boar in the UK. The number of wild-boar farms has been increasing since the 1970s, driven by a market for their strong, wild-flavoured meat. While in captivity they are subject to the Dangerous Wild Animals Act and require a licence. However, if they break out into open countryside they become just another non-notifiable wild animal like deer, badgers and foxes. Since they can weigh 280lb fully grown, jump six feet and reach a speed of 30mph, this is not an unusual occurrence. Every now and again, farmers find they are too much to handle or that the cost of keeping them fenced is beyond them. No one knows the true figure for how many wild boar have broken out and are roaming Britain, but in the Forest of Dean alone the number is thought to have reached 1,500.

Our best bet was to hope that a feral individual in our area would arrive at Knepp on his own. If a wild boar wanted to break in, we were advised – and the scent of our Tamworth sows should prove irresistible – a deer fence would present no

The Canadian 3rd Division stationed at Knepp Castle during the Second World War parade in front of the first crop of wheat grown in the Repton Park as part of the British government's campaign to Dig for Victory. *(Knepp archives)*

Like so much land on heavy Sussex clay, much of Knepp had been allowed to scrub up during the agricultural depression between the wars. But in the Second World War even the most unproductive land was cleared for ploughing. Under rewilding, thorny shrubs are now returning to these areas, providing a haven for wildlife. *(Knepp archives)*

BEFORE: Our old water-meadows, or 'laggs', had never been agriculturally productive, despite being drained for the purpose in Victorian times. When we released pigs into the Middle Block in 2004 they had a field-day rootling in the wet soil. *(Charlie Burrell)*

AFTER: Our restoration of 1.5 miles of the River Adur has returned the flow of water from a steep-sided Victorian canal to its original floodplain. The land now acts like a natural sponge again, holding water and preventing flash floods downstream. Numerous associated shallow ponds, or scrapes, on the floodplain provide habitat for kingfishers, herons and other water-birds. *(Charlie Burrell)*

BEFORE: the reconstructed Hammer Pond in summer 2004, a year after the first fields in the Southern Block were left fallow after we abandoned conventional farming. *(Knepp archives)*

AFTER: Autumn 2017, fourteen years after being left fallow, the delineation of the fields is beginning to blur as hedges billow out and thorny scrub emerges. In the foreground an eruption of sallow (native hybrid willow) provides habitat for purple emperor butterflies. *(Charlie Burrell)*

Charlie and our daughter Nancy rejoice in a bumper crop of wheat in 1996
– a rare year when Knepp Home Farm actually made a profit.
(Isabella Tree)

This old oak sat in the corner of an arable field, assaulted by ploughing and chemicals for fifty years. It began dying just as we began restoring the Repton park. Under the old regime we would have chopped it down without a thought. Now it is rich dead-wood habitat and a symbol of our change of heart. *(Charlie Burrell)*

The Dutch ecologist Frans Vera, whose grazing ecology theory inspired the Knepp project, stands in the Southern Block demonstrating how naturally regenerating thorny scrub provides protection for young trees from browsing animals – proof of the medieval adage that 'the thorn is the mother of the oak'. *(Charlie Burrell)*

Fallow deer, inhabitants of Britain before the last Ice Age, were reintroduced to our islands for hunting by the Normans. The most numerous of the large herbivores at Knepp, they are predominantly grazers. The bucks generate considerable vegetation disturbance during the rut with antler-rubbing and lekking. *(Charlie Burrell)*

Roe deer, also native to Britain, are predominantly browsers. Already present at Knepp in low numbers, they add another mouthpiece to the mix of herbivores, contributing to vegetation complexity. *(Charlie Burrell)*

A native species, red deer were introduced to the project in 2009 when we judged the emerging vegetation was ready for some heavy-hitting disturbance. Red deer break branches, dig up turf and de-bark trees. *(Bill Brooks)*

Old English longhorn cattle, a hardy ancient breed, survive through the winter by browsing on vegetation. They act as proxies for their extinct ancestor, the aurochs. *(Charlie Burrell)*

Our Tamworth pigs create the same disturbance as the original wild boar. The first thing they did when released into the park was rootle along the verges – areas that, having never been ploughed, were rich in invertebrates and rhizomes. *(Charlie Burrell)*

obstacle. Until then, the Tamworth would stand in as its proxy, rootling and disturbing the soil of Knepp as their wild ancestors had in the time of King John.

We had chosen Tamworths, as we had the Exmoors, as an old breed renowned for their hardiness and their close relationship to their original ancestor. Their long legs and snouts, narrow backs, long bristles and surprising ability to sprint for short distances as fast as a horse, are characteristic of European forest swine. Registered as a breed in the early nineteenth century on the Prime Minister Sir Robert Peel's estate at Tamworth in Staffordshire, they have lost out to fast-growing, large-littering modern breeds specifically designed for intensive farming. The Rare Breeds Survival Trusts estimates that there are fewer than 300 registered breeding Tamworth females in the UK.

When the Tamworths appeared, the Exmoors acted as if we had introduced them to a pack of grizzly bears. One glimpse of the vast, bristly, ginger farmyard sows and the ponies were running for the hills. Domesticated horses, too, shied away – a response triggered, we imagined, by some atavistic memory of wild boar predating on new-born foals. Like hyena, wild boar are omnivorous. Their meat-eating is usually of carrion – their teeth are for grinding rather than killing – but they are opportunists, and a tender, unresisting new-born wild foal would, a thousand years ago, have been a delicacy to a hungry wild boar.

Eventually, the Exmoors realized that the Tamworths posed no real threat. They relaxed a little and would even graze in the same area as the pigs – but if a piglet was foolish enough to stray into their herd they did not hesitate to boot it to death, as I witnessed to my dismay one morning when I was showing some adorable new piglets to my four-year-old goddaughter.

People have a famously soft spot for pigs. Intelligent, inquisitive, imperious, myopic, sociable, gluttonous, grunting, ungainly, it is easy to recognize ourselves in them. From Miss Piggy to the Empress of Blandings we have celebrated the comedy of our similarities. But there may, indeed, be real biological grounds for the sense of connection. Recent genetic research has identified a close relationship in pig and primate evolution. Whether we are actually descendants of an ancient common ancestor of pig and chimpanzee will require a detailed search of the human genome but it seems we are certainly much closer to pigs than we originally thought. Which is why, perhaps, the Tamworths are constantly forgiven their antics at Knepp. The instant they were let out of the acclimatization area in the Rookery, they applied themselves to destroying Charlie's manicured verges along the drives with the unstoppable momentum of forklift trucks. Then, two abreast, they unzipped the turf down the public footpaths, following the exact routes on the Ordnance Survey map, heading diagonally across the fields. We realized that what they were doing, with the undeviating propulsion of slow-motion torpedoes, was zeroing in on slivers of the park that had never been ploughed – margins rich in invertebrates, rhizomes and flora. In the first few days of their release the pigs drew an accurate blueprint of what modern farming had done to our soil.

The ornamental grass circle in front of the house, another patch of pristine turf, proved to have a magnetic attraction, too, and Charlie was compelled to take to his bicycle, jackeroo stock-whip in hand, to impress upon them that this area was sacred ground. There aren't many effective ways of turning around a 500lb beast compelled by appetite, and the alternative – a bucket of pig-nuts – would only have encouraged them to return. The two sows – nicknamed 'Big Mama' and 'Sweet Face' by our children – got the point, however, and passed on the message to their piglets. On this score at least, we'd come to an understanding. As Winston Churchill once observed, 'A cat looks down on you. A dog looks up to you. A pig looks you straight in the eye.' We had met our equals.

Their ingenuity often got the better of us, however, when it came to public events in the park. The pigs could spot a marquee going up a mile away. Though we electric-fenced the showground for the summer Craft Fair we didn't think to fortify the pond on one side of it. The pigs swam across in the middle of the night, broke into the confectionery tent and hoovered down two sacks of Mr Whippy powdered ice-cream. At the annual Polo Ball held on the field in front of the lake they would mingle with the black ties and ball-gowns, begging for canapés and stealing the show with their party trick of crashing over onto their sides for a belly rub. When the phone rang the morning after a big tented Indian wedding in the park with news that the pigs had snaffled two trays of onion bhajis, we braced ourselves for demands for a refund and possibly a court summons. The mother of the bride, however, was congeniality itself. The visit from the pigs had added to the delights of the day. She was only worried that the spices might have given them tummy-ache. Could we give them some Alka-Seltzer?

The Tamworths' opportunistic snacking, however, was a real concern – and not just because it might give them indigestion or lose us our recently accredited organic status. Like Duncan, we worried that the Tamworths might just be too familiar with humans to be left to their own devices in a rewilding project. Walkers had begun bringing crusts to feed them and Big Mama and Sweet Face – and their rapidly growing offspring – were starting to charge up and head-butt people's pockets. They meant no harm, but they could easily knock over the elderly or infirm, or a child. And a protective dog might not be so forgiving. We put signs up on all the footpaths begging people not to feed any of the animals. In time, and with wild-born generations, we hoped, the pigs might grow more reserved and perhaps even develop a flight distance of their own.

Once the pigs had exhausted the verges they cast their snouts further afield. We were dismayed at first to observe their capacity for damage, particularly in the wet, when ten individuals could churn acres into the battlefield of the Somme in a matter of hours. But the land's ability to regenerate was equally astonishing and in the growing season it was only a matter of days before a patchwork of pioneer plants would appear where the sward had been opened. Invertebrates, including solitary bees, colonized the exposed ground. Some of these bees, now rare in the UK, need large patches of open ground in which to burrow and, in the absence of wild-boar disturbance, resort to farm gateways where heavy traffic and bottlenecks of livestock have the same earth-churning effect. In winter, wrens, dunnocks and robins trailed in the wake of the pigs, picking for insects in the furrows.

Ants began to use the clods of earth turned over by the pigs to kick-start anthills that have grown, in some places, over a foot in eight years – their colonies thriving in micro-climates of sun-warmed, aerated soil. The anthills, in turn, attract mistle thrushes and wheatears, and especially green woodpeckers, whose diet, particularly in winter, can consist of as much as 80 per cent grassland ants. In flight the green woodpecker is easy to spot: a flash of vivid yellow-green dipping through the air with a loud cackling cry – the 'yaffle' which gives the woodpecker its Sussex dialect name. It is not so easy to spot once it has landed. Perfectly camouflaged against the grass, it drills into the ant mounds, breaking into the galleries and gathering up ants with a flick of a tongue four inches long and coated with glue. At rest, in order to fit inside the bird's head, the tongue coils behind the skull, over the eyes and into the right nostril. The adult collects ants for its nestlings too – in astronomical amounts. In one study, carried out in Romania, seven green woodpecker chicks consumed an estimated 1.5 million ants and pupae before leaving the nest. The droppings of a green woodpecker look like cigarette ash on top of an ant mound. Break them open and they are full of sad little ant faces looking like they don't know what hit them.

The sun-warmed soil of the anthills is also a favoured basking spot for the small copper butterfly and the declining 'common' lizard, and provides a place for the widespread common field grasshopper to lay its eggs. Very occasionally, in a reversal of fate, the pigs will excavate the anthills for beetles, and then the ants bustle about to repair the damage. The anthills have a different soil composition from the surrounding acid grassland, favouring different species of fungi, lichens, mosses, grasses and other flowering plants such as wild thyme which colonize and help to bind the surface. Suddenly, miraculously, thanks to the unexpected association between ants and pigs, we were seeing light, complex soils rising out of our heavy Sussex clay.

The pigs were having an impact on vegetation, too. They have a penchant for plants that other grazers cannot find or stomach, like the stubborn, subterranean roots of docks and spear thistles. Unlike other ungulates they can also eat bracken and its rhizomes, neutralizing the toxins and carcinogens in their gut. While even they can't tackle poisonous rhododendron as a mature shrub, they have proved an effective ally in eradication programmes in conservation projects, suppressing rhododendron regrowth by eating the new shoots.

It was clear to us from the outset that the pigs were creating opportunities for other species. But the browsing, trashing and trampling of the other grazing animals was also having an effect. In places where the low branch of a tree provided a scratching post for the cattle, for example, the compacting of the clay by their hooves created saucers in the ground which periodically filled with water. For once we were happy to see water lying on the land. We began to learn that these clean-water 'ephemeral ponds' – sometimes no bigger than a large puddle and so shallow as to be prone to evaporation – are an important habitat (now increasingly rare in the UK) for plants like water crowfoot, water starwort and stoneworts, and a whole range of specialist snails and water beetles, as well as the endangered and ethereal fairy shrimp. All the grazing animals would spend at least some time investigating the margins of the lake and other ponds in the park, and their trampling and browsing challenged the supremacy of reed mace, creating opportunities for other aquatic plants.

But the biggest change of all came from simply not drenching the land with fungicides and pesticides, as we had since the 1960s. As our insect populations exploded, we were seeing pipistrelle bats flicking outside the house at night and Daubenton's bats skimming the surface of the lake for midges and mosquitoes. And, according to local chiropterologists (bat scientists), rare barbastelle bats had begun flying in from the Mens woodland reserve, fifteen miles away, to feed on night-flying micromoths and small beetles over our water meadows. A candle-lit dinner in the garden was now an invitation to a host of moths we were useless at identifying, apart from hummingbird hawkmoths – which were conspicuous and self-explanatory. In autumn, we can now pick field mushrooms in the middle of the park and, every year, an eruption of parasols fringes the edge of Spring Wood with fairy rings.

With the grazing animals no longer taking avermectins – the powerful wormers and parasiticides with which most domestic horses and all livestock on non-organic farms are habitually dosed – we were seeing cowpats and horse dung unlike anything we had seen outside Africa, latticed with the holes of dung beetles. For Charlie this became something of a fixation, taking him back to the bug obsessions of his childhood in Africa and Australia. He would lie next to a pile of fresh Exmoor dung and count the minutes (the record was three) that it would take for the dung beetles to arrive. Summoned by the smell and zeroing in like attack helicopters, the beetles fold their wings and plop straight into the dung. If a crust has already formed, they bounce off and then have to scamper back into it, burying themselves headfirst in nourishing excrement. Before long the kitchen counter was forested with glass vials containing all the species Charlie could find, to be dispatched to Professor Paul Buckland at Bournemouth University for identification. Triumphantly, after a summer of faecal rummaging, he had identified twenty-three species of dung beetle from a single cowpat.

There are about sixty species of native dung beetle in the UK, we learned. Unlike African dung beetles, which are famous for rolling away dung balls up to fifty times their weight over long distances, some using the Milky Way to guide them, most of our dung beetles are tunnellers – pulling the dung down into the soil to nest chambers that can be up to two feet deep, either near or directly underneath the dung site. The dung provides a food supply for the beetle's larvae, allowing them to develop deep inside the nest, away from predators.

There have been dung beetles on the planet for 30 million years. They exist on every continent except Antarctica and specialize in every form of animal dung there is, though the majority prefer the plant material contained in the dung of herbivores. Dosing livestock and pets with parasiticides that pass into their excrement, killing any insect that eats it, including dung beetles, is one of the most serious problems affecting our soils. The process of a dung beetle's tunnelling, eating and digesting adds organic matter, increases soil fertility, aeration and structure, and improves rainwater filtration and the quality of groundwater run-off. Ironically, by eating the parasites harboured in dung and by swiftly processing the dung itself, dung beetles also reduce the transmission of parasites and hence the need for chemical livestock wormers. Only now, when several of our dung species are on the verge of extinction, are farmers beginning to appreciate their value. Dung beetles are estimated to save the British cattle industry £367 million a year simply by encouraging the growth of healthy grass. And of course they are part of the food chain. For the first time we were seeing little owls – beetle specialists – breeding at Knepp, perching with their chicks on the tree-guards of the new generation of oaks we had planted in the park.

Other insectivorous birds were returning too, including a species once familiar to the ear of everyone living in the country. The skylark is the subject of Britain's favourite modern classical piece of music. Yet this beloved bird declined 75 per cent between 1972 and 1996, and still the decline continues. People are now more likely to have heard 'The Lark Ascending' in a concert hall than in the countryside. Walking over tussocky grass in what was once the large arable field next to Tumble-down Lagg overlooking the floodplain of the River Adur, and

Town Field – so named for the medieval town (all trace of which has vanished) that once thrived in the curtilage of Old Knepp Castle – we were hearing skylarks again, their vertical ascent pulsating with urgent song. The very air, it seemed, was being recolonized with the sounds of the past.

7

Creating a Mess

The question is not what you look at, but what you see.

Henry David Thoreau, *I to Myself*, August 1851

Woe to you who add house to house and join field to field
till no space is left and you live alone in the land.

Isaiah 5:8

How far we could proceed with rewilding the Middle Block
was dictated in large part by the designation of the nineteenth-
century park around the house. Our grant from Countryside
Stewardship required the Repton features of rolling deer lawns,
which meant keeping the numbers of grazing animals high,
allowing no opportunities for unsightly scrub to emerge.
Thrilling as it was to see insects, birds, bats, reptiles and fungi
on the rise, and to have found respite for our ancient oaks, from
a rewilding point of view the landscape itself still felt constrained, bound to an ideal of human artifice.

In the Northern Block, since it had never been part of the
Repton plan, but had once, it was thought, been part of old
Knepp Castle's more rugged medieval deer park, we were freer
to experiment. In 2004 Frans Vera came to stay and advised us to
put only a small herd of longhorns in this area for the time
being, to give the vegetation a chance. In five years' time, he
hoped, we would begin to see the hedges growing out, thorny
scrub developing and pioneer species entering the sward. At that

point we could decide whether to introduce deer, ponies and pigs, or wait even longer. It was like weighing the contenders before putting them into the ring. We managed to persuade the Countryside Stewardship Scheme that this strategy – of establishing a fairer contest between vegetation succession and animal disturbance – might, ultimately, create something more dynamic and biologically interesting than the static, 'game-over' landscape of a nineteenth-century deer park and consequently received a derogation to allow scrub to appear in this area. We released our second herd of twenty-three longhorns to roam the 235 hectares (580 acres) of the Northern Block, and sat back to await events.

The Southern Block was a completely different story. Even though it was likely to have been part of the original twelfth-century deer park, it was not featured on the 1754 Crow map – the only clue the estate had of its medieval past – which meant we could not offer it up to Countryside Stewardship as a park restoration. We were making little headway, meanwhile, persuading government to support a naturalistic grazing experiment across the whole estate. Despite several more visits, encouraging discussions and a pledge to fund a baseline survey of wildlife at Knepp, English Nature was still tentative about publicly backing the project. In January 2005 Keith Kirby wrote: 'We have had informal discussions with various people in the Rural Development Service and the Countryside Agency about "rewilding" ideas; some people enthusiastic, some less so.' Anticipating the 'new, integrated rural delivery agency' in 2007 he went on, 'as part of the run-up to this integration we are talking about what issues we will want to take forward practically as joint ventures between now and then . . . I hope rewilding will be part of this.' But clearly nothing was going to happen soon and without funding we had no means of erecting the £100,000 deer-fence around the Southern Block boundary, plus the £50,000 needed to remove culverts, bridle gates, fences, field gates, river gates and bridges.

We had begun taking the least productive fields of the

Southern Block out of conventional farming in 2001, continuing in increments over the following five years. With no immediate prospect of introducing herbivores into this area we decided to avoid the cost of re-seeding with a native grass mix as we had in the Middle and Northern Blocks and simply left the fields as they were after the last harvest of maize, wheat, barley or whatever crop had happened to be growing. By 2006 all 450 hectares (1,100 acres) had been left to their own devices for between one to five years, while we continued to petition the powers-that-be for the wherewithal to put a conservation grazing strategy into action.

Ironically, this frustrating hiatus proved the most positive move of all for rewilding. Our haphazard process of freeing the land in stages, combined with no re-seeding of grass and a delay in introducing the heavy-hitting grazers, proved to be rocket-fuel to natural processes, generating opportunities for wildlife that were far more exciting than anything we were doing elsewhere.

In just a few years a completely different landscape began to stir in most of the Southern Block. The very wettest fields, compacted after years of farming, and now deprived of the rotavator and starved of oxygen, were proving slow to change. Fifteen years on, some have barely moved at all and we imagine that, if soil invertebrates are still unable to colonize and aerate them, these waterlogged pans will eventually form shallow, standing ponds – a very different kind of habitat. But in all other areas, to a greater or lesser degree, thorny scrub was taking off. With no cover of thick grass sward to hold them back, fists of hawthorn, blackthorn, dog rose and bramble were punching through fields that, only two or three years earlier, had been blanketed with maize and barley. Miles of hedgerows, previously flailed every autumn before the ground was too wet to take the hedge-cutter – thereby depriving birds of the vital resource of winter berries – were now exploding into the welcoming humus, billowing out like a dowager liberated from her stays.

Every field was responding differently, depending on the

land use over the years, its last crop, subtle differences in soil type, the weather conditions of the particular year it was taken out of agriculture and whether that year was a 'mast' year (a year of exceptional seed production) for certain trees and shrubs – all of which encouraged different assemblages of vegetation colonizing at a different pace. Complex communities of flora were emerging in close proximity to each other: the knock-on effect was astonishing. Bicycling across the area or driving in the 4WD mule in summer we had to keep our mouths shut and wear glasses against the splatter-cloud of insects. The 'moth snowstorms' remembered by environmental journalist Mike McCarthy as a common feature of summers before pesticides took their toll were back in force. There was birdsong, even in winter. Flocks of fieldfares, meadow pipits and redwings – winter visitors we had rarely seen here before – were descending for berries and invertebrates, and bullfinches – a bird that was fast declining elsewhere in the south-east of England, down 35 per cent in the years 1995–2010 – were feasting on buds, blackberries and seeds. March brought out skylarks by the dozen and in summer the yellowhammer – one of our most rapidly declining farmland birds (a drop of 60 per cent nationwide since 1960) – pleaded for 'a-little-bit-of-bread-and-no-cheeeeese'.

Most significant of all, from the Vera perspective, as the scrub began to appear, tiny oak trees began popping up by the thousand all over the Southern Block. Some may have erupted from larders of acorns stashed by field mice that had subsequently been predated by a barn owl or buzzard – birds that were also now appearing in numbers. But by far the most significant distributor of the oak is the jay. The most strikingly handsome and colourful of the crow family, dusky pink with white throat and black moustachial stripe, and black and white wings emblazoned with blue, the jay was persecuted throughout the nineteenth century – and continues to be by some gamekeepers – as a robber of birds' nests, eating eggs and even chicks. Like most corvids it is an impressive all-rounder, also feeding on a variety of invertebrates, seeds and fruits, and occasionally small mammals. But it has one particular speciality – its habit of burying acorns. Other corvids may do this but none with the skill of the jay, which makes it the single most import-ant agent in the generation of natural wood pasture.

Pedunculate and sessile oaks, left to their own devices, have a surprisingly poor ability to reproduce. An oak can be twenty years old before it bears its first crop of acorns and then most of the tens of thousands of seeds that fall to the ground every autumn are eaten by animals or simply rot away. Since it is light-demanding, any seedling that manages to take root beneath the parent canopy is doomed to fail. The acorn needs, somehow, to be buried in the earth to escape predation and germinate. To perpetuate itself the oak must rely on other spe-cies and this has given rise to its remarkable symbiotic partnership with the jay.

A single jay can plant over 7,500 acorns in four weeks, living up to its Latin name, *Garrulus glandarius*, 'the chattering acorn-gatherer'. It is particularly choosy, selecting ripe acorns that are not too small and have not been affected by parasites, those with high calorific value that also – hence the symbiosis – have the best chance of germination. Carrying up to six at a time – the largest or longest acorn visible in its beak, the rest in a stacking system down its gullet – the jay flies to a spot any-where between sixty or seventy yards to a few miles away from the parent tree. It seeks out areas of open ground where the oak can germinate, and then buries the acorns at the base of thorny bushes like hawthorn which, projecting vertically from the grassland, act as beacons to jog its memory at a later date. It buries each acorn separately, about eighteen inches to three feet apart, hammering them deep into the ground where they are less likely to be found by mice and squirrels, and, incidentally, are most likely to take root.

Jays eat these stored, carbohydrate-rich acorns throughout the year. But from April to August, when there is plenty of other food available, they do so far less – and this is when the excess acorns can germinate. The stem of the seedling generally appears in May and by June the first crown of leaves has unfolded. This timing is key. June is when the jays start looking for the seedlings to feed their young. They are interested not in the seedling itself but in its cotyledons – the fat, primal leaves containing stored food reserves from the seed that most plants depend on for their initial burst of energy to grow.

For an oak, however, the cotyledons are not so crucial. Immediately after germination a young oak growing in full daylight puts down an extensive root system with a long taproot, and this nourishes the seedling from the start. Scientists have recently shown, by removing the cotyledons during the early stages of an oak sapling's growth, that they contain far more energy reserves than the seedling needs. It can survive perfectly well without them. An oak's cotyledons remain in the ground. When a jay finds a seedling it takes hold of the stem with its beak and lifts the plant, raising the remains of the acorn and the cotyledons above the ground so it can pluck them off to feed to its young. Because of the strength of the oak seedling's taproot, this yanking up of the plant does not, in the majority of cases, kill it and the removal of the cotyledons does not hamper its growth. It seems these cotyledons may be the oak's reward to the jay for its careful midwifery.

All over the Southern Block, now, we were finding jay-planted oak seedlings. In 2009 Charlie, Ted and a group of volunteers counted 1,600 in a single field. On some we could even see the scar on the stem where the jay had picked it up with its beak to remove the cotyledons. Many had been planted next to a little burst of hawthorn, blackthorn or bramble and it was easy to see how the thorny shrub would, in just a year or so, begin to envelop the oak – a tangle of nature's barbed wire, protecting the gangly sapling as it grew.

As yet, with only a few resident roe deer, and a tiny population of rabbits (compared with the thousands on the grasslands of the Middle and Northern Blocks), the browsing impact on the emerging scrub was very low. What we were seeing, in effect, was the kind of vegetation pulse that, in fully functioning ecosystems, erupts when a population of grazing animals has been decimated by some extreme event or epidemic – like the murrains and plagues that affected deer in the royal forests of medieval England; or, more recently, the myxomatosis outbreak that devastated rabbit populations during the 1950s and led to the regeneration of juniper and hawthorn across southern England; or the pathogen that wiped out over 200,000 saiga antelope (88 per cent of the population) on the steppes of Central Asia in 2014. The resulting eruption of scrub produces a wealth of margins for wildflowers and invertebrates, particularly those with complex life cycles that require two or more habitats close to each other for different stages in their growth. Invertebrates attract other invertebrates and small mammals, amphibians and reptiles, which in turn attract birds and other predators. As we were about to discover, emerging scrub is one of the richest natural habitats on the planet.

Modern farmers and landowners, however, are prejudiced against scrub because it is considered unproductive. As a result it has been almost entirely eradicated from Britain. Scrubland is almost ubiquitously described as wasteland. It was not always so. In medieval times, scrub species were highly valued, and scrub was anything but a dirty name. The iron-rod stems of blackthorn were used for walking sticks and its fruit – sloes – for medicines and flavouring wine and gin. Brambles, like elder, produce edible berries that were also useful for dyes. Hawthorn makes good walking sticks, as well as tool handles, and was used for stock-proofing, and produces hawberries for preserves and sauces. Hazel was for hurdles, thatching spars, basketry, furniture and charcoal; willow for charcoal-making and basketry, cricket bats and medicine. Charcoal from alder and dogwood made gunpowder. Broom, of course, made excellent brooms. Juniper was for smoking meats and making pencils, its berries for distilling oil, and flavouring game and gin. Spindle was for skewers, toothpicks and baskets. Wych elm made bows, furniture and threshing floors. Birch provided cotton reels and bobbins, firewood, brooms and roofing thatch; its bark was for waterproofing and tanning. Birch wine, fermented from sap, was used as medicine and young birch leaves were a diuretic. From the dog rose came rosehips – which we now know are exceptionally high in vitamin C – for syrups, sauces and jellies. Gorse – known as 'furze' in Sussex – was fodder for animals and fuel for kilns and ovens. A buffer of thorny scrub was often encouraged around woodland to prevent the ingress of grazing animals. Place names like Thorndon, Thornden, Thornbury, Haslemere, Hazeldon, Spindleton, Hathern (hawthorn), Hatherdene, Brambleton, Barnham Broom, Broomhill, Broompark, pepper the map of Britain. Our own field names at Knepp recall the days when scrub was an asset – Benton's Gorse, Broomers Corner, Broom Field, High Reeds, Cooper Reeds, Faggot Stack Plat, Bramble Field, Rushett's, Rushall Field, Little Thornhill, Great Thornhill, Stub Mead, Barcover Furzefield, Swallows Furzefield, Coates' Furzefield, Greenstreet Furzefield, Constable's Furze, Pollardshill Furze, Old Furze Field, Furzefield Plat, Great Furzefield and lots of Little Furzefields.

Most importantly of all, in the days of commons grazing, thorny scrub was valued as a nursery for the regeneration of trees. The agricultural writer Arthur Standish (fl. 1611–1615) reminds his readers of 'an old forest proverb – the thorn bush is the mother of the oak'. Thorny bushes, he proclaims, Vera-like, are 'the mother and nurse of trees' and 'but for them, there would be no timber in the common land'. To supplement natural regeneration, forest officers in the seventeenth century were instructed to 'caste acornes and ashe leyes into the straglinge and dispersed bushes; which (as experience proveth) will growe up, sheltered by the bushes, unto suche perfection as shall yelde in times to come good supplie of timber'. So important were thorns and holly to the regeneration of trees that a statute established in the New Forest in 1768 imposed three months' forced labour on anyone found guilty of damaging them, starting every month with a number of lashes of the whip.

Yet in modern times even conservationists have struggled to promote the value of scrub. Part of the problem is its ephemeral nature. Scrub, by definition, is habitat on the move. In the absence of grazers and browsers it is vegetation on the way to becoming closed-canopy woods. Grasslands, water meadows, marshland, woods, downs, moorland, even heath can be delineated. They can be self-sustaining, easier for humans to lock into a holding pattern. Scrub doesn't stand still. The more you cut it down, the more prolific it becomes. Even defining it is difficult and mapping it virtually impossible. Where does it begin – at the margins, with grassland, bare ground and marshy spaces, with bracken, reeds and low-lying bramble, or with the shrubs themselves? Where does it end – when the nascent trees are taller than the shrubs, or as the understorey in closed-canopy woodland? It is – endlessly morphing, on its way to being something else – a discomforting notion for the modern mind.

Conservationists, bent on keeping a landscape in stasis for the preservation of targeted species, have, for decades, regarded encroaching scrub as the enemy. Vast sums have been spent on its eradication, with scrub-bashing a staple activity of conservation volunteers. The champion of margins, scrub itself has been marginalized, exiled to the no-man's-land of railway sidings, slag heaps, spoil tips, gravel pits, docks and abandoned quarries and mines. Ironically it is these shunned, overgrown, unprotected places that are now notable for wildlife, bastions for species on the verge of extinction across the countryside at large, like cirl bunting, red-backed shrike, black redstarts, willow tits, natterjack toads, great crested newts and the very rare horrid ground weaver spider, and other rapidly declining species like linnets, willow warblers and bullfinches, and Dartford warblers. 15 per cent of all nationally scarce insects are recorded from brownfield sites, some of which have now been designated Sites of Special Scientific Interest. Conservation groups like Buglife find themselves in the bizarre position of petitioning for the preservation of post-industrial areas for wildlife while our so-called greenfield sites, supposedly protected from development, have close to no wildlife value at all. Brown is the new green.

Paradoxically, too, zero tolerance towards thorny scrub deprives conservation of its most effective ally when it comes to planting trees. Fortunes are spent every year buying bare-root 'whips' – young saplings grown in nurseries – to plant or restore woodland. Looking after young nursery trees is far more challenging than is generally appreciated. The whips are vulnerable and can easily dry out and die before, or even after, they are re-planted. They are not as well connected to the soil as naturally established seedlings, and often lack the appropriate fungal associates. They can be bruised and damaged and open to infection. They have to be individually protected by tree-guards, invariably carbon-intensive polypropylene cylinders, attached to tanalized wooden stakes with plastic ties – another financial and environmental cost; another labour-intensive process. Even if the area to be planted is fenced against deer, tree-guards are poor protection against wind, flooding and disturbance from rabbits, voles and badgers; and high moisture content inside the cylinder can induce rot and mildews, and harbour insect pests. If neglected, the tubes can rub against the saplings' etiolated stems and inflict damage of their own. Whether or not the trees survive, there is, ultimately, the labour-intensive task of removing the tree-guards from site, and the carbon cost of disposing of or recycling them. Most tree-guards are supposed to degrade with exposure to sunlight but in practice this doesn't seem to happen. If the trees have grown well, the tree-guards are not exposed to enough sunlight; if they die, the cylinders simply topple over and are subsumed by thickets of grass. But even if they do start to decay, allowing tree-guards to degrade on site leaves polluting plastic residues in the soil.

As Knepp was beginning to demonstrate, thorny scrub does a far better job of providing protection and a growing environment for saplings. Officers from the Woodland Trust and other tree charities have marvelled at the speed of regeneration at Knepp, as well as the variety of species spontaneously establishing themselves – including wild service and crab apple. However, tempted as these conservation organizations may be to sit back and allow the brambles and blackthorn to do their job for them, and at no cost, their fund-raising model does not encourage this. Charities rely on grant aid to plant woodland. The messy, robustly competitive and variable responses of nature do not fit with a grant system that requires precise costs, targets and predictability. Charities rely, too, on public donations to buy the trees, and volunteers to plant and maintain them. The appeal of digging a hole and planting a tree is a crucial part of their story. If charities simply left it to nature, the mechanism from which a large tranche of their funding is derived would vanish.

Until recently, one important mitigating factor against scrub loss in our landscape was the practice of coppicing, in which trees – typically oak, hazel, ash, willow, field maple and sweet chestnut – are regularly felled to near ground level, so that shoots (known as 'spring wood') regrow from the stump, or stool. Archaeologists have traced the practice back to the early Neolithic. Some of the earliest evidence of coppicing comes from the Somerset Levels where, 4,000 years ago, our ancestors laid elaborate wooden tracks across boggy ground. These walkways were made of oak timber lashed together with even-length poles of ash, lime, elm, oak and alder and smaller poles of hazel and holly. Coppicing, as Britain's first people discovered, supplies fast-growing, accessible, malleable, multi-purpose timber, with the added advantage of prolonging the trees' life. A small-leafed lime, still coppiced to this day at Westonbirt Arboretum in Gloucestershire, is thought to be thousands of years old. In effect, coppicing mimics the browsing and breaking impact of Britain's megafauna, harvesting the branches, not the stem. The very fact that so many of our trees and shrubs respond so well to such damage shows they co-evolved with vast numbers of animals. In the last interglacial, these animals were particularly substantial. In addition to the aurochs, horses, red deer, bison, elk, boars and beavers that recolonized Britain as the ice retreated in the early Holocene, in the Middle to Late Pleistocene (781,000–50,000 years ago) Britain was home to straight-tusked elephants, hippopotami and Merck's and narrow-nosed rhinos. They browsed on familiar trees such as hazel and lime, hornbeam and blackthorn, alongside dog rose, bramble and hawthorn, pulled down branches of oak and elm and smashed through holly and box. The savage spikes of blackthorn, over-engineered for even the hide of an aurochs, would have given a rhino pause for thought.

From Roman times to the eighteenth century, Sussex's famous iron industry depended on coppice. Far from eradicating woodland – as is often believed – iron masters who required constant, accessible supplies of charcoal and wood fuel actually preserved them. Cut at intervals ranging anywhere between four years for birch and up to fifty for oak, our most prized ancient broadleaved woods may have been coppiced seventy or more times across their history. Our county, still one of the most wooded in the country for this reason, has coppicing enshrined in place names like Underwood, Nutbourne, Maplehurst ('hurst' being Old English for a wood on a hill), Lyndhurst (lime wood) and Kilnwood – and our own Knepp place names of Lindfield Copse, Pollardshill, Alder Copse, Shoots, Spring Wood, Wickwood, Coppice Plat and Coppice Field. Coppicing created an eternal cycle of regenerating scrub, benefitting numerous butterfly and invertebrate species, as well as so-called 'woodland' birds. But it was still a contrived and heavily managed environment where thorny species like bramble were not tolerated. Even honeysuckle (which provides the nest materials for dormice, and is the most plant of white admiral butterflies) was, until well after the Second World War, rooted out as an undesirable weed. Mixed coppice was obviously the most biodiverse but often coppice was restricted to just one or two of the most commercial species – in our part of Sussex, hazel.

The advent of the coal industry in the nineteenth century heralded the gradual demise of coppicing in Britain. In France, which only has coal in the very north, there is still a thriving wood-fuel industry based on coppice. But the invention of plastics and modern techniques of mass production sounded its final death knell in Britain. Almost all the purposes for which coppice and scrub had been used in the past were suddenly satisfied by cheap plastic alternatives and over the second half of the twentieth century 90 per cent of traditional coppice in the UK disappeared. Ancient coppices like Spring Wood in the park at Knepp were left to grow into blocks of mature trees or cleared to make way for subsidized farming or development. Populations of nightingales, marsh tits, garden and willow warblers, pearl-bordered fritillaries, silver-washed fritillaries, wood white and purple emperor butterflies plummeted, along with anemones, bluebells, ground ivy, yellow archangel, violets, spurges, ragged robin, meadowsweet, cow-wheat and bugle – prolific flowerers in the sunny, open conditions created after a coupe, or section of woodland, has been coppiced.

Supposedly useless, scrub became demonized in the twentieth century. Once, untidy margins were tolerated, even encouraged. Now, armed with motorized tools, we have become a nation obsessed with orderliness and boundaries. Systems of rotational growth that mimic nature's cycles of boom and bust have been replaced by a landscape that appears, within a human lifespan at least, unchanging. A patchwork of neatly hedged fields dotted with mature trees and small copses, framed by bare, rolling hills and slow-flowing rivers has become the archetype of England's green and pleasant land. It is etched in our subconscious, the bar-code of stability, prosperity, control. Rooted in this idyll is our notion of mankind, subjugator of wilderness, bending nature to our sway. Our area of the south-east is, according to the author of *The Kent & Sussex Weald* (2003), 'beautifully man-made'. It is 'one of the longest-running and best recorded examples of the unremitting labour of generations of farmers to clear and settle a great expanse of wild country'. It was not surprising, then, that locals who had gazed all their lives on what they considered the epitome of English landscape, the picture postcard of resolute agricultural endeavour, were outraged when Knepp was invaded by scrub.

Interviewed anonymously, a cross-section of local villagers

vented their anger, particularly about what was happening in the Southern Block. It was not because they were anti-conservation per se, they explained to the student conducting the survey on reactions to our rewilding project for her MA. Most of them considered themselves wedded to the countryside, lovers of wildlife. 'I love wildlife, I love the countryside, I love to go somewhere and see butterflies and moths and hedgehogs,' said one, 'I'm not saying I want that all wiped away.' It was just that Sussex was not the place for wild, untrammelled land. 'I don't believe in this scheme, not in the south-east of England,' one of the participants declared. 'It's turning into quite a mess . . . a fair old mess really,' said another. 'It's not even a wild mess, you just don't see it . . . I mean I've been all over the world and you get jungle and you get different things but actually this is completely different because you don't feel it should be here.' Others, writing to Shipley Parish Council, said 'it feels like a foreign land' and 'it looks totally abandoned, like nobody cares for it anymore.' Some said it looked as though the land was for sale, or the farmer had died. The park restoration around the castle generally received a favourable response. 'Where you've got the deer running around and the cattle, it's a lovely sight.' To most people, the Repton deer park conformed to a romantic ideal. Like an agricultural landscape it was orderly and unthreatening. It was 'more normal, more liveable'. Abandoning the land to nature, on the other hand – 'letting it go' – smacked of laziness, irresponsibility, even immorality. It was uncivilized, a 'backward step'. To some it was 'wanton vandalism'.

Time and again, locals expressed dismay at the 'ruination' of farmland. The messy look of the place betrayed lost productivity. 'A lot of my farmer friends cannot believe that he's got all these thousands of acres and he's done what he's done with it . . . to see this perfectly good ground, just being abandoned basically.' 'It's not like it's scrap land. It's not scrap land. And yet he's turning it into this wilderness.' To many, Charlie was undoing the labours of his ancestors. 'Shipley Parish reverberates with the past . . . and this particular estate farmed by this particular family has been a model estate until only a few years ago. It was the pride and joy of the Burrell family.'

In a letter to the *County Times* another disgruntled observer wrote: 'When it was farmed first by Sir Merrik and then Sir Walter and Lady Burrell, [Knepp] was an estate admired and worked by people proud of its high standard of farming and general care . . . In this day and age when we are asked to grow all the food we can, to save importing and help feed starving countries, he has turned a fine working estate into a wasteland . . . Someone needs to stop him.'

To evaluate the mounting local opposition to Knepp, Shipley Parish Council canvassed local opinion on, among other things, 'the benefits or otherwise of the contributions of public money to the project'. Time and again people expressed the same complaint: 'The money would have been better used training Knepp Castle staff in traditional farming methods so that they understood how to use the land profitably making a contribution to the world shortage of food'; 'food production should be a priority in the busy south-east of England, and in general I feel "feed the world" should be our guideline'; 'It is taking reasonable agricultural land out of production thereby increasing the need for imported products'; 'Rewilding a section of South East England which has been prime agricultural land, made up of ancient field patterns and homesteads dating back to the Anglo-Saxon period, is to me a misuse of taxpayer's money . . .'

The consensus was that 'the Sussex Weald, an area famous for its productive mixed farming, being turned back to weeds is difficult to comprehend. Tax payers' money being used to encourage landowners not to farm their land . . . does not seem sensible when we are told we need to produce more food with a rising population.'

It is an argument that lies at the heart of much of the hostility towards rewilding. Yet this conviction, keenly and compassionately felt, is based on a misleading narrative promulgated largely by the food and farming industry. Fear of starvation, food shortages or, at very least, increased commodity prices flies in the face of facts established by, among others, the United Nations. Until this issue is properly understood by the public, allocating land to conservation projects like ours, whatever the wider benefits, is likely to continue to engender passionate opposition.

The notion that we must work every inch of the land for our survival, ingrained in us since the Second World War, is highly emotive, and distressing images of famines in war-torn and politically unstable regions of the world daily reinforce the idea that there is not enough food to go round. With the global population predicted to rise from 7 billion people to 10 billion by 2050 the message being driven by food producers and retailers, agri-business and farmers' unions is of the need to increase global food production by 70–100 per cent.

But this message does not reflect the experiences of farmers like ourselves, driven out of business by the global market – by low commodity prices resulting from subsidies and over-production. This is the other side of the coin that vested interests in the food industry do their utmost to ensure remains face down. The largely unpublicized reality is that the world already produces enough to feed 10 billion people. The shocking sub-text is that a third of this food – 1.3 billion tonnes every year – is wasted. This is a discomforting, almost incomprehensible fact and one that is often swatted aside. How can mere 'waste' possibly account for so much? But it underpins one of the greatest scandals of our time.

According to the UN Food and Agriculture Organization, industrialized nations annually waste 670 million tonnes of food. By waste, the FAO means perfectly edible food, needlessly thrown away. 20 per cent of oil seeds, meat and dairy, 30 per cent of cereals, 35 per cent of fish produced for human consumption and 40–50 per cent of root crops, fruit and vegetables never meets the mouths it is intended for. A third of fruit and vegetables are discarded because they fail to conform to cosmetic standards. Supermarket chains are some of the worst culprits, driving perfectionism – straighter carrots and blemish-free apples – and squandering mountains of both fresh and cooked products post-delivery. Though publicly committed to reducing waste, in the fiscal year 2015/16 Tesco admitted they had thrown away 50,000 tonnes of food from their UK stores. Across the developed world, restaurants routinely waste food by over-ordering supplies, dishing out portions that their customers can rarely hope to finish and throwing away everything left over at the end of the day. The BSE crisis of 1996 and the foot-and-mouth outbreak of 2001 put paid to feeding these leftovers to pigs – a tradition centuries old. Now it goes to landfill. And more crops are needed to grow our bacon. Almost all (97 per cent) global soy production is used for animal feed, and European imports of soymeal increased almost 3 million tonnes in the two years following the 2003 pigswill ban.

The profligacy continues in the home where we, as consumers, routinely over-buy, tempted by two-for-one bargains and loyalty points. We store food improperly and take 'use by' dates literally, though these are only intended to indicate peak freshness. And we have forgotten how to cook with leftovers. With food as cheap as it is, there is little incentive not to toss the scraps that confound us straight into the bin. This would have been unconscionable during the Second World War. From 1940 till 1954, the year rationing ended, wasting food was a criminal offence. Yet in rich countries today, consumers alone throw away 222 million tonnes of food each year – very nearly the net food production of sub-Saharan Africa. In the UK, 7 million of the total 15 million tonnes of food and drink wasted in 2013 was thrown out by households. This level of wastage costs the UK around £12.5 billion, emits some 20 million tonnes of CO_2 and uses around 5,400 million cubic metres of water – two and a half times the entire annual water discharge of the Thames – every year. And this is without taking into consideration the switch to a meat-centred diet, which consumes far more grain than if we ate the grain ourselves, and the excessive amount we eat – far more calories than we need, according to the medical profession, now battling the epidemic of obesity, with its associated diabetes, cancers and heart disease. The average American eats at least 20 per cent more calories today than in 1970, mostly as highly processed junk foods, and the British are rapidly following suit.

In developing countries food tends to be lost at the front of the food chain, rather than at the end. Poor infrastructure – lack of refrigeration, transportation, storage, food-processing plants and communications – equates to a loss of 630 million tonnes, almost the same as in the developed world. Here, though, the wastage of food induces hunger rather than obesity. In sub-Saharan Africa, 10–20 per cent of its grain – worth $4 billion and enough to feed 48 million people for a year – succumbs to mould, insects and rodents. India loses an estimated 35–40 per cent of its fruits and vegetables before they reach markets.

Waste, however, is a problem that the food and farming industry is reluctant to resolve, for fear of driving itself out of business. Instead, it seeks to encourage even greater human consumption and secure additional markets for its food. Just as cereal producers in the 1960s and 70s promoted intensive farming systems, feeding grain to cattle in the cereal glut that followed the Green Revolution, now they look to the automobile industry for an outlet. Once we ate food. Now, often, we burn it. The car has become the new cow. Already 40 per cent of US maize – grown on land the size of Iowa or Alabama – is used to feed cars, while in the European Union consumption of biodiesel (mostly home-grown rapeseed oil and palm ooil imported from Indonesia and Malaysia) increased 34 per cent between 2010 and 2014. In 2013 the Organisation for Economic Co-operation and Development (OECD) estimated that if we continue down this path, by 2021, 14 per cent of the world's maize and other coarse grains, 16 per cent of its vegetable oil and 34 per cent of its sugar cane will be burned as fuel. In the UK, the National Farmers' Union has been lobbying government to lift its 2 per cent cap on the volume of crops (mainly wheat, sugar beet and oilseed rape) allowed to be grown here for biofuel processing, to the 7 per cent level allowed by Europe. This is hardly the position it would take if, as a nation, we were threatened with serious food shortages. The cap imposed by government, again, is not because of fears of food scarcity. It is in response to climate-change scientists, including those from the European Federation for Transport and Environment, who point out that biodiesel, made primarily from vegetable oil, and heralded by its producers as 'green energy', is, in fact, 80 per cent worse for the climate than fossil diesel.

The unsung reality that the world is currently producing enough food to feed 3 billion more people than are alive has come about largely through remarkable advances in agricultural technology. New varieties of crops, GPS-guided precision sowing and fertilizing and hi-tech farm machinery have all contributed to enormously higher yields. The world cereal harvest has grown by 20 per cent in the last decade. In the UK, in 2015, wheat yields rose by 6 per cent. Across the country the average harvest of wheat is now 3.7 tonnes per acre – compared with the 2.75 tonnes per acre we were averaging at Knepp in the 1990s. This abundance would astonish our ancestors. A grain of wheat planted in England today yields 60 to 70 grains compared to four grains in the 1300s.

Bumper crops inevitably lead to lower prices, driving farmers on marginal land like ours – where the costs are higher and the efficiencies harder to come by – out of business. The simple reality is that we need less land for food. While yields have continued to rise year on year, the acreage devoted to wheat and barley in Britain has fallen by 25 per cent since the 1980s. Even with the UK population increasing by nearly 20 million since 1939 we now have the smallest area of land (6 million hectares) devoted to arable since before the Second World War. And it's not just arable land that is decreasing. In 2014 the area under permanent pasture in the UK was 5.8 million hectares compared with 7.4 million at the end of the 1920s, and we have only 22,000 hectares of productive orchards now, compared with 113,000 hectares in 1951.

Knepp is a casualty of a global process of extraordinary rises in agricultural productivity and the resulting abandonment of marginal land. By 2030 Rewilding Europe estimates there will be 30 million hectares of abandoned farmland in Europe. Already, much of northern Scandinavia lies fallow. What happens to all this land is an issue concerning most European governments, including Britain. It is an opportunity for nature unprecedented in modern history – if only we can overcome our deepest prejudices about what our land should look like.

8

Living with the Yellow Peril

Ragwort, thou humble flower with tattered leaves
I love to see thee come and litter gold,
What time the summer binds her russet sheaves;
Decking rude spots in beauties manifold . . .

John Clare, 'The Ragwort', *Poems of the Middle Period*
vol. IV, 1832

Many of our neighbours' concerns were allayed over the first few years. No one was gored by fallow bucks during the rut. The Exmoor ponies, with Duncan removed from the herd, were giving no bother to riders on the bridleways. We heard no more from the woman who insisted children should walk with escorts on the footpaths because of attacks from free-roaming animals. Longhorn cows with their calves – once a 'disaster waiting to happen' – were even welcomed by some, glad to see these handsome cattle back in an area where dairy farming was continuing to decline. We were mindful of potential flashpoints. On the footpaths and green lanes we did our best to roll areas that had been churned up by the pigs or badly 'poached', or trampled, by the traffic of animals in wet weather. Neighbouring landowners told us that on their lands, too, complaints about mud, uneven ground and the potential for twisted ankles were on the rise – an indication, it seemed, of an increasingly urban attitude to the countryside.

But one particular aspect of the project refused – and continues to refuse – to lie down. The furore was so intense that at one point it threatened to derail the project altogether. To many people, the most offensive aspect of the Knepp project, epitomizing our neglectful ways and ranging in locals' minds from a 'great disappointment' to an 'unmitigated disaster', is the appearance of 'injurious' weeds. 'Sir Charles has turned a well-farmed estate into a wasteland of thistles, docks and ragwort,' wrote an observer to the *County Times*. Of these three offending species, by far the worst seems to have been – and continues to be – common ragwort. One *County Times* reader was so incensed he was stirred to poetry:

> Knepp Castle, ragwort shame
> Spread like a plague, and who's to blame?
> A sea of yellow, such a disgrace
> This poisonous weed takes over the place.
> They leave it growing for the 'ground-nesting birds'
> But where are they? Never seen nor heard.
> Meantime it spreads onto neighbours' land.
> Stop this pollution! This we demand.
> 'Conservation', they cry – a convenient excuse.
> Not in my book – it's neglect and abuse.
> Readers write letters to the *County Times*
> But what about DEFRA – shouldn't there be fines?
> This year worst of all, they've had a bad press
> But will Knepp Castle tackle this mess?
> Mr Burrell take action, this I implore
> Or next year we'll be on to you, like never before.

Common ragwort (*Senecio jacobaea*) is native to the Eurasian continent. In Europe it is widely spread from Scandinavia to the Mediterranean, and is naturally abundant in Britain and Ireland. Standing generally around three feet tall, it produces dense, flat-topped clusters of bright yellow flowers from June onwards, and is commonly found on wasteland, waysides and in grazing pastures, where even a rabbit scrape provides enough bare ground for it to germinate. With rootling pigs and the disturbing hooves of herbivores, not to mention thousands of burrowing rabbits, the opportunities for it to flourish on our post-agricultural land are manifold. But in 2008 it was particularly virulent. Being a biennial and responding vigorously to stress, it abounds two years on from a drought summer, like the one we had in 2006. The dry April of 2007 had facilitated germination even further and, in the words of another *County Times* reader, we were seeing 'field after field of ragwort blowing in the breeze'.

The moral outrage ragwort engenders in Britain is usually aimed at alien invasives like Japanese knotweed. Hostility to a plant that has been part of our environment since the last ice age is a peculiar new phenomenon. Less than two centuries ago the poet John Clare was extolling its 'shining blossoms . . . of rich sunshine'. The Isle of Man knows it as 'cushag' – its national flower. Yet to the rest of Britain ragwort is an evil to be expunged from the world. Its sulphur-yellow flowers are rags to irascible bulls. Feelings run so high that recent attempts by DEFRA and the Wildlife & Countryside Link – a coalition of forty-six conservation organizations – to encourage a sensible approach have failed to dent anti-ragwort propaganda.

The loudest accusation of all is that it is a killer of livestock. Ragwort is, indeed, a poisonous plant. It contains pyrrolizidine alkaloids – toxins that, when eaten in large quantities by mammals, cause liver-failure and death. But grazing animals have lived with it for tens of thousands of years. Our own longhorns, Exmoors, Tamworths, roe, fallow (and subsequently red) deer graze amongst ragwort with no adverse effects whatsoever. They know to avoid it. The plant itself warns them away with its bitter taste and a smell so bad it has been immortalized in British history. After the Battle of Culloden in 1746, when the victorious English are said to have renamed the garden flower 'Sweet William' in honour of William, Duke of Cumberland, the defeated Scots retaliated by naming ragwort 'Stinking Willy'. In Shropshire and Cheshire its name is 'Mare's Fart'.

The problem of poisoning arises not in the wild but where

fields and paddocks are overgrazed and the animals have no choice but to eat it, or when ragwort is cut into silage or hay and the animals are unable to detect and avoid it. Even then, the animal has to eat an excessive amount – an estimated 5–25 per cent of body weight for horses and cattle and 125–400 per cent for goats – for it to be fatal.

The source of the most recent wave of ragwort hysteria can be laid at the door of the British Equestrian Veterinary Association and the British Horse Society. In 2002 they published the results of a survey claiming that as many as 6,500 of the UK population of around 600,000 horses die every year from ingesting ragwort. It was an astonishing leap from the average of ten ragwort-associated horse deaths per year estimated by the Ministry of Agriculture, Fisheries and Food in 1990. The BEVA's claim – it emerged – was based on bad science. 4 per cent of BEVA members had responded to the survey, reporting that they had seen, on average, three 'suspected' (note, not 'confirmed') cases of ragwort poisoning (note – not deaths) that year. The BEVA had then simply multiplied this average by the full BEVA membership of 1,945 to produce a total of 6,553 cases for that year. No one at the BEVA seems to have considered the most likely reason that the majority of vets failed to respond to their survey was that they had no cases to report. Despite the fallibility of their reasoning and their having subsequently removed the misinformation from their website the BEVA-based myth has developed a life of its own, particularly in the folklore of horsiculture. As the old adage goes, a lie can get halfway round the world before truth has got its boots on.

But then British antagonism towards John Clare's 'humble flower' has stubborn roots – as difficult to grub out, it seems, as the roots of ragwort itself. The ground in which the prejudice first germinated was opened up by the Weeds Act back in 1959. The Weeds Act singled out ragwort and four other species – broad-leaved dock, curled dock, creeping thistle and spear thistle – and labelled them 'injurious'. Back then, the Act had, specifically, agricultural interests in mind. These are weeds that, if uncontrolled, can have a significant impact on arable production in terms of lost revenue from lower crop yields. Creeping thistle, for example, exudes pheromones which inhibit the germination of most grain crops. In the case of ragwort, the cost is in eradicating it from fields and paddocks so it is not processed into animal fodder.

But 'injurious' is a provocative word, a fluttering skull and crossbones that has waved a welcome to all sorts of scaremongering over 'pernicious' plants ever since. A common misconception is that ragwort is poisonous to human touch even though the plant's pyrrolizidine alkaloids (which occur naturally in 3 per cent of all flowering plants) cannot be absorbed through the skin. Breathing in ragwort pollen, it is claimed, can give you liver damage, though this, too, is a physical impossibility. Honey from bees feeding on ragwort was recently headlined in the *Daily Mail* as poisonous to humans, though DEFRA has described this risk as both 'highly unlikely' and 'negligible'. Bees invariably take nectar and pollen from numerous other poisonous flowers including foxgloves and daffodils. Yet none of these have ever been accused of poisoning honey.

Opponents of ragwort, pointing the finger at the offensive weed on other people's land, routinely claim the moral high ground. Landowners and local councils, they insist, are obliged by law to eradicate it wherever it occurs. But this is categorically not the case. Neither are the five weed species listed under the Weed Act 'notifiable' – there is no such concept in UK law.

The Ragwort Control Act of 2003 – an amendment to the Weeds Act of 1959 – has done little to clarify the situation and allay public fears despite publishing a Code of Practice, under pressure from the Wildlife and Countryside Link, which clearly states that 'common ragwort and other ragwort species are native to the British Isles and are therefore an inherent part of our flora and fauna, along with invertebrate and other wildlife they support. The Code does not propose the eradication of common ragwort but promotes a strategic approach to control the spread of common ragwort where it poses a threat to the health and welfare of grazing animals and the production of feed or forage.'

The government's own guidelines still appear somewhat conflicted and inflammatory about ragwort and other 'injurious' weeds. 'It's not an offence to have these weeds growing on your land', it states in 2014 Land Management advice, but 'you must . . . prevent harmful weeds on your land from spreading onto a neighbour's property'. While stating it will only take action if these weeds are threatening land used for livestock, forage or agriculture, at the same time it encourages people to 'complain about harmful weeds' on their neighbours' land, and provides an 'injurious weeds complaint form' with which to do so.

It seems that the damage is done. Few people in the countryside nowadays are able to accept common ragwort's place in nature, let alone celebrate it as John Clare did. No one sees it as a beautiful, dazzling explosion of sunshine and – perhaps more importantly – no one values its ecological contribution to our lives. Though we protest that we love nature it seems that this is only on our own terms. We have become a nation of gardeners, more interested in exotic flowers than natives. Plantlife, the environmental organization that seeks to safeguard our wild vegetation, has a membership of 10,500. The Royal Horticultural Society has 434,000. Even Prince Charles, champion of wildflower meadows, patron of Plantlife, in 2015 petitioned Natural England to change its stance on ragwort and 'tackle the problem more proactively'.

Yet the very fact that ragwort is not grazed, leaving it standing when other flowering plants have been nibbled away (and therefore glaringly conspicuous to its critics), should be cause for celebration. Ragwort is one of the most sustaining hosts to insects we have. Seven species of beetle, twelve species of flies, one macromoth – the cinnabar, with its distinctive black-and-yellow rugby jersey caterpillars – and seven micromoths feed exclusively on common ragwort. It is a major source of nectar for at least thirty species of solitary bees, eighteen species of solitary wasps and fifty insect parasites. In all, 177 species of insects use common ragwort as a source of nectar or pollen. When most of the other flowers have died, ragwort continues on into late summer, providing a vital source of nectar. We have it at Knepp sometimes as late as November. Even at night its bursts of luminous yellow attract nocturnal moths – forty species of them. The effect of this boost to insect life is colossal. Natural England, itself, describes the number of predators and parasites dependent on the invertebrate resource supported by common ragwort as 'incalculable'; while its attractiveness to carrion-associated insects plays a key role in supporting the decomposition cycle.

Despite these benefits to our wildlife, anti-ragwort propaganda has, in recent years, inspired eradication programmes anywhere that ragwort appears, including on roadsides and in wildflower meadows, and – incredibly – in areas designated for conservation as Sites of Special Scientific Interest. Broad-spectrum herbicides are often the chosen agent of destruction, causing – inevitably – collateral damage. But even when uprooted by hand there can be losses to other flora. Other native yellow flowering plants – like hoary ragwort, marsh ragwort, tansy, St John's wort and hawkweed – are commonly mistaken for it. Weeds, as the saying goes, are plants in the wrong place – only now, it seems, everywhere is the wrong place for ragwort.

To put ragwort in context, it is only one of a considerable number of plants that can be fatal if eaten by horses and other livestock. In Southern England common species that can kill grazing animals include foxglove, cuckoo pint, ivy, black bryony, white bryony, bracken, elder, spindle and yew. In March our woods in the Northern Block are carpeted with native wild daffodils – a rare sight since nineteenth- and twentieth-century plant collectors dug most of them up elsewhere in the country. The daffodil – both wild and domesticated versions – is one of our most poisonous plants. A few years ago they almost killed a local vicar, who ate a bunch of daffodils to enliven his Easter sermon and had to be rushed to hospital to have his stomach pumped. Yet no one thinks to denigrate them.

The negative reputation of the ragwort derives partly, perhaps, from its method of reproduction. It is not a bulb like the daffodil, and so is thought to be profligate and unpredictable. The number of seeds it can produce varies widely but most reliable sources cite up to 30,000 seeds per plant. They are commonly thought to be carried huge distances by the wind. The explosion of ragwort around Shipley in the summer of 2008 was identified by numerous locals as being a result of seed drifting from Knepp.

A letter Charlie received from the owner of a local stud farm on 8 September 2008, when the ragwort was in full bloom, was one of many:

> Sir,
>
> The weed season is here again and may I congratulate you on another bumper crop.
>
> It seems that everyone else is doing their hardest to eliminate ragwort, thistle and dock while you and yours are doing nothing.
>
> I am sure that as part of a Stewardship Scheme you are entitled to do what you are doing but please spare a thought for the people and land all around you to where these seeds are blowing.
>
> I had friends down for the weekend who farm on a large scale near Cambridge and they were appalled at the neglect of the land in the area.
>
> I am sure this letter will have little or no affect but I will of course be finding out from DEFRA how you are able to neglect in this fashion.

Once again, prejudice and alarm outpace science. It was virtually impossible, according to the government's own guidelines, for ragwort to be colonizing the countryside from Knepp. Research has shown that 60 per cent of ragwort seeds fall around the base of the plant, and it is the seed source in the soil, rather than the source from windblown seed, that generally germinates. The seed being blown on the wind is lighter and likely to be infertile. It is estimated that, for a plant producing 30,000 healthy seeds, 18,000 of them land at the base of the plant, 11,700 at 4.5 metres (15 feet) away, and so on, decreasing with distance, until 36 metres (120 feet) away only 1.5 seeds land. In accordance with the code of practice published by DEFRA we had created a 50 metre buffer zone inside our boundary that we keep regularly topped, allowing no weed seed sources to develop, and to further reassure our neighbours we voluntarily pull up ragwort by hand in a further 50 metres. In areas of particular sensitivity where, for example, our land abutted a llama farm, we cut a 100 metre strip – twice the area recommended by DEFRA. Our ragwort seed, viable or not, was – and still is – highly unlikely to be travelling beyond our boundary. According to Professor Mick Crawley, Emeritus Professor of Plant Ecology at Imperial College London, whose ragwort research project, begun in 1981, still continues, 'In our experience, ragwort comes from seed more often from the soil seed bank than from last year's seed production.' The seed can survive for at least ten years in the soil. All it takes is a tiny bit of soil disturbance, which could be no more than the scratchings of a rabbit, and the seed can germinate and recruit to the rosette stage. 'Recruitment in ragwort', he says, 'is usually microsite limited and there are usually plenty of seeds in the soil seed bank to fill up all of the available microsites.'

In the Repton park, where opinions of how a cultural landscape should look are even more acute, and the appearance of ragwort in the closely cropped sward even more conspicuous, we have had to adopt a more Draconian approach. We simply cannot risk jeopardizing the whole project because of the public reaction to a single plant. To this day, across the estate, in a prolific ragwort year, we can spend around £10,000 pulling up a native flower that has countless benefits for wildlife, and is doing no harm to us, our neighbours or our livestock.

We tried our best to explain all this to those who wrote to

us but our efforts to allay their anxieties fell, more often than not, on deaf ears. It seemed that there was something more fundamental driving the complaints. Ragwort, like concerns about free-roaming animals, other injurious weeds, unevenness of the ground, even lack of food production, seemed to be symptomatic of some greater sense of unease. What seemed to exercise our neighbours most about the new regime of management – or lack of it – at Knepp was more nebulous, though perhaps even more disquieting for those living alongside it. It was a question of aesthetics, of what people wanted or were prepared to live with. We were, it seemed to many of our detractors, destroying the native character of our countryside – something they considered to be beautiful, balanced and harmonious; qualities integral to our very existence. 'To my mind,' a local wrote candidly to Charlie in 2007, 'your ex-arable land hurt my sensibilities.'

Aesthetic sensibilities are deeply subjective, and hard to acknowledge and analyse clearly. They take root in us from the moment we're born. They bind us to a particular view of the landscape, something we begin to think of as 'natural' or, at least, benign. What we see as children, particularly where we grow up, becomes what we want to continue to see, and what we want our children to see. Nostalgia, and the sense of security that nostalgia brings, binds us to the familiar. We are persuaded, too, by our own absorption in this aesthetic that what we are seeing has been here for ever. We believe the countryside around us, or something very similar to it, has persisted for centuries and the wildlife within it, if not exactly the same, is at least a fair representation of what has been here for centuries. But the ecological processes of the past are hard for the layman – and often even conservation professionals – to grasp. We are blinded by the immediacy of the present. We look at the landscape and see what is there, not what is missing. And if we do appreciate some sort of ecological loss and change, we tend to go only as far back as our childhood memories, or the memories of our parents or grandparents who tell us 'there used to be hundreds of lapwings in my day', 'skylarks and song thrushes were ten-a-penny', 'the fields round here used to be red with poppies and blue with cornflowers', 'cod was the poor man's fish when I was a nipper'. We are blind to the fact that in our grandparents' grandparents' day there would have been species-rich wildflower meadows in every parish and coppice woods teeming with butterflies. They would have heard corncrakes and bitterns, seen clouds of turtle doves, thousands of lapwings and hundreds more skylarks. A mere four generations ago they knew rivers swimming with burbot – now extinct in Britain – and eels, and their summer nights were peppered with bats and moths and glow-worms. Their grandparents, in turn, saw nightjars settling on dusty country lanes and even hawking for moths around the street lamps in towns, and spotted flycatchers in every orchard, and meadow pipits everywhere from salt-flats to the crowns of mountains. They saw banks of giant cod and migrating tuna in British waters. They saw our muddy North Sea clear as gin, filtered by oyster beds as large as Wales. And their grandparents, in turn, living at the time of the last beaver in Britain, would have known great bustards, and watched shoals of herring five miles long and three miles broad migrating within sight of the shore, chased by schools of dolphins and sperm whales and the occasional great white shark. We don't have to look too deeply into the history books, into contemporary accounts, for scenes dramatically different to our own to be normal. Yet we live in denial of these catastrophic losses.

This continuous lowering of standards and the acceptance of degraded natural ecosystems is known as 'shifting baseline syndrome' – a term coined in 1995 by fisheries scientist Daniel Pauly, who noticed that experts who were charged with evaluating radically depleted fish stocks took as their baseline the state of the fishery at the start of their careers, rather than fish populations in their original state. Hundreds of years ago an area of sea may have been heaving with fish. But scientists' reference point for 'natural' population levels is invariably pinned to levels dating back no more than a few decades from the present. Each generation, Pauly realized, redefines what is 'natural'. Each time the baseline drops it is considered the new normal. Something similar has happened with the British Trust for Ornithology setting 1970 as its baseline year for monitoring British bird populations. Of course, a baseline has to be set somewhere – and the declines since then, meticulously recorded, have been dramatic – but the baseline itself begins to encourage pre-baseline amnesia. We forget that there was once more. Much, much more.

Evidence of shifting baselines was apparent on our first tractor-and-trailer tours of Knepp in the early 2000s, when we began to take mixed generational groups from NGOs like the National Farmers' Union and the Country Landowners' Association around the project.

We were familiar with the usual reaction from our own generation, the forty-to-sixty-somethings. Children of the agricultural revolution were aghast at what we were doing. The twenty-somethings were often more responsive. For them the idea of national food security, of digging for victory, was an anxiety from a bygone age. They had grown up in a time of plenty – an era of globalization, cheap clothes and cheap food, their supermarket shelves stocked with Spanish tomatoes in winter, asparagus from Peru, lamb from New Zealand, tiger prawns from Thailand and beef from Argentina. But they had never heard a turtle dove, and rarely a cuckoo. Most had never seen a living hedgehog. The emptiness of British skies, the absence of birds and butterflies, was their normal. Yet they had also been educated, at school at least, to worry about the environment. Knepp was something new and we watched their confused delight as they waded through insect-filled air, picked up grass snakes and slow-worms, and raised their voices above surround-sound birdsong.

But the real surprise came from the oldest generation. Those in their eighties could remember the agricultural depression between the wars, when marginal land across the country had been abandoned – the era of Charlie's great-grandfather, when most of Knepp had been allowed to revert to scrub. To them, clumps of dog rose and hawthorn, thickets of hazel and sallow – even swathes of ragwort – were not offensive at all. The land-scape recalled them, instead, to their childhood ramblings in a countryside heaving with insects and birds, to the days when there was a covey of grey partridges in every field. There was nothing threatening or alarming about what they were seeing. Quite the reverse. To some, it was positively beautiful. 'You don't know what you're talking about,' one old boy berated his son – a baby during the war – who insisted what they were seeing was 'unnatural'. 'This is how the countryside always used to look!'

9

Painted Ladies and the Perfect Storm

We rarely hear the inward music but we are dancing to it
nevertheless

Jalaluddin Rumi, thirteenth century

With the project now well under way we needed guidance on stocking capacity for our expanding free-roaming herds, as well as on UK legislation, particularly in regard to land reversion and derogations; we needed to lobby for funding for the enclosure of the Southern Block; and – evidently – we needed to get better at public relations. We pulled together a small group of conservationists with different areas of expertise who were intrigued enough by what was happening at Knepp to give of their time. On 10 May 2006 we held our inaugural Steering Group meeting for the Knepp Wildland project. The day's programme for 'Establishing a Biodiverse Wilderness Area in the Low Weald of Sussex' began with a morning safari.

As we wandered around the emerging scrub of the Southern Block pondering various issues – including our exuberant ragwort – it became obvious that the group was capable of far more than basic advice. The likes of Dr Tony Whitbread, CEO of Sussex Wildlife Trust, Theresa Greenaway from the Sussex Biodiversity Record Centre, Jonathan Spencer from the Forestry Commission, Matthew Oates from the National Trust,

Jim Swanson from the Grazing Animals Project, Emma Goldberg from Natural England, Paul Buckland, Professor in Environmental Archaeology at Bournemouth University, Hans Kampf, Policy Adviser on Ecosystems to the Dutch Government, and Joep van de Vlasakker from the Large Herbivore Foundation would be the ideal panel to help us carry the project forward. New avenues of thinking were opening up. Suddenly we were looking at our evolving habitat through the eyes of professionals, seeing Knepp as part of a bigger picture, through the wider scope of 'living landscapes' and 'connectivity' – new buzz words for us – and assessing its implications not just for conservation in our region but for other parts of Britain.

This group was the nucleus of what was to become the Knepp Wildland Advisory Board. Over the next few years they were joined by another twenty or so eminent naturalists attracted by what was happening at Knepp, including our old friend Ted Green and, of course, Frans Vera. We had to pinch ourselves, on occasions, seeing the level of expertise in the room. In crucial ways their involvement gave Knepp credibility and was a huge boost to morale. The atmosphere was galvanizing. Here was a coterie of serious-minded naturalists fired up by what we were doing. One board member described our meetings, with the dining-room table at full extension and late-night whiskies by the fire in the library, as *Life on Earth* meets *The Big Chill*. Arguments about definitions and values, processes not targets, monitoring and baselines, degrees of management, costs and benefits, and new concepts like 'natural capital' and 'ecosystems services' were chewed over, often until the early hours of the morning. There was a sense of subverting old habits and preconceived ideas, redefining the rules.

Discussions were not always harmonious. One adviser described the effort to gain consensus on any given topic like trying to get frogs into a bucket. The specialists, inevitably, were coming at the experiment from their own angles and frequently the desire for a specific outcome would get the better of them. To stretch the analogy – all the frogs came from different ponds, and they all had different views about what it was to be a frog and what their pond should look like. Time and again, the board had to be reminded of the over-riding principle of non-intervention, of the need to accept uncertainties and think outside the parameters of a specific scientific discipline – basically, to loosen up and forget about the day job. The Dutch contingent proved indispensable in this. They had several decades of open-ended experimentalism under their belt and spoke convincingly about the concept. Already, thanks to the influence of the Oostvaardersplassen, other conservation-grazing projects were starting up in Holland and elsewhere in Europe, with natural processes as their driving principle. Surrendering management of nature to nature was becoming part of European thinking.

One of the initial discussions of the Advisory Group centred on the definition of 'rewilding' itself, and whether it was appropriate for us to be using the word to describe what was happening at Knepp. The word is common currency now, and more nuanced. But just a decade ago it was grabbing headlines in the UK, mostly in connection with a Scottish landowner who had announced his intention to release a pack of wolves on his estate. There was clearly no scope for introducing big predators at Knepp. A wolf pack's territory covers 20–120 square miles and they can travel 50 miles in a day. The hunting range of the Eurasian lynx (a far more likely candidate for reintroduction to Britain, being a solitary, reclusive, forest-dwelling animal preying almost exclusively on roe deer) can be anything from 8 to 174 square miles. Nevertheless, the strong association of 'rewilding' with predator reintroductions was already fuelling speculation that Knepp was about to become some kind of Jurassic Park. Charlie and I had been pussy-footing around the word, sometimes feeling we should be grasping the nettle and using it with confidence, sometimes worrying that adopting the term for Knepp would only add to our mailbag.

There is an uneasy response to the 'R' word in the conservation world, too. Many scientists consider it provocative and nebulous, leading to 'confusion and contradictory views'. 'Practitioners, proponents and journalists too often play too loose with rewilding terminology', a group of scientists wrote in an article entitled 'Rewilding is the new Pandora's box in conservation' published in *Current Biology* in 2016. Many argue that the stubborn little prefix 're-' reveals a naive ambition to recover the past. 'Rewilders', they claim, are idealists calling for the impossible – a return to a state of nature that, because of species and habitat losses down the centuries, irreversible changes to soil and climate, and the incalculable impositions of 'The Anthropocene', can no longer exist. We knew we were not guilty of that. Our landscape in Sussex is so heavily influenced by human beings, so altered by its history and the prevailing conditions of the present, we could only ever hope to create something for the future out of the ingredients remaining to us. Should we, perhaps, just call it 'wilding'? Could we really describe what we were doing on a relatively small area of post-agricultural land sandwiched between the creeping conurbations of Horsham and Worthing, under the Gatwick stacking-system, criss-crossed by roads and with no apex predators, as genuinely 'wild'?

The word 'rewild' was coined in the 1980s by the American conservationist Dave Foreman, one of the founders of the group Earth First!, who went on to help establish the Wildlands Project (now the Wildlands Network) and the Rewilding Institute in the United States. It first occurred in print in *Newsweek*, in an article titled 'Trying to Take Back the Planet' in 1990. It was subsequently adopted by American biologists Michael Soulé and Reed Noss who, in a *Wild Earth* article in 1998, refined it as conservation based on the 3 Cs – 'Cores, Corridors and Carnivores'. They emphasized the importance of ecological networks – joining up hotspots of biodiversity and isolated patches of wilderness so that natural processes can function on a significant scale again. And they championed the role of apex predators in the system – something that the father of modern conservation and, arguably, the first 'rewilder', the American author and ecologist Aldo Leopold, had identified half a century earlier. Yellowstone National Park has since become a flagship example of the rewilding movement in the States ever since it was seen that the reintroduction of wolves in 1995 led to a staggering increase in biodiversity – a phenomenon that has become known as the 'apex predator trophic cascade'.

The concept of rewilding in America is on a gigantic scale and for the most part focuses on areas of existing wilderness. The most ambitious wildlife corridor, the Yukon to Yellowstone Conservation Initiative, or Y2Y, established in 1997 for the benefit of wide-ranging animals like wolves and grizzlies, is 1,988 miles long, between 310 and 496 miles wide and covers an area of 502,000 square miles, taking in the entire range of the Rockies, five American states, two Canadian provinces, two Canadian territories and the reservations or traditional lands of over thirty Native American governments – well over five times the size of the UK.

One would be excused for thinking that such opportunities are limited in densely populated, heavily industrialized, historically fragmented Europe. But suddenly, in the last few decades, possibilities for American-style rewilding on this side of the pond have blown wide open. The same effects that have influenced us at Knepp – increased competition through globalization and a collapse of farm commodity prices – have precipitated a widespread withdrawal of farming on marginal land throughout Europe. Huge areas of the Alps, Pyrenees, Portugal, central Spain, Sardinia, the former East Germany, the Baltic States, the Carpathians, northern Greece, Poland, north Sweden, north Finland and the Balkans are being – or have already been – abandoned. The process has been accelerating as younger generations with new aspirations are moving to the cities to escape the hardships of subsistence farming and the loneliness of the nomadic or pastoral life. All across Europe remote villages are emptying, with only a handful of the oldest occupants remaining. By 2020 it is estimated that four out of every five European citizens will be living in urban areas. According to Rewilding Europe, by 2030, more than 30 million hectares (116,000 square miles) of farmland will have been abandoned – 5 million hectares more than the entire area of Britain.

Already Europe is seeing the effects of this unprecedented land release in rising populations of birds of prey, species like otter, beaver, elk and boar and, notably, large predators. A study in 2013 by the Zoological Society of London and Birdlife International found brown bear, wolf, wolverine and the Eurasian lynx in nearly one-third of mainland Europe, with most animals living outside designated nature reserves. Brown bears (*Ursus arctos*) are the most abundant. Europe now has around 17,000, compared with just 1,800 grizzlies (*Ursus arctos horribilis*, the larger subspecies) in the United States – an area twice the size of Europe. Bears now live in twenty-two European countries. Wolves number 12,000 – almost double the number in the US – and lynx, 9,000 of them, now roam across twenty-three European countries. The population of 1,250 wolverines (the largest land-dwelling species of the weasel family, also known as the 'skunk bear'), so far, remains restricted to northern parts of Scandinavia and Finland. But the hope is that they, too, will recover some of their southern range.

The resurgence of predators has, of course, not been universally popular. While tolerance for wild animals amongst Europeans has been rising since the environmental movement began in the 1970s, there is still deep-rooted hostility in some parts of the community – particularly amongst sheep farmers, some reindeer pastoralists and hunters. But their outrage is also, perhaps, indicative of their own beleaguered position. Sheep farmers find it easier to blame wolf attacks (almost always exaggerated) for a decline in profitability than the arrival of cheaper lamb from New Zealand. Agricultural ministers, too, find it expedient to point the finger at rising numbers of predators, rather than acknowledge the fundamental malaise affecting the whole of the European farming industry, about which they can do very little.

The presence of predators in Europe remains a subject of heated debate and though they are persecuted in places, their range and overall numbers continue to increase. The study, conducted by fifty leading European carnivore biologists, places great emphasis on the role of legal protections under the European Union, particularly the EU Habitats Directive, which protects over 1,000 animal and plant species, as well as 200 habitat types – something that is of great concern to UK con-servationists as they consider the implications for wildlife in a post-Brexit Britain. Animals in non-EU countries like Norway and Switzerland that are exempt from this directive have lagged far behind the recovery seen elsewhere in Europe. In Germany, on the other hand, where there is a €15,000 fine for killing a wolf, the number of wolf packs has risen from one in 2000 to forty-five in 2015.

On the surface of it, this process of land abandonment and resurgence of predators in Europe may seem as though rewild-ing is happening all by itself, that we can sit back and simply let it happen. But in terms of water systems, soil types and com-munities of plants, animals and invertebrates, human interference has, over time, changed the stage, establishing a different state of equilibrium – something that is known as a 'catastrophic shift'. Left to its own devices, the land could take tens of thou-sands, if not millions, of years to re-establish dynamic, biodiverse ecosystems. The question is whether reintroducing absent elements into these areas can accelerate the process, and which elements these could be. The reintroduction of the wolf into Yellowstone National Park, where it is credited with changing the course of a river, is much-trumpeted. But this hap-pened largely because it returned to a near-fully functioning eco-system complete with wild herbivores – it slotted back into its ecological niche, and the domino effect on wildlife was con-sequently dramatic. Vast natural ecosystems – true wildernesses – like this are almost unknown in Europe. Predator numbers may be rising on the Continent but, on their own, they cannot change closed-canopy woods into anything else.

Large herbivores – as Vera explains – play a more fundamental role in the creation of habitat. If used in the right way,
they can solve the locked-in problems of catastrophic shift.
Reintroducing grazing animals – proxies of missing megafauna
– and other keystone species like the beaver have been shown
to recover biodiversity and, consequently, they can expand
ideas about what rewilding can mean, and the scale at which it
can operate.

Bison are a good example. Standing on a sandy ridge on the
Dutch coast with our tree expert friends Ted Green and Jill
Butler, and Frans Vera himself, one blustery November day in
2015, a few miles from the city of Haarlem and half an hour's
drive from Amsterdam airport, Charlie and I were witnessing a
small miracle. We were standing in the middle of the 330 hectare
nature reserve of Kraansvlak – an area less than a third the size
of Knepp. Behind us, outside the perimeter fence, rattled a com-
muter train; in front of us, overlooking the slate-grey North
Sea, the casino town of Zandvoort fringed the dunes with tower
blocks; and in between, less than 60 metres away, grazing down
a hummocky slope next to a grove of Corsican pines, was a
herd of twenty-two bison and their calves. Their arcing silhouettes with woolly heads, black crescent-moon horns and
colossal shoulders sloping to a narrow rump conjured up story
books and Westerns and ochre figures on smoky cave walls. As
they inched down the slope, twisting their tongues around tufts
of grass, the sea wind fanned their tails and the fringes – faintly
ginger – under their chins, as though bringing ghosts to life.

The bison were here to perform a specific role – as 'chain-
saws on legs'. A die-off of rabbits had led to Kraansvlak's
celebrated wildflower lawns being smothered by coarse grasses,
and had allowed sycamores, white poplar and shrubs to march
into the sensitive dune landscape. A massive ecological shift
was taking place. The two principal bullying species of grass
that had taken over – bushgrass (*Calamagrostris epigejos*) and
European beachgrass (*Ammophila arenaria*) – were too tough
for even Highland cattle to deal with. Concerned about the

deterioration of the dune ecosystem and the negative impacts on the water table, PWN, the Dutch water supply company that owns the reserve, entered into partnership with the ARK Foundation and in 2007 introduced bison into the area – the first free-roaming herd in Holland.

The result has been full of surprises. Not only have the bison reversed the encroachment of trees as hoped – ring-barking the sycamores and poplar, creating cemeteries of top-pled spindle and trampling, pawing and ripping through the suffocating rough grasses – they have also kicked off a far more dynamic ecosystem than under the previous regime of grazing rabbits. Beneath a grassy bank where the feathers of a pigeon betrayed a fresh goshawk kill, the ARK Foundation's ecologist, Leo Linnartz, pointed to a patchwork of lichens, mosses and violas colonizing a sandy hollow, reminiscent of a golf bunker. 'This is what we didn't anticipate,' he told us. Bison create wal-lows, pawing with their front hooves and tossing away the turf with their horns, shouldering into the banks and rolling around in the exposed dirt – or in this case, sand – to rid themselves of itches, old fur and parasites. To avoid re-infestation by parasites they continually rub out fresh wallows, impelling dunes that had become anchored by a crust of heavy grass matting to shift and move once more – destabilizing the landscape.

Life surfaces in their wake. Sand wasps, mining bees and tiger beetles colonize the sand baths, and bison trails between the bunkers become highways for sand lizards and small mam-mals. Birds, including woodlarks and red-backed shrikes, gorge on the resurgent insects, and fallow deer snuff out fungi amongst the grass roots exposed by their excavations, dispers-ing the spores in their faeces. Like all herbivores the bison act as vectors, carrying plant seeds in their guts, hooves and fur (roughly half the plant species in the Netherlands and Central Europe have seeds with hooks to facilitate transport by fur), and transferring minerals and nutrients from one area to another in their dung, urine and bones. In the depressions cre-ated by their hooves during the wet winter, seeds of lady's bedstraw, common milkwort, hound's tongue, carline thistle and basil thyme germinate. As the result of the reintroduction of this single species of large grazing mammal, a mosaic of habitats has re-emerged. From a landscape of impenetrable rough grass and monotone stands of sycamore and poplar, a complex system of wet dune 'slacks', or hollows, alternating with thickets of thorny scrub, groves of pine and deciduous woods, sandy plains and wildflower meadows has emerged.

Visiting the Oostvaardersplassen had demonstrated to us that a suite of herbivores can create a biodiverse ecosystem from a blank slate. The Kraansvlak goes several steps further – it proves that the presence of even one herbivore species can alter and diversify the rate of change in a landscape, stimulating a variety of previously absent natural processes in an area less than a hundredth of the size and in a habitat even as sensitive as sand dunes. Connection with larger areas of nature would almost certainly open up even greater opportunities for bio-diversity (and there are plans to connect Kraansvlak by land-bridges to a neighbouring 2,000 hectare nature reserve); and a small herd of Konik horses added to the mix in 2009 have increased the ecological complexity even further and improved the grazing for the bison.

The grazing relationship of equines and bovines is a new revelation that could be of huge benefit to both conservation and domestic livestock production. Studies by Princeton University in Kenya in 2012 showed that cattle gained 60 per cent more weight when grazing with donkeys – an easy-to-weigh, easy-to-study proxy for the zebra – than grazing on their own. The donkeys (hind-gut fermenters) ate the tough, upper portion of grass that cows (ruminants) had difficulty digesting. Similarly, in the wild, at a greater distance, they observed that the rough grazing of zebras made the softer, leafy grasses more accessible to wildebeest. This dynamic, known as 'facilitation', has also recently been recognized on Dartmoor, where feral Dartmoor ponies facilitate the grazing of free-roaming domestic cattle. The grazing 'lawns' created by the ponies on the moor are also vital habitat for a rare butterfly species, the marsh fritillary – one of the fastest-declining species in England, recorded as losing 66 per cent of its colonies between 1990 and 2000. That different herbivores, once denizens of the same landscape, have developed complementary grazing techniques is, perhaps, unsurprising. It is wonderful to imagine, in the great landscapes of the distant past, herds of aurochs and bison trailing in the wake of herds of tarpan.

The effect of this European version of rewilding is clear: the right number of the right species of grazing animals introduced into even a relatively small, isolated area can have an exponential impact on biodiversity. They can provide that initial impetus to kick-start natural processes, like a plane pulling a glider into the air.

Bison are, unfortunately, out of the running for Knepp – another of our original aspirations we have been forced to shelve for the time being. As ever, the concern is dog-walkers. Kraansvlak, with its simple, three-strand electric cattle fence, demonstrates how safe these animals are. But bison are uneasy with dogs or, as they see them, wolves. Every year 4,000 tourists walk the bison trail through the Kraansvlak reserve, and on our visit Leo's wife had happily headed off to search for them on her own with their new baby in a sling. But dogs are not allowed. Dutch policy-makers and conservationists are braver than the British. Excluding dog-walkers from Knepp, even if it were to enable us to have free-roaming bison, would be, almost certainly, too contentious to countenance.

Even without bison, however, our own free-roaming herbivores were clearly having a dramatic effect on biodiversity. But there remained the question – academic, perhaps, but still a concern to us – of whether we could, or should, follow the European example and call what was happening at Knepp 'rewilding'. We asked a member of the Advisory Group to formulate an alternative phrase for our project. He came up with the phrase 'a long-term, minimum intervention, natural process-led area' to describe Knepp – a punctilious definition that nevertheless sparked off more leaping in and out of the frog bucket. The Advisory Group argued heatedly amongst themselves about what 'long-term' meant; who was to determine 'minimum intervention'; and, of course, the specifics of 'natural' and 'process-led'. Even the word 'area' proved contentious – how big did a project need to be for it to manifest natural processes? Surely we weren't talking about people's back gardens here? No matter what phrase we chose to describe Knepp, it was clear it would always provoke heated debate and a call for refinement. Perhaps 'rewilding' was, by its very nature, a slippery, unpredictable concept. We agreed, ultimately, that it was a useful shorthand, and to hell with the consequences. But 'perhaps, for the time being, just to be on the safe side,' Charlie mumbled resignedly to me one sombre winter's evening, 'let's call the experiment the Knepp "Wildland" Project and leave the 're-' out of the equation.'

Keith Kirby had been unable to attend our first Steering Group meeting but sent Emma Goldberg to represent Natural England in his place. A year or so later, Jim Seymour, Programme Manager for Natural England in the South-East, joined her on our Advisory Board. Their presence was a vote of the civil service's continuing curiosity about Knepp – confidence was too strong a word and we were frustrated not to be making any further progress with funding. In February 2008 Keith wrote to Charlie: 'I cannot pretend that we are going to be in a position to say whether or not we can "adopt" the Knepp Project as a potential demonstration site in the next 6–12 months. I realise that this will be disappointing to you and that you will need to plan accordingly . . . .'

Keith would certainly not have been encouraged by the continuing furore over our proliferating weeds and, in particular, a spectacular outbreak in 2007 of creeping thistle. Creeping thistle, a native throughout Europe and northern Asia, known in some places as 'cursed thistle' or 'lettuce from hell thistle', is a classic pioneer. It loves grazed land, arable fields and areas of disturbed ground where there is little competition or complexity of species to suppress it. When conditions are right – moderate temperatures, plentiful groundwater and not too much sunlight (in other words, a typical Sussex summer) – its spread can be breathtaking. It sends down a deep taproot on germination and though its seeds are windblown, it also breeds clonally using lateral roots – so strides of hairy, dusky-pink flowers bobbing off into the distance can be, in effect, a single plant. And digging it up, as any gardener knows, is rarely the end of it. Its roots are brittle and can regenerate from the tiniest fragment.

By 2008 the advance of three-foot-high thickets of creeping thistle was jaw-dropping and by 2009 it had covered acres of the Repton park, down the length of west and north drive, and swathes of the Northern Block beyond Pondtail Farm buildings. It was the biggest challenge yet to our rewilding ethos. We looked out on the day of the triffids and knew what our neighbours would be saying and the threat the thistles could pose to our Countryside Stewardship Scheme funding with their unashamed invasion of the Repton park. Less than a decade earlier, under the old regime, we would have been out with the toppers and weedkiller for all we were worth. It took all the courage we could muster to hold our nerve and do nothing.

While we were furrowing our brows over our prickly conundrum, across the English Channel, another invasion was coming our way. At speeds of up to 30mph, 11 million painted lady butterflies were gliding towards a land they had never seen before. The painted lady, a famous long-distance migrant, is one of our summer-visiting butterflies. About 1 million individuals drift over to our islands every year. But once every decade, when a population boom in the desert fringes of North Africa and Arabia (in this case, in 2009, the Atlas Mountains in Morocco) combines with the perfect weather conditions for trans-continental flight, millions more come and Britain is treated to a bonanza.

It was 24 May, a warm, clear Sunday morning, under a ridge of high pressure after the showers of the previous day. We woke to butterflies streaming past our windows at the rate of one a minute. Out in the park thousands upon thousands of painted ladies, a shivering miasma, had descended on the swathes of creeping thistle. As we approached, the dogs ran into the prickly cover, bouncing about looking for rabbits, sending up puffs of orange and brown wings like autumn leaves.

An older name for them in Britain, before the seventeenth-century fashion for ladies painting themselves with make-up, is 'bella donna' – pretty lady. Though for a brief period in the eighteenth century we cut short the romance and called them the 'thistle butterfly', or just 'the thistle'. The butterflies, while feeding on a wide variety of flowers, zone in on thistles to lay their eggs. The flowers provide nectar for the adults but the leaves are food for their caterpillars.

Standing in the middle of a butterfly blizzard, eyes closed, as I did that extraordinary day, is discombobulating. The sound of a single butterfly is imperceptible. But tens of thousands have a breath of their own, like the back-draught of a waterfall or an accumulating weather front. It feels as though the oscillating susurration of their wing-beats, pounding away on their supernatural wavelength, might dissolve the world into atoms. If the beat of a single butterfly's wings can raise a hurricane on the other side of the world, one wonders, what might tens of thousands do in your own backyard?

We walked for half an hour that morning, parting curtains of butterflies. For days everyone around us, from Brighton to Worthing, on the Downs and in the Weald, was talking painted ladies. People were going butterfly mad, drawn to hotspots like ours. On 28 May, on a Butterfly Conservation reserve near Laughton in East Sussex, Neil Hulme from our Advisory Board counted 1,590 butterflies streaming in per hour, at rates of up to 42 per minute, 'coming at me like tracer'. Across Europe that year 60,000 public sightings of painted ladies were recorded, with 10,000 from observers in the south of England alone. It was an exercise in citizen science that helped solve one of the most enduring mysteries of this butterfly's life cycle.

Until that bonanza year the migration was thought to be a one-way trip for the painted ladies. Few had ever been seen returning to the Continent. People widely believed in the 'Pied Piper hypothesis' – that the butterflies came to the UK on a wing and a prayer, hoping to colonize, only to be killed off cataclysmically every winter. In 2009, though, the numbers were so great that people did begin to observe the new generation, even though they were in much looser concentrations than on arrival, taking off and heading back south. That autumn, high-resolution Vertical Looking Radars based at Rothamsted Research in Harpenden, Hertfordshire confirmed what people were noticing from the ground. Once airborne the ladies ascend to test the availability of favourable tail-winds. The VLRs can 'see' up to 1.2 kilometres into the air and detect flying insects within fifteen different height bands, each of 45 metres depth. The radar 'signatures' of different species can be identified or checked using nets suspended below helium balloons. This research was ground-breaking and explained why the return migration had gone unnoticed for so long. Most of the butterflies returning southwards do so at high altitude, out of sight, often at more than 500 metres above the ground.

A picture began to emerge. What we were seeing at Knepp and what people were recording up and down the country was part of the greatest butterfly migration on earth – a round-trip that, in its best years, can stretch 15,000 kilometres from the arid expanses of Africa to the Arctic Circle, almost twice the distance of the famous monarch butterfly migrations in North America. The painted lady is the only butterfly species ever recorded in Iceland. It can take up to six successive generations to make the journey. But other, less spectacular forays may involve only four life cycles. One of the reasons the painted ladies had proved so difficult to trace is that, unlike the monarch butterflies, their migration does not involve synchronized breeding. Some migrants may decide to 'put down', mate and egg-lay at any point in the journey, while others continue. In really warm weather the entire life cycle can be played out within a month, and the freshly emerged individuals may immediately continue northwards. Broods will overlap and by mid/late summer young, pristine butterflies may be migrating alongside older, worn specimens. Some individuals will go much further than others on the north-bound journey. Staggering their annual movement in this way helps spread the risk for the species.

But mysteries remain to be fully explained. How can a creature, weighing less than a gram, with a wingspan of about six centimetres and a brain the size of a pinhead, find its way to a land it has never known, to which even its parents and grandparents have never been? New research suggests they might be steering using a solar compass in the club-ends of their antennae.

This was our first loudhailer lesson in the phenomenon of boom and bust, Nature's cardiograph of population explosions and cliff-falls. That summer, spiky black caterpillars swarmed over the thistles, spinning silken webs like tents, which soon filled with frass and inedible leaf spines. The whole area took on the appearance of a chaotic army encampment. By autumn, after the caterpillars had wolfed down their leaves, pupated and flown, our creeping thistle fields were in tatters, their stalks draped in dirty silk, the pink flower-heads nodding on skeleton stems – easy pickings for the ponies. The following year, our sixty acres of creeping thistle had vanished entirely. The devastation caused by the caterpillars had quite possibly weakened the plant's immunity, opening the door to some pathogen – a virus, pest, rust or fungus – which spread through the clonal colony like wildfire. Sooner or later, it seems, a perfect storm of weather, pathogen and predation converges to wipe creeping thistle out. Its clonal method of reproduction – its most pernicious characteristic to most people – is also its greatest weakness. It was a lesson that has since saved us a great deal of unnecessary stress. Now, when people stand shaking their heads in our fields of ragwort or – latterly – acres of the pioneer fleabane, we smile benignly and shrug off their concerns. Not even plagues of injurious weeds last for ever.

We had been given a ringside seat at one of nature's greatest spectacles thanks to sitting on our hands and keeping the glyphosate under lock and key. But even without the painted ladies, those three years of thistles had proved a gift. The prickly cover had protected other butterflies, day-flying moths and fellow invertebrates – including an explosion of grasshoppers – from the preying beaks of birds, creating the perfect opportunity for the common lizard. Gravid females with dark stripes scuttled between the thistle stems along tracks made by field mice, hunting for insects in preparation for the birth of their wriggling young. Though Exmoor ponies and pigs are partial to thistles, they hesitate to wade through robust swathes of them and tend to nibble only at the fringes. Protection from the hooves of herbivores gave an added boost to anthills. Ants could build new mounds – vulnerable to being knocked down and kicked over in their early, soft-soil stage – without disturbance. Making a nest himself, on his wax jacket, Charlie watched for hours as, mandible by mandible, the worker ants cut down thistle and grass stalks to add structure to the new mounds. By the time the thistles died back in autumn the anthills had gained height and stabilized, capped by a coating of living moss and grass like the rind of a cheese. Now, back in the post-apocalyptic expanse of the park you can tell where the outbreak of creeping thistle once was, from the density of anthills.

10

Purple Emperors

Dipt in the richest tincture of the skies,
Where light disports in ever-mingling dyes;
While ev'ry beam new transient colours flings,
Colours that change whene'er they wave their wings.

Alexander Pope, *The Rape of the Lock* II, 1714

By 2009, eight years after we'd begun the shift from intensive farming to rewilding, we could boast some astonishing results. Redwings, fieldfares and lesser redpolls were back at Knepp for the first time in decades. These are all on the UK's red list for birds of the highest priority for conservation. The number of skylarks (another red-listed species) on a single transect in the Southern Block rose from two (recorded in 2005) to eleven, and Robbie Burns' 'sweet warbling woodlark' was causing a birding stir in our emerging scrub. In winter, gadwall were dabbling on the lake, jack snipe, common snipe and woodcock were feeding on our laggs, or water meadows, and that spring, a pair of ravens nested exactly where Ted Green had predicted they would, in the gigantic cedar of Lebanon outside our bedroom window. It was the first time ravens had been seen here for over a hundred years. An assault of *kraa*s and *grunk*s now wakes us on cold February mornings, ricocheting off the brick walls. In my dozing half-sleep, the sound carries me to medieval England, King John and the old castle, to the days before ravens were shot by gamekeepers, when these were birds of myth and portent, scavengers of corpses on the gibbet and the battlefield and treasured street-cleaners of London. If ravens at the Tower safeguard crown and country, their arrival at Knepp was assuredly auspicious.

Birds resident here had begun to change their habits, adapting to the influx of new arrivals. Crows and rooks seemed to be less conspicuous, harried – perhaps – by the territorial ravens. Though their numbers remained the same, the herons on the lake had, for the first time in the thirty-five years that local birders Alf and Iris Simpson had been watching them, deserted their tree-top roosts in the heronry and were nesting a few feet above the water – protecting their eggs and young, presumably, from the buzzards wheeling overhead.

Frank 'Batman' Greenaway, husband of Theresa, our species recorder on the Advisory Board, spent the summer identifying the rocketing number of bats and on warm July nights we would wander down to the lake or laggs to watch him at work. Activating a detector clicking with sonic frequencies like hyperexcited Morse code, bats skimmed towards us into the invisible harp trap strung with fine nylon lines, tumbling harmlessly into the canvas collecting bag at the base. The harp net is an ingenious device, safer than mist nets that can sometimes entangle the captive's membranous wings and tiny fingers. In Frank's gloved hand, the screwed-up features of a whiskered bat, or a pipistrelle weighing less than a £1 coin, peeked out in startled affront. The visceral recognition of a bat, face to face, is a surprise. It is not like looking at a bird in the hand, with dinosaur genetics, cold-eyed, beaked and feathered, oviparous, clawed, inscrutable. Here is a warm-blooded mammal, glistening-eyed, with questing nostrils, a complaining mouth revealing tiny pointed teeth and furry body and – if it's female and lactating – tiny breasts and minuscule nipples. Somewhere, in the darkness, lying flat under some boarding or in a cavity in a tree or in someone's roof, is a baby waiting to be suckled. This winged creature of the night is, endearingly, one of us.

Thirteen out of our total eighteen UK bat species were

recorded on the estate that summer; two of them rare not just in Britain but in Europe as a whole. Bechstein's, a tree-living bat associated with old-growth broad-leaved woodland, is so rare little is known about it. It has a long pink muzzle and reddish brown fur, big ears and feeds on spiders and day-flying insects resting in the trees. Barbastelle bats, with endearing, upturned noses like a pug and wide, rounded ears joining on the top of the head (a useful distinguishing feature) roost behind the loose bark of aged trees and can live to twenty-three years. Their black fur, frosted white at the tips, feels slightly greasy to the touch – raincoat protection for their long distance travels across the countryside at night.

By 2009, our rewilded 3,500 acres of former arable farmland could claim fifteen 'UK Biodiversity Action Plan Priority' species – four bats and eleven birds – and sixty invertebrate species of conservation importance. Seventy-six new species of moths were added to our records in 2009, bringing the total to 276. Occasional visitors were on the rise, too, with little egrets, a bittern on Brookhouse Scrapes, scaup ducks on the lake and a green sandpiper puddling in the scrapes along the Adur.

Non-natives – escaped exotics or their descendants – were also finding us. Some, like a Himalayan bar-headed goose – the 'hamsa' of Indian mythology and one of the world's highest-flying birds, said to have been seen flying over Mt Everest – stayed for just a few days, a new kid on the block, skirting awkwardly around the grazing flocks of greylags and Canadians. Others, including a pair of flamboyant, tree-nesting Egyptian geese, made themselves at home. The first feral pair in the county to breed, they bray like donkeys all winter, flapping indecisively between the castle turrets and the cedars, their twenty or so offspring now adding to their clamour every spring.

We were committed to sitting on our hands and just observing what turned up, and doing so, the exotics began to challenge our perceptions about what should rightfully be here. Typically in Britain, our judgement on the subject is bewilderingly subjective. We rail against 'alien, invasive' species like Himalayan balsam and *Rhododendron ponticum*, while turning a blind eye to pheasants, rainbow trout, snowdrops and sweet chestnut. Snake's head fritillaries are a defining feature of 'medieval wild-flower meadows' protected by SSSIs. Yet they are no more native than the Loddon lily, the county flower of Berkshire.

Sometimes it is a question of rarity. Rabbits, introduced by the Normans, with a population in the UK now of 37.5 million, are often considered a pest. Brown hares, most probably introduced by the Romans 2,000 years ago, have loped into our affections and have their own UK Biodiversity Action Plan.

Sometimes it is just a question of timing. Recent arrivals, like the edible dormouse, which escaped from Lord Rothschild's collection at Tring in Hertfordshire in 1902 and is currently labelled a threat, may, in fifty years' time, seem as adorable and worthy of our protection as the little owl, introduced into Britain in 1842. The American signal crayfish, introduced in 1976, is denigrated for out-competing our native white-clawed crayfish even though there were already five other non-native crayfish in our river systems when it arrived and our 'native' itself was – genetic analysis has now shown – most probably introduced from Europe in the 1500s. And sometimes it is just a question of aesthetics and annoyance. British cornfield weeds are mostly ancient human introductions. Why do we champion blue cornflowers, golden corn marigolds, red poppies and the pretty pink (but poisonous) corncockle, while insisting that the wild oat, which has been here since the Bronze Age, is an undesirable alien?

While we merrily ring our houses with gardens full of exotics, the countryside is considered a place apart. If a plant escapes into the wider landscape from a park, garden or arboretum, it is suddenly undesirable. At our own back door the exotic is in neutral territory, like an illegal immigrant camping out in an airport. One of the underlying problems is confusion about our own role in introductions. Human agency usually identifies a species as alien. It is interesting how, in delegitimizing or denying ourselves a role as vectors for other species – be it intentional or unintentional – we exclude ourselves from the rest of the animal kingdom. Only not all humans are considered this way. Introductions made by pre-technological, pre-European societies, however advanced and whatever they may have got up to, are generally considered legitimate. Even tribal communities living today are considered exempt from the finger of blame, no matter that they, too, may travel and trade over great distances. But if anyone touched by modernity – anyone akin to those deciding the labels of 'native' and 'non-native' – introduces a new species, well, that is illegitimate.

There is confusion, too, over the degree to which introduced plants and animals upset the ecological status quo. The tabloids revel in headlines about invasions and attacks and aliens taking over the world. But scientists increasingly argue that the impact of non-natives is vastly exaggerated and largely a matter of perception. Studies show that even Himalayan balsam – large, flowery and conspicuous as a new arrival – ultimately has negligible effect on the diversity and composition of riverbank vegetation, and is positively beneficial for native pollinators.

It is often assumed that a new species will inevitably take over the niche of another. But ecosystems, even on islands, do not necessarily work this way. The space may not be 'full', the niche may be new. New arrivals may simply add to the diversity. The picture, too, is often blurred by other causes of ecosystem change. Are exotics responsible, or are they merely taking advantage of instabilities caused by pollution, climate change and habitat degradation? When a flock of ring-necked parakeets squawked over our heads in the Southern Block a few years into the project, we persuaded ourselves to keep an open mind. In the event, they vanished after a couple of weeks, seen off, perhaps, by our growing population of raptors. Maybe these colourful escapees have succeeded in establishing in Richmond Park and Kew Gardens precisely because there are fewer species there to harry them.

Other exotics have been more successful and, since the overall number of birds and other species at Knepp continues to climb year on year, we have no reason not to be relaxed about them. Who is to say that the mandarin ducks that have, in the last few years, taken to nesting in the oaks at the head of the lake are undesirable or un-British? Like fallow deer, rabbits, hares and even *Rhododendron ponticum* they have been here before, during the last interglacial period, over a hundred thousand years ago. Some would regard that as the ultimate claim to native status. We decided our best policy was to take a leaf from ecologist Ken Thompson's 2014 book *Where Do Camels Belong?*. 'We should stop thinking that we can turn the clock back to some pristine, pre-human golden age, even if we had any idea what that pristine state looked like', he says. 'We should instead focus on getting the best out of our brave new invaded world.'

One particular alien, however, was so appealing he managed to shake us from our resolution of non-intervention. Percy the Peacock arrived out of nowhere in a flourish of self-confidence and has stayed for years. His mournful cries and trembling fan-tailed displays, staged from the roof of the old stallion box, got to us after a couple of years and against our better judgement we softened and bought him a couple of peahens for company. They survived until they nested. One was taken by a fox almost immediately after she began sitting in a patch of nettles in the orchard. The other, more cleverly hidden in the yew hedge in our garden, was taken just a few days before her clutch was about to hatch. The fox must have jumped the six-foot-high ha-ha to get her. We renewed our vows not to meddle with nature, however unnatural nature seemed, and these days Percy seems to have found his own consolations – alternating between flirtatious foreplay with a shiny, electric-blue BMW convertible parked outside the Stable Yard flats (its car alarm drives him to a frenzy) and flying into the chicken enclosure for consummation with our amenable white Sussex hens. Thankfully there will be no issue, though the hens, annoyingly, keep going broody. We have no idea how old Percy is, but I read with mixed emotions that, domesticated (if that is what he is), a peacock can live for fifty years.

It was surprise encounters with more common species, though, that most seemed to characterize the diversity and abundance of life now bumping against ours: a gigantic, fat female grass snake four foot long, slithering at head-height through our yew hedge, searching for birds' eggs; female glow-worms – actually bioluminescent beetles – waving their torches for mates by the tennis court; a spectacular spew of bubbly, sulphur-yellow dog vomit fungus, a plasmodial slime mould, erupting all over the grasses in the park one summer, never seen before or since; kestrels nesting in the oak opposite the front door; treecreepers and flycatchers in the wisteria; badger cubs playing on the drive.

My writing shed in the old apple store on the far side of the walled garden, overlooking an abandoned paddock, its windows shielded by buddleia, has become a de facto bird hide. I now have binoculars and field guides on my desk, undermining my own attempts to avoid distraction. In 2008, a pair of little owls, nesting in the stallion box, taught their young to fly from the garden wall. I watched one of them catch a tiny grass snake and wrestle with it on the ground, clearly challenged beyond its usual deftness with earthworms. Occasionally the scream of a rabbit alerts me to a stoat attack and I watch the David and Goliath struggle, the tiny predator locked onto its prey, surprised only if the rabbit gets away. In a hole in the wainscot a blue tit nest flags up tufts of blue wool it has scavenged from my dog's blanket. Next door, in the wood shed, swallows keep me company through June and July, burbling away over their young. I watch them dive over the paddock for insects, swirling about with the house martins and swifts. On a good July day I can count ten species of butterfly without moving from my desk.

Sometimes it is the numbers that take my breath away. We used to watch murmurations of starlings over Brighton pier or the Somerset levels. Now they morph against our March skies, rolling and breaking like aerial waves until darkness siphons them down into the bamboo grove behind North Lodge in the park like a genie disappearing into a bottle. One October a flight of pink-footed geese, thousands strong, clamoured for an hour or more in circles over the lake, sending down scouts to test the water until finally splashing down just before nightfall. They were migrating south from the expanding ice-belt and dropping temperatures in Greenland, en route to Holland, perhaps, or western Denmark. Their cries and wing-slappings filled the night. They were gone before morning, leaving the ghost of their presence behind them, like an evacuated army.

But even as these apparitions were becoming a fact of life we were worried for the future. The clock was ticking down on our ten-year Countryside Stewardship Scheme agreement for the Middle and Northern Blocks, due to expire in 2010, and there was still no funding on the horizon for the Southern Block. The alternative, going back to the plough – if there was even someone out there prepared to farm our land at this stage – seemed unimaginable, though Jason Emrich, our estate manager, intelligently continued to investigate all options.

We had been pinning our hopes on Higher Level Stewardship, the more targeted level of DEFRA's Environmental Stewardship Scheme which was launched in 2006. Aimed at funding more active and demanding agri-environment projects under a fixed ten-year agreement, with a higher per acre grant than the Countryside Stewardship Scheme, it would also, we hoped, cover the crucial cost of fencing the Southern Block. Frustratingly, however, we were told that Knepp was not in one of their target areas for habitat management and was therefore ineligible.

It took a visit by Andrew Wood, Natural England's Executive Director of Science, Evidence and Advice, who had been adroitly collared by Jason at a land agents' conference, to flick the switch. Andrew spent one morning with Charlie in June 2008 looking around our wetlands and emerging scrub in the Southern Block and declared it 'exactly what HLS was designed for'. And he should know, because he had designed the programme. The target areas, he told us, were only a guideline to maximize efforts in places where environmental schemes already existed. It was not designed to penalize efforts like ours. Indeed, the very existence of the Knepp Wildland project has now singled out the Adur catchment in West Sussex as an HLS target area. Natural England's initial reluctance had been a typical example of the bureaucratic tail wagging the dog. The day after Andrew's visit we received a phone call from our regional manager at Natural England, offering us a capital grant to fence the Southern Block and giving the green light for us to apply for HLS funding for the entire estate. The HLS agreement, of ten years' duration, would begin on 1 January 2010.

Charlie was like a greyhound out of the slips. By March 2009 the nine-mile perimeter fence was finished and at the end of May, fifty-three head of longhorn cattle from a farm on the Scottish borders near Hadrian's Wall were unloaded from trailers into the Southern Block. Twenty-three Exmoor ponies joined them at the end of August, twenty Tamworth pigs in September, and forty-two fallow deer, caught up from the Middle Block, the following February. By then, jay-planted oak saplings and a few ash, wild service and birch were thrusting up, Vera-style, through their thorny nests. Thickets of dog rose, bramble, hawthorn and sallow provided the introduced herds with a smorgasbord of browsing, with the added treat of tender unprotected saplings stranded out in the open. The battle between vegetation succession and animal disturbance could begin.

Before long we were using animal trails to walk through the Southern Block just as we would gravitate along elephant and buffalo tracks through the African scrub. The feeling was totally different to the landscape of the park and the Northern Block. Here, there is density and complexity fizzing with life. Birds and insects throw up a wall of sound. Broken branches, dung, hoof-prints, scratching posts and wallows indicate the presence of large animals that have melted into the bush. It is a feeling so alien to us in Britain, used to seeing all our livestock in open fields that, searching for analogies, it inevitably transports you abroad. Time and again, visitors encountering this scenery for the first time describe how they expect to turn a corner and see herds of zebra or wildebeest, or look up to see a leopard in a tree.

In July 2009, a few months after the introduction of long-horn into the Southern Block, Matthew Oates, National Specialist on Nature at the National Trust and member of our Advisory Board, was sequestered deep inside one of the stands of hybrid sallow whips, now six to ten feet tall, magnifying lens in hand, a jay's feather tucked inside his lucky purple bandana hat band and a beam of delight across his face. He had made an exciting discovery. Matthew is best described as a butterfly enthusiast, but one that carries his enthusiasm to the borders of insanity. After fifty years in pursuit of butterflies he is famous for his studies of rarities like the pearl-bordered, marsh and high brown fritillaries, and the rapidly declining Duke of Burgundy. But there is one butterfly that, for him, eclipses even these dizzy delights. And in 2009, in the Southern Block, amidst the proliferations of gatekeepers, ringlets, meadow browns, marbled whites, small and Essex skippers, common blues and small tortoiseshell, he had found it and, more specifically, its breeding ground.

The scarce and elusive purple emperor, the second largest of our native butterflies and arguably the most spectacular, is often seen in modest numbers on our north-western border in places like Marlpost Wood, Dog-barking Wood and Madgeland Wood, snatches of ancient woodland around the expanding conurbation of our nearest big village, Southwater. This is where Matthew first saw them, as a young boy escaping from lessons at Christ's Hospital boarding school in the early 1970s. The encounter sparked off a lifetime obsession that introduced him to other 'sacred groves' of the purple emperor – Alice Holt, an ancient woodland on the Hampshire/Surrey border; the New Forest in Hampshire; Savernake Forest in Wiltshire; Bookham Common near Leatherhead, Surrey; Bernwood Forest, north-east of Oxford; and the purple emperor mecca, Fermyn Woods, once part of Rockingham Forest, near Brigstock in Northamptonshire.

Such is the purple emperor's magnetism that these sites are, from the end of June to mid-July, besieged by hundreds of butterfly-watchers bristling with telescopic lenses and a bizarre range of ingredients to attract the insects. Befitting an emperor, the butterfly has decadent tastes. It is one of only two of our British butterflies that does not visit flowers to feed on nectar. Instead, it behaves like a butterfly in the tropics, drinking aphid honeydew on the leaves of trees or descending to the ground to sip on the stinking juices of rotting meat, rotting fruit and excrement. The Emperor's Breakfast experiment, laid out on a linen tablecloth by Matthew one summer in the heart of Fermyn Woods, identified the emperor's preference for pickled mudfish and Big Cock shrimp paste from Thailand over rotten bananas, Stinking Bishop cheese, fresh horse manure, crushed grapes, a wet bar of soap and Pimm's No. 1. But the secret amongst aficionados is 'belachan', a putrid fermented-krill relish from Malaysia that spreads easily on gate-posts – and on oneself if really desperate for a close encounter.

So it was with almost uncontainable excitement that Matthew announced he had seen a couple of purple emperors at Knepp where they had never, in living memory, been seen before, and that he had seen them flying at low level through our young sallow scrub. Until that moment, purple emperors were considered to be exclusively a woodland species, if not an ancient-woodland indicator species. They might descend to feed on a muddy puddle or some putrescent carcass in a ride or clearing, and the female to lay her eggs on sallow shrubs – the food plant for her caterpillars – but ancient, closed-canopy woods were the emperor's undisputed domain.

It was late in the season and a wet one at that, so we saw no purple emperors ourselves. But Matthew showed us their eggs, single green dots with a distinctive purple band around the base, laid on the upper surface of deeply shaded sallow leaves. How he ever found them is a mystery. But Matthew has seemingly psychic antennae when it comes to butterflies and has peered into mottled foliage for decades. The empress – or 'Her Imperial Majesty', to Matthew – is choosy about the nursery for her offspring. She selects leaves that are mid-green in colour, of a certain thickness, soft to the touch and with a matt rather than shiny finish – 'apple leaves' the naturalist-writer-artist and emperorphile Denys Watkins-Pitchford, who wrote as 'BB', called them. Matthew demonstrated the pinch test between his thumb and forefinger. These are presumably the leaves that are most palatable for tiny young larvae. They don't occur on all sallow. Sallow taxonomy is a tangled phenomenon. The term 'sallow' refers to two closely related species – the goat willow (also known as 'great sallow') and the grey willow (also known as 'common sallow') – which often hybridize. The types of leaves hybrid sallow produces are multiple and random. The form of leaves that are selected by the purple empress for egg-laying amount to only a tiny proportion in any given stand of sallow. In late July the caterpillars hatch in Lincoln green livery, an exact match for a sallow leaf. Ingeniously they ensure their own leaf won't fall early by binding it to the stem with silken thread. In early November, the caterpillar sits in raindrops to help it morph to a brownish colour, and then it hibernates in the forks of the sallow twigs, strapping itself, a subtle bulge, onto the bark with skeins of silk so it can ride out the storms of winter. Knepp's now extensive sallow groves, with such a wide diversity of leaves, Matthew suspected, could prove a significant attraction for the purple emperor.

Sallow, like scrub, is rarely tolerated on the land today. Its flowering 'catkins' used to be an important nectar source in early spring, but the significance of its loss is entirely forgotten. Once used for making hurdles and wickerware, sallow is now confined to the niche market of country craft fairs. In commercial terms it no longer has value, and, at Knepp, sallow had been relegated to a scattering of trees left to senesce in the laggs, in hedges and along the old droving lanes. The 'invasion' of young sallow marching into our former arable fields was another cause of disgust to local farmers and landowners. To our animals, it is clearly an important source of browse in winter and early spring, before the grass flushes. One has to wonder whether sallow played a similar role back in the days of pasture-woodland systems.

Sallow also requires specific conditions to seed. The seed is only viable for a couple of weeks in May. Every few years or so it occurs in great blooms of fluff, drifting on the breeze like a snow storm. But it needs to find wet, bare ground to germinate – it is a pioneer colonizer of bare clay. In most of the Southern Block there is no sallow at all. The areas where it has established would have had wet and open soil during the crucial two-week window in a given mast year. By removing fields from farming in stages, and leaving them exposed after their last harvest rather than blanketing them with grass, we had, accidentally, created the right conditions – the randomness upon which natural pulses like sallow mast thrive.

The summers following 2009 were wet in West Sussex, not great for butterflies, and Matthew was on the chase elsewhere. Charlie and I, having no idea where or how to look for them, failed to spot any purple emperors at all. That they were very much here and poised for takeover burst upon us in the butterfly summer of 2013.

On 20 July Matthew Oates came to Knepp with Neil Hulme to check up on the emperors' progress. A fellow member of our Advisory Board and Conservation Advisor to the Sussex Branch of Butterfly Conservation, Neil claims the counter-intuitive distinction of having seen sixty-six out of the UK's fifty-nine regularly occurring species of butterfly, with the excess including rare and exotic vagrants such as the scarce tortoiseshell, Queen of Spain fritillary, Camberwell beauty and a hybrid cross between an Adonis blue and a chalkhill blue which, in terms of scarcity, is the lepidopterist's unicorn. Emperors were already fully out in other sites across the country and numbers that July were reportedly good. Neil and Matthew anticipated seeing a dozen or so at Knepp, perhaps even twenty. But in five hours, over a small area and in cloudy weather, they counted eighty-four – a purple emperor explosion. To their satisfaction, the butterflies were not only numerous but 'seriously violent'.

Purple emperor-watching with Matthew and Neil is not your average butterfly entertainment, ethereal and somewhat effete. Theirs is a raucous, adrenaline-fuelled spectator sport. The emperors themselves seem to play to the crowd. Pugnacious males dart around the crowns of oaks, staking out their territory, jetting about with muscular flicks of their wings, twirling on their own axes, elevating a hundred feet into the air. They are the SAS of butterflies, fit, fearless and chemically armed. 'Think testosterone,' says Matthew, 'multiply it by πr^2 and double it. Forget boys locked in boarding schools. They've spent ten months as a caterpillar waiting for this. They've pupated, they're mature and they're desperate. They're squaddies in the disco on a Saturday night. They're sailors in port after a nine-month voyage.'

High up, skimming a tree's silhouette and framed against the sky, the emperors look black – like a rainforest butterfly. At a glimpse, they can be mistaken for birds. This is lekking taken to the skies. The males attack anything that comes near them, defending their territory and the pick of the females. An unwary chaffinch is chased away. Blue tits shriek in alarm – a comeuppance for them, since, from October through to April, when the emperor larvae hibernate, they are the butterfly's main predator. Emperors have even been known to attack sticks and bricks thrown up into the air. From time to time a couple, or even three, male emperors lock horns, tussling in flight – 'having a bundle', as Neil puts it; 'beating the shit out of each other', says Matthew. Just as in a deer lek, the weaker animal is eventually intimidated by the stronger.

While emperors may favour a particular tree for their displays, the felling of a 'master oak' does not – as is commonly believed – result in the demise of a colony. At Knepp, the butterflies have plenty of oaks to choose from and they charge

around the leeward branches of 400-year-old veterans grown
out of ancient hedges, around giants on the edges of woods or
fringing the green lane – always within yards of the sallow
stands – in territories identified on Matthew's purple emperor
map as 'Serial Offenders' Institute' and 'Mindless Violence', a
short walk from 'Bonked Senseless'.

Only when a male swoops down to search for females in the
sallow does his purple raiment come to light, refracting through
his wing-scales at angles with the sun. Or when several settle
together with opened wings at a sap-run on an oak tree, sipping
the sugary bleed from a torn-off limb or lightning strike. The
predilection for oak sap may explain why the Sussex emperors
are more violent than their cousins elsewhere. With veteran
oaks still relatively plentiful in Sussex the emperors here are
primarily sap-feeders. They are, for want of a better term,
pissed. Drunk with sap, the butterflies stagger in their flight,
almost crashing into branches. Occasionally a male will descend
to feed on fox scat or take minerals from the rubble on a track
but it's only since 2016 – and who knows why? – that they've
begun to do this at Knepp.

The empress in more demure brown-and-white livery lacks
his Imperial Majesty's purple sheen and, though she can chase
off birds too, once she has mated – a tail-to-tail congress that
lasts a tantric three and a half hours – she lurks in the sallow
shadows, avoiding the master oaks and the attentions of other
sex-starved males, and laying her eggs carefully on selected
leaves.

We saw another exciting increase in numbers in 2014 but the
red-letter day for the purples came on 11 July 2015 when Matthew and Neil clocked up 126, followed by another
record-breaking count of 148 individuals on 21 June 2017. The
tally established Knepp as the largest breeding colony in the
UK, displacing the mighty Fermyn Woods – 'from zero to
hero', as Matthew put it, in less than a decade. Thanks to Neil
and Matthew's observations of butterflies rampaging around
open-grown trees and through sallow scrub at Knepp, the

emperor can no longer be described as a woodland species. And here, again, is the magic of rewilding. Like the white-tailed eagles nesting in willows below sea level in the Oostvaarders-plassen, process-led conservation allows nature to reveal the limitations of our own understanding and the plasticity of species. We assume we know what is good for a species but we forget that our landscape is so changed, so desperately impoverished, we may be recording a species not in its preferred habitat at all, but at the very limit of its range. Naturalists believed the purple emperor was a woodland butterfly only because – with no significant areas of sallow left – that is where it has clung on. Now, thanks to the emperor butterflies' spontaneous colonization of Knepp we know a little more about how to mitigate, should we so choose, this rare insect's decline. We know more – but by no means everything – about their life cycle and preferences, and the narrow niche of sallow types and situations favoured for breeding. And we can dwell on the delightful thought that, in times past, purple emperors would have been a feature of the English summer, present in huge numbers in every sallow-strewn county.

But there is another surprising aspect of Knepp's purple emperor story that could be key to their continued success here. 2014 was another conspicuous mast year for sallow, with blizzards of fluff floating on the wind in May. The areas where seeds successfully germinated, where new sallow saplings are just now beginning to grow, were damp patches of earth exposed by the rootling of pigs. Pigs – and presumably in the past, wild boar – provide opportunities for sallow succession. The expansion of the purple emperor's empire at Knepp may well depend, in part at least, on the accommodating diggings of our Tamworths.

It was becoming clear to Charlie and me that had we set out with the intention of creating the perfect habitat for purple emperors, we would never have achieved the numbers that have spontaneously emerged through rewilding. The phenomenon is an example of what we are learning to refer to as 'emergent properties'. An emergent property is a property which a complex system has, but which the individual constituents of that system do not have, like the cells of the heart which, on their own, do not have the property of pumping blood but which together create a higher level aggregate – a complex organ – that does. At Knepp, previously missing or dormant components were coming together, striking up extraordinary and unexpected outcomes. In effect, two plus two was making five – or more; and this imposed on us, as midwives of the system, acceptance and humility about our role. There may well be other factors involved in the success of purple emperors at Knepp that we have not yet identified, perhaps may never identify – a preference for certain types of animal dung, minerals or sap-runs, temperatures, moisture or some other tiny cog in the wheel, or a fortuitous combination of any number of things. What seems imperative is that we take care not to fall into the trap of assuming, as conservationists have so often in the past, that a couple of specifics – some tall trees and a massive amount of sallows – is basically all the purple emperor needs. This is tantamount to asserting that the individual cell of a heart has the property of pumping blood – an assumption known as the 'fallacy of division'. The purple emperor butterfly, with its complicated life cycle involving numerous stages requiring different conditions over the course of almost a year, beats its wings to the tune of the entire symphony orchestra that has conjured it into being.

11

Nightingales

Thou wast not born for death, Immortal Bird!
No hungry generations tread thee down;
The voice I hear this passing night was heard
In ancient days by emperor and clown.

Keats, 'Ode to a Nightingale', 1819

Standing in the Southern Block on a still, late April night, sil-houettes of oak trees and shaggy hedges framed against a glittering sky, the outpourings of a nightingale throwing its notes to the heavens are discombobulating. It 'sends' you, in the old-fashioned Sam Cooke sense, somewhere beautiful but also distant and unsettling. Thoughts flutter. Longings and misgivings, doubts even, hover in the air. The looming forms around you, the very ground feels unsteady, rocked by the challenge this twenty-gram bird projects into the enormity of space.

The song of a nightingale is not an easy ride. It throws the ear with unexpectedness – phrases fired off, one after the other: florid trills, first rich and liquid, then mockingly guttural and discordant; now a sweet insistence of long, lugubrious piping; then bubbling chuckles and indrawn whistles; and then, suddenly, nothing – a suspended, teasing hiatus before the cascades and crescendos break forth again. The mind tries to anticipate but there is no sense, at least no human sense; no pattern, no repetition. A single nightingale has around 180 'riffs' or song phrases in its repertoire, from a total of 250 for the species, which it sequences differently each time it sings. It is a display of astonishing mastery, heart-rending in its energy and volume – these pulsating strains issuing from tiny vocal cords belting out like organ pipes, throwing the music of the tropics into the English night air. And the performances can be marathon. Though a typical aria lasts thirty minutes, one nightingale has been recorded singing non-stop for twenty-three and a half hours.

Like its fellow African migrant the turtle dove, the nightingale has nested in our culture, become ours. It wings its way through Shakespeare, Milton, Matthew Arnold, Coleridge, Tennyson, Shelley, Keats, John Clare, T. S. Eliot, our greatest poets adding their transports to those of Aesop, Aristophanes and Pliny, the Persian poets and all the minstrels and troubadours down the ages whose imaginations have been teased, provoked and disturbed by the 'joy that is almost pain'.

But few people in Britain today are familiar with the exquisite unease of a nightingale's song. Like the turtle dove, it is now almost a miracle to hear one. Between 1967 and 2007 the number of nightingales in the UK fell 91 per cent. For every ten birds that were singing when I was a child, there is now only one. This isn't supposed to have happened. England, it is true, has always been at the northernmost reach of the nightingale's range. The breeding capacity of this warm-climate bird is restricted to areas where the temperature in July is between 17 and 30 °C – so, conventionally, nowhere north of Yorkshire, and rarely above an altitude of about 600 feet. But with global warming ornithologists had expected this to change. By now, they had predicted, we should be hearing nightingales in the borders of Scotland and expanding into Wales. Instead, its territory has retracted, shrivelling south and eastwards, with Kent, Sussex and Suffolk the last bastions of its communion with England.

It's sobering – and surprising – to remember how common they once were. Only a century or two ago nightingales were serenading Londoners. The land on which the royal palace now stands was, when the Duke of Buckingham acquired it in 1703, 'a little wilderness full of Blackbirds and Nightingales'. The bird that possessed the feverish, tubercular Keats in the spring of 1819 was singing near his house on Hampstead Heath. As the heaths and commons of London contracted or were vigorously tidied up, the Victorians, yearning for its song like the emperor in Hans Christian Andersen's tale, made pilgrimages to hear nightingales in the countryside and imported them to sing in their parlours and drawing rooms. In the 1830s, a gamekeeper in Middlesex could catch a hundred and eighty nightingales in one season, receiving eighteen shillings a dozen for them in London – a lucrative supplement to his wages. The trade continued towards the turn of the century. According to Richard Jefferies, a naturalist writing in Surrey in 1886, 'a couple of roughs would come down from town and silence a whole grove.' A nightingale makes a poor prisoner and the majority battered themselves to death against the bars of their cages. 'The mortality was pitiable,' describes Jefferies. 'Seventy percent of these little creatures that were singing a week before in full-throated ease in the Surrey lanes would be flung into the gutters of Seven Dials or Whitechapel.'

Mercifully, the market for caged birds fell away in the twentieth century and there were still nightingales left to sing in the countryside through the Second World War. The voice of a nightingale can reach 95 decibels, way above the levels requiring industrial workers to wear ear defenders. Technically, it can be classed as noise pollution. On a night in May 1942 a BBC sound engineer accidentally made what has become a famous recording: a nightingale in a Surrey back garden poignantly raising its love-song against the approaching thrum of the engines of war – Wellington and Lancaster bombers on their way to bomb Cologne. The live broadcast was suddenly terminated when the BBC realized they could be alerting the Germans to the raid.

By the Second World War the possibility of hearing a nightingale in the capital was no more than a dreamy illusion, though romance had it otherwise. There is something in a nightingale's song that seems to strain for the sublime, as though it might lift the world away from the pains of reality.

> That certain night, the night we met,
> There was magic abroad in the air.
> There were angels dining at the Ritz
> And a nightingale sang in Berkeley Square.

Somehow, these lyrics of 1939, recorded by Vera Lynn, Glenn Miller, Frank Sinatra, Nat King Cole and a host of others down the decades (including, more surprisingly, Rod Stewart and Manhattan Transfer), have developed a life of their own, as if wishful thinking has made the fantasy, fact – that nightingales really did sing their hearts out to lovers in Mayfair during the Blitz.

Berkeley Square, though, is not, and never has been – at least not since the seventeenth century – nightingale habitat. The British Trust for Ornithology describes the nightingale as a woodland species – shy, reclusive, hiding deep within thickets in the understorey of woods. Its decline is linked, once again, with the decline of coppice. The proliferation of nightingales at Knepp on open, formerly arable land has therefore been something of an ornithological thunderclap, as surprising as the purple emperor's appearance here to lepidopterists. Knepp is only the second place in England – after Lodge Hill in Medway in Kent, owned by the Ministry of Defence and where plans for the development of 5,000 houses have, for the moment at least, been suspended – where the numbers of nightingales have been rising. Their rapid colonization of Knepp has shaken up what we thought we knew about this bird and, like the purple emperor, thrown up wider questions about where conservation has been going wrong.

In 1999 a national nightingale survey carried out by the British Trust for Ornithology recorded nine territories on Knepp. But Charlie and I can only remember hearing them here once in the 1990s, one memorable year when, standing at midnight on the dam wall at the end of Knepp lake, we heard three singing in concert, two from the heronry on one side and one from the rookery on the other. It is possible they had been displaced by the harvesting, that year, of large areas of coppice over at Arundel – one of the few significant areas of coppice left in the county. Our delight at the manifestation of their pure, penetrating song, amplified over the Mill Pond under a full May moon, was dampened by the notion that these tiny birds had flown across two continents to find their habitat demolished. The farmland of Knepp was clearly no substitute. We went down to listen to them the following night but they had moved on.

By 2001, the year we started rewilding, nightingales seemed to have disappeared from the estate altogether, in line with the national decline of 53 per cent between 1995 and 2008. The suspected causes of the nightingale crisis were the usual: declining availability of food resources due to widespread use of pesticides and livestock wormers, housing development on habitual nesting grounds, loss of coppicing, changes to nightingale wintering grounds in Africa and climate change affecting the migration route.

So it was a surprise, seven or eight years later, suddenly to be hearing nightingales again at Knepp – and this time in numbers. In the Southern Block we could hear three, four, sometimes five competing with each other. Anticipating their arrival in late April we began to have nightingale dinners, taking groups of friends out after supper to listen. Most had never heard one before. Contrary to poetic convention, only a male nightingale sings. He sings both night and day whilst he is trying to attract a mate, but it is at night that his arias, disentangled from the racket of diurnal birdsong, burst forth with such clarity and conviction upon the human ear.

Conservationists began to show an interest and in 2012, the year of another national nightingale survey conducted by the BTO, the biology department at Imperial College London was sufficiently intrigued to send one of their MA students, Olivia Hicks, under the auspices of her tutor, Alex Lord, to investigate. Olivia stayed with us for two weeks in May, keeping nightingale hours, often returning to bed just as we were getting up for breakfast. Her goal was to identify nightingale territories and the type of habitat they had chosen at Knepp, and then to work out if the males had successfully paired, to give an indication of breeding rates. For this, she returned for another bout of insomnia in the last week of May and first week of June.

Nightingales are notoriously difficult to spot. An unassuming LBJ ('little brown job', in twitching terminology), they melt into their cover. Nests are even harder to find. But their song is a giveaway, and the fact that they are deeply territorial, rarely straying from their chosen nesting site, makes them relatively easy to count. The male nightingales arrive in England in an advance cohort in early to mid-April, having flown from wintering grounds in equatorial Senegal, Guinea-Bissau and Gambia, to take possession of a suitable nesting site. Not all nightingales leave Africa to breed. But millions do take on the Herculean challenge of the 3,000-mile migration for the chance to raise chicks in Europe where there are far fewer predators (even insects eat fledglings in Africa) and less intra-species competition for territory and food. The female follows a week or so later, flying at night to escape avian predation. In the inky vastness she catches the notes of males singing below. She'll drop down to join one, attracted, recent research suggests, by the virtuosity of his performance – volume and complexity being an indication of physical strength and maturity: signs of a good father. In daylight she'll inspect his choice of breeding spot. If she doesn't approve, she'll fly on in search of a more discerning mate.

Nest-building is done exclusively by her, while her mate continues to sing. After pairing, though, his song is territorial, conducted only during the day, and without the depth and urgency of his earlier broadcasts. As soon as the young are hatched – about thirteen days after the eggs are laid – he joins in feeding them and virtually ceases to sing altogether. This is key to estimating breeding success. By June the only nightingales left singing are bachelors – lonely hearts, failed homemakers, vainly hoping to attract a straggling female.

Olivia's findings were astonishing. She found thirty-four nightingale territories on Knepp. From having no nightingales at all, we were now, after just nine years, hosting between 0.5 and 0.9 per cent of the UK population. Of these thirty-four territories, twenty-seven of them were paired – a 79 per cent success rate compared with the European average of 50 per cent. Two of our neighbours allowed Olivia to use their land – an area totalling 1,040 hectares (2,600 acres) of intensive arable farmland – to use as a comparison. Here she found nine territories (significantly higher than the 1999 BTO survey) but with only two of them (18 per cent) paired. Her findings showed that Knepp had not only become a breeding hotspot for nightingales. It also suggested that males, perhaps juveniles or late arrivals, were spilling over onto neighbouring land once the prime territories at Knepp had been taken.

Deep inside the exploding skirts of an overgrown hedge, a nightingale's nest – a tangle of twigs and moss, a few feathers and dry oak leaves, just a foot above the ground – identifies why the nightingales are attracted to Knepp. The majority (86 per cent) of the birds had taken up sites in overgrown hedgerows, twenty-five to forty-five feet deep, where there is around 60 per cent blackthorn with thorny cover extending right to the ground (no browse-line from deer or rabbits), fringed with brambles, nettles and long grasses, and where the cavernous, cathedral-like structure of the thicket's interior offers a safe haven for adults and their fledgling chicks to peck about for insects in the leaf-litter.

So a nightingale – Knepp reveals – is not a woodland bird. Trees need not play a part in the picture at all. But what does this mean? Are nightingales changing their habits? Is Knepp a truer picture of their ideal habitat? Or is it just an improvement on conventional woodland? Is this information really new to science? In Knepp's library, looking back through the giant illustrated folios of *The Birds of Great Britain* by my old friend, subject of my very first book, the Victorian ornithologist John Gould, the nightingale nest is described in simple terms as 'generally placed on the side of a bank, and occasionally in a shrub or bush'. In our well-thumbed volumes of *Birds of Sussex* published in 1938, nearly a hundred years later, the Sussex ornithologist John Walpole-Bond, son of a vicar of Horsham, describes how the 'favourite breeding-haunts . . . are supplied by woods, particularly their outskirts; spinneys; shaws; thickets on down; common and waste ground generally, even expanses of shingle like the Crumbles; and certain sorts of hedgerows, double hedgerows especially'. Their nests, he says, are 'usually in wild sloes, brambles, heaps of debris, even on ivied walls'. Nightingales were all over the place.

Yet these observations, made by punctilious field naturalists only a century or so ago, are rarely consulted by modern science. In academic papers the onus is on referencing contemporary research. Another example of shifting-baseline syndrome. The nightingale – like the purple emperor – has been labelled a woodland species today, because that is where we see it. We study it there, make all our calculations of its behaviour there. Woodland coppice has become, to our minds, perfect nightingale territory because, in the absence of open-grown thorny scrub, thickly vegetated banks and double hedgerows replete with insects, that is all we have been offering the birds. And where – does anyone consider? – would nightingales have nested before wood coppice came along? Our baselines are entrenched in a landscape of human activity. We talk of 'woodland', 'wetland', 'heathland', 'moorland' and even 'farmland' birds. But their true context, before man began parcelling up the landscape and assigning bio-geographical and 'habitat' categories for species, may be much more complex and amorphous, as denizens of the shifting margins where one habitat blends into another.

Our views in the UK are constrained, too, by insularity. On the Continent, in places where nightingales are still plentiful, they quite obviously appear to favour the habitats described by Gould and Walpole-Bond. I've heard them singing in scrub on the salt pans of the Camargue; even seen them, bold as brass, on shrubs around orchards in Bulgaria. A German research paper of 1973 describes them, categorically, as a bird that disdains closed-canopy woods. Yet, somehow, in Britain we seem to regard our islands as an exception to the rule, as if species change their preferences halfway across the Channel. Had we set out with the intention of attracting nightingales to Knepp we would almost certainly have been encouraged by British conservationists to create woodland coppice – and most likely been disappointed with the results.

The following year another Imperial MA student, Izzy Donovan, continued Olivia's work on nightingales at Knepp. She added to her study another six birds of European conservation concern: two of them – the green woodpecker and whitethroat – amber-listed; four of them – cuckoo, linnet, song thrush and yellowhammer – red-listed. Calculating densities of birds per ten hectares she compared numbers at Knepp with densities given in the *Atlas of European Breeding Birds*, and on the site of a neighbouring intensive farmer. The results, once again, were astonishing. Knepp performed at least as well as, if not better than, what are considered good habitats elsewhere:

Species	Densities in good habitats	Knepp density estimates	Local farm (control) estimates
Linnet	5.5–9.2	8	1.3–2.2
Yellowhammer	4.7	4.5–7.5	3.6–6.1
Song thrush	15	3.5–5.8	None
Green woodpecker	0.3	3.8–6.38	1–1.6
Whitethroat	10	8.5–14.2	2.6–4.4
Cuckoo	0.3	3.5	None observed
Nightingale	2	7–11	1.3–2.2

The only, as yet unexplained, anomaly was the song thrush, numbers of which, according to our 2016 survey, are now conspicuously high.

The findings about the nightingale's habitat were so exciting that on 1 May 2014 we held a Nightingale Workshop at Knepp, attended by several of the top brass from Natural England, as well as representatives from the National Trust, Wildlife Trusts, Country Landowners' Association, National Farmers' Union, the British Trust for Ornithology, the RSPB and a number of interested landowners. We hoped Natural England – whose response so far had been extremely positive – would be able to feed this new information into their grant system, to incentivize farmers and landowners in areas where nightingale populations were still clinging on, into growing out their hedgerows to the prescribed twenty-five feet or more to provide extra habitat. To us it seemed a relatively simple step that could halt the decline of one of our loveliest birds and benefit a host of umbrella species.

But the reality in conservation is never that simple. Shortly after the meeting one of the landowners, who had several nightingales on his farmland in Suffolk (one of the most northerly sites for the species), applied for a grant to allow some of his hedgerows to scrub up. His local Natural England office turned him down, arguing that the lack of nightingales for five miles around his land would make it a bad use of their funds. Despite encouraging signs at first, the nightingale hedgerow initiative failed to gain traction at Natural England. Enthusiasm for the project amongst all those sitting around our table gradually fizzled out. And sadly, it seems, without incentives and direction from above, most landowners, even those who are conservation-minded, rarely have the time, drive or resources to devote to conservation measures – even when they are as simple and rewarding as this.

12

Turtle Doves

I, an old turtle,
Will wing me to some wither'd bough, and there
My mate, that's never to be found again,
Lament till I am lost.

Shakespeare, *The Winter's Tale*, c. 1609

More exciting even than the nightingales has been the arrival, from the very brink of extinction, of turtle doves. There are estimated to be fewer than 5,000 pairs left in the whole of Britain, and only 200 pairs in Sussex. Knepp may be the only place in Britain where numbers have increased in recent years. From none at all in the days of farming, we counted sixteen singing males in 2017. Turtle doves, however, are much harder to monitor than nightingales. The males stake out large territories so they are never reliably in the same place. Their gentle *turr-turr*-ing often falls beneath the register of the older human ear so it's harder for some birders to track them. What the birders are missing is a sound at the furthest end of the spectrum from a nightingale's cacophonous serenading, as close as the bird world gets to a lullaby. 'The cooings of the Turtle Dove', according to the Victorian ornithologist John Gould, 'relieve the mind by calling up soothing and pleasing thoughts not easily described.' To R. Bosworth-Smith, classics master at Harrow and author of *Bird Life & Bird Law* (1905), the 'low crooning' of the turtle dove is 'one of the most soothing sounds in nature'. It is balm to the soul.

In Gould's day turtle doves were a familiar sight, arriving in spring in pairs with 'various broods assembling in considerable flocks' for migration in the autumn. But even in the 1930s Walpole-Bond describes 'batches' of them arriving in the Sussex Weald, 'small parties and flocks of even several hundred individuals' feeding on vetches in fields of grain all through the breeding season, and the 'rush' of young broods off to Africa in July, followed by a second brood heading off in September. He watched courting males in their 'show-off flight' clapping their wings above their backs, ascending and descending on rigid pinions, with a suspended floating halfway, or simply sliding on motionless wings from a tall tree to a lower one. Their nests were so numerous that not all were hidden in impenetrable cover and it was 'by no means unusual' for Walpole-Bond to approach close to a sitting turtle dove on a more open nest without disturbing her. 'In highly favoured areas I have fairly frequently found from six to ten nests in tolerable proximity, whilst a friend of Millais' once near Horsham actually discovered seventeen – incidentally, in the short space of an hour!'

The turtle's cloak of invisibility today is no doubt a response to its drastic decline over the last few decades. Deprived of safety in numbers it has become more reclusive than ever. In just the five years between 2005 and 2010 there has been a 60 per cent drop in turtle doves in the UK, and the trajectory continues in free-fall. Bird conservation bodies like the RSPB have been frantically searching for clues in the hope of finding a way to turn the species back from the brink.

Hunting along the migration route is undoubtedly a factor. In 2007 it was estimated that up to 3 million turtle doves are shot in Europe every year. Despite a European ban on spring shooting, in Mediterranean countries the culture of dove-hunting runs deep and the bird is routinely shot as it flies in both directions. One September a friend in Greece served us a special supper of turtle doves, shot by him, and was dismayed that his treat was not rapturously received. Though these little roasted birds dressed with mountain thyme would have been flying south from Central Europe, it was impossible not to look at them and think of our turtles cooing to us in Sussex a few weeks earlier.

Severe droughts in the Sahel zone are another possible factor. Turtles are remarkably tolerant of the heat and have been observed in Africa to feed in direct sunlight until temperatures reach 45 °C. But they cannot last long without water. Loss of trees around oases and loss of groves in arable landscapes may also be affecting their ability to recuperate on migration. Competition with Eurasian collared doves – one bird species that is on the rise – has been cited. Then there's the protozoan parasite *Trichomonas gallinae*, a cosmopolitan bird parasite, believed to be an ancient pathogen that affected the dinosaurs. It appears to be hitting turtle doves particularly hard. Since 2011, of 106 turtle doves in East Anglia screened for the presence of the parasite, 96 per cent have tested positive, with 8 birds displaying fatal symptoms.

Trends since 1980 show that populations of turtle doves across much of Europe have undergone moderate to serious decline. But this is as nothing compared with the rapid and almost total loss in the UK. This has thrown British bird conservation into disarray. What is responsible: is it a particular problem with our habitat, lack of food, increased competition or parasites, or a combination of some or all of these? Contrary indicators abound. Recent RSPB radio-tracking shows turtle doves in East Anglia travelling large distances – up to 10 kilometres – in search of food, leading observers to believe that they are naturally wide-ranging foragers. But another report by the RSPB in 2017 declares that, in order for them to rear their fledglings successfully, their food source has to be within 127 metres of the nest: 'In our study area, seed-rich habitats included semi-natural grassland, quarries, fallow areas and areas of low-intensity grazing – mostly horses, with the occasional alpaca – that allow wild flowers and grasses to flower and seed. However, the birds still returned to the area near their nests, spending around 50 per cent of their time within 20m of their nest.'

It seems we are still confused about their diet – presumably because in Britain these days it's rarer than ever to see turtle doves feeding. The RSPB describes them as 'obligate granivores' – feeding on seeds and nothing else. However most of the weed seeds believed to be their main food source in nature (if they can find them these days) – like common fumitory, knotgrass and red fescue – don't start to ripen in the UK until July. There are strong indications that turtle doves are, indeed, having difficulty finding food when they first arrive in May. After their long migration they must pile on the calories as fast as they can if they are to make breeding condition. In peak health, turtle doves may have two or three broods in a season. In the UK, nowadays, they are lucky to make one.

So what has changed since the 1960s, when the UK had an estimated 125,000 breeding pairs with two or more broods a season? Certainly, routine use of chemical herbicides up and down the country since the 1970s – not just in agriculture but on every patch of managed ground – has had a dramatic impact on the availability of so-called 'arable' weeds. Changes in agricultural practices have also made a difference. As arable weeds have declined, turtle doves have begun feeding on cereals, scavenging particularly from spillage around grain depots and farmyards where they can find shattered grains crushed under wheel or foot. Greater efficiency – bigger combines, less wastage, fewer messy farmyards – are denying them this opportunity, too.

So the decline in this 'farmland' bird is commonly attributed to the industrialization of agriculture and, in particular, the loss of traditional, wildlife-friendly farming practices. But, once again, this skews the picture. Once again, we cast ourselves in the position of God. The baseline most ornithologists refer to is within living memory, a generation or two ago, in the 1960s. Many consider that era, when arable farming peaked but before the onset of chemical herbicides and the misleadingly named Green Revolution, to be the turtle dove's 'Golden Age'. Others look back to the 1930s – the swansong of traditional farming.

No one seems to cast their mind back further, to consider what turtle doves may have eaten before they found themselves in this cultural landscape, where 'arable' weeds existed before there were arable fields; what opportunities might have propelled these migrants to our shores in the first place, possibly thousands of years ago, or what they may still be eating under wilder conditions in the present day.

There are those who argue that the turtle dove has evolved alongside agriculture, that, as a species, it was only able to extend its migration into Britain with the availability of crops and greater opportunities for weeds provided by ploughing: it may never have existed here in the distant past in significant numbers. But this is again to consider the turtle dove in an isolated context. It overlooks the fact that this bird is multinational, an intrepid traveller. For six months of the year, it lives in natural – or at least much more natural – conditions in sub-Saharan Africa. Twice a year it switches from a wild diet to whatever food is available in agrarian Europe, and back to a wild diet again. If you were peering through your binoculars at a turtle dove in the savannas and thickets of the Sahel, you would not tick it off as a farmland bird.

There are strong suggestions, too, that the turtle doves' scavenging of arable grains in Europe is a measure of desperation, following the eradication of arable weeds with herbicides. The great distances flown by the radio-tracked birds in East Anglia to find food may not be normal behaviour at all but an indication of the scarcity of food in that landscape. Grain may be their food of last resort. A dove has a much more delicate metabolism than a pigeon. Ask most dove fanciers and they will tell you of the hazards of feeding wheat and corn to doves. The whole grains are indigestible and the sharp edges of cracked grains can tear the throat and crop and induce canker. Grains can also absorb moisture in the gut and generate fungal disease. With large, cultivated grains of wheat, barley and oilseed rape difficult for turtle doves to metabolize, the wild population may be filling their bellies but not improving their physical condition – another contributing factor, perhaps, to the declining number of broods. It may also explain why so many are being affected by diseases such as *Trichomonas gallinae.*

We don't have to go far, however, to find a more complex profile for the turtle dove. A quick glimpse in the library, even only as far back as the Victorian era, describes a far more varied diet than most British conservationists currently imagine. According to Gould, the turtle's principal food consists of 'the seeds of the vetch and wild plants, the tender shoots of herbs, and small-shelled snails'. Birdlife International, observing turtle doves across the continents of Europe and Asia in the present day, also attributes to them wider tastes – 'seeds and fruits of weeds and cereals, but also berries, fungi and invertebrates.'

Habitat, like food, is broader in Gould's world. The turtle dove was 'a frequenter of woods, fir-plantations, and the thick and high hedges between cultivated lands' and its territory was expanding – presumably due to a warming climate – as far as the Scottish borders. A century later, in the 1930s, Walpole-Bond was seeing them nesting 'in tall, straggling quickset [hawthorn hedges] or in one of those scattered thorns so prevalent in woods' in West Sussex, as well as in conifers, elders, birches, hollies and hazels, occasionally pear and apple in orchards and twice in gorse. David Armitage Bannerman, author of *Birds of the British Isles* (1953–63), waxes lyrical about his first encounter with numbers of turtle doves in 'a lowland waste of sandy heath, with scrub and thorn-bushes dotted here and there.' It seems that, just like the nightingale, as the turtle dove's territory has shrunk, so has our understanding of its true range and habits.

On 10 May 2012 the RSPB and Natural England launched Operation Turtle Dove, 'a project which aims to reverse the decline of one of England's best loved farmland [sic] birds', and in January 2015 they approached us with an idea intended to give the turtle dove a leg up. They had identified the Adur Valley, our local river-catchment area, as one of the turtle doves' last strongholds and come up with a scheme to provide them with sustenance on their arrival in late April and early May to help get them into breeding condition. The proposal was to scatter a special mix of wheat, oilseed rape, millet and canary seed at selected sites including, they proposed, on Knepp. The seed would be 'spun out' over farm tracks and on bare, fallow ground – places the turtle dove is known to prefer to feed, perhaps because of its short legs and/or so it can more easily detect a threat from predation.

The idea seemed to us to illustrate perfectly the principal failings of conventional conservation. Though designed with the best intentions – desperate times calling for desperate measures – it was short-sighted, rooted in the agrarian paradigm, compromised by depleted baselines, driven by the mentality of 'man knows best', and ultimately unsustainable.

The choice of seed mix – arable grains – seemed particularly ill-advised given that turtle-dove numbers are continuing to plummet on an arable diet. The trial proposal itself, while recommending a proportion of at least 75 per cent wheat and oilseed rape in the mix, confesses 'wheat is likely to contain very few of the vitamins and antioxidants a turtle dove needs for good health'. Little consideration is given to the bird's aboriginal diet other than a suggestion of 25 per cent red millet, white millet and canary seed in the mix – crops not conventionally grown in the UK. Even if turtle doves are attracted to these random scatterings of grain (provided they aren't eaten by non-target birds, rats and other small mammals first), supplying them with an artificial food source that is not, anyway, naturally available at that time of year might draw them away from food that may be more beneficial to them in the run-up to breeding. Might they not be seeking young weed shoots and starchy cotyledons as part of their early season diet, for example, or even, as one eminent ornithologist suggested when I posed the question, the high-calorific buds of shrubs like hawthorn – one of the turtle dove's favoured nest sites and a food source used by numerous other birds in spring to get themselves breeding fit? Without knowing what the turtle doves are looking for in spring, supplementary feeding them with what we would like them to be eating – because it fits with our agricultural paradigm and is readily available from commercial seed stockists – might do them more harm than good.

And even if the scheme proved successful, what then? Bird-table conservation on this scale is expensive and clearly not sustainable for any length of time. How much grain scattering would need to be done and across how large an area to have an impact on turtle doves' breeding success, let alone halt the decline? When would one stop feeding the doves? Who would be responsible for their decline when it stopped?

Whatever the merits of Operation Turtle Dove's proposal, our Advisory Board were all agreed that it was wrong for us. Against a background of cataclysmic loss, the number of turtle doves at Knepp – possibly the greatest density of birds currently surviving in England – demonstrates that they have found something here that works for them. The occasional sightings of fledglings proves they are successfully breeding. We don't yet know what they're eating, whether their diet changes through the season or how important the habitat is for them. Do they like our big, open-grown thorny hedgerows and scrub for nesting, perhaps? Or our short, grazed turf for feeding? Is it our plentiful water sources? Or is it a combination of all of these – or more? We do know that, whatever it is, they are finding it here at Knepp. One suggestion is that the pigs might yet again be playing a role. Their rootling may be producing the right conditions, in the right habitat, for the germination of the annual and biennial weed species the turtle dove likes to eat during the summer. It may even be providing that vital early source of seeds – lying dormant in the soil since the autumn – for the turtle doves' arrival. Or some other provision, like tiny snails. The pigs' disturbance of the soil provides the same opportunities as ploughing did in the age before herbicides; and, once again, points to the ecological role that free-roaming wild boar might have played in our landscape before agriculture. How turtle doves are behaving at Knepp could, our

Advisory Board felt, be key to understanding their decline elsewhere. Subscribing to Operation Turtle Dove's feeding trial would only compromise the lessons we are yet to learn.

We received a friendly and understanding reply to our refusal and, in a conciliatory gesture, the RSPB agreed it would consider including a buffer around the estate to minimize any effects on our population. Disappointingly, though, they have not taken us up on our suggestion of funding a tracking and recording programme at Knepp. With so many other desperate measures being considered and time running out for the turtle dove, one can't help but feel this is another wasted opportunity. Meanwhile, we rely on a small but engaged group of local birding volunteers, led by Penny Green, our ecologist, who assemble at a heroic hour on still mornings throughout the breeding season to try to map the turtle doves, hoping one day to catch them feeding unawares, perhaps even locate a nest.

Conscious though we are that Knepp could provide precious information for the conservation of the turtle dove, we are equally aware of the dangers of becoming disproportionately consumed with the preservation of a single species. One of British conservation's most conspicuous failures in the twentieth century has been to concentrate on individual species to the neglect of ecosystems. This shift in focus is sometimes hard for conservationists visiting Knepp to accept. More important to us than any of the charismatic species appearing within the project is the continuation of self-willed natural processes on the land. If we had not allowed a dynamic ecosystem to establish here, we would never have had turtle doves in the first place.

Another failure of conservation, and one of which we are increasingly aware, is isolation. Almost every site of nature in Britain is, in effect, an island. Islands tell us a great deal about evolution, and about environmental collapses. Generally, the smaller and more remote the island, the fewer the species and the more vulnerable its ecosystem. Climate change, drought and other extreme events can wreak disaster on species if they are unable to move. The introduction of a single new species can bring down an entire ecosystem if that system is isolated. Rats or goats arriving on a rocky outcrop in the middle of the ocean dramatically and rapidly devastate it – when they arrive on a continent, the continent shrugs them off. Populations, on the whole, are less likely to bounce back if they cannot be seeded from elsewhere. Small, remote populations may also be prone to inbreeding. A small genetic pool might gradually decrease in variation as it becomes more inbred and this lack of ability to respond to change can mean that the entire population is more likely to suffer a final descent to extinction.

In Britain, most of our areas of nature conservation are tiny and isolated. Of England's 4,100 Special Sites of Scientific Interest, generally designed to save a precious patch of habitat such as the culm grasslands of Devon, an endangered species like a bittern or a unique geological feature, the majority are less than 100 hectares (250 acres). Other nature reserves, like the 2,000 sites run by the Wildlife Trusts, are even smaller – with an average size of just 29 hectares (72 acres). Like David Quammen's cut-up fragments of carpet, they are susceptible to all the associated unravellings.

Of course, some species can arrive on and leave islands at will. Birds, and even some butterflies and other insects like bees and wasps, can fly considerable distances when a habitat no longer suits them or when compelled by a desire to colonize. Many types of seeds, pollen and fungi spores can be carried far and wide on the wind. In scientific terms, they have a high 'permeability index'. There are more opportunities for small mammals to travel between areas of nature on land than across open sea, but crossing an inhospitable landscape with no food or cover and criss-crossed by roads also poses dangers. Other species, with a still lower permeability index, may be trapped on the sinking ship. Lichens and saproxylic beetles living on ancient oaks need to find other old trees within a few hundred metres. But nowadays there are none. The violet click beetle, which gets its name from its faint blue-violet sheen and an endearing habit of springing upwards with an audible click if it falls on its back, is found on ancient ash and beech trees in only a few locations in Europe and three locations in Britain – in Windsor Great Park, Bredon Hill in Worcestershire and Dixton Wood in Gloucestershire (all SSSIs). Desperate attempts are being made to drag fallen hollow trees up to the host trees to encourage it to spread. Though they have a higher permeability index, the long-term future of the rare fungi *Phellinus robustus* and *Podoscypha multizonata* on our ancient oaks at Knepp will depend on the ability of the spores to find another generation of veteran trees to colonize within their range.

Having only isolated pockets that are rich with life – putting all your eggs in one basket – is a risky business. Wildlife hotspots can become species 'sinks' – even for those species that are blessed with mobility. With no competition from apex predators like the wolf, lynx and bear to keep them in check, Britain has relatively high populations of versatile, medium-sized predators like foxes and badgers – generalists with numerous prey species that travel easily through the human landscape. The UK has around 240,000 foxes and, protected by law since 1973, an estimated 400,000 badgers. But the most overlooked and possibly most significant predator in terms of environmental impact is one whose numbers have risen commensurate with the human population: the domestic cat. According to the Mammal Society, the UK's 10.3 million cats catch up to 275 million prey items a year, 69 per cent of which are small mammals and 24 per cent birds. The smaller and more isolated the habitat, the more conspicuous it is as a hotspot for life and the fewer the possibilities of escape from predation. A meadow may advertise itself as ideal habitat to breeding lapwing or a copse for woodcock or dormice while being, at the same time, a magnet to cats, badgers and foxes. Our isolated habitats may be attracting endangered species, only to hasten their demise.

Another factor is the 'edge effect' – the impact that a surrounding hostile environment has on an isolated habitat. A wood stranded in a cereal field often has a very different micro-climate at its centre than at its edges where it is exposed to wind, extreme heat and frost. The hard, linear boundaries of our modern landscape – with no messy, broad margins to soften the transition – mean chemical sprays easily drift into a habitat, reducing its effective size. The larger the area of habitat, the smaller the relative area of its edges, and therefore the less impact on the site.

There's a problem, too, for species that need different habi-tats at different stages in their life cycle, and for those – like some species of butterflies, bumblebees and freshwater amphib-ians and molluscs – that are unable to survive in a single isolated habitat. These multi-habitat life-cycle species are a phenomenon scientists are only just beginning to understand in terms of landscape-scale conservation. It seems that if one patch of vital habitat in a connected system of habitats is destroyed or deteri-orates, whole populations may decline or go extinct, even if the surviving patches remain in good condition. Colonies linked through exchanges of individuals – so-called 'meta-populations' – are also vulnerable to breaks in the habitat chain. If the colo-nies become separated from each other, if the links in the chain of migration are broken, the larger population loses the capacity to rebound.

The desperate need to connect pockets of nature and build resilience back into ecosystems began to impress itself on British conservationists a quarter of a century or so ago; indeed it is one of the fundamental principles of the EU Habitats Directive of 1992, to which the UK is currently bound. In 1996 the Sussex Wildlife Trust published a document, *A Vision for the Wildlife of Sussex*, promoting the idea of much bigger spaces for nature, and in 2006 the UK federation of Wildlife Trusts launched the con-cept of 'Living Landscapes' – connecting isolated wildlife sites together using 'corridors' such as river valleys, green lanes and hedgerows, and creating 'stepping stones' like copses in open grassland to provide stopping off places for birds – to allow species to travel through areas transformed by human activity.

As well as restoring ecological dynamism, connectivity (they urged) would improve species' chances in the face of climate change. As temperatures increased, it would allow them to move north or even, in some cases, gain altitude to survive.

This drive for connectivity was underlined in an influential report, *Making Space for Nature: a review of England's Wildlife Sites and Ecological Network*, chaired by the eminent, and eminently likeable, biologist Professor Sir John Lawton – a recent member of our Advisory Board. It was submitted to the Secretary of State at DEFRA in 2010. Improving the state of nature overall in England and connecting up existing wildlife sites, he urged government, would not only restore biodiversity and build resilience into the system, it would provide benefits vital to the economy – like flood mitigation, water and air purification, carbon sequestration, soil restoration, crop pollination, as well as improvements to human physical and mental health.

The report formed the basis of the Environmental White Paper, *The Natural Choice*, in 2011, which remains government policy today. Some of Lawton's twenty-four recommendations have been implemented, at least in part. A dozen 'Nature Improvement Areas' (out of a total of seventy-six applications) – Birmingham and the Black Country, Dark Peak, Dearne Valley, Greater Thames Marshes, Humberhead Levels, Marlborough Downs, the Meres and Mosses of the Marches, Morecambe Bay Limestones and Wetlands, Nene Valley, Northern Devon, South Downs Way Ahead and Wild Purbeck – were, as he suggested, set up within three years of the report, largely under the aegis of the Wildlife Trusts. The government has begun trialling a system of payments for ecosystem services and biodiversity offsetting, and identifying potential areas for natural flood-management. In the corridors of power and the meeting rooms of NGOs, Lawton's mantra for nature – 'more, bigger, better, joined' – is beating a rhythm for change.

But for the most part the vision remains aspirational. Most of Lawton's recommendations concerning habitat creation, local government planning for nature, tax incentives to landowners, the simplification of Environmental Stewardship Schemes, increased protection and monitoring of Local Wildlife Sites and ancient woodland, the ecological improvement of National Parks and Areas of Outstanding Natural Beauty, the large-scale restoration of river systems and reduction of their nutrient overload seem to have disappeared into the black hole that is Whitehall. Though other 'Nature Improvement Areas' have been earmarked, funding has not been forthcoming. In the six years since *Making Space for Nature* was published there have been four Secretaries of State at DEFRA, making mincemeat of ambitions and wrecking any continuity of thought. A substantial volume of relevant policy may now be in place, the words may be there, the sentiment ripe. But lack of political will, lack of funding and lack of integration between government sectors and policy-makers continues to scupper implementation. Nature remains on a losing wicket, largely undefended against growing cumulative pressure from the more powerful lobbies of intensive agriculture, fisheries, forestry and urban development.

At four o'clock one early summer morning I dragged our daughter Nancy out of bed to accompany me on one of our ecologist Penny's surveys for turtle doves. The air was spectacularly still, the clarity magnifying the caw of every jackdaw, the crooning of every collared dove ('I-don't-know, I-don't-know') and wood pigeon ('I-*really*-don't-know'), isolating the teasing notes of blue tits and the insistence of chiffchaffs, the odd possessive *cronk* of a raven. We dispersed with our clipboards, Nancy and I, to cover an area in the furthest reaches of the Southern Block. Before long we had criss-crossed our chart with the initials for jackdaws, rooks, carrion crows, jays, magpies, buzzards, ravens, collared doves, wood pigeons, feral pigeons, stock doves and pheasants, with arrows indicating their direction of flight – a battalion of predators, competitors and transmitters of disease considered by Operation Turtle Dove to have a possible influence on turtle-dove numbers. In the avian rush-hour of dawn, this exercise seemed to be clutching at straws. Apart from the collared dove (which began colonizing the UK in 1955), all these species, present now in large numbers at Knepp, would have been present in large numbers in the glory days of the turtle dove. If they were having a significant impact on turtle doves today, it was surely only because turtle numbers were now critically low. Pointing a finger at these peripheral species seemed to be like accusing spectators at the scene of a crime.

After an hour of roaming, a throaty *turr-turr*-ing from a stand of sallow took us both by surprise. Creeping through the thicket we emerged in a grove of ash saplings, offspring of a fifty-year-old tree that seemed to be showing the first signs of dieback from *Chalara* – the fungal disease that has been spreading through ash trees across the country since 2012. The dead branch of the tree was providing the dove with the perfect territorial perch. After a few moments of *churr*-ing it flew on, beyond the grove, to the twisted limb of a stag-headed oak standing out in the open on an ancient hedge-line.

We watched it through our binoculars, barely 60 yards away, caught, it seemed, in the crosshairs of time, a thread from the earliest books of the Bible to the tales of Chaucer and the sonnets of Shakespeare intersecting with our world at Knepp. Nancy's great-grandparents would have heard this sound here every summer without fail. Her great-great-grandparents would have seen flocks of them and thought nothing of it. Embodied, it seemed, in these murmurings of loss were the hardships of a journey across deserts, the bristling of guns, the promised land a shrinking world. The gentle mournfulness of its call seemed to plead for a change of heart. A lament from the wild. An unrequited love song. A swansong.

13

Rewilding the River

Man cannot live by marsh alone, therefore he must needs live marshless. Progress cannot abide that farmland and marshland, wild and tame, exist in mutual toleration and harmony.

Aldo Leopold, *A Sand County Almanac*, 1948

The autumn of 2000, the year we stumbled into rewilding, turned into the wettest since records began in 1766. The skies that had blackened over the farm sale at the end of September had advanced a chain of convective storms that stalled over the south-east of England in early October, bringing days of downpours, culminating in a terrific deluge on the night of 11 October. Plumpton in East Sussex, eighteen miles south-east of Knepp, had been hardest hit, receiving 156.4 millimetres of rain in forty-eight hours. Combined with the high spring tide and aquifers already full after three wet years, the water had found nowhere to go. Twelve major rivers in Sussex and Kent, including the Ouse, Cuckmere, Arun and our river, the Adur, burst their banks. Ditches filled; storm drains burst; roads became rivers; streets and driveways sped the rain into tributaries of the gathering flood.

Downstream, coastal towns were inundated. In Lewes the water rose from ankle deep to six foot in less than half an hour. Rush-hour motorists clambered onto the roofs of their cars. Firkins floated out of the devastated Harvey's brewery, bobbing off down the streets, ramming against walls and front doors in a bizarre parody of the barrel-rolling tradition of bonfire night. Emergency services were scrambled, with the army and volunteers drafted in to shore up defences around Lewes, Tunbridge Wells, Maidstone, Shoreham, Littlehampton, Newhaven and Medmerry, near Chichester. Lifeboats evacuated people through their downstairs and even upstairs windows. In Uckfield, a lifeboat rescued twenty nightshift workers stranded in a supermarket, and a shop owner, swept away by the flood down the high street, was lifted to safety by helicopter.

The Adur, like its sister rivers the Ouse and the Arun, was quickly overwhelmed. At Knepp, the canalized stretch of the Adur that runs for one and a half miles from Capps Bridge past Old Knepp Castle and under the A24 swelled into a 150 acre lake stretching from Shipley to Pound Farm. Sheets of water swept down our floodplain, swirling around the embankments of the old castle, recreating the twelfth-century moat. The torrent crashed over the weirs and roiled into the culvert under the dual carriageway. The village lane by Tenchford was breached and at Floodgates, water began lapping at the edges of the A24. In a moment of madness, encouraged perhaps by a sudden burst of sunshine between downpours, we took to the flood in the little rowing boat from the lake. Marooned voles and field mice were clinging to fronds of vegetation as the water rose around them. We were too concerned with navigating the eddies and currents to heed them. We swung off, inches above a submerged barbed-wire fence, just short of the A24, pulling the boat up onto the causeway of the old castle, thankful not to have capsized.

As November approached, storms continued rolling over from Western Europe, venting their worst on Shropshire, Worcestershire and Yorkshire. Peak flows on the Rivers Thames, Trent, Severn, Wharfe and Dee were the highest for more than fifty years. The River Ouse in Yorkshire rose eighteen feet – the highest level since the seventeenth century.

Inches away from being deluged, sixty-five thousand sandbags defended the city of York. It rained, continuously, for three months. Between September and November an average of 503 millimetres fell across the whole of England and Wales, exceeding the previous record by 50 millimetres. Weather-related insurance claims for the autumn of 2000 totalled £1 billion. In all, in 700 villages, hamlets and towns across Britain, 10,000 homes were flooded.

As farmers throughout our county kissed goodbye to their winter crops (insuring against crop loss is prohibitively expensive for most farmers), worried about the cost of buying in extra feed for animals deprived of autumn grazing and – worse – agonized over the drowning of sheep and cattle, we realized the full implications of our escape from farming. Authorities declared this a 1-in-200-year event. The Environment Agency, however, with uncanny timing, published a report on 10 September 2000, announcing that climate change had made Britain a hotspot for flooding. The risk to lives and property would increase tenfold over the next century. The south-east of England, it warned, was likely to see more sudden intense thunderstorms. Flooding of low-lying areas was increasingly likely, due to an anticipated rise in sea level of 15–50 centimetres this century, as Arctic glaciers continue to melt. The frequency of dangerously high tides would rise from once a century to once a decade, threatening even flood-defence structures as formidable as the Thames Barrage.

In the aftermath of the storms local MPs, local authorities and devastated householders pressed for funding to shore up flood defences. They called for levees along river banks and for raising existing levees with more boulders to keep rivers in their channels. Rivers must be dredged, they urged, revetments built and remaining meanders straightened to carry floodwater faster out to sea. Major roads needed to be raised, bigger storm drains installed and reserve electrical supplies buried underground, out of the water's reach. The cost would be high. But, it was argued, cheap at the price of protecting lives, businesses, infrastructure and property. There were universal outpourings of frustration and indignation, a sense of a battle lost for lack of reinforcements. The water had got away with it – this time. But the war was yet to be won.

Controlling flows of water is a war humans have been waging the world over, ever since they first began draining land for agriculture and improving rivers for navigation. In Britain, the Romans flung themselves at land drainage, cutting the Car Dykes in the Fens and the ditches of Romney Marsh among many others. But it was the Victorians who took hydrological engineering to its zenith.

Eighteenth-century canals – 4,800 miles in all – saw the blossoming of waterways that would, until eclipsed by the railways in the 1840s and 50s, serve as the commercial arteries of the nation. By the mid-nineteenth century canals criss-crossed Britain, linking ports and navigable rivers with inland industry. In West Sussex even small rivers like the Adur were adapted for barges carrying coal, sand, gravel and salt upstream, and timber, grain and produce downstream. In 1807 the River Adur Navigation Act permitted local agencies and landowners 'to cleanse, scour, enlarge, widen, deepen and render more straight, the Current of the said River . . . so as to maintain a more effectual Navigation for boats, Barges, Lighters, or Vessels drawing three feet of water'.

The works exceeded expectations and within three years barges drawing four feet were using the improved channel. Wharves were dug at two termini, with another added in 1811 for importing lime, chalk and coal. Fifteen years after completion, the Adur canal was extended to West Grinstead by widening and dredging the shallow stream to the north of Bines Bridge. The canal was extended again under an Act of 1825, widening and straightening the stretch from Bines Bridge to Bay Bridge on the Horsham to Worthing Road – a project that took five years. Two brick locks were built, large enough to admit craft up to seventy feet long – one near West Grinstead church where the early Burrells are buried, and the other near

Lock Farm at Partridge Green. Another wharf was created at Bay Bridge at the terminus near the Burrell Arms, just short of the old Knepp castle, together with a basin in which the barges could turn before heading back downstream.

It was no mean feat to render the Adur navigable even for shallow vessels. By the nineteenth century, the Adur was a ghost of its former self. Long ago, during the reign of Edward the Confessor, it had been a powerful tidal river, carrying large ships inland as far as Steyning, six miles south of Knepp. The name Adur is thought to come from the Celtic word 'dwyr' meaning 'flowing waters'. Barges had plied the river as far as Shipley, exporting iron and timber to the coast. In Shipley church, built by the Knights Templar, where modern generations of Knepp Burrells are buried, an ironstone mooring bollard recalls the draught boats that would have carried pilgrims and soldier-monks off to the crusades. In the early thirteenth century, King John used ships to transport the great oak timbers from Knepp Forest thirteen miles down to the estuary to reinforce his defences at Dover.

During the fourteenth and fifteenth centuries, though, erosion caused by longshore drift along the coast shifted the mouth of the Adur eastwards, away from the run of tides and the prevailing wind, creating a shingle bar that impeded the flow of tidal water. Though salt water was still reaching old Knepp castle in the 1530s the volume had fallen away dramatically. The reclamation of tidal marshes by a process called 'inning' (throwing up embankments around the marshes and installing one-way drains) exacerbated the silting up of the estuary, and the old port at Bramber had to be moved four miles downstream to Shoreham on the coast.

With the loss of the powerful effects of the tide, the flow of the Adur was limited to whatever freshwater trickled into it. There are few natural springs in our part of the world and most streams and rivers rely almost entirely on rainwater run-off. To make the Adur navigable again the Victorians had to 'cleanse, widen, and deepen the Sewers, Cuts, Streams, Trenches and

Passages for water leading into or towards the said river, and to alter and change the course thereof by new Drains, Trenches, or Passages, where the same may be expedient for securing a good and effectual Drainage of and through the said Levels and Low Lands.'

It was a process that was being enacted across the length and breadth the country. For the Victorians, land drainage was a win-win situation. It supplied the means by which shallow, slow-flowing rivers and canals could be used for transport and it made land available for agriculture. With the population of Britain doubling in just fifty years, from 9 million at the time of the first census in 1801 to 18 million in 1851, the race was on to find land to produce more food. The canalization of our stretch of the upper reaches of the River Adur, west of old Knepp Castle, was part of a colossal nationwide effort, stimulated by interest-free, short-term loans from the government to landowners, to improve the land for agriculture.

Sir Charles Merrik Burrell, first occupant of the new Knepp Castle built by Nash, was one of the most vociferous proponents of land drainage. On 16 May 1845, he appeared before a Select Committee of the House of Lords to give evidence on the merits of Pearson's draining plough – an invention that was revolutionizing his estate at Knepp. In the twelve years since he had started using Pearson's plough, Sir Charles said, the Home Farm's yield of wheat had increased from five sacks per acre to seven or eight, and in some cases nine. He could now grow 'White Belgian Cattle Carrots and very good Swede Turnips . . . this in a District where, when I first took Land in hand in 1803 and 1804, no Farmers in the Neighbourhood attempted to sow Turnips of any Kind, except in their Gardens for domestic Use.' His observation reveals how different the soil must have been, how much richer the organic matter. Had he gazed into a crystal ball, after a hundred and fifty years of ploughing, he would see land where growing vegetables is again unthinkable.

But back then there was fertility to be unleashed, and the principal obstacle was drainage. The wonder plough was the brainchild of Mr John Pearson, a farmer on a hundred acres of sodden Weald clay in Kent. His land was clearly much like Knepp's, 'very wet and stiff', with no fresh springs and yet the water 'caused by the rain and snow is held on the surface of the ground, owing to the retentive quality of the clay beneath, which hinders it sinking away'. Without artificial drainage, crops came late in the summer when the sun had evaporated the surface water, and even then they were scant. Wheat crops could be grown only about twice in every seven years, with the land remaining fallow in between. Draining, if it could be done at all, was carried out 'by Hand with Frith or Bushes at much Expense' – digging trenches and filling them with rubble, twigs and branches.

Pearson's invention, pulled by six (Sir Charles recommended eight) draught horses, pioneered a way of excavating drains two foot below ground. This was far more efficient than trying to drain water off the surface by digging open ditches and grips by hand, and it helped prevent the run-off of topsoil and manure. Draining the clay soil went beyond increasing the potential for arable and other crops. Drier pastures eradicated foot rot in livestock and reduced the expense of buying winter fodder since animals could be turned out to grass earlier in the spring and remain out several weeks longer in the autumn. The drainage plough had considerable impact on human well-being, too. 'The Health of my Farmers and Cottagers, with their Families, has been much improved', Sir Charles told the committee, 'so that Agues, which had been common, no longer prevail, and low Fevers also have greatly diminished.' Landowners, he urged the committee, must encourage their farm tenants to use this plough and install tiled drains and outfalls on their land. He was, himself, making pipe tiles (the cylindrical clay pipe was invented in 1810) in the clay brickworks at the centre of the estate, to gift to any tenants wishing to drain their holding. A statute in 1826 had already exempted from duty 'those bricks and tiles made solely for draining wet and marshy land – provided they are legibly stamped in making with the word DRAIN.' A large number of people could be employed installing drains, he added, and this 'has been a very great Inducement to me to do it, because it has kept the Poor off the Parish. I have employed sometimes Two Ploughs going, and the Work that each Pearson Plough will do at a fair Morning's Work will require Twenty-two Hands to fill it up by Night.'

The commercial effect of land drainage on the countryside was incalculable. On Kent and Sussex clay it also opened up possibilities for roads that would, for the first time in history, be viable all year round. Between 1847 and 1890 thirteen separate Land Improvement and Drainage Acts were passed and nearly £16 million – £1.44 billion in today's money – was spent on land improvement in Great Britain. In the Burrell archives, loan agreements and repayment schedules chronicle the enthusiastic take-up of the schemes at Knepp which, at some point, included the canalization of our stretch of the upper reaches of the Adur. By November 1875 Sir Charles' son Percy Burrell had taken up his father's baton and was subject to three charges under the Public Money Drainage Act, two under the Lands Improvement Company's Act, and six under the General Land Drainage Company's Acts. A further £1,529 14s 2d charge was made the following year for drainage, grubbing and road-making on the Estate. In all, he borrowed £8,000 – half what it had cost his father to build the castle. Further loans, mainly to continue the drainage work, were taken out by his son and heir, Sir Walter, in 1877, 1879, 1880, 1883 and 1884.

By the second half of the nineteenth century another plough was making waves. John Fowler, a young agricultural engineer from a Quaker family in Wiltshire, moved by witnessing first-hand the horrors of the Irish potato famine, devoted himself to inventing ways of reducing the cost of food production. In 1851 he exhibited his new drainage 'mole' plough at the Great Exhibition – a horse-powered winch-driven machine that could tunnel drainage channels three feet six inches deeper than Pearson's and avoid digging large, messy trenches. By 1852 he had replaced the horse-drawn winch system with a coal-fired steam engine and the industrial revolution began transforming the countryside. Between 1840 and 1890, 12 million acres of land were drained in Britain, most of it made over to agriculture.

Until we sold it in 2000, we used the same basic mole plough, now pulled by tractor, in our fields whenever they showed signs of waterlogging. The torpedo-shaped 'mole' is mounted on a steel plate suspended from a frame. The frame itself is pulled along a few inches above the soil, with the steel plate beneath it slicing a thin cut through the surface. Beneath the steel plate, the mole torpedo cores through the clay, smearing and compacting the sides of its tunnel into a smooth, hollow tube – in effect, a drain without infrastructure. Our neighbours still use a mole plough every ten to twenty years or so, maintaining a lattice-work of ducts running between ditches and above the main drainage pipes.

In other respects, too, British farmers today have simply maintained, and sometimes improved, the drainage systems the Victorians put into play. Canals have had their day as commercial transport systems. But they are still maintained so they can receive water drained off the land by the intricate networks of ditches and underground drains. And so it flows from canals and rivers, out to sea. When the Victorian drainage pipes break or become silted up they are simply replaced with more durable plastic ones. The same ditches around field perimeters are cleared and re-excavated by mini-digger every year; the same Victorian outlets routinely cleared. Only fifty years ago Charlie's grandmother Judy would, like most farmers, spend her winter weekends in a ditch with a spade, keeping the outlets clear and running. Some still prefer to do this by hand. One misjudgement by a digger driver and the holding pipe can be dislodged, changing the angle of the outflow and wrecking a system that has worked for centuries.

The Victorian obsession with getting excess water off the land as fast as possible has entered our DNA, and in times of excessive rainfall, with water flowing into all the outlets and all the rivers all at once, fuelling floods, our instincts tell us we simply need more of the same. We need, or think we need, to get the water off the land even faster. The sooner the water can disappear away from us out to sea, we feel, the safer our homes, farms, property, livestock and land, will be.

But there is another way of dealing with water. Charlie's and my first tentative defection against the principle of drainage at any cost was made long before we had any thoughts of rewilding. Drainage on our floodplains had never worked well enough for arable crops. The soil remained soggy and prone to surface water no matter how many drains were cored into it. In the summer it was possible to graze livestock on the laggs but there was always a risk of liver fluke, a harmful parasite transmitted by water snails. Fencing was a problem, too. Water meadows running alongside a water course are inevitably long and thin and require a greater quantity of fencing than the conventional square field. By the 1990s, the peak of our arable and dairy production, we had 260 acres of laggs that were just not worth the cost of fencing. When the fence around an eight-acre water meadow near Brookhouse dairy fell into disrepair we decided, instead, to break up the drains and dig out some scrapes to create opportunities for waterfowl. From the moment there was standing water, we had teal, mallard, wigeon and moorhens. Once vegetation like reed mace and rushes had grown up around the edges, we were seeing reed warblers, and long-tailed tits in the scrub. A visiting ornithologist pointed out goldcrests – a bird normally associated with coniferous woodland. The goldcrests were our first clue, though we didn't register it at the time, that species may not always keep to the habitats designated them in modern guidebooks.

The immense satisfaction of re-creating bodies of standing water on the land encouraged us to embark on a carp-farming enterprise – another attempt at diversifying on the farm. There were native crucian carp in Knepp lake, and faster-growing mirror carp from Europe had been introduced in the 1930s to sell on to angling ponds. Extending the carp business would, we hoped, be a solution for some of our problematic water meadows. We received planning permission to restore the dam wall of Hammer Pond at Shipley, fallen into disrepair following the demise of the iron industry, and set to work excavating the shadow of the old five-acre pond behind it with a digger.

Smashing up the Victorian drains felt, at first, unnervingly like vandalism. These were the arteries that, it was inculcated in us, allowed the blood of our fields to flow. But watching the lake, last described in 1849, resurface and lap around the edges of the laggs was hugely gratifying. It felt as though this is what the clay had been yearning to do. In all, we restored eighteen ponds and lakes. Not all of them were stocked with carp. Some we restored just for the sheer fun of it: from old watering-holes on ditch lines at the corner of fields and ancient ponds along the green lane that would once have refreshed livestock on their long plod to market, to the delightfully named Honeypools and the elegant expanse of Spring Wood Pond in the park. Ultimately, the carp enterprise has proved a successful addition to the diversification of the estate, but the reappearance of water on the land and all the wildlife it attracts is reward of another kind.

It was not until we had embarked on the rewilding project, though, that we began to think in a deeper way about the water crossing our land. A conversation with Hans Kampf, one of the early members of our Advisory Board, the summer after the floods of 2000, as we walked along the edge of the canalized Adur, set us thinking about the movement of water from the moment it fell as raindrops on our soil, through its progress into drains and ditches, streaming into the river and down towards the sea.

Hans is a man of many dimensions. He grew up on polder land three kilometres from Amsterdam airport, son of an air-traffic controller. Somewhere between picking fungi in the autumn woods next to the airport and forays to a local pond to collect water fleas for his schoolteacher's fish tank, he was stirred, he says, by a pressing desire to 'give more freedom to nature'. At the time he joined our board in its first year he was senior policy advisor to the Dutch Ministry of Agriculture, Nature and Food Quality, and about to become Executive Director of the Large Herbivore Foundation, an advocacy for endangered megafauna in Eurasia. His experience working with natural processes at the Oostvaardersplassen and establishing large-scale ecological networks across borders in Europe gives him a rare ability to relate micro with macro. Above all he is, like Frans Vera, both thinker and doer, and a man of unqualified optimism. 'What's impossible today might be possible tomorrow, and if not, next week,' he says brightly. He also has, like most Dutch ecologists, a profound understanding of the behaviour of water.

With 17.7 million people crammed into 16,000 square miles (one sixth the area of the UK), the Netherlands is the most densely populated country in Europe. Since half the country is at or below sea level, it is also one of the most vulnerable in the world to flooding. For a thousand years, since Dutch farmers built the first dykes, the Netherlands has been fighting back the water. The entire country is a complex system of man-made dykes, dams and floodgates, drainage ditches, canals and pumping stations. Dutch water engineers are the best in the world and their expertise is exported around the globe. In the 1620s the English imported a Dutch engineer, Cornelius Vermuyden, to drain the Fens of East Anglia for agriculture. But what the Dutch are currently advocating for river systems challenges centuries of accepted wisdom about water control – including their own.

Catastrophic floods in the Netherlands in 1993 and 1995, in which 200,000 people were evacuated and hundreds of farm animals died, exposed the inherent weakness of the existing river-dyke system. Increased rainfall resulting from climate change supercharged the country's four main rivers and put pressure on flood defences as never before. The threat for the Dutch is no longer just from the sea. With the frequency of severe freshwater flooding predicted to increase, Dutch engineers have realized there is no way of building dykes big enough and stable enough to resist these cataclysmic floods. A different approach is needed. Instead of channelling water off the land as fast as possible, they are now reversing the process and trying to keep it on the land for longer. Like the Germans and the Chinese, the Dutch are giving back hard-won reclaimed land – polders – to the rivers, cutting meanders back into the floodplains and restoring the old marshes and wetlands. Houses built on floodplains are being demolished and their inhabitants resettled on higher ground. The boy is taking his finger out of the dyke. There is still much work to be done. But already the 'Room for the River' project has reduced the risk of extreme flooding in the Netherlands from once every 100 years to once every 1,250 years.

As we walked beside our diminutive canal, twenty-five feet across at its widest, its banks so steep the dogs need a helping hand getting out after a swim, the ghost of the Adur's old meanders snaking down the floodplain alongside us seemed to sketch an alternative. Ahead of us the ruin of the old castle on its grassy knoll stirred up visions of the days when the river beneath it would rise and fall of its own volition, following its own rhythm. Fill in the canal, Hans suggested, and return the river to its floodplain. This, he said, would not only create enormous opportunities for wetland birds, flora and invertebrates, it would mitigate flooding downstream. The laggs would soak up excess water like a sponge, holding it back from general spate in times of heavy rainfall, releasing it slowly and safely, while also storing up water for drier seasons. The marshy vegetation would act as a filter, purifying the heavy nitrate run-off entering our land from intensive farms around us. And removing the weirs would encourage the migration of salmonids again, moving up from the sea.

The response from the Environment Agency was enthusiastic. They had maintained the canal into the twenty-first century at huge expense to the taxpayer without really knowing why they were doing it. No one at the EA could remember the reason for the five high-maintenance weirs on our stretch of the

Adur, other than the weak justification that it provided coarse fishermen with deeper pools to fish in. Such is the excruciating process of civil-service decision-making, however, that it took nine years of bureaucracy and convoluted feasibility studies before the project got under way. Finally, in September 2011 we stood, watching Reg, the digger driver, making his first impressions in the floodplain.

The aim was to create a more natural, shallow riverbed with softer banks so the river would readily spill over in heavy rains, as it used to. But naturalizing anything is a challenge, particularly when it falls to an Environment Agency digger driver who has spent most of his working life applying himself to the exact opposite. 'Natural' was not in Reg's mindset. No matter how often Charlie stood exasperated by his side, trying to reinforce the concept, Reg could not be persuaded to commit the Hymac excavator to creating a messy, shallow channel. Instead he constructed – over two long years and at huge expense to the taxpayer – what looked more like a separate, winding, steep-sided canal. After he had finished, no doubt looking back over his shoulder with intense satisfaction, we brought in another digger at our own expense to soften some of his edges, hoping that our grazing animals, once they had easier access to the water, would continue the process by trampling and puddling the margins. A team of volunteers from the Ouse and Adur Rivers Trust installed artificial 'woody debris blockages' of fallen trees to create a more dynamic flow of water and help deposit silt in the channel. The excavation of shallow scrapes elsewhere on the floodplain adds a further dimension to the evolving wetland but several dry patches of meadow indicate where old drains still managed to evade the digger.

Nevertheless, the results have been astonishing. The year after completion we saw green sandpipers on the muddy banks and a little egret stalking the scrapes. Mallard were soon nesting in the reeds and mandarin ducks flew down to feed from their nests in the trees at the head of the lake. Lapwings followed soon after – in 2016 Penny, our ecologist, managed to ring two fledglings – and the shallow scrapes, colonized by small fry and amphibians, are now patrolled by up to sixteen herons at a time. In 2012 the Environment Agency removed the largest of the weirs and decommissioned three of the others – including the self-regulating donkey weir in Shipley – allowing fish to cross them for the first time since their construction. By 2013 sea trout were migrating up the river in numbers. One volunteer saw six of them wriggling up over the Hammer dam wall spillway in just half an hour.

Data from a flow box installed at Bay Bridge where the Adur leaves Knepp has not yet been analysed by the Environment Agency. But anecdotally, at least, it seems the re-naturalization of our section of the river is having an impact on the flow of water around and below us. Estate cottages at Tenchford and Knepp Mill, notoriously prone to flooding in the past, haven't flooded since the project began. Even after severe storms the A281 downstream at Henfield, often closed because of floods, has remained passable.

Our project, however, covers just a modest one-and-a-half-mile stretch of a small river. For another fifteen miles from us to the sea, the remainder of the Adur is a featureless, canalized conduit with sheer banks virtually devoid of wildlife. When Charlie and the children paddled in blow-up canoes under the A24 to Shoreham-by-Sea one spring they saw three mallard, a couple of swans and a skylark in all those fifteen miles. To appreciate the grand potential of river re-naturalization Charlie and I visited an upland rewilding project in the Lake District begun in 2003, around the same time as Knepp. 'Wild Ennerdale' is a partnership between Natural England and three landowners – the Forestry Commission, the National Trust and United Utilities (the north-west's water and waste-water company). The partnership's aim is 'to allow the evolution of Ennerdale as a wild valley for the benefit of people, relying more on natural processes to shape its landscape and ecology'. Since the 1920s, conifer plantations, including non-native sitka spruce, had, in the words of author and fell-walker Alfred Wainwright, thrown 'a dark funereal shroud of trees' over the seventeen-square-mile valley. Forestry tracks carved up the land and, like much of upland Britain, sheep had grazed the remaining land to the bone.

Looking out over Ennerdale today, from slopes a couple of hundred feet above the old plantations, Wainwright would hardly recognize the place. The great headwall still shadows the top of the dale, of course, with the 3,000 foot fells of Great Gable, Haystacks, Pillar and Kirk Fell shedding snow and rainwater into the valley; and seven miles downstream at the end of the valley the repository of Ennerdale Water, a glacial lake two and a half miles long surrounded by farmland, looks eternally placid. In between, however, the dale is slipping the yoke of human control. The management policy is now as light as the partners dare. Forestry tracks have been abandoned, and boundary fences, bridges and a concrete ford have been removed, allowing Arctic char and other fish back up to their old spawning grounds. Larch plantations (now uncommercial), wrecked by storms in 2005 and battered by an outbreak of blight in 2013–14, have been left to decline, allowing large areas to regenerate with native species like hazel, aspen, ash, birch and Scots pine – favourite of the red squirrel. Sheep numbers have been dramatically reduced and the once intensively grazed valley floor and woodland is now much more lightly grazed by a small herd of old-breed Galloway cattle. Their trampling breaks through the sward to initiate further vegetation recovery.

On the hillsides the former billiard-table surface of sheep-cropped grass has erupted into riotous 3D. Browsed domes of holly, birch saplings and rowan trees punctuate a bulbous ground cover of sphagnum and star moss, heather, ferns, fungi and lichens – splashes of pillar-box red and mustard yellow against a busy spectrum of greens. Dark purple splatterings of thrush and grouse droppings on the rocks indicate that we are not the only ones gorging on wild bilberries. Here and there, clumps of juniper evoke the original Norse meaning of

Ennerdale – Juniper Valley. Walking across this spongy hillside carpet you feel like there are springs in your boots.

The resurgence of natural vegetation on the sides of the valley is now holding back the soil and soaking up rainwater, dramatically reducing the amount of run-off into the river. But the river at Ennerdale is also putting on the brakes. When we descend to walk along it, the Liza looks more like a river in Alaska or the Himalaya. It flows in fingers over gravelly, boulder-strewn courses between impermanent islands of birch, spruce, heather and grasses. Gravel banks shift and build, waiting for the next flood to smash them to smithereens and reassemble them in another formation. Without bridges or revetments, unpiped, unchannelled, the river chomps freely all around it, clawing at the forest, creating new margins, reinventing itself with every big rainfall. Fallen trees and woody debris create blockages and diversions, absorbing and neutralizing the water's energy, taming the monster.

The devastating floods hurtling off hillsides in the Lake District in 2009 threw up obvious comparisons with the singular response of rewilded Ennerdale. On 18 and 19 November, cataclysmic rain descended in the high fells (Thirlmere, five miles from Ennerdale, received the record – 405 millimetres over the course of thirty-eight hours). With the hillsides grazed to short grass swards and compacted by huge numbers of sheep over several centuries, there was nothing to intersect the passage of water into streams and rivers, most of which had been modified into narrow, high-energy drainage channels. Within hours the pulse of floodwater had burst from the channels, and was bringing down bridges and buildings and cascading down lanes and roads. Soil and gravel poured into the torrent from the unstable, eroded hillsides and scoured down the valleys, unleashing a cement-mixer tsunami on towns and villages downstream. By contrast, at Ennerdale, where the soft, absorbent land acted like a sponge, the flood flows quickly dissipated and the Liza was still clear and fordable the day after the downpour. When terrifying floods struck Cumbria again in

2015 during Storm Desmond, and towns like Appleby, Penrith, Carlisle, Keswick, Kendal, Cockermouth and Workington suffered all over again, none of the villages below Ennerdale, including Ennerdale Bridge and Egremont, flooded.

In Pickering in the Yorkshire Dales, a community-led project based on the same principles of naturalistic flood management has proved just as effective. Stuck at the bottom of a steep gorge draining much of the North Yorks Moors, Pickering was flooded four times between 1999 and 2007, with the last disaster causing £7 million in damage. The solution, the local authorities insisted, was to build a £20 million concrete wall – a Berlin Wall of sorts – right through the lovely old town centre to keep the water in the river. None of the inhabitants, understandably, were enamoured of the idea so, instead, they researched a plan to slow the flow of the water from the hills and persuaded the Environment Agency, Forestry Commission and DEFRA to support them. In the becks above the town, Forestry Commission staff built 167 leaky dams of logs and branches – letting normal flows through but slowing down the high ones – and added 187 lesser obstructions, made of bales of heather in smaller drains and gullies. Elsewhere, off the Forestry Commission estate, they planted 29 hectares (72 acres) of woodland upstream and, after much bureaucratic tangling, built a bund – or embankment – near the bottom of the catchment, to store up to 120,000 cubic metres (26 million gallons) of floodwater, releasing it slowly through a culvert.

Three months after it was inaugurated, on the fateful Boxing Day of 2015, it rained for twenty-four hours. The chairman of the Pickering and District Civic Society climbed up to the bund to check it and, finding it working well, returned home, switched on the TV and saw the devastation being caused by floodwaters all over northern England. Pickering, alone, was spared. The total cost of the Pickering scheme had been around £2 million. That was a tenth of the cost of the concrete wall proposed by the local authorities – a wall, most inhabitants are convinced, that would not have coped with the floods anyway.

Meanwhile, over in Wales, studies at Pontbren in the Brecon Beacons have proved that, by simply removing the sheep and planting trees, the rate at which water infiltrates the soil is sixty-seven times greater than on pastures tightly grazed by sheep, where their stiletto hooves compact the soil.

On average, flooding costs the UK economy £1.1 billion a year. The cost of the 2015 floods alone was £5 billion. One in six properties in the UK is now at risk of flooding. But this need not be. The evidence, both in the UK and abroad, is incontrovertible: naturalizing rivers and rewilding river-catchment areas prevents flooding. It is far cheaper, safer and more resilient than engineering hard flood defences. And it brings with it other huge economic benefits in terms of water purification, soil restoration, drought resistance and wildlife. Yet in the UK we are still being disastrously slow on the uptake. While forward-thinking countries like the Netherlands, Germany and China are giving over huge amounts of money and land to re-naturalize their rivers and wetlands, we continue to allocate the bulk of our grant money for flood defence to conventional, large-scale, hard engineering schemes.

River re-naturalization projects, meanwhile, have to rely on levering funds from local authority or Lottery Fund grants and corporate donations. The Sussex Flow Initiative – a partnership between the Woodland Trust, Sussex Wildlife Trust and the Environment Agency, begun in 2014 to promote natural flood management in the River Ouse catchment – receives funding from Lewes District Council and the Royal Bank of Canada, and nothing from the Environment Agency or any other government agency. As I write, in 2017, sixteen years after we first applied for funding for our project, there are still precious few incentives from government for landowners and farmers to store water in ponds or on floodplain fields. On the contrary. Strong disincentives to avoid re-naturalizations still persist, since water bodies of any description are categorized as 'Permanent Ineligible Features' and so exempt from farm subsidies. While grants do exist for planting trees on uplands and along rivers, there is little or no proactive engagement with farmers and landowners to encourage their uptake, and there are still no grants to promote natural regeneration. The re-naturalization of a meagre mile and a half of the River Adur at Knepp remains, shamefully, one of the largest stretches of river restoration on private land in the UK.

14

Bringing Back the Beaver

I guess that beavers do instinctively what mankind must learn to do eventually.

Eric Collier, *Three Against the Wilderness*, 1959

Derek Gow stood on the churned-over slicks of mud on the banks of our 're-naturalized' stretch of the Adur, watching a ten-ton Hymac excavator scraping away at our over-engineered meanders and a gang of volunteers dragging saplings into the water to create woody blockages, his face a picture of bemusement. He was too diplomatic to pour cold water on our endeavours. There was enough of that swilling about on site already. But in his eyes this was hydrological burlesque. He knew there was a much easier and more effective way to achieve what we were after – one that would not only provide greater complexity, naturalism and efficiency in the system, but would also cost next to nothing. The solution was another keystone species missing from our landscape.

Beavers were once widespread in Britain. Once again our place names echo their presence, from Beverley and Bewerley in Yorkshire to Beverston in Gloucestershire and Beverley Brook running through Richmond Park down to the Thames. Exploited long before the Middle Ages, they were hunted to the brink of extinction in the sixteenth century, prized for their dense, silky fur and castoreum – the secretion from scent sacs close to the tail used for making perfume. Castoreum was also used as medicine – the concentration of salicylic acid, from which aspirin is derived, from the beaver's ingestion of willow bark and leaves makes it an effective anti-inflammatory and analgesic. Beavers were also eaten by Catholics, who categorized them as fish, thus making them permissible for Holy Days and Lent, and were generally considered a pest for their interference in drainage schemes. A few beavers, nonetheless, may have clung on in backwaters into the eighteenth century. The very last record is in Bolton Percy in Yorkshire in 1789, when a church warden paid a bounty of tuppence for 'a bever head'.

Derek, an ecologist and reintroduction specialist, has devoted much of his life to returning this lost animal to Britain, though he began his conservation work in the service of water voles. 'It was the water vole that introduced me to the beaver,' he says. The connection between the two is, for Derek, an example of the complex inter-species relationships our modern environment has lost.

Water voles had entranced Derek ever since he was startled to tears as a young boy on holiday in his native Scotland by a couple of fighting males falling into the stream beside him as he fished for sticklebacks. Galvanized by a survey in 1992 showing a 95 per cent crash in a species once common throughout our waterways, Derek devoted himself to re-establishing sustainable colonies in Britain. 'It's not often you can call a wee furry mammal a keystone species, but the water vole is definitely one.'

The deep, convoluted burrow systems water voles excavate in river banks provide habitat for grass snakes, amphibians and other small mammals, as well as fertilizing the soil and stimulating different plant and invertebrate communities. Even the collapse of banks from over-burrowing creates opportunities for nesting sand martins and kingfishers. At 330 grams for an adult male, compared to 30 grams for a male field vole, the disappearance of water voles is a huge prey loss for species like herons, buzzards, owls, kestrels and foxes. As numbers continue to plummet – from 1.2 million in the UK in the early 2000s to around 300,000 today – the impact on our ecology, Derek believes, is incalculable.

Water voles have been devastated by repeated releases of American mink – both escapees and those liberated by animal-rights activists – from fur farms in Britain from the 1950s until fur farming was banned in 2000. Their natural defence mechanisms – springing out from the river bank into the water with a surprisingly loud plop, fondly remembered by canoeists and fishermen a generation or two ago, or diving and resurfacing in dense vegetation with their ears, nose and eyes barely breaking the surface – are effective to a degree against native predators. But they offer little protection against a non-native, fast-breeding, notoriously efficient killer like the mink. When mink first appeared on Knepp Lake in the 1980s, water voles were the first to vanish. Next were ducklings, moor-chicks and goslings. Gone were the days when Charlie's grandfather would take him out in the rowing boat to prick the eggs of crop-destroying Canada geese. Suddenly there were no eggs of any water fowl to be found. With no national strategy – even now – for managing wild populations of mink, control is left in the hands of landowners and local communities. Through the 1990s the local mink hounds, a motley bunch of enthusiastic mutts, would flounder about our waterways in search of quarry, hallooing with excitement. It was a grand day out for all involved but their efficacy was doubtful. We once watched a mink slide unnoticed straight through the splashing, yelping melee. Traps were more successful. We caught thirty-five in a month one winter.

But again, questions arise as to whether this alien, efficient killer as it is, is the prime cause of the water voles' decline. Had we otters, polecats and pine martens thriving in our ecosystem still, one wonders whether the mink would have colonized so successfully. Otters, in particular, kill mink kitts and occasionally adults too. Where otters have a presence in Britain, mink numbers are conspicuously low. Perhaps, like so many other 'invaders', the mink has simply scampered through an open door.

It is loss of habitat that Derek considers the fundamental threat to the survival of the water vole. The water vole is another 'meta-population' species that depends on habitats connected together like links in a chain. Colonies expand in summer to interbreed with nearby colonies and then contract in winter. By the 1990s Britain's ubiquitous loss of wetlands meant that these colonies had become isolated and fragmented, the chain links broken. Water voles now have to cross vast, hostile landscapes to find mates, and the chances of breeding are growing slimmer and slimmer. Derek began raising captive water voles (10,000 to date) at his farm in Devon for release into restored areas of wetland where mink could be controlled. So far he has successfully established colonies in twenty-five sites in the UK, from Aberfoyle in Scotland to the River Meon in Hampshire and our neighbouring river, the Arun. It was during the course of this work that he began to consider the water vole's association with another keystone species.

'There I was, building dams and opening up ponds in sunny wetlands as habitat for the water vole and I realized there must have been a mechanism doing this before us,' says Derek. 'It's obvious, really. It's the beaver.'

Close observation suggested another, subtler relationship between the species. 'Water voles rescue their babies from floods. They carry them off to secondary nests created specifically for this purpose. The readiness with which they do this, at the slightest sign of rising water, indicated to me they were used to living in very dynamic water-systems. It isn't just rainfall they're prepared for. Beavers can build a dam in hours. Suddenly, overnight, a small channel can become a pond. Water voles have evolved to react instantly, and regularly, to the engineering work of the beaver.'

It is almost impossible, now, to imagine how profoundly our British landscape has been shaped by the beaver. Throughout human history the fortunes of the beaver, tied to the fortunes of men, have waxed and waned. Already in the Mesolithic period (10,000–8,000 BC) in Britain there are signs of land under human drainage. From then onwards the beaver's dominion of our wetlands came under increasing pressure. Under Roman rule, as farmland expanded, marshes were drained, and wilderness was hunted out for meat and pelts, beaver numbers declined dramatically. They recovered again in Saxon times and were still evident in the eleventh-century Norman countryside. But by the twelfth century, at the latest, the beaver was no longer the landscape manipulator it had been. And by the sixteenth and seventeenth centuries, when England began importing Dutch engineers to drain its marshlands, beavers throughout Europe had been persecuted to the verge of extinction. Nevertheless, in 1577, William Harrison, Canon of Windsor, a contributor to the Act for the Preservation of Grain (also known as the Tudor Vermin Acts) which declared public enemies of numerous species in Britain from harvest mice to sparrows, gives a vituperous description of the beaver as a 'monstrous rat . . . of such force in the teeth, that it will gnaw an hole through a thicke planke, or shere through a dubble billet in a night'.

We get an inkling of the beaver's enormous creative potential, though, from the landscape of North America at the time of European settlement. The North American beaver is a distinct species, with forty chromosomes to the Eurasian's forty-eight. The two never interbreed, even in captivity. They are thought to have diverged about 7.5 million years ago when beavers crossed the Bering Strait land bridge into the North American continent. Nevertheless, in visual appearance, behaviour and environmental impact, the American beaver is virtually indistinguishable from its European cousin.

For millennia Native Americans had lived alongside the beaver without significantly impacting its numbers. Before the arrival of European fur trappers in the 1600s, there are estimated to have been at the very least 60 million beavers in the continent of North America, from the Arctic tundra to the deserts of northern Mexico, from the Atlantic to the Pacific, with beaver dams every hundred yards along most small rivers. Many ecologists put the figure higher – in the hundreds of millions. In the drier Western states beaver dams stabilized water levels, prevented streambed erosion and provided vital systems for water storage. In the mountain states, they provided protection from flooding by storing the spring flush of water from melting snow. Native Americans considered them 'the sacred centre' of the land.

'If we take this beaver density and apply it to Britain before the dawn of human agriculture, we can envisage complex systems of ponds and channels in all our valleys. The landscape would have looked totally different. And the effect the beaver's manipulation of our wetlands would have had on wildlife is simply immense,' Derek says. 'Beavers can literally breathe life into the land.'

He dreams of the day when beavers will be paddling, again, in every river in England. We wondered whether Knepp might be suitable for a beaver reintroduction. It had been on Charlie's letter of intent to DEFRA back in 2000. But, like the bison and the wild boar, the beaver had fallen off the agenda as a dream too far. Gazing out across Knepp Mill Pond at the rapidly silting margins and the bow-lake choked with scrub and weeds, Derek's eyes lit up. 'They'd coppice that willow carr in a trice and you'd have open water again,' he said. 'They'd love it here.'

The prospect of beaver reintroductions in the UK has been a subject of controversy for some time. Anglers particularly oppose the idea, convinced that beavers adversely affect fish stocks. A surprising number of people, perhaps confusing them with otters, think that beavers are pescatarian. Even C. S. Lewis portrays Mr and Mrs Beaver in Narnia tucking in to trout and potatoes. In reality, though, their characteristic buck teeth would be useless in a fish fight. Self-sharpening secateurs, their bright orange gnashers, fortified with iron, are designed for chopping timber, bark and woody vegetation. Those fishermen that acknowledge beavers as plant eaters still insist that their dams place barriers in the way of salmon and trout migration.

Land managers are concerned about damage to trees, water courses, ditches and crops. And then there is that pervasive general British nervousness about loss of control. Who knows what might happen? We have lived without the beaver, too long, people say, to start reintroducing it now.

The genie, however, is already out of the bottle. Introductions, both accidental and intentional, are already upon us. The catalyst, according to Derek, was in 1982, when the UK ratified the Berne Convention on the Conservation of European Wildlife and Natural Habitats. Under the convention, countries must consider the reintroduction of extinct native species, particularly keystone species, wherever feasible. By the 1990s, reintroductions in Europe had demonstrated how easy – and beneficial – it is to return beavers to the wild. In Scotland, Dick Balharry, chair of the John Muir Trust and the National Trust for Scotland, broached the idea with Scottish National Heritage who, however, strongly opposed it, citing, amongst other worries, problems of quarantine. Still, small independent zoos and wildlife parks in Scotland and England began, with Derek's help, to import animals from Poland, to demonstrate that beavers can happily survive quarantine, and to begin to acclimatize the British public to the idea of beavers in the landscape. They were, Derek says, 'lighting candles in the dark'.

It was 2001 when word began to spread of beavers on the loose. Hugh Chalmers of the Borders Forest Trust phoned Derek from his canoe in the middle of the Tay. 'Have you lost a beaver?' he said. ''Cos one's just swum right past me.' Several years earlier, it is thought, beavers slipped out of Auchingarrich Wildlife Park in the southern Scottish highlands after one of the keepers, having electrocuted herself climbing an electric fence, switched off the power. But the beavers, notorious escapologists, could have come from a number of sources, including another two enclosures on private estates, both with water courses that flow into the Tay. There is, of course, also the possibility that frustrated advocates for the beaver had taken matters into their own hands – 'black ops' as it is known in the conservation world. Wherever they came from, by 2001 there was a thriving colony, untagged and unchipped, living on Tayside – Britain's largest river catchment and close to the site of Britain's earliest carbon-dated remains of beaver dams and lodges (between 1,500 and 8,000 years old) in the submerged woodlands of Loch Tay. The success of the escapees from private collections embarrassed the Scottish government into action. In May 2009, a trial release by Edinburgh Zoo and the Scottish Wildlife Trust was sanctioned on Forestry Commission land at Knapdale in Argyll. The Knapdale beavers – originally sixteen from Norway – gave birth to at least fourteen kitts in the first four years after their release, created 13,045 square metres of new freshwater habitat, equivalent to about ten Olympic swimming pools, and built numerous dams and lodges, the largest of which is the size of a double garage. Altogether, there are now thought to be several hundred beavers living free on Scottish rivers – though no one knows the exact number or precisely where they have spread. Tourists were already flocking to see the beavers in their natural habitat. But uncertainty about these immigrants' status – whether the Scottish government was, ultimately, going to grant them leave to remain, or have them deported – was fuelling resentment in local communities. With no compensation for flooded agricultural land, farmers had already shot a number of beavers in and around the Tay.

In 2009, when we met him, shortly after the Knapdale beaver trial had begun, Derek was looking for a trial site where he could lobby support for a beaver reintroduction in England. On closer investigation the River Adur, porous in its upper reaches and over-engineered from Knepp to the sea, was not ideal. A more natural and self-contained catchment area involving a variety of land managers and public access in order to gauge response would be more useful. While Derek continued his search, he proposed setting up an organization that would act as a forum for discussion about the beaver in England and that would try to bring all the vested interests together, avoiding the polarization that seemed to be happening in Scotland.

This 17,500-year-old cave painting of a wild horse at Lascaux in France is remarkably evocative of the Exmoor pony, one of Europe's oldest breeds of horse. Herds of horses, or tarpan, once roamed our landscape and the Exmoor can provide the same beneficial stimulus to our ecosystem today.
(Top: Granger/REX/Shutterstock. Bottom: Charlie Burrell)

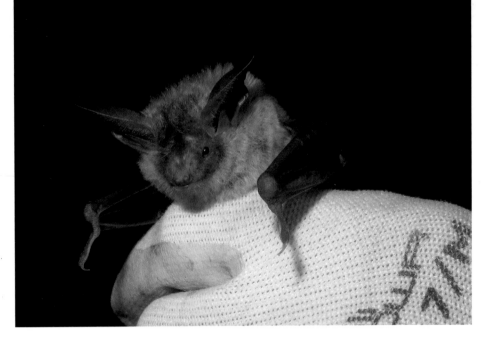

Thirteen out of the UK's seventeen bat species are now found at Knepp, feasting on our huge populations of insects. Bechstein's bat, a species associated with old-growth broadleaved woodland, is rare throughout Europe.
(Ryan Greaves)

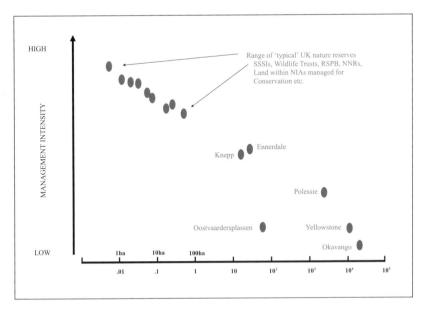

Schematic diagram of a variety of protected areas scaled by size and by a qualitative indication of management intensity; very broadly, the larger the protected area, the less human intervention is required to manage it per unit area of habitat. *(Diagram produced by Professor Sir John Lawton)*

Dragonflies and mayflies are particularly sensitive to pollution and the appearance at Knepp of species like the scarce chaser – a blue-eyed dragonfly found only in six places in the UK – is testament to the improved quality of our water. *(Charlie Burrell)*

Dung beetles have suffered dramatic declines nationwide due to widespread use of wormers and parasiticides in livestock. Since we gave up conventional farming they are now thriving at Knepp, with twenty-three different species found in a single cowpat. The appearance of *Geotrupes mutator* (pictured) in 2017 was the first record of this beetle in Sussex for fifty years. *(Penny Green)*

The astonishing success of nightingales at Knepp offers new insights into the preferences of this rapidly declining African migrant. Classed in the UK as a 'woodland' bird, it thrives in our thorny scrub. Our national intolerance for scrubland has been responsible for the cataclysmic decline of numerous species of birds. *(David Plummer)*

Having suffered devastating losses over the past few decades due to loss of habitat and the native seed-bearing plants on which it feeds, the turtle dove is expected to be extinct in the UK by the middle of the century. Knepp could be the only place in the UK where numbers are actually rising, with sixteen singing males recorded in 2017. *(Ben Green)*

A pair of peregrine falcons began breeding at Knepp in 2016. Usually associated with nesting in cliffs, or on pylons and cathedrals, at Knepp they're nesting in a pine tree – yet another example of how much more expansive and multifarious wildlife might be, given half a chance. *(Gerard Lacz/REX/Shutterstock)*

All five UK owl species can now be found at Knepp, including little owls feasting on our burgeoning populations of dung beetles. *(Ned Burrell)*

The presence at Knepp of rare fungi like *Phellinus robustus* (pictured left), which grows only on veteran trees, and *Podoscypha multizonata* (pictured above) is an indicator of biological continuity, a link with generations of old oaks going back thousands of years. *(Ted Green)*

Ted Green leads an Ancient Tree safari under the Knepp oak, the five-hundred-year-old tree that sparked off our restoration of the Repton park. *(Charlie Burrell)*

Long considered a butterfly dependent on woodland, at Knepp the purple emperor favours our emerging sallow scrub, demonstrating how misleading our ideas about species can be when our observations are made in a landscape depleted of habitat options. Knepp now has the largest population of purple emperors in the UK.
(Neil Hulme)

The appearance of common spotted, southern marsh and early purple orchids – plants that depend on subterranean mycorrhizal fungi – in our former arable fields is a clear indication that our soils are reviving. *(Charlie Burrell)*

The rare water-violet, a lovely aquatic plant with spikes of delicate lilac blossoms, provides shelter for dragonfly nymphs, water beetles and tadpoles. It began appearing in ponds in the rewilding project as water quality improved. *(Charlie Burrell)*

In July 2010 the Beaver Advisory Committee for England was set up. I had petitioned for 'Nice Beaver' as a more engaging title but was overruled. Charlie was chair, and Derek Gow and Roisin Campbell-Palmer, conservation projects manager at Edinburgh Zoo and one of the managers of the Scottish Beaver Trial, also joined the board. Over the next few years, representatives from the National Farmers' Union, Country Landowners' Association, Farming and Wildlife Advisory Group, Wildlife and Wetlands Trust, Wildlife Trusts, RSPB, Environment Agency, National Trust, Friends of the Earth and the Forestry Commission met at Knepp to chew over the hopes and fears of beavers in English waters. Counterintuitively, perhaps, the Forestry Commission has long had an interest in beavers as forest engineers and is broadly, if cautiously, supportive, with their only real concerns being about the possible impact on expensive infrastructure such as culverts and roads. In their view the benefits could far outweigh the difficulties, provided an unsentimental attitude towards the management of beavers through relocation or culling could be adopted.

Though the Scottish Beaver Trial was being forensically documented, it soon became clear that nothing other than English evidence would sway English stakeholders. DEFRA, however, remained reluctant to grant a licence to release beavers in a trial on an English river. So, in 2011, the Devon Wildlife Trust, with Derek as consultant, set up a project to test the impact of beavers in a 2.8 hectare (7 acre) enclosure on farmland in west Devon.

A sign on the garage door announced a 'BOLD VENTURE'. But when Charlie and I visited the Devon site in October 2014 the location was still a closely kept secret. Every precaution had been taken against escape. A rodent Colditz, the enclosure was ringed with a £35,000 steel mesh fence, 1.25 metres high reinforced with three strands of electric wire and a skirt of double sheets of weld mesh buried 90 centimetres underground.

Threading our way around felled saplings and gnawed tree

stumps, over intricate canals and the odd sink-hole, it was hard to believe this was once soggy, secondary woodland along a trickling, 200 metre-long, canalized stream. In little over three years two adult beavers and their three offspring had created a braided system of channels, willow coppice and ponds – 1,000 square metres of open water – held by more than a dozen dams. In the middle of it all they had built their lodge, a heap of mud, sticks and moss, where – since we were visiting during the day – the nocturnal beavers were holed up, waiting for nightfall to resume their labours.

The effect on wildlife has been astonishing. In summer the air of this tiny beaver kingdom is thick with butterflies, hover-flies, damselflies and dragonflies. Banks grow water mint, bog pimpernel and orchids. Amongst the diverse mosses and epiphytes, a tiny oceanic liverwort, fingered cowlwort, has appeared. Ducks paddle the ponds, and marsh tits, willow tits, spotted flycatchers, grasshopper warblers, great spotted wood-peckers, tree creepers and lesser redpolls hunt insects in the trees. Grey herons and kingfishers dive for fish. Woodcock overwinter here, eating worms, beetles, spiders, fly larvae and small snails. The number of aquatic invertebrate species has risen dramatically, from fourteen in 2011 to forty-one in 2012. As have beetles – from eight species in 2011 to twenty-six in 2015. Five species of bat, including the rare barbastelle and Natterer's bat, have been recorded on the site. Common lizards hunt through the deadwood understorey. Amphibians have proliferated. In the first year, 2011, project recorders counted ten clumps of frogspawn. In 2014 there were 370; in 2016, 580. There is even frogspawn dripping from the trees – spillage from the predation of herons on gravid frogs.

Most exciting of all for the Devon Wildlife Trust has been the reappearance of tall herb fen vegetation including purple moor grass and sharp-flowered rush – characteristic flora of Culm grassland, an endangered habitat of western Britain and Northern Ireland that has, through drainage, cultivation, over-grazing, burning and afforestation, declined 90 per cent over the past hundred years. Only 3,500 hectares (13.5 square miles) of Culm grassland survive in Devon.

But it is the impact on water that is likely to be most persuasive in the beaver's favour. Careful monitoring of water flow across the site by hydrologists at the University of Exeter has shown that when slurry effluent flushes into the enclosure from the adjacent farm, the filtration system created by the beavers dramatically reduces pollution levels leaving the site. Levels of nitrates and phosphates in the water, entering the site as run-off from the surrounding farmland, are also reduced to virtually nothing. Soil run-off is captured, too. During storm events, surface water leaving the beaver-modified site contains three times less sediment than the water entering it. The three-hectare area, fed by a tiny headwater stream that would once have held only a few hundred litres of water, now holds a million. The series of a dozen or so leaky dams regulates outflow, reducing flood peaks and increasing base flows during droughts; so the graph of water volumes leaving the site, once a rollercoaster, now gently undulates. Over all, the water table has risen 10 centimetres. It is precisely the strategy that the inhabitants of Pickering and the Stroud Sustainable Drainage Project (an enterprise covering the whole of the 273 square kilometre catchment area of the River Frome in Somerset) have been implementing – by hand – to protect themselves from flooding.

The work being carried out by Exeter University at this tiny site in Devon is the most detailed ever conducted on the hydrology of beaver dams and will certainly add to our understanding of the beaver as the ultimate flood-control engineer. But in terms of the arguments in favour of restoring beavers to ecosystems, it is icing on the cake. Evidence from Europe and America is plentiful already, and on a much larger scale.

In North America by the 1930s only 100,000 beavers survived in remote areas of Canada after three centuries of trapping and shooting. Between 1853 and 1877 the Hudson Bay Company alone shipped 3 million beaver pelts to England. Today, beaver numbers have recovered to between 6 and 12 million across the Continent. There are now 70,000 beavers in the state of Massachusetts alone. The resurgence has triggered hundreds of scientific papers. At the University of Rhode Island, scientists have demonstrated how beaver ponds act as nitrogen sinks, with up to 45 per cent of nitrogen in water taken up by bacteria and aquatic plants proliferating in the standing ponds and stored in sediment. Their findings have been independently verified by the Soil Science Association of America. At Colorado State University, studies have focused on the carbon sequestration of beaver dams. The process of locking up carbon in the sediment of beaver ponds, geoscientists claim, could have a significant mitigating effect on climate change. At the Wildlife Conservation Society in Montana, scientists have demonstrated how beaver dams raise underground water levels, increase water supplies and substantially lower the cost of pumping groundwater for farming, as well as improving habitat for songbirds, deer, wapiti and – significantly – fish. In Wyoming, streams where beavers live have been shown to harbour seventy-five times as many water birds as those without, and the total biomass of all the creatures living in the water may be between two and five times greater in beaver ponds than in undammed sections. Other studies show how the silting up of beaver ponds, abandoned over time when supplies of vegetation ran out, is one of the primary ways in which new soils are created.

In Europe, reintroduction programmes in 161 locations in twenty-four European countries including France, Germany, Switzerland, Romania and the Netherlands have restored beaver numbers to more than 1.2 million from only 1,200 in eight relict populations in 1900. There are now beavers in river systems in almost every country of Europe. Scientific studies on free-living European beavers echo the findings of the United States. But perhaps more significantly for the recalcitrant British, densely populated Europe is demonstrating that it knows how to live with beavers.

There can be few landscapes as intensively managed as the German province of Bavaria. As far as the eye can see, the plains of the Danube are cultivated to the millimetre. Arable fields are vast and hedgerow-less; roadside verges are manicured, flower-less runways. Cows, pigs and sheep are generally reared indoors, even in summer. Forestry in the uplands produces around 4.85 million cubic metres of timber every year and counts for nearly 3,000 permanent jobs in administration and 2,300 in logging. Yet somehow, here, in an area substantially smaller than Scotland, humans are living alongside 18,000 beavers.

Gerhard Schwab is Derek Gow's German counterpart. A mountain of a man with a forested beard and long grey hair snaking down to his waist, he introduces us to 'Airport Beaver' in a patch of woodland just minutes from the flight arrivals hall in Munich. We visit many beaver sites on our whirlwind three-day tour – from Bavaria's highest beaver at 1,456 metres in Great Arber Lake to beavers in quarries, beavers on the Danube and beavers living free in community parks in town suburbs. But the most surprising site has to be where beavers have set up home in an angling club. Middle-aged men sit with their flasks and sandwiches, casting for zander and rainbow trout, mani-festly unconcerned about the bank of logs and sticks looming over the far end of the pond. True, some of the most pictur-esque willows have had to be chain-link fenced to protect the fishermen's shade and regulate the water temperature. Trout will not tolerate high temperatures as carp, pike and catfish do and would suffer in water exposed to direct sunlight. But this inconvenience is a price Bavarian anglers are entirely prepared to pay to accommodate the beaver.

'Fishermen were some of the fiercest opponents when beavers returned to Bavaria in the 1960s,' says Gerhard. 'But the reality of living with them has changed their minds.' Fish stocks in beaver ponds, where dams and lodges provide habitat for invertebrates and micro-organisms as well as protection for small fry against predation by larger fish, kingfishers and herons, have increased up to eighty times. Elsewhere, dams are proving no obstacle to fish migration – unsurprising, perhaps, considering that salmonids and beavers have co-existed for tens of millions of years. Providing voluntary services for an angling club for between seven and fifteen days a year is a condition of the fishing licence in Bavaria, and anglers now spend that time fencing trees and filling in beaver holes and runnels around ponds and rivers with bricks, so they can walk the banks and pitch their umbrellas. 'Symbiosis,' says Gerhard.

Bavarian farmers, too, are learning to live with beavers, thanks to an ingeniously simple and inexpensive flow device – the 'beaver deceiver' – pioneered in the US, which regulates the water level of beaver dams and keeps culverts open where arable fields are threatened.

'Nine times out of ten, beavers do not cause a problem for farmers,' says Gerhard. 'And where they do, the problem is usually easy to rectify.' An important tenet behind the confidence of Bavarian farmers is that ultimately, should all else fail, a beaver can be trapped or killed. 'That knowledge alone has brought a far greater degree of acceptance,' says Gerhardt. 'It's vital that farmers and landowners know the law is not going to slap a preservation order on the beaver and dictate that people have them on their land, come what may.'

Our little NGO, the Beaver Advisory Committee for England, was attempting to demonstrate to the British that European, Canadian and American anglers and farmers live perfectly happily with beavers when events leapt spectacularly ahead of us. A family of beavers was discovered living wild on the River Otter in Devon. A grainy, black-and-white night-vision video clip taken by retired environmental scientist Tom Buckley in February 2014 shows three beavers frolicking in the water, grooming each other and gnawing at trees. Unsurprisingly, it went viral. Many locals had known about the beavers for almost a decade but had kept quiet, fearing media attention and, above all, the authorities' adverse response. They were right to worry. Shortly after the discovery DEFRA announced plans to trap the colony and return them to captivity on the grounds that they were an invasive species and could be carrying a disease which posed a risk to human health.

Once again, how the beavers had got there was a mystery. Suggestions they had escaped from a nearby nature reserve are probably less likely than the theory that wildlife vigilantes, or 'beaver bombers', as the press dubbed them, were responsible. Whatever their origins, Devon Wildlife Trust and locals in the nearby town of Ottery St Mary – including the farmer on whose land the beavers were filmed – rallied to oppose the government's decision, signing petitions and posting 'Save Our Beavers' signs in shop windows. Ten thousand people sent messages to the Minster for the Environment urging that if the beavers had to be caught up for testing, DEFRA should re-release them straight back into the Otter if the tests proved negative.

Rising support for the beavers, not just in Devon but around the country, encouraged Friends of the Earth to challenge the government on the legality of their position. Britain, they argued, forms part of the 'natural range' of the Eurasian beaver and removing them would be against EU laws governing protected species.

As the flak began to fly, Devon Wildlife Trust held a number of public meetings to try to reach a consensus on pressing for the post-testing release of the beavers. In Derek Gow's view, the groundwork done by BACE during the course of five years played a key part at these meetings in deciding the fate of the Devon beavers. 'Ten years ago, you'd never have got environmentalists sitting down with anti-beaver pressure groups like the National Farmers' Union. But we all knew each other from Knepp. We'd got along fine and there was an element of trust there. Everyone still had positions but they were willing to go along with an official trial release. DEFRA hadn't a leg to stand on.'

On 23 March 2015, on the upper reaches of the River Otter, the silhouettes of the trees began to thicken in the gathering dusk, intensifying the cloak and dagger atmosphere. The film crew from BBC *Springwatch* were killing time, taking mood shots. The air of expectancy amongst the select band of onlookers – staff and trustees from the Devon Wildlife Trust, the young farming couple who owned this land, and Charlie and me – was almost unbearable. We paced the shingle spit, side-stepping fallen timber – evidence of the beavers' previous years of industry – glancing at our watches, fretting about last-minute glitches. The phone call had come from Devon Wildlife Trust with just twenty-four hours' notice. They had been waiting for the all-clear from tests carried out on the captured beavers at Derek's farm by Roisin and her colleagues from Edinburgh Zoo. Now the animals, stamped with a clean bill of health and conspicuously ear-tagged, were ready to go. The government had finally agreed to a trial release on the Otter. Devon Wildlife Trust's courageous position and their earlier investment in the 'Bold Venture' had paid off. It was a huge commitment for the tiny organization. Submitting the highly detailed licence application had been challenging enough, but they also under-took to provide financial and organizational resources, and pledged to manage all the complex licence conditions. In part-nership with Clinton Devon Estates, Derek Gow Consultancy and the University of Exeter, Devon Wildlife Trust would lead the trial over a period of five years – at a cost of £500,000 – and measure the impact of beavers on the local environment, economy, community and wildlife.

At the end of those five years, in 2020, the government is expected to make a decision about the future of the beaver in England and, assuming the beavers in England behave as they behave everywhere else in the world, begin issuing other licences for release. Meanwhile, on 24 November 2016 the Scot-tish government finally gave the European migrant beavers in Scotland indefinite leave to remain, putting yet more pressure on England to do the same.

The thrum of an engine broke the stillness at last and Derek Gow's pick-up pulled alongside the river. Three travelling cages were lifted out of the back and placed gently on the ground, exit hatches to the water. Rigid with anticipation on the opposite bank, cameras fixed on the cages, we stared into the twilight. This was history in the making. The first ever government-sanctioned reintroduction of an extinct mammal in England. One by one Derek lifted the flaps and three low shadows loped into the water and paddled away. The others would be released the following evening.

Two of the beavers slid down river and disappeared within seconds but the largest, a pregnant female, after a lap of honour, emerged onto the sand-spit in front of us to preen. The size of a portly spaniel, she sat up, whiskers diagnosing the air and, balanced by the flat scaly tail on the ground behind her, began to comb through her long, slick fur with a back claw. Perhaps the dream of having beavers at Knepp was not so far away. I could see her in the willow carr of Knepp lake or gliding the length of Hammer Pond, beavering away with a cohort of industrious little offspring, her youngest kitts sneaking a ride on her tail. Our concrete dams and Lego block slipways would be things of the past, the floodplains punctuated with woody debris blockages not of our own making, our clumsy, artificial scrapes a staircase of pools, Spring Wood a resurgence of coppice. And with this watery refinement a whole habitat would spring to life, an aqueous kingdom such as Knepp has not seen since the early Middle Ages, a place of vegetative complexity where even water voles would have a sporting chance to outwit the mink.

15

Pasture-fed

We need a better way to talk about eating animals. We need a way that brings meat to the centre of public discussion in the same way it is often at the centre of our plates.

Jonathan Safran Foer, *Eating Animals*, 2011

We had made a lucky choice with our longhorns, it turned out – and not just for their docility. The distinctive white 'finching' down their backs was a welcome clue to their whereabouts in our increasingly wild terrain and they were surviving the winters with flying colours. Hardy and resilient, they rarely used the empty barns available to them for shelter, preferring to hole up in a wood or grove of sallow to see out a storm or a cold snap.

But most important of all, from an economic point of view, longhorns produce exceptional beef. In his 'Perfection' series of programmes for TV in 2013, the chef Heston Blumenthal chose longhorn above all other traditional beef including Aberdeen Angus and Japanese Kobe as the best-tasting steak in the world.

By 2010, with three herds now comprising a total of 283 head (69 cows, 36 in-calf or bulling heifers, 9 bulls and the rest followers of between six and twenty months old), we felt we had reached the maximum stocking density for the project and needed to start culling. Suddenly a by-product of rewilding began to present itself as a potentially significant income stream. We were, in effect, producing premium organic longhorn beef with no feed or infrastructure costs and barely any veterinary costs at all. A small family-run butcher specializing in conservation-grade meat approached us to rent one of our defunct farm buildings and we found the perfect partner. We built a cutting room and maturation chiller where our beef is hung for five weeks – an almost forgotten practice in the fast-food age. We now have waiting lists for our prime cuts and supply restaurants, pubs and a top-end butcher's shop in our area.

But more than the taste and tenderness of the meat, or even the fact that it is organic, the key selling-point for us is that our animals are 'pasture-fed'. It is a distinction that to date has been overlooked by the UK government and the food and farming industry, but one that has far-reaching consequences for both human and animal health. In the 1990s scientists in the United States began to identify a difference between the fats put down by livestock pastured on grasslands and grain-fed animals in intensive systems. The findings, coming together with concerns for animal welfare, sparked off the 'grass-fed' movement in America. Now, in most US supermarkets, sections of the beef counter and dairy shelves are dedicated to 100 per cent grass-fed produce. Typically, the British were sceptical of research done abroad. But in 2009 an independent study carried out in the UK by the Economic and Social Research Council verified the US findings.

Chemical analysis of meat from cattle grazed on pasture shows far higher levels of vitamins A and E, and usually double the levels of beta-carotene (the precursor of vitamin A) and selenium – all powerful antioxidants. It also contains higher levels of healthy fatty acids including the long-chain omega-3 fatty acid DHA, which protects against heart disease and plays a key role in brain function and development. The human brain is half fat, and one quarter of that fat is made up of omega-3. Since the body cannot make its own omega-3, it has to derive it from food, but there are very few foods that contain it. Oily fish like tuna, mackerel and salmon have high levels of omega-3 DHA. However, fish stocks across the planet are crashing, and farmed salmon, even if it is organic, is generally fed on meal comprised of unsustainably sourced wild fish. It is also highly polluting, producing concentrated amounts of fish faeces and waste food which alter the marine biology, as well as spreading disease amongst wild fish. Producers of omega-3 supplements are increasingly turning to krill – small crustaceans found in all the world's oceans – and environmental campaigners are lobbying to protect this vital resource at the base of the marine food chain. Pasture-fed meat is, in contrast, highly sustainable and, crucially, presents omega-3 in a balanced ratio with omega-6 fatty acids. Current research suggests the modern diet contains far too much omega-6, found predominantly in vegetable oils. Nutritionists maintain that the key to health is food with a ratio of omega-6 to omega-3 no greater than 6:1. Pasture-fed beef consistently measures below a ratio of 4:1; while beef fed on grain generally registers above 6:1, and can be as high as 13:1.

Perhaps most significant of all are the considerably higher levels in pasture-fed animals of conjugated linoleic acid (CLA) – a fatty acid with proven benefits for the immune and inflammatory system, as well as bone mass. Considered to be one of the most powerful anti-carcinogens in nature, CLA is also proven to reduce body fat and the risk of heart attack. Further, grass-fed beef contains greater amounts of vaccenic acid than conventional beef, which is also converted into CLA by bacteria in the human digestive tract, raising the total amount of CLA received from eating wholly pasture-fed meat.

In contrast, modern intensive methods of rearing cattle on grain hamper the development of healthy fats, vitamins and other important compounds in the animal. Grain contains very little omega-3 compared with natural pasture. Even 'finishing' cattle on grain – the conventional practice of fattening beef for market – can reverse the benefits of a lifetime on grass. There's a logical explanation for this. Animals that evolved to eat grass struggle to metabolize grain – even if it's organic. The 'performance feeds' of barley, wheat, soybean, rape, molasses with added proteins and vitamins given to animals in intensive systems load on the weight but lead to all sorts of health problems, lowering their natural immunity and producing far higher rates of illness and disease which, in turn, may require routine administration of antibiotics, avermectins and other costly interventions. Humans, too, find the kind of fat that animals put down when they are fed grain difficult to metabolize. It is now clear that eating grain-fed animal fat can be positively detrimental to human health, with increasing evidence of links to obesity, cardiovascular disease, diabetes, asthma, autoimmune diseases and cancers, as well as depression, ADHD and Alzheimer's.

The implications of these findings are enormous. We should not be cutting out animal fats from our diet, as almost all recent medical advice insists. We should simply be taking care that we're eating the right sort of animal fat. And it's not just meat this applies to. In the US, cattle grazed entirely on grass were found to produce milk with five times more CLA and 30 per cent more omega-3. When children changed their diet from commercial pasteurized milk to raw milk from pasture-fed cattle, asthma and allergies declined dramatically. Consumers who consider themselves lactose intolerant may not be allergic to milk entirely – only the type of milk produced by grain-fed animals. Importantly, the richer the pasture in terms of wildflowers, herbs and diversity of grasses, the higher the levels of healthy fatty acids in the milk.

In the UK the term 'grass-fed' is used by meat producers whose animals may have had access to grazing but that may be also fed or finished on cereals, manufactured feeds and/or by-products from food manufacture. According to DEFRA, livestock only need to derive 51 per cent of their diet from grass to be sold as 'grass-fed', and there is no evidence that 'grass-fed' claims are ever investigated or policed. So the nascent British movement for a natural diet for ruminant livestock has adopted the term 'pasture-fed'. 'Pasture for Life' accreditation by the Pasture Fed Livestock Association, founded in 2011, ensures that animals have never been fed anything that does not come from pasture. That pasture, moreover, has to be managed in a way that minimizes – and preferably eradicates – the application of herbicide sprays and fertilizers so as to preserve natural grasses, herbal complexity and mineral availability for the herbivores' diet. It may not only be grains that give animals indigestion. A rich diet of purely agricultural grasses may be almost as bad, as our own cows memorably demonstrated to us.

Charlie had kept a close eye on our second herd of longhorns when they were released into the Northern Block, curious as to how they would behave. We had seeded almost the entire 235 hectares of the area under our extended Countryside Stewardship Scheme with the standard CSS mix of eight species of native grass – except for a single field of rich Italian ryegrass that had been used for silage-making and that we knew would simply revert to native grasses once it was deprived of artificial fertilizers. Just like the herd in the Middle Block, the cattle familiarized themselves with the external boundary before venturing into the interior. Charlie was sitting under an oak having a sandwich when he saw them discover the field of luscious, emerald-green ryegrass. Lowing with delight they put their heads down and dived in like children let loose in a chocolate factory. But twenty minutes later, they walked out again, bellowing complaints, and headed for the roughest grasses they could find. They stayed on the tussocky thatch on the floodplain for several weeks until their stomachs recovered and, all summer, avoided that field of rich Italian ryegrass like the plague, only returning to it once it was safely colonized by native grasses. It was as clear a demonstration as any of how the protein- and sugar-rich grasses we impose on cattle in modern farming systems, let alone what we feed them intensively indoors, is like us being made to eat foie gras and Christmas pudding every day of the year.

More than indigestion, it seems chemically fertilized ryegrass monocultures may also contribute to the production of methane in the ruminants' digestion process – one of the most harmful greenhouse gases behind climate change. Methane emissions are lower in biodiverse pasture systems largely because of fumaric acid – a compound that scientists at the Rowett Institute in Aberdeen identified as leading to faster growth and reducing emissions of methane by 70 per cent when added to the diet of lambs. Fumaric acid occurs widely in many plants and herbs of the field and hedgerow, including angelica, common fumitory, shepherd's purse and bird's-foot trefoil.

Scientific evidence that fats from pasture-fed animals are good for us – as any of our lard-, cream- and butter-eating grandparents and great-grandparents could have told us – and that 'healthier' alternatives like margarine and vegetable oils may be anything but has hardly, as yet, gained any traction in the UK. The shift away from pasture-based systems that began after the Second World War with the intensification of farming (and which was hotly opposed at the time by many farmers and conservationists) has led us down a path entrenched in grain production. Small meat and dairy producers who used to keep hardy breeds of cattle and sheep on herb-rich pasture (and if housed in winter, fed them hay and, latterly, silage) have been systematically displaced by large-scale arable farms growing grain for refined food products and feed for cattle. Although much of our land in Britain is ideal for grazing – and historic-ally we have depended on a diet of vegetables, meat and fruit – much of our land is now cultivated, irrigated and chemically fertilized to produce cereals, half of which are now fed to live-stock.

With so much land given over to arable across the planet (globally, around a third of all grain produced is fed to live-stock), we are now also encouraged to eat more meat than we ever did before – around 1 million tonnes of beef a year in the UK. Yet feeding cattle on grain is expensive, carbon-demanding and fraught with inefficiencies. It takes around 7–8 kilograms of grain to produce 1 kilogram of beef. Over the last fifteen years, 5.5 million hectares (21,235 square miles) of pastureland have been ploughed up in Europe, a process which released twice the amount of greenhouse gases emitted in the UK in a year, mainly for growing grain to feed livestock. Agri-business and the food industry are expanding intensive grain-fed meat production as consumers in the developing world begin eating more meat. It is a serious concern from both a health perspective and an environmental one. Suggested alternatives range from hi-technology artificial meat to universal veganism. But the answer could be much easier. Rather than redesign the future, we could heed the accumulated wisdom of the past. We could eat less meat, and return to traditional methods of rearing animals.

To the importance of herb-rich pasture for a sustainable system of raising healthy livestock Charlie and I would also add, from observing our animals in a wilder regime, the benefits of browsing. To begin with, we had worried as scrub and pioneer plants like fleabane began to take over in the Southern Block that there would not be enough grass left for the cattle. But experience has shown that the Southern herd often outperforms the herds grazing in the parkland of the Middle and Northern Blocks. Browsing on twigs, bark and leaves appears to provide cattle, deer and horses alike with nutrients and minerals that grass alone cannot give. This would have been stating the obvious to farmers in the past. Collecting 'tree fodder' for livestock by pollarding – cutting the branches of living trees higher than animals can reach – pre-dates haymaking by thousands of years and was once common practice across Britain. This sustainable, two-tiered system of agriculture is still used in parts of Europe and subsistence regions of Africa and Asia, where lopping off branches in full leaf to store as animal feed for winter or the dry season extends the life-span of the tree and is a valuable insurance against drought and poor grass growth.

Like herbs in meadows, the leaves of many trees and shrubs have medicinal properties. Laying hedges as field boundaries using a rich variety of tree and shrub species would, in the not so distant past, have served the additional purpose of providing livestock with an extra source of nutrition and opportunities for self-medication.

It was only over snowy days in January 2010 and again in December 2011 that we needed to fork out bales of organic hay cut from fields around the village outside the project. While the ponies and deer could survive a period of extended snow cover in the park, the longhorns have forgotten how to dig through snow to find grass, and in the Middle and Northern blocks, with high deer browse-lines, vegetation was less available to them. The only other times we have provided supplementary feed was after months of solid rain, such as in the spring of 2013, when the ground was poached to hell and the new grass was slow to appear.

All herbivores naturally lose condition in the winter but studies show that a cycle of weight loss and gain may actually be beneficial to their health. Evolved over millennia to cope with the boom and bust of the seasons, the metabolism of grazing animals may be unsuited to cope with high calorific intake all year round. The test is in the animals' overall health at the end of winter and how quickly they put on weight with the first flush of spring grass and new foliage.

However easy the animals were proving to be, naturalistic grazing threw up intractable problems with modern British livestock regulations. Allowing a number of bulls to run with the herd makes it impossible to identify the sire of calves, which means our longhorns have had to lose their pedigree status. According to the pedigree rulebook, too, longhorn bulls are required to reach 310 kilograms in 300 days – a weight gain that can only be achieved by intensively feeding them grain, hence the importance to those in the know of the term 'slow-grown', both as a matter of taste and of animal welfare.

Though naturalistic grazing is, for the most part, extremely low maintenance, some aspects take far longer than in an intensive system. Ear-tagging is a regulation from which only the ancient Chillingham cattle in Northumberland – a wild-roaming herd emparked in the Middle Ages – are exempt. For the eight years it took our cows in the Middle Block to recover their natural rhythm and synchronize their cycle to give birth in spring, locating their calves for ear-tagging within days of being born was a frustrating game of hide and seek. Even if we knew where a certain cow liked to give birth, the random calving pattern scattered across the year meant we never knew quite when she would.

Conforming to regulations for domesticated livestock has, ultimately, demanded a departure from our non-interventionist ethos. Leaving the herd to their own devices meant that heifers sometimes as young as six or seven months old were being covered by bulls. There was a risk that a heifer might gestate a comparatively large calf and her immaturity could lead to problems giving birth. How significant this risk is, is impossible to determine. We had two such calving problems in a herd of 50 cows and heifers over eight years – very little in the scheme of things – but the question was whether we could or should allow this to happen at all. In May 2007 we invited a group of vets from DEFRA, RSPCA, Natural England and several conservation grazing projects to see our naturalistic system in practice. This was the only concern they identified and we decided to follow their recommendations. The bulls are now segregated from the herd, grazing on 400 acres of organic conservation land geographically separated from the project by the village, until the breeding season begins. When the bulls join the herd in June or July the young heifers are taken out, and swapped over again in September. Breaking up the herd, though, has an inevitable impact on relationships. When the heifers are taken away, at around six to twelve months, even though they are now almost entirely dependent on grass, they can still be suckling from their mothers. When they return to the herd ten weeks later it is sad to see that mothers and daughters no longer seem to recognize each other.

Rounding up free-roaming cattle for TB testing every four years, vaccinations for common cattle diseases like black leg, and general husbandry and health checks, is also a challenge – and increasingly so, as areas of scrub and wetland expand. A visit to Tour du Valat in the Camargue in southern France –

the wetland conservation project started by Luc Hoffmann, co-founder of the World Wildlife Fund – introduced us to the wonders of the Camargue horse. An ancient breed, designed for rounding up fighting bulls in the rough terrain of the Rhone estuary marshlands, Camargues are undaunted by water and thick scrub, instinctively know how to behave with cattle, and are generally unafraid of pigs, habituated as they are to wild boar.

Cattle respond to Camargue mustering like a dream. Unfortunately, neither our stockman Pat Toe nor Craig Line his trusty assistant are horsemen and while we call in the cowboys, usually Charlie, his PA Yasmin Newman and our son Ned, to ride our three Camargues for big round-ups, the regular business of cattle management was carried out by all-terrain vehicle and quad bike. Round-ups by vehicle tended to be a frantic chase inducing panic and fear in the cattle and an equivalent amount of adrenaline in their handlers until the wisdom of Bud Williams revolutionized our process. Bud, a cattle rancher from Oregon who died in 2012 at the age of fifty-six, preached a method of moving cattle that is a million miles from the 'yeehaah' dust-kicking stampedes of Westerns. Based on an empathetic understanding of herd mentality, Bud could gather animals of any description – from cattle, sheep and 'hogs' to reindeer, elk and bison – on foot and over any kind of terrain. He grazed his own cattle on rotation, without fences.

The Bud Williams videos – hours filmed on a shaky camera by his wife Eunice, unexpurgated and with intriguing noises off – are, for those in the business of mustering cattle, compelling viewing. Using just the right angles of approach, always in sight, never directly behind them, Bud stirs the herd into pacific motion, gauging just the right pace, not too slow, not too fast, to magnetize them. Stray animals are sucked into the direction of travel like drops of mercury. 'They don't know where they're going or why,' he says, never prone to embellishment, 'but they don't wanna miss out.' It is the atavistic compulsion of migration in action, hard-wired into their DNA.

It is something nomads and pastoralists also have in their bones. Watching Romanian herdsmen driving cattle and water buffalo through the wood pastures of Transylvania is to witness the same unflappable ease of the tortoise defeating the hare. The enlightened Australian cattle-rancher who put us on to Bud Williams is appalled at the macho stick-wielding, adrenaline-fuelled culture that prevails over cattle management in most modern systems. 'It shows that cattle-handlers don't understand their animals any more. The more hollering and whip-cracking a stockman does, the more fearful I think he is.'

Just how much time and energy is wasted in modern cattle-handling systems by this frenetic approach, not to mention the stress imposed on the animals, was brought home by our experience with Temple Grandin, one of the world's most famous cattle-whisperers, who visited us in July 2011. Temple was born in Massachusetts in 1947, severely autistic. Unable to speak until the age of three and a half, and intolerant of any physical contact, her astonishing insights might never have surfaced had it not been that her mother rejected medical advice to incarcerate her in an institution and insisted, instead, on a normal education. A eureka moment in Temple's early life was watching animals enter a cattle crush on her aunt's farm. Designed to keep the cow 'stock-still' while being branded, de-horned or receiving veterinary treatment, Temple observed how the close confinement of the cage, pressing against the animal's body and clamping tightly around the neck and head, also calmed it down. She developed her own 'squeeze machine', a contraption she could crawl into at times of unbearable stress or panic, releasing a lever that would collapse the frame to her body. It was, for Temple, a safe substitute for the human hug.

Her affinity with animals expresses itself most often in her anxieties. Feeling threatened by her surroundings, reactive to light and unexpected flashes, and hypersensitive to noise, touch and changes in visual detail, she instinctively understands what spooks and frightens them. Temple's designs have revolutionized more than half the handling and slaughter systems across the United States, transforming a stressful and dangerous process into an efficient, humane and ultimately cost-saving exercise.

Temple had expressed a desire to visit Knepp at the end of her UK lecture tour. Her handshake was vice-like, a social ritual she has taught herself to endure, though she still averted her eyes as she introduced herself, 'Temple Grandin. Temple Grandin. Pleased to meet you, pleased to meet you.' At school she was nicknamed the 'tape recorder' for her habit of repeating herself. Words, she claims, are her second language. Like an animal she thinks primarily in pictures. She was wearing a cowboy shirt with Texan longhorns on the lapels, a bootlace tie and a big brass belt-buckle embossed with a longhorn head. I was keeping an eye on the clock because her companion had told me Temple was anxious to be at Gatwick at 7pm exactly, in time for her flight back to the States. Temple's train fever is off the spectrum. Her flight wasn't until the following day.

We take Temple and her companion on a tour of the rewilding project but it is difficult to gauge what she makes of it. She has a new fixation – a theory she is developing about 'whorls', the spirals of hair on cows' foreheads. The higher up the forehead the whorl is, she maintains, the more aggressive or temperamental the animal. The theory is not as quirky as it sounds, since hair patterns in a foetus form at the same time as the brain. Paediatric studies have discovered a similar development in children, with natural hair partings or 'cowlicks' on their scalps corresponding to the underlying structures of the brain. In cows, the direction of the whorl may also denote right- or left-handedness, indicating not only the way an animal prefers to turn, but the dominance of the cerebral hemispheres – geared towards social interaction and food-finding in the left side of the brain, and detection of danger and avoidance behaviour in the right. Temple has tested her theory on thousands of cattle and is keen to see where the whorls are located on our longhorns.

As we wander through the herd lying placidly in the summer sun the whorls do, indeed, seem to be between the eyes or even lower down. All except one – a dark grey cow with sweeping, upright horns, who warily rises to her feet as we approach. The Black Bitch is notoriously shirty and prone to charging anyone who comes near her calf. We have tolerated her because she is such a good mother. There's a spirit about her we can't help but admire. But this is rewilding in the Anthropocene with footpaths and dog-walkers to consider. The lofty whorl, like an Indian *bindi* in the middle of her forehead above her eyes, confirms what we already instinctively know. We have to cull her, Temple suggests, and, to ensure her over-protective genes are not passed on, all her progeny must go, too. Temple's advice is eminently practical though she is aware of the dangers of single-mindedly selecting for any one trait in a breed, even if that trait is docility. Who knows what other important, useful or healthy characteristics may be lost on the way? In intensive systems, selective breeding manipulates genes at break-neck speed with little thought of the long-term losses to the breed or the physical side effects. It is a primary cause of pain, ill-health and neurological disorders in modern livestock.

When we finally distract Temple from the cows' whorls we take her to see the cattle-handling system we have created from designs in her book *Livestock Handling and Transport*. She spots a problem immediately. The entrance is, just as she dictates, at an encouraging angle of thirty degrees. But in our case, she tells us, there is no need to board the sides of the race – which most of the longhorns are tall enough to see over, anyway. The large barn wall to one side of the race is enough of a block to reduce distraction. If we leave the race exposed, she adds, the animals will be reassured by the sight of the rest of the herd turning around the bend and walking back towards them up the parallel race. They will assume they are all returning to where they started. We say goodbye to Temple (more uncomfortable handshakes before she bolts for the car with undisguised relief) unaware of the impact her simple suggestion is to have. Ultimately, her tiny adjustments shave another half-hour off our handling time. The overall difference is staggering.

Before Temple's system it took five people a whole stressful day to process the herd. Now, two or three people can process a hundred relaxed longhorn cattle in under two hours with considerably less risk to themselves.

Meanwhile, the other animals in the project are also thriving. Finding a nest of marmalade piglets snoozing in the sun or trotting purposefully behind a colossal Tamworth sow, belly-grunting her encouragement, never fails to tug the heart strings. The sows are scatty mothers, perhaps because they have between four and six offspring. They seem unbothered if they lose one – the onus is on the piglets to keep up – but they are remarkably communal and often suckle each other's young. They have certainly taken to rewilding. Walking beside a pond one day Charlie and I were startled by a jacuzzi of bubbles. Snorting like a hippo, one of the old sows broke the surface, a giant freshwater swan mussel in her jaws. Paddling to the bank she expertly prised it open with her trotters and teased out the flesh with her teeth. Her companion surfacing beside her was less picky and scrunched down the delicacy, shell and all. How they discovered the mussels lurking in the silt at the bottom of our ponds is a mystery but they are now a favourite part of their foraging repertoire. The pigs can hold their breath underwater for up to twenty seconds, revisiting, perhaps, an aquatic stage in their evolution.

We had hoped to sell our 'wild range' organic pork commercially but it soon became clear that, critical as our Tamworths are for soil disturbance, the project can only sustain a certain number of these marauding ploughs at one time – more like six adults rather than sixty. This was a disappointment because our early experiments at making air-dried *pata negra jamón*, salted in wine boxes, then hung in a fly-proof cage under the oak in the garden for the summer, consistently outshone Spanish versions in blind tastings in our kitchen. The delicious oaky fat put down by the pigs after feasting on Sussex acorns melts on the slicer. Joints and chops have a deep, nutty flavour – entirely unlike the pallid pork in supermarkets. Now we simply produce Tamworth sausages and bacon for home consumption and visitors to our campsite shop. We're less inhibited, too, in our use of pasture-fed pork lard and beef dripping in cooking – a ready source of omegas 3, 6 and 9, and a cheaper, more sustainable alternative to fish oils.

Our Exmoor ponies, too, are strikingly self-assured. Once they began breeding there was even less cause to worry about the possibility of obesity and laminitis. Suddenly there was plenty of action – mares fighting for the role of dominant matriarch, colts play-fighting, the lead stallion looking over his shoulder for an upcoming challenger. Natural stress and interaction: the essence of a dynamic herd. Some level of stress hormones in animals boosts the immune system. The same is true for humans. Recent studies have shown that short-term bouts of stress can protect against Alzheimer's by flooding the brain cells with chemical stimulants and can prevent breast cancer by suppressing the production of oestrogen. Physical problems arise, for both humans and animals, when levels of stress chemicals in the body are either chronically very low or high and sustained.

However, by 2010 our herd had grown to more than thirty Exmoors – the maximum we felt the project could sustain. Like other conservation areas with wild horses, we faced the problem of what to do with the excess stock. With no demand for semi-feral, unbroken horses a live Exmoor will fetch a pitiful £25 – roughly what it costs to draw up its passport for market. Like the ponies of the New Forest and Dartmoor, the carcass of a wild-living Exmoor will generally go to zoos or packs of hounds, or be sent to France. It seemed a sad and wasteful end for our animals, compounded by our concerns about long transportation and unknown abattoirs. To keep our numbers at a sustainable level, the only other option – it seemed – was castration.

Castration is a stressful experience for both the animal and the handlers involved, and expensive – it costs about £200 to dart and operate on each stallion – but it was, at least, a one-off exercise. To the vet's alarm the stallions took more than double the amount of tranquillizer normally required for a domesticated horse and half the amount of antidote. The stallions appeared to recover faster than the ashen-faced men holding them down but it was still a regretful moment. We no longer have the joy of seeing foals at foot but most lowering of all is to watch the herd losing its dynamism, stress levels falling to virtually zero, the spark of natural interaction and acquired wisdom halted in its tracks – a 'wild' animal going nowhere.

But there is another way. In 2015, Charlotte Faulkner, a horse enthusiast living on a farm near Tavistock in Devon, took a bold step that could safeguard the future of semi-feral herds. For years she has run the Dartmoor Hill Pony Association, trying to find ways to support wild ponies on Dartmoor, rescuing neglected animals and securing homes for unwanted foals. Sixty years ago, there were thousands of ponies grazing on Dartmoor. In the 1930s, when the granite and coal industries flourished, they were used as pit ponies, as well as for riding and driving carts. That number has now dwindled to 800, with 400 foals shot every year by farmers. As a breed the Dartmoor pony is in crisis, and without grazing, the moorland faces the prospect of being overcome by rough grasses and, much as the Kraansvlak did, suffering a loss of important habitat and biodiversity.

Mastering her own sensitivities, Charlotte embraced the only solution – to eat the ponies. 'If I thought there was another way, believe me, I'd have done it.' She confesses to drinking two pints of cider before braving her first mouthful of pony steak but her initiative has paid off. An enthusiastic market for pony sausages and roasts in restaurants, pubs and farmers' markets around Dartmoor has provided farmers with a source of income from the ponies and given the wild herd a new lease of life. Criticism from horse lovers has at times, though, been vicious. Sometimes she rings the abusive callers back and suggests they visit her farm to understand the rationale. 'They never take up my invitation,' she says.

The horsemeat taboo in the UK is difficult to explain. Horses are eaten in countries across Europe, South America and Asia. The top eight countries (including China, Mexico, Italy and Argentina) consume about 4.7 million horses a year. In Britain, as in the rest of Europe, horse was eaten throughout the Middle Ages despite a papal ban on horsemeat in 732 (it was associated with Germanic pagan cults) and strict taboos amongst Romany and Jewish communities. In France horse-eating received a boost during the Revolution when aristocrats' stables were opened to the starving. In the Napoleonic campaigns the army resorted to eating its horses, and the general populace tucked into their ponies during the 1870–71 siege of Paris. Nowadays butchers' shops advertise horsemeat with sign-boards of galloping horses or horses' heads. There is no sentimentality across the Channel: 100,000 live horses are transported into and around the European Union for human consumption.

But perhaps the British public are less sensitive than one imagines. In 2007 a readers' poll in *Time Out* magazine showed that 82 per cent of respondents supported Gordon Ramsay's decision to serve horsemeat in his restaurants. The vogue for 'nose to tail' gastronomy may be changing our tastes and sensibilities. When a spate of food scandals in 2013 revealed that beef and other products on sale in British supermarkets had been contaminated with horsemeat, consumers seemed more concerned that they had been duped into eating untraceable products, quite possibly from sick and dying animals treated with dangerous chemicals, than at the idea of eating horsemeat per se. In the weeks following the media frenzy Twitter was awash with witticisms – 'too much salt and Shergar in our food', 'Findus lasagne made with marscapony and boloneighs', 'frozen meat importers should face more hurdles', '*Horse & Hound* – trade magazine of the French beef sector', 'Tesco say their burger sales remain stable', 'lack of confidence in frozen meat won't last furlong'. But restaurants in the UK selling horsemeat were booked out. The horsemeat debacle was music to our ears. It broke a great taboo, exposed the irony of 'good' horsemeat going to waste and 'bad' ending up in dodgy burgers and pies, and suggested that the British public might be persuaded to consider top-quality, traceable, conservation-grade British horsemeat for the table and that, one day, we might again have a breeding herd of Exmoors at Knepp.

In 2010 we introduced red deer into the park and a small herd into the Southern Block where the Advisory Board judged that the vegetation had grown robust enough to handle another big hitter. We now had the confidence to override the naysayers. Red deer present no more of a threat than any other animal in the project. As ever, lack of familiarity, it seems, breeds unbridled fears – but we were also beginning to appreciate the reverse. Nothing dispels those fears faster than experience itself. As Hans Kampf puts it, this is 'thinking by doing'.

The red deer surprised us, though, in one respect. On their release from the trailer they plunged into the nearest body of water. Even now they are habituated to Knepp they spend much of their time up to their haunches in the lakes and ponds. It is an odd sight when you are used to seeing red deer on craggy hillsides in Scotland, but observations of them at Knepp and elsewhere in the lowlands seem to confirm suspicions that they are – or were – a riverine species, pushed into the uplands as humans took over their habitat. Across Eurasia, red deer are still key grazers in reed beds and marshes, just like the sambar in South-east Asia, Père Davids in China and sitatunga antelopes in central Africa.

The red deer's remarkable growth in lowland conditions adds weight to this theory. The stags at Knepp are twice as heavy as Scottish stags, their antlers up to three times the weight. Deforestation and chronic over-grazing in the Highlands, combined with artificially high numbers supported, in some cases, by supplementary feeding in winter, restricts the growth of red deer in Scotland and, knowing no different, most people in the Highlands have come to accept these numbers and sizes as normal.

The Norwegians see it differently. They see a lot of things differently. In Norway, Duncan Halley, a Scot who has been working for the Norwegian Institute for Nature Research for the past twenty years, walked us through a landscape that was, until the mid-nineteenth century, barren sheep-grazed hillsides punctuated by the odd wind-blasted tree, with the only shrubs wedged in inaccessible gullies and ravines. On the same latitude as Scotland, with the same volcanic or metamorphic geology, acid, peaty soils, similar seasonal temperature changes and, in some cases, even higher rainfall and stronger winds, this corner of south-west Norway used to look exactly like the Highlands. But in the mid-nineteenth century an agricultural depression sparked a mass emigration of farmers to the United States and widespread land abandonment. There was no aristocratic culture of deer-stalking here – this is very much yeoman country – and most of the deer had already been hunted out. With the removal of sheep there were barely any grazing mouths left in the region. Changes in social and economic conditions from the 1950s onwards completed the human population drift from countryside to town. The result is a vegetation pulse that has astonished scientists, historians and foresters alike.

In Scotland the received wisdom is that trees do not belong in the Highland landscape. The panoramas of Landseer are part of our subconscious. The Caledonian forests disappeared so long ago, it is thought, as to have no relevance to the present, and if there ever was a seed source for trees in those soils, it is now long gone or the soils have changed so much that succession is no longer possible. It has been generally accepted that no tree could ever have grown above 650 metres (2,100 feet).

Norway proves otherwise. After a century or more of no grazing pressure, trees cover every inch of available land, from sea level to 1,200 metres. They grow on open hillsides, on escarpments and even on scree, on wind-blasted cliffs and on the spray-dashed shoreline – a triumph of vegetation succession. Wherever the seed source has come from for all these trees, it has clearly not been a problem. We walked through woods of birch,

Scots pine, rowan and aspen, the floor spongy with moss and lichens, trees growing even on top of granite boulders. On anthills taller than a man, a spray of pellets betrayed the lekking site of a capercaillie. And higher up, closer to the treeline, where patches of snow were clinging on even in June, amongst dwarf willows, tortured birch and juniper we disturbed red-spotted bluethroats, bramblings, redstarts, wheatears, fieldfares – and grouse. Heather is the understorey here, a very different scenario from the open grouse moors of Britain. The grouse are likely seeking willow buds, a higher source of protein than heather. These birds used to be considered a different species to our own – the Norwegians call them 'willow grouse' – but now they are acknowledged as a subspecies. Grouse just behave differently in Norway because different opportunities are available to them.

What has happened in Norway reveals how an ecosystem can flip from one end of the spectrum to the other – from a landscape so dominated by grazers as to prevent any kind of vegetation succession at all, to a landscape where grazers have been successfully excluded long enough for it to turn into closed-canopy forest. Scotland and Norway, once identical twins, are now poles apart. And each country thinks its own landscape is natural.

Inspiring as it is to see the potential for vegetation in Scotland, Norway faces problems at the other extreme. As trees take over the last remaining patches of open ground, and scrubby margins revert to closed-canopy woodland, the potential for dynamism reduces. Current levels of animal disturbance in Norway are not significant enough to halt the progression of trees, open up new areas, stimulate complexity and redress the balance of unfettered vegetation succession. It is a landscape crying out for bison and wild boar.

Some disturbers have returned. Beavers are making their way north from Sweden and red and roe deer have colonized the new forests. Half a million people in Norway, 9.5 per cent of the population, are registered hunters. But the hunting culture in Norway is very different from Scotland, quite apart from the differing techniques and challenges of stalking – one in dense woodland, the other, in an open landscape. In Norway, weight dictates the numbers of red deer shot. When carcass weights go down, indicating excessive competition for food, the number of shooting licences issued rises until a population of deer of optimum weight has been regained. In Norway, the dressed carcass of a stag two and a half years old is expected to weigh at least 80 kilograms – around 20 kilograms heavier than the carcass of a Scottish stag dressed in the same way and of the same age. Some Scottish estates have, in an effort to re-establish natural vegetation, brought deer numbers right down and have found, as a consequence, that the weight of their deer has risen commensurately. But for the most part, across the Highlands, the practice remains as it has since Victorian times and Scottish red deer are encouraged in artificially high numbers such that trees and vegetation have little or no chance to rebound.

The Norwegian system, on the other hand, faces a catastrophic shift towards a closed-canopy landscape. By sustaining deer populations on grounds of optimum weight, the natural boom-and-bust rhythms plateau, and with such low numbers the animal impact on the forest becomes insignificant. What, primarily, is missing from both the Norwegian and the Scottish paradigms is an equal fight between vegetation succession and animal disturbance, where natural dynamics and population fluctuations are free to perform, stimulating and sustaining biodiversity over the longer term.

In the UK we have a curious north–south divide in approach, both of which result in excessively high populations of deer. While we keep numbers of red deer artificially high in the Highlands for the purpose of stalking, elsewhere in the country, where populations of other deer species are rocketing, we are reluctant to control them. In the Second World War the numbers of roe deer in Britain were negligible but since the 1960s populations of the native roe and escaped exotics have exploded. The British deer population is believed to be at its highest level for a thousand years, with some 1.5 million red, roe, fallow, sika, muntjac and Chinese water deer roaming the countryside. Because there is so little natural habitat left, their impact on our precious pockets of nature is considerable and they may well be contributing to the decline of ground-nesting birds such as native woodcock and nightingales, which need dense cover and are easily disturbed. Unlike the rest of Europe, the British public (apart from sporting estates) seem to have lost their taste for hunting for the pot and this readily available source of healthy, free-roaming protein is entirely overlooked. Without effective culling and without predators to harry them, deer colonize the countryside at will and, again, vegetation is not allowed a chance to recover. It is a landscape crying out, first and foremost, for the lynx, the natural predator of roe.

Large predators are an aspect of rewilding clearly absent at Knepp. Our 3,500 acres are, for our grazing animals, the antithesis of a landscape of fear. Sociability rather than survival keeps them to their herds. They wander loosely, grazing at will, covering whatever ground they please, with only a fox to make a play for a piglet or fawn. Who knows what impact we are missing, what properties would emerge if we could add this piece of the jigsaw, if Knepp could be connected to a truly living landscape replete with predators once again?

16

Rewilding the Soil

Upon this handful of soil our survival depends. Husband it and it will grow our food, our fuel and our shelter, and surround us with beauty. Abuse it and the soil will collapse and die, taking humanity with it.

Atharva Veda, Sanskrit scripture, c. 1200 BC

The Nation that destroys its soil destroys itself.

Franklin D. Roosevelt,
President of the United States, Letter to all State Governors
on a Uniform Soil Conservation Law, 1937

When we began rewilding, our attention, like most people who visit Knepp for the first time, gravitated towards the large mammals, their physical presence, lumbering through the landscape at will, bringing a jolt of reconnection.

Then came the birds, augurs of resurgence – skeins of geese and flights of duck descending in autumn, the raptors with their wild cries, now in numbers, kettling in the thermals over-head, songbirds thronging the scrub and surprise visitations: a Montagu's harrier (Britain's rarest breeding raptor), a pair of great white eagles, a black tern, migrating white storks and even a black stork in 2016 – one of the rarest birds in Western Europe. In 2014 we saw our first long-eared and short-eared owls. Knepp could now boast the presence of all five British owls, as well as two breeding pairs of lesser spotted woodpeckers, and peregrine falcons nesting in an oak (some of the very few tree-breeding peregrines in the UK). In the spring of 2017, nightjars – a so-called 'heathland bird' – added their *churr*-ing to the nocturnal arias of our nightingales and, for several weeks that summer, a male red-backed shrike, known as the 'butcher bird' for its habit of lardering insects on thorns, staked his territory in a bramble bush. Red-backed shrikes were once common throughout Britain but declined to virtual extinction in the late 1980s. Only four pairs are known to have bred in England since then. So rare is this bird we were advised by the RSPB to keep watch over the site to protect it from egg-collectors and over-zealous photographers. From a safe distance, through binoculars, we watched him deftly catch an emperor dragonfly on the wing and transfix it on a bramble thorn. We're praying he returns to his spot next year, and that twitchers, if they discover him, will exercise restraint, and that, one day, a female will join him.

Gradually, however, our attention began to be drawn to other creatures, too – small predators like stoats, weasels, polecats, now evident in numbers, and the water shrew rebounding in our streams and ponds, its venomous frog-paralysing bite belying its furry-snouted cuteness. Or other small mammals like the harvest mouse, emphatically tiny pale ginger *Micromys minutus*, weighing less than 10 grams – the smallest rodent in Europe, a Priority Species in the UK Biodiversity Action Plan. Surveys showed our harvest mouse population was rocketing. In February 2016 our ecologist Penny Green and four volunteers counted fifty-nine breeding nests and twenty-nine shelter nests in just five hours surveying reeds around Knepp Mill Pond and Hammer Pond. Astonishingly skilful, the harvesters weave their nests, the size of a cricket ball, onto the swaying stalks of living reeds. If you look inside, the nests are lined with thistle-down or soft, finely chewed grass.

The Southern Block was proving by far the most productive for small mammals, the rebounding vegetation providing them with food and nesting habitat as well as protection from predators. Aerial mapping by an independent environmental consultancy showed us that woodland and scrub cover here had increased from 10 per cent in 2001 before the start of the project to 35 per cent in 2012, and by 2016 it was 42 per cent. However, the loose definition of 'woodland and scrub' is deceptive. The vegetation here is much more complex than this. Within these structures, sometimes even deep inside groves or underneath bushes, are areas still regularly grazed by the animals. To our minds, this is wood pasture in action. By 2016/17 we noticed the recruitment of scrub and trees beginning to level out; complexity, itself, putting the brakes on the early pioneers.

Compared with the Southern Block, the re-seeded grasslands of the Middle and Northern Blocks have changed relatively little. A small-mammal survey carried out in the summer of 2016 showed just how dramatic the effect of the increased vegetation structure in the Southern Block has been. Forty Longworth traps baited with gerbil food, blowfly pupae, hay and chopped apple and carrot were set in each of the three blocks over a total of seven days. Over the five times that they were checked during that period, between seventeen and thirty-two of the forty traps in the Southern Block contained either a wood mouse, yellow-necked field mouse, bank vole, field vole or common shrew, compared with two to five captives in the forty traps in each of the Northern and Middle Blocks.

Hedgehogs – known in old Sussex as 'prickleback urchins' – had once been plentiful at Knepp. When we first moved here in the mid-1980s, our Labrador would bring them into the house, his gentle mouth protecting both himself and the hedgehog. But they had vanished completely in our last years of farming. In 2016 we saw our first hedgehog footprints in our hedgehog-monitoring tunnels, though we are yet to see their owners. Slow-worms and grass snakes are now a common sight warming themselves, sometimes in knots of a dozen or more, under our *refugia* – small pieces of corrugated iron scattered around the project to help us record them. Common toads and frogs and common and palmate newts are plentiful, and from one recorded site for the rare great crested newt in a pond in the middle of a wood in 1987, we now have two thriving colonies in ponds where they have never been seen before.

Botanists alerted us to rare plants like adder's tongue fern, marsh speedwell, water violet and the lesser water parsnip – a species which seems to be in decline in Sussex as a whole. Eighty-nine bryophytes (mosses, hornworts and liverworts) have been identified, including several rarities, suggesting that Knepp may ultimately prove to be one of the richest sites in Sussex.

With an increasing number of entomologists descending on us, our attention began sliding further down the food chain towards invertebrates and the accumulating list of insect rarities. Removing pesticides and avermectins, and leaving deadwood on the land, has triggered a rise in notable beetles: the first record in Sussex for fifty years of the dung beetle *Geotrupes mutator* (in three different sites on Knepp); the rare chestnut brown *Calambus bipustulatus* click beetle, whose larvae live in the soft, rotting stumps of old oaks; and *Korynetes caeruleus*, the predatory steely blue beetle feeding on the larvae of wood-boring insects. The invertebrates' is a bewitching world of orb weavers, crab spiders, leafhoppers, soldier beetles, froghoppers, harvestmen, bush crickets and outlandish creatures like the fungus weevil *Platystomos albians*, a bird-dropping mimic, and *Trematocephalus cristatus* – a striking red and blue-black money spider with a hole straight through its head.

Mayflies and dragonflies, too, throng the messy, vegetative margins of our lakes and ponds now rejuvenated by clean water. Two species of damselfly, the banded and the beautiful demoiselle, particularly sensitive to pollution, flit in hundreds over the streams and the surface of the River Adur. Rarer species like the scarce chaser, a blue-eyed dragonfly found only in six places in Britain, have appeared out of nowhere. Eighteen were counted here in a single day.

Butterflies were suddenly rising in number and variety. The

first survey of the North and Middle Blocks in 2005 recorded thirteen different species; by 2014 we had twenty-three. Surveys of the Southern Block, begun in 2012, increased the tally of butterfly species for the whole of Knepp to thirty-four. Some of them are new arrivals, like the marbled white (first recorded here in 2005), the small heath (another species deceptively tagged to a particular habitat), the dark green fritillary (first recorded here in 2015) and the walled brown (first recorded in 2017). And some – such as green-veined whites, Essex skippers and, of course, purple emperors – have exploded in numbers. In 2015 Neil Hulme counted 790 small skippers – a spectacular increase from the 62 he counted the previous year which was, in itself, a great year for butterflies. By 2017, brown hairstreaks – denizens of blackthorn – were rocketing, making Knepp now most likely the largest population centre of these butterflies in the UK. Purple hairstreaks are also flourishing, with more than 500 individuals counted on a single day in June 2017. This lovely blue-purple butterfly, less than half the size of a purple emperor and normally only ever seen as a speck flitting around the canopy of an oak where it feeds on honeydew, delights visitors to Knepp by regularly descending to ground level.

By 2016 our number of moth species had climbed to 441, including moths that are rapidly declining nationally, like the dusky thorn, figure of eight, cinnabar (exclusive to ragwort) and the ghost moth. On summer nights, white male ghost moths live up to their name, hovering around Hammer Pond, lekking over yellow females sitting patiently in the grass. In 2017 we were excited to find the extremely rare rush wainscot, a Red Data Book moth, whose larvae feed inside the stems of common club-rush, yellow iris and reed mace. While the names of butterflies are often disappointingly prosaic (small white and large white hardly make the heart sing) moths' names flutter with romance – from the swallow prominent, coxcomb prominent, beautiful china-mark, canary-shouldered thorn and maiden's blush to the waved black moth, whose larvae feed on fungi around rotting trees, or my favourite, the setaceous Hebrew character, named for the black mark on its forewings resembling the Hebrew letter *nun*.

Of particular interest to both conservationists and farmers are the pollinators. Surveying nine areas of the Southern Block over several days in 2015 and 2016, Dave Goulson – Professor of Biology at Sussex University, and author of *A Sting in the Tail* and *Bee Quest* (with a chapter on Knepp) – recorded sixty-two species of bee and thirty species of wasp, including seven bee and four wasp species of national conservation importance. This was a remarkable tally, in his estimation, considering that the land was little over a decade out of intensive agriculture. Colonizers of some of the rarer species could have come from miles away. Finding suitable habitat at Knepp, they have swiftly proliferated. Some, like the red bartsia bee, are specialists in particular flowers now present at Knepp. Others, like the ridge-cheeked furrow bee, need desiccation cracks in the soil to nest in – something amply provided by our clay in summer. One unusual 'solitary' bee (*Melitta europaea* – so unusual it doesn't have a common English name) likes to nest in damp or even partially flooded soils. It visits exclusively yellow loosestrife for pollen but also for floral oils with which it waterproofs its nest. And then there's the rough-backed blood bee (*Sphecodes scabricollis*), exceedingly rare across Europe as well as in the UK. Distinguished by the bright red band around its black abdomen, the tiny 6 millimetre female of the species lives up to its sinister name by entering the nests of other bees – in particular the bull-headed furrow bee – and killing the host's offspring before laying her own egg inside. Other species were surprising to find in our clay landscape. One, *Crabro scutellatus*, is associated with damp heathland; another – a very scarce sand wasp (*Gorytes laticinctus*) – with light soils. Even 'specialist' wasps and bees, it seems, can defy the neat categorizations assigned to them by science.

The multitude of insects thronging their floral hosts, skating on the water's surface tension, scuttling through undergrowth or crawling between crumbling layers of deadwood is a universe overlooked by most of us as we walk through the landscape, though it remains within the sphere of the naked eye. There is another realm of invertebrates that we cannot see at all, however, and of which we are even less aware, yet it is more fundamental to natural processes than any other – the soil itself.

Early on, we had seen dung beetles tunnelling through cow-pats and dragging nutrients into underground chambers for their larvae, and ants raising hills out of the earth, but it was evidence of the machinations of earthworms in the ground beneath our feet that signified the return of our inert, post-agricultural land to fertility. Several years into the project we started to see worm casts – tiny pyramids of worm excrement like squiggles of piped chestnut puree – erupting on the surface. In a few of the wettest areas of the Southern Block the ground is still too compacted and anaerobic after decades of farming for these surreptitious pioneers to break through but almost every-where else the earthworm has made astonishing inroads. Studies by Master's students from Imperial College London in 2013, using as a baseline neighbouring farmland with the same soils and under the same system of conventional agriculture as previ-ously at Knepp, found a significant rise in the abundance and variety of all three categories of earthworms – epigeic (surface dwellers found in leaf litter and rotting logs), endogeic (soil dwellers that burrow horizontally and rarely come to the sur-face), and anecic (deep, vertical burrowers that leave their casts on the surface) – in all three areas of the project. In total, we have now found nineteen species of earthworm – a diversity that, according to soil scientists, is extraordinarily high.

Earthworms struggle to survive under intensive farming. Epigeic worms, deprived of surface compost, are virtually non-existent in agricultural fields; while, year on year, the process of ploughing and rotavating chops up anecic worms and exposes endogeic worms to predation. But simply disturbing the soil, whether by spade or rake in the garden or by mouldboard, ridging- and chisel-plough in the fields, breaks up the organic matter that sustains ground-living worms. Soil compaction caused by farm machinery also causes problems for worms. Applying chemical fertilizers and pesticides is more harmful still, suppressing many beneficial types of bacteria, mycorrhizal fungi, protozoa, nematodes and other living organisms in the soil, including worms. High-nitrogen fertilizers are prized by golf courses not just for establishing luminous billiard-table greens but as the surest way of eradicating bothersome earthworms whose casts can get in the way of a putt.

Over the years modern farming has reduced soil to what Elaine Ingham, one of the world's leading microbiologists, dismisses as 'dirt' – a sterile medium in which plants struggle to grow without artificial fertilizers. It is a self-perpetuating cycle of destruction and chemical dependence. Without soil organisms and soil structure to retain them water and nutrients leach away, and the soil compacts and becomes prone to erosion. Muddy run-off spreading like ink blots from the mouths of rivers into the sea is a sight familiar to aeroplane passengers anywhere in the world. According to the Food and Agriculture Organization of the United Nations' report in 2015 on the Status of World Soil Resources, a third of land across the planet is moderately to highly degraded due to erosion, salinization, compaction, acidification and chemical pollution, and around 25–40 billion tonnes of topsoil are lost to erosion every year. Land degradation costs up to $10.6 trillion a year, equivalent to 17 per cent of global gross domestic product. In the UK, that cost is between £900 million and £1.4 billion a year – half of which is caused by the loss of organic matter, over a third by compaction and about 13 per cent through erosion. In England recently, an estimated 2,000 tonnes of topsoil slipped into the River Wye during a single rainstorm. That soil is gone from the land for ever, carried out to sea. The depletion of topsoil is so severe in the UK that in 2014 *Farmers' Weekly* announced that we have only a hundred harvests left in the country.

The humble earthworm may seem an unlikely saviour but it could quite possibly turn the crisis around. Throughout history, ancient civilizations have valued earthworms as champions of healthy soils. Aristotle described them as 'the intestines of the earth' in the fourth century BC. Cleopatra, ruler of Egypt in the first century BC, recognizing the earthworms' contribution to Nile Valley agriculture, declared them to be sacred, and any harm done to them punishable by death. In the late nineteenth century Charles Darwin, who devoted the best part of his declining years to earthworms, identified them, in effect, as ecosystems engineers: 'It may be doubted whether there are many other animals which have played so important a part in the history of the world, as have these lowly, organised creatures.' Based on enterprising experiments in his garden at Down House in Kent he claimed that their role as digesters of vegetative debris was fundamental to the creation as well as the fertility and friability of our soils. 'All the vegetable mould over the whole country has passed many times through, and will again pass many times through, the intestinal canals of worms.' A single acre of earth, he calculated, can contain over 50,000 worms which, in a year, can move almost twenty tons of soil.

Darwin's estimations of earthworm populations, improbable though they seemed at the time, are modest compared to twentieth-century findings in some parts of the world. Scientists have counted 670,000 worms per acre of topsoil in tropical rainforests in Malaysia and an incredible 8,000,000 per acre in a New Zealand pasture. In the Nile Valley, earthworms in one acre deposit up to 1,000 tons of casts per year – a process which goes some way to explaining the astonishing fertility of Egypt's agricultural land.

From the 1950s, however, industrial farming the world over was convinced it could function without worms or any of the other organisms that naturally inhabit the soil. It is only now, faced with diminishing topsoil, declining fertility and rising costs of inputs, that soil analysts are beginning to rethink the modern agricultural approach and consider ways of employing earthworms and other naturally occurring organisms to improve our soil and drive a more sustainable system of agriculture.

Since Darwin, worms have been desperately neglected by

science. That they aerate the soil, acting as sub-surface ploughs and rotavators, is well known to any gardener. Their burrows become tubular pathways which also facilitate the movement and storage of water – leading to improved drainage as well as retention of moisture in the soil. They also enable the downward passage of plant roots. This tunnelling action, on its own, defends soils against flooding and erosion.

But it is only in the last couple of decades that oligochaetologists – earthworm scientists – have begun to understand more about the biology of earthworms and the miracles they can perform. As they travel through the soil, worms excrete coelomic fluid – mucus that helps them move, digest, respire, hydrate and detoxify. This mucus, rich in glycoproteins, lines the walls of their burrows and encourages the growth of bacteria and fungi. Bacteria also thrive inside the worm's intestinal tract. Up to fifty different species of bacteria have been found inside the common earthworm, also known as the lob worm (*Lumbricus terrestris*).

Bacteria and other soil microbes are enablers of plant growth. They mineralize nutrients in the soil, breaking down soluble and insoluble organic matter into inorganic forms that plants can use. Some convert organic compounds like amino acids into ammonium and nitrates, the form of nitrogen that plants use to build up proteins, and some fix nitrogen in a plant's roots. Others break down carbon, sulphur, hydrogen and other compounds into an absorbable form for plants, while at the same time stabilizing and making these nutrients available in the soil for longer periods. Soil microbes produce enzymes which catalyse the mineralization of phosphorus, another nutrient that is of high importance to plant growth. Different microbes switch on and off in response to different temperatures and moisture levels, affording a greater level of resilience for soil and plants as the conditions change hour by hour, day by day and year by year. They are present in healthy soils in astonishing diversity and astronomical amounts. A single handful of soil can hold billions of bacteria, millions of microscopic nematodes and protozoa, thousands of mites, collembolans and enchytraeid worms, hundreds of species of fungi and algae, as well as countless springtails, tiny spiders, ants, termites, beetles, centipedes and millipedes – the whole gamut of life that makes up what scientists call the 'Soil Food Web'. In that handful of soil are more organisms than the total number of human beings who have ever lived on earth.

Not all soil organisms are beneficial. Some spread pathogens that can kill or cause a plant to wilt and collapse. In some conditions, particularly in anaerobic, waterlogged soil – soil that is generally devoid of worms – denitrifying bacteria can break down nitrates and return nitrogen to the air. Many human diseases originate in the soil, from fungi, viruses, protozoans and, especially, bacteria that spend some part of their life cycle there.

Worms, however, seem to have a selective effect on the kinds of bacteria that prevail in the soil. Not all bacteria can survive a worm's digestion. Those that are harmful to the worm tend to be killed while those that are beneficial reproduce rapidly, so there are many more of these beneficial bacteria coming out of the worm than went in at the beginning. This bias can change the very nature of the soil. Studies using worms in sewage-treatment plants have proved their ability to eradicate harmful bacteria such as *E. coli* and salmonella, converting raw sewage into nutrient-rich organic matter that is safe enough to be spread on agricultural land.

Different species of worm host different bacteria, so agronomists believe it may one day be possible to select for particular bacteria – those that will benefit particular crops – by inoculating the soil with particular types of earthworm. This research is still at an early stage but other studies have quantified the more basic benefits of worms for agriculture. According to a 2014 report by the Soil Biology group of Holland's Wageningen University – a research team that included scientists from the United States and Brazil – earthworm presence increases crop yields by 25 per cent on average, and above-ground biomass by 23 per cent.

Worm casts on their own provide a kind of super-fertilizer – a manure that holds up to five times the nitrogen, seven times the soluble phosphate, three times the magnesium, one and a half times the calcium and eleven times more potassium than the surrounding topsoil. Elaine Ingham, the queen of vermicompost, whom we met one blustery January day as keynote speaker of the 2015 Oxford Real Farming Conference, on her way to advise struggling potato-growers in Jersey, advocates 'compost tea' – a dilution of worm castings – to restore microbial life to depleted soils. She finds it inexplicable that conventional farming continues to champion expensive chemical fertilizers to the neglect of the natural potential of the soil, and to consider just three basic elements – nitrogen, phosphorus and potassium – as necessary for growing crops.

Artificial fertilizers are not only costly – a crippling expense for the world's poorest farmers – they are also extremely inefficient. Conventional agriculture uses more than 150 million tonnes of chemical fertilizers (almost exclusively nitrogen, phosphorus and potassium, or 'NPK') every year, yet much of this is wasted. Often, fertilizers are applied at the wrong time, when the plants are not taking up nutrients, or applied in excess of plant demands. But it is also a question of biology. Much of the phosphorus in chemical fertilizers quickly binds to minerals in the soil and becomes unavailable to plants, unless there are micro-organisms present in the soil to convert it. Without a healthy soil biology up to half of nitrogen inputs are lost, washed into rivers and the sea where they cause algal blooms which suck oxygen out of the water and suffocate other forms of life. Every spring, around 16,800 square kilometres (6,500 square miles) of the Gulf of Mexico becomes an anoxic 'dead zone' caused by fertilizer run-off from the Mississippi. There are over four hundred of these dead zones in coastal waters worldwide, including huge areas of the Black Sea that may never fully recover from the catastrophic algal blooms – the 'red tides' – caused by massive agricultural discharges in the 1970s.

Nitrates are also lost from the soil in the form of gas. Under

waterlogged or saturated soil conditions some bacteria transform nitrate fertilizer into nitrous oxide, a greenhouse gas, each
molecule of which is almost 300 times more powerful than
carbon dioxide in its greenhouse warming effect. Nitrogen is
lost from the soil as ammonia gas, too, which is produced from
the volatilization of urea, the preferred fertilizer of many farmers. The cost to the world, from the effect on people's lungs to
the depletion of the ozone layer, from dead zones in coastal seas
to polluted drinking water and damaged soils, is astronomical.
According to the European Nitrogen Assessment published in
2011, pollution caused by nitrogen-based compounds cost the
European Union €70–320 billion a year. The bill for the whole
world could top €1 trillion.

Apart from the environmental damage they cause, synthetic
fertilizers are also limited in the range of nutrients they provide
for crops. They can replenish macronutrients, like nitrogen
and phosphorus, but not micronutrients such as magnesium,
calcium, zinc, sulphur and selenium that are also taken up by
plants. In intensive farming, repeated harvesting strips the soil
of these micronutrients, and eventually crop yields begin to
decline. Elaine Ingham points to the panoply of nutrients in a
healthy soil that micro-organisms make available to plants, all
of which are likely to be important, in some way, for human
health. 'The more we learn,' she says, 'the more we realize that
everything is important. The list of elements we measure for
soil health will probably increase until it includes the entire
periodic table. There's a reason for yttrium on this planet. We
don't need much, but we probably need some.'

Even as munitions factories swung into agro-chemical production after the Second World War, scientists voiced their
concerns about the declining nutritional value of food grown
with artificial fertilizers. This has been one of modern farming's
most persistent blind spots. A landmark study by the Department of Chemistry and Biochemistry at the University of Texas
in 2004 analysed US Department of Agriculture nutritional data
from both 1950 and 1999 for forty-three different vegetables

and fruits and found 'reliable declines' in the amount of protein, calcium, phosphorus, iron, riboflavin (vitamin B_2) and vitamin C over the past half century. A similar study in Britain using nutrient data from 1930 to 1980 found that in twenty vegetables the average calcium content had declined 19 per cent, iron 22 per cent and potassium 14 per cent. Another study, analysing data from *The Composition of Foods*, a reference manual published by UK Government biochemists every few years, identified that during the period 1940–1991, potatoes had lost 47 per cent of their copper, 45 per cent of their iron and 35 per cent of their calcium, while the declines for carrots were greater still. Broccoli – considered a superfood rich in micronutrients and antioxidants – suffered an 80 per cent drop in copper, with the calcium content a quarter of what it was in 1940. The same was true for tomatoes. We would have needed to eat ten or more tomatoes in 1991 to receive the same amount of copper as we would have derived from one tomato in 1940. Yet another study calculated we have to eat eight oranges today to receive the same amount of vitamin A as our grandparents did from eating one. Levels of other nutrients, not measured in the first half of the twentieth century, such as magnesium, zinc and vitamins B_6 and E, are also likely to have declined considerably.

On their own, without the aid of bacteria, mycorrhizal fungi and all the other microbes and animals – the worms, protozoa, nematodes, mites, springtails and the like – that occur naturally in the soil, plants are less able to absorb these essential nutrients and the effects on human health are only just being considered. US government figures suggest a correlation between declining magnesium levels in foods like spinach, cabbage, tomato and lettuce in the American diet and increases in deficiency conditions like asthma, cardiovascular diseases and bronchitic and orthopaedic deformities. Meanwhile pesticide residues, nitrogen concentrations, linked with an increased risk of certain cancers, and toxic heavy metals like cadmium in our food are also likely to be having a detrimental effect on our health. Livestock fed on intensively grown crops will be affected in the same way.

Inoculating the soil with bacteria- and fungi-rich vermicompost, a practice that began amongst gardeners, is now being used in large-scale agriculture in the United States, Canada, Italy, Japan, Malaysia and the Philippines. It has resulted in dramatic increases in yields in organic systems and higher nutrient take-up in crops, and shown potential for pest control as well. Sap-sucking insects, in particular, appear to be repelled from plants grown in vermicompost. Studies are being carried out to see if a leafhopper called the glassy-winged sharpshooter, which has spread phylloxera through the vineyards of California, may also be deterred from attacking vines fed with vermicompost.

Even more astonishing, perhaps, than the earthworm's role in the plant-nutrient cycle are recent findings from Oxford University that identify the ability of the earthworm and its associated battalions of bacteria to clean the soil of toxic pollutants. In 2000 the UK pledged to phase out the use of a dangerous synthetic chemical, polychlorinated biphenyl (PCB), commonly used in paints, dyes, plastics and electrical equipment. PCBs accumulate in the fatty tissues of animals and humans, affecting the nervous system and brain functions, and inducing genetic defects and cancers. The clean-up operation from PCBs on the land presents huge logistical problems. The conventional approach is to excavate contaminated soil and store it in large containers to be taken, eventually, to landfill or for incineration. The discovery that earthworms can metabolize toxins like PCBs, as well as DDT and organochlorides like dieldrin (originally used as an insecticide and banned in the UK in 1989), provides a simple, low-cost solution to the detoxification of our soils. Worms are now being used in the restoration of open-cast mining and industrial sites as both creators of soil and removers of pollution – taking the concept of ecosystem engineer to an entirely new level.

So it was with a deeper appreciation for earthworms that we celebrated their return to work at Knepp. In these mysterious, deaf, blind, spineless, toothless creatures we have another – and perhaps our most crucial – keystone species, one that can bring about changes at the microscopic level that utterly transform life above ground.

Of the three broad categories of earthworm it is the vertical-burrowing anecic worm – the one on which Darwin focused his experiments – that seems to be producing the surprises at Knepp. Scientists had anticipated at the beginning of the project that anecic worms would take about a year to advance a single metre into our degraded post-agricultural soils. At this rate it would be a century or more before they progressed a hundred metres out from the old hedgerows, if they had managed to survive there at all. Yet after only a little more than a decade we are now finding worm casts in the middle of the old arable fields, well over 50 metres from the hedge-line.

We are desperately keen to have proper soil analysis and monitoring carried out at Knepp because it seems the implications of these findings are huge. If soils can be restored at very little cost by a few decades of rewilding there could be enormous benefits for agriculture. A former senior advisor for Natural England, Gwil Wren, has suggested the idea of 'pop-up Knepps'. An area of degraded land could be rewilded for, say, twenty, thirty, forty or fifty years or more – enough time to regenerate the soil and provide a period of emerging scrub habitat for birds and other wildlife – and then be returned to agricultural production. The land to be rewilded would be strategically planned over a much larger area – such as a river catchment, selecting specific areas that could become stepping stones or corridors of nature to re-connect the landscape. As one piece of land is taken out of rewilding and returned to sustainable agriculture, another in the vicinity embarks on re-wilding; ensuring the same amount of land remains under rewilding to balance the amount of land under agriculture – comparable to the traditional rotational system of leaving fields fallow, only much more extensive and on a longer time-scale. Returning scrub to conditions for agriculture is remarkably easy with modern machinery. In 2011, in preparation for a biomass plantation trial with the Forestry Commission, a single gigantic forestry mulcher turned 15 hectares of scrub at Knepp (a separate piece of agricultural land abandoned at the same time as the rewilding project land) into a fine, workable tilth in just a few hours. Since it amalgamates the mulch into just the top 30–50 millimetres of soil, the process also has minimal impact on existing earthworm populations and their unseen companions, as evidenced by the numbers of snipe and wood-cock feeding on invertebrates in the soil amongst our plantation eucalypts.

Science is only just beginning to get to grips with the universe of soil organisms, the services they perform and how they interact with each other and affect the plant life above them. For decades, research into soil biology – 'one of the most neglected components of the global system', according to envir-onmentalist Tony Juniper – has been woefully underfunded, sidelined by other, less complex fields of natural science, sexy projects like space technology, and the agro-industry's funding of research into artificial systems. Only now are scientific tech-niques coming into play that allow the observation of soil microbes – microbial 'dark matter' – in their natural environ-ment rather than within the limiting scope of the laboratory. 99 per cent of microbes will not grow in laboratory conditions. In 2015 the journal *Nature* reported the first discovery for thirty years of a new antibiotic in the soil – teixobactin – capable of killing *Mycobacterium tuberculosis*, *Clostridium difficile* and methicillin-resistant *Staphylococcus aureus*. Most antibiotics are derived from soil microbes and the great hope is that now many other antibiotics new to science can be uncovered in the soil in this way.

At last, things seem to be changing. Several of the United Nations' Sustainable Development Goals for 2016 to 2030 relate to soils, and the UN's Intergovernmental Technical Panel on Soils' report documents how soils are changing globally and the consequences of this for humanity. According to a report published by the Economics of Land Degradation Initiative in September 2015, if sustainable land management was rolled out around the world, as much as $75.6 trillion could be added to the global economy every year through jobs and increased agricultural output. In the UK, major funding programmes – like the Natural Environment Research Council's Soil Security Programme, and the Biotechnology and Biological Sciences Research Council's SARISA (Soil and Rhizosphere Interactions for Sustainable Agri-ecosystems) programme – focus on the biology of soil and how to integrate this understanding into agriculture.

For Ted Green, the most exciting evidence of recovering soils at Knepp is the eruption of fruiting bodies of fungi. Walking with him along the edge of Hammer Pond in the Southern Block we discovered the rare *Boletus mendax*, a mycorrhizal mushroom associated with old oaks that, he suggested, could have waited as mycelia amongst the trees' roots for decades until the right conditions above and below ground enabled it to grow. In a stand of ten-year-old sallow we were surprised by a semi-circle of milk-caps and a cluster of red fly agaric – the lurid red hallucinogenic mushroom of fairy stories. These are Ted's 'recyclers', the agents of decay. They release enzymes that can break down some of the most durable substances in nature – the fibrous lignin and cellulose of plants, the hard shells of insects, animal bones and even broken rock in the soil.

Encouraging, too, is the presence of orchids – southern marsh, early purple and common spotted orchids, and the much rarer bird's nest and greater butterfly. These are plants that depend on an exclusive, symbiotic relationship with mycorrhizae. Orchid seeds do not contain nutrition to support germination. This gives them the advantage of having minuscule seeds – weighing only a few millionths of a gram – which they can spread far and wide on the wind. Germination depends entirely on mycorrhizae which colonize the seeds and supply them with food. The appearance of orchids is visible evidence that creeping underground mycorrhizae, Ted's 'food-gatherers', are spreading their web beneath our fields. Like soil bacteria, the mycorrhizae are freeing up essential elements in the soil, phosphorus, copper, calcium, magnesium, zinc and iron, making them available in a form that plants can absorb.

But mycorrhizae also contribute a final compelling argument to the value of rewilding the soil – that of carbon sequestration. One of the secrets, as Graham Harvey explains in his book *Carbon Fields* (2008), is an extraordinary substance called 'glomalin'. For such a revolutionary substance glomalin is still, amazingly, little discussed. It was discovered in 1996 by soil scientist Sara Wright at the US Agricultural Research Service. A sticky glycoprotein, it is produced by mycorrhizal fungi from carbon extracted from the roots of plants. Its gluey proteins coat the hair-like filaments or hyphae of the mycorrhizae, protecting them from decomposition and microbial attack. Acting as microscopic underground conduits, the hyphae extend the reach of a plant's roots to areas in the soil that the roots are unable to exploit on their own. Glomalin reinforces the hyphae, sealing the conduits to prevent leakage and ensuring the efficient transport of distant water and nutrients back to the plant.

Glomalin has profound effects on soil as well. As plants grow, the fungal hyphae creep down the plant's roots establishing new networks near the extending tips. Higher up the root, the defunct hyphae slough off their protective glomalin, which falls back into the soil and attaches to particles of sand, silt, clay and organic matter, forming lumps of soil, or 'aggregates', allowing water, air and nutrients to infiltrate the spaces between. Protected by their tough, waxy coating of glomalin these aggregates are what give soil its structure – the kind of friable tilth a farmer or gardener crumbles appreciatively between their fingers.

Glomalin is extraordinarily durable. Tests have shown it can survive intact in the soil for more than forty years. Its very toughness seems to be the reason it has gone undetected by science for so long. Back in her laboratory in Beltsville, Maryland,

Wright found she could only separate glomalin from the soil by immersing it in citrate solution and subjecting it to intense heat for over an hour.

Glomalin is made up of protein and carbohydrate sub-units, both containing carbon, the total of which comprises 20–40 per cent of the molecule – a considerable proportion compared to the 8 per cent in humic acid, the element once thought of as the main storage material for soil carbon. Aided by glomalin, the 'superglue of the soil', aggregates protect organic carbon from decay by soil microbes. More mycorrhizae in the soil produce more stable aggregates, and more aggregates result in higher soil carbon storage. Amazingly, the world's soils hold more carbon as organic matter than all the vegetation on the planet, including rainforest. 82 per cent of carbon in the terrestrial biosphere – that is, the part of the earth's land surface including the adjacent atmosphere where life exists – is in the soil.

One of the remarkable features of mycorrhizae is their ability to respond to rising carbon-dioxide levels in the atmosphere by increasing their production of glomalin. In a three-year experiment, scientists at the University of California used outdoor chambers to control carbon-dioxide levels on small areas of natural grassland. They found that when the gas reached a concentration of 670 parts per million – the level it is predicted to reach by the end of this century – the fungal hyphae grew three times as long and produced five times more glomalin than those exposed to today's levels of carbon dioxide.

Improving the structure of our soils and returning unproductive agricultural land to permanent pasture could be a crucial weapon in the battle against rising levels of CO_2. According to the Royal Society, carbon capture by the world's farmlands, if they were better managed, could total as much as 10 billion tonnes of carbon dioxide a year – more than the annual carbon-dioxide accumulation in the atmosphere. Carbon Farmers of America, a company selling 'Carbon Sinks' to clients interested in helping reverse climate change, endorse this. They estimate that if organic matter in the world's farmed soils was increased by as little as 1.6 per cent, the problem of climate change would be solved. Alan Savory, Zimbabwean ecologist, proponent of holistic land management and, in particular, a rotational, natural grazing system with the power to return areas of desert, or 'brittle zones', to productive grassland (a system that has come to be known as 'mob grazing'), goes one step further. He estimates that restoring the world's 5 billion hectares (19 million square miles) of degraded grasslands to functioning ecosystems could return ten or more gigatonnes of excess atmospheric carbon to the terrestrial sink annually. This, he claims, would lower greenhouse-gas concentrations to pre-industrial levels in a matter of decades.

Recently, after the Paris Climate Change talks in 2015, the French launched the '4 per 1000' initiative. Its aim is less ambitious but the reasoning is the same: the quantity of carbon contained in the atmosphere increases by 4.3 billion tonnes every year. The world's soils contain 1,500 billion tonnes of carbon in the form of organic material. Increasing the quantity of carbon contained in soils by just 0.4 per cent a year – through restoring and improving degraded agricultural lands – would halt the annual increase of CO_2 in the atmosphere. This would go a considerable way to achieving the Climate Change objective of limiting the global temperature increase to 1.5/2 °C, while at the same time increasing global food security by improving soil fertility and stability.

The potential for rewilding projects like Knepp to provide carbon sequestration is of increasing interest to our own government, under pressure to meet its ambitious target of reducing carbon emissions by 57 per cent of 1990 levels by 2030. In 2012, researchers from Bournemouth University and the Centre for Ecology and Hydrology prepared a report for DEFRA looking at large-scale restoration projects such as Ennerdale, the Great Fen, the Frome catchment, Pumlumon in Wales and Knepp. They quantified eight key 'ecosystems services' – carbon sequestration, recreation, aesthetics, flood protection, provision of food, energy/fuel, raw materials/fibre and fresh water – provided by these projects. Scores were awarded from 0 (not relevant) to 5 (very high importance).

Under the previous intensive farming system Knepp scored 1 for carbon sequestration, 3 for recreation, 5 for aesthetics, 1 for flood protection, 5 for provision of food, 2 for energy/fuel, 3 for raw materials and 2 for fresh water. Under rewilding, most of these scores have risen significantly, up to 5 for carbon sequestration, 5 for recreation (and this was before we began our eco-tourism business), 4 for flood protection, 5 for energy/ fuel and 4 for raw materials. Provision of food remained the same with a top score of 5, and so – interestingly – did aesthetics. The fresh water score – concerned with water reserves for human consumption – remains the same at 2, as we don't have reservoirs. But we are able to show that rewilding Knepp has improved water quality, something that is of huge ecological importance. Much of the water entering Knepp comes from adjacent farms and built-up areas and is significantly polluted. Testing in 2016 gave all standing water on the Estate the highest reading for water purity, indicating that our land is now providing an effective system of filtration and purification.

The greatest leap in the DEFRA assessment is in carbon storage – an estimated 51 per cent rise resulting from the 'increased carbon storage capacity of neutral grassland and broadleaved woodland under rewilding'. Over a period of fifty years, the report estimated, Knepp Wildland will have stored an additional £14 million worth of carbon.

The great concerns of our time – climate change, natural resources, food production, water control and conservation, and human health – all boil down to the condition of the soil. It seems we are, at last, beginning to reappraise the essential medium of earth's biology, that thin, living skin. We are starting to appreciate its potential for doing many of the things we thought, arrogantly, we could do on our own. By returning to the soil we are beginning, after centuries of exploitation and technological hubris, to seek an understanding of how our species can survive in the world not just for the next few decades but for the thousands of years to come, how we can combine our creative intelligence and expertise with systems that have benefitted, unlike us, from millions of years of R and D. It is perhaps unsurprising that the Latin word for soil – 'humus' – gives us 'human' and 'humility'. The soil is, quite literally, what grounds us.

For Charlie and me it is the closing of the circle. It was a conversation about mycorrhizal fungi that set us thinking in the first place. Now, nearly two decades later, rewilding has returned us to a deeper appreciation of the ground beneath our feet. It is the invisible foundation of all that we see emerging before our eyes; it is the great recycler, the connector, the key to life itself.

17

The Value of Nature

No man is an Iland, intire of it selfe, everyman is a peece
of the Continent, a part of the maine.

> John Donne, Meditation XVII,
> *Devotions upon Emergent Occasions*, 1624

We have come to see ourselves as lords and masters of the
Earth, entitled to plunder her at will. The sickness evident
in the soil, in the water, in the air and in all forms of life are
symptoms that reflect the violence present in our hearts.
We have forgotten that we ourselves are dust of the Earth;
that we breathe her air and receive life from her waters.

> Encyclical from Pope Francis, 2015

Gradually, ten years after we started rewilding, local criticism
of Knepp Wildland began to simmer down as people grew more
familiar with it and the vegetation became more complex and
established. Aesthetic sensibilities, as the DEFRA ecosystems
services report suggested, began to shift and even the wild look
of the Southern Block no longer seemed such an affront. In
2009 we had added another 4 miles of permissive footpaths to
the existing 16 miles of public Rights of Way on the estate to
help connect the routes together, and designated an additional
4.7 miles for the Toll Rides Off-road Trust for horse riders.
Today, many people traversing the rewilding project tell us they

find it as pleasing, in its own way, as the Repton park or even the former farmland.

Exciting though it is, we feel Knepp is still not wild enough. There is so much more it could, and should, be. One day, we hope to have wild boar and beavers; perhaps even bison and elk. And to be able to leave carcasses out on the land, providing a source of food for neglected scavengers that would also return minerals to the soil. We would prefer to shoot our cattle and pigs on site, to save them the stress of transportation to a slaughterhouse. And to be able to make wonderful charcuterie from our breeding herd of Exmoors. We haven't lost hope for land bridges to connect up the three areas of the project; or for more of our neighbours to join in. We dream of leading safaris from Knepp across rewilded land all the way to the sea, linking habitats from the clay to the chalk to the shingle; for our long-horns to be browsing in our sallow scrub one week and seaweed on the beaches of Shoreham the next. And to reintroduce species that are unlikely to be able to come back on their own. One day there could be osprey snatching fish from the lake, and white storks nesting on the castle turrets and the square tower of Shipley church. This is just the beginning.

Our wildlife successes have, no doubt, been largely respon-sible for people's change of heart. There is plenty for naturalists to celebrate, but it was the resurgence of particularly rare and charismatic species like the nightingale, purple emperor and turtle dove that began to attract media attention and persuade the public at large that there was method in our madness.

Some enthusiastic responses, however, have not been so welcome. To some, it seems, the idea of rewilding is a licence to behave wildly. Dog-walkers, exhilarated by the unbridled landscape, often allow their pets to rampage off the footpaths, chasing the free-roaming herds and putting up ground-nesting and water birds. It is a constant surprise to us how many people do this, even those we know well, and that they never consider themselves or their dogs to be in the wrong. No association is made between their beloved 'letting off steam' and the impact on wildlife. In a depleted environment beset by pollution, fragmentation and climate change, uncontrolled dogs are yet another burden, to add to predation by free-roaming domestic cats, putting unwarranted pressure on wildlife.

The larger animals are sometimes targets too. When one of our older sows tried to protect her piglets from repeated harassment by a pair of dogs, she charged at the owners who 'feared for their lives'. In an effort to staunch the escalating drama and protect the long-term interests of the project we decided not to contest the owners' allegations, though there had been witnesses on several occasions. Instead, we took the sow off to slaughter. Once, we encountered a father and son on horseback living the cowboy dream, chasing our cattle at break-neck speed through the Southern Block, their dogs snapping at the calves' heels. Poaching is a distressing occurrence. We've found snares set in the Southern Block, fallow shot with a .22 rifle, often left hideously wounded, and the local abattoir reported that a couple of our Tamworths had air-rifle pellets embedded under their skin. One year, in a bizarre reversal of 'rustling', six unwanted, malnourished sheep were dumped in the Southern Block.

Lack of empathy and knowledge of nature seems to be at the root of much of this behaviour, and again it separates us from the era of our grandparents and great-grandparents. How many trees, flowers, birds and insects can an average person identify today – let alone know the breeding season for ground-nesting birds or how to pick up a slow-worm without harming it? In 2007 the *Oxford Junior Dictionary*, aimed at seven-year-olds, dropped 'almond', 'blackberry' and 'crocus' in favour of 'analogue', 'block graph' and 'celebrity'. The 2012 edition continued writing nature out of young minds, replacing 'acorn', 'buttercup' and 'conker' with 'attachment', 'blog' and 'chat room'. Instead of 'catkin', 'cauliflower', 'chestnut' and 'clover' they now have 'cut and paste', 'broadband' and 'analogue'. Heron, herring, kingfisher, lark, leopard, lobster, magpie, minnow, mussel, newt, otter, ox, oyster and panther have all been deleted.

The *OJD*'s edit mirrors the shift in children's perceptions and activities over the past few decades. Since the 1950s, 80 per cent of the population in the UK have lived in towns and cities but only a generation ago, 40 per cent of children still regularly played in natural areas. This has dropped to 10 per cent today, with 40 per cent of children never playing outdoors at all. When I was a child it was normal to cycle miles from home to meet up with friends. Weekends were spent scavenging on waste ground and gravel pits, damming streams, building dens, making camp fires, swimming in rivers and ponds – none of it under adult supervision. Today's children, even if they live in the countryside, are under almost constant surveillance, protected from the perils of adventure and independence. A fear factor has entered our lives, even though there is no evidence to suggest the world is more dangerous for children than it was fifty years ago. In 1971, 80 per cent of eight- and nine-year-olds walked to school alone. By 1990 this had dropped to 9 per cent and now it is even lower.

This 'extinction of experience' in childhood has a direct bearing on attitudes to the environment in later life. Studies show that children who spent time in green spaces between the ages of seven and twelve tend to think of nature as magical. As adults they are the people most likely to be indignant about lack of nature protection, while those who have had no such experience tend to regard nature as hostile or irrelevant and are indifferent to its loss. By expurgating nature from children's lives we are depriving the environment of its champions for the future.

But we are also doing something devastating and costly to society itself. On grounds of health alone, nature provides a service we cannot afford to ignore. Evidence shows that people are healthier, physically fitter and better adjusted, and children's behaviour and schoolwork improve, if they have access to the countryside, parks or gardens. According to Public Health England, poor air quality in urban areas is said to be a factor in 29,000 premature deaths in the UK every year. A recent report in the *Lancet* associates the noise and air pollution of busy roads with Alzheimer's disease. Fresh air, long considered a tonic, is not just about avoiding pollution. Toxicologists are discovering that air provided by nature is loaded with microbes produced by plants, fungi and bacteria that are beneficial to health and boost the immune system. Even the remote sight of nature has curative effects. Health services have found that hospital patients need fewer painkillers after surgery and recover much faster if they have views of nature from their beds. In 2007 Natural England and the RSPB compiled studies from the UK, US and Europe in a report called 'Natural Thinking', highlighting the effects of nature on mental health. One in six of the UK population suffers from depression, anxiety, stress, phobias, suicidal impulses, obsessive compulsive disorders or panic attacks – sometimes in deadly combination. This costs the National Health Service £12.5 billion, the economy £23.1 billion in lost output and £41.8 billion in the human costs of reduced quality of life and loss of life. The studies show that symptoms of all these disorders are alleviated with time spent in nature. Measurements of blood pressure, pulse rates and cortisol levels of young adults demonstrate a decrease in anger and an increase in positive mood when walking in a nature reserve, while the reverse is true walking in an urban environment. Low levels of self-discipline, impulsive behaviour, aggression, hyperactivity and inattention in young people all improve through contact with nature. Studies on children who were being bullied, punished, relocated or suffering from family strife all showed that they benefitted from closeness to nature, both in levels of stress and self-worth.

It is perhaps unsurprising that so many of the naturalists and environmental journalists who walk through our door discovered nature either as unhappy or restless youngsters or in moments of crisis in later life. Many – like Matthew Oates, Ted Green, Dave Goulson, Peter Marren, Mike McCarthy, George Monbiot, Patrick Barkham, Chris Packham and Simon Barnes – have written movingly about nature's ability to restore a sense of connection and balance the mind, and for those of us with access to this natural health service, self-prescription at moments of stress is instinctive. In late July 2010, barely a week before the end of my mother's life and finding the strain hard to bear, I left her bedside in Dorset for a day or two at home. In search of a distraction Charlie walked me to Spring Wood in the middle of the park, where an extraordinary spectacle had just materialized. Through shafts of light angled through the 140-year-old oaks dozens of silver-washed fritillary butterflies were looping through their courtship display.

Our largest fritillary, once found as far north as Scotland and in numbers so profuse it was common to see forty on a single bramble bush, the silver-washed was, until recently, unknown beyond a line between the River Mersey and the Wash. The crash of the population was linked, as with the white admiral and pearl-bordered fritillary, to the demise of coppicing. Thankfully it is now on the increase and once again moving north, having recently recolonized much of East Anglia. It has also reappeared at Knepp. Spring Wood, un-coppiced for generations, had been a closed-canopy oak plantation for most of the twentieth century but at the start of the park restoration we had thinned it in accordance with the Repton ethos and now the butterflies had what they needed: well-spaced oaks, the deep crevices in their bark a place for laying eggs; and, in dappled shade protected by low-lying brambles, a carpet of violets – food source for their caterpillars.

Deep, rich orange and speckled with black, every now and again a flick of their wings flashed an underside of green and mother-of-pearl – the silver wash that gives the fritillaries their name. The female flies straight and level, the slow semaphore of her wing-beats and the scent from the tip of her abdomen exuding allure. The male swoops in tight loops under and up in front of her, stalling so she can pass beneath him through a shower of intoxicating scent-scales shed from his forewings. Nothing, I felt, could have encouraged me at that moment beyond shafts of sunlight spun with the dust of butterflies.

For Harvard biologist E. O. Wilson the human connection with nature – something he calls 'biophilia', the 'rich, natural pleasure that comes from being surrounded by living organisms' – is rooted in our evolution. We have been hunter-gathers for 99 per cent of our genetic history, totally and intimately involved with the natural world. For a million years our survival depended on our ability to read the weather, the stars and the species around us, to navigate, empathize and cooperate with our environment. The need to relate to the landscape and to other forms of life – whether one considers this urge aesthetic, emotional, intellectual, cognitive or even spiritual – is in our genes. Sever that connection and we are floating in a world where our deepest sense of ourselves is lost.

Stephen and Rachel Kaplan take the psychological implications of this dislocation further. Their research, begun in the 1980s, focuses on the burden that living outside the natural world imposes on the brain. Modern life, loaded with stimuli, multiple forms of communication and information requiring rapid processing and selection, demands what they call 'directed attention' from the right frontal cortex of the brain – the same part of the brain that appears to be affected in children with attention deficit hyperactivity disorder. This kind of focused attention is tiring and requires enormous effort to block out distractions, resulting in symptoms of impatience, planning impairment, indecision and irritability. The natural environment, on the other hand, holds our attention indirectly, providing what the Kaplans call 'soft fascination', a broad absorption that demands little or no effort and provides plenty of space for reflection and mental recovery. Their studies showed that even comparatively effortless pastimes like listening to music or watching TV are not as effective as nature at clearing the mind and recovering the powers of direct attention. There is an evolutionary explanation here, too: being focused on any subject or activity too closely or for too long would have rendered early humans vulnerable to attack. Much less costly, in terms of brain energy, would have been the broader, softer 'indirect attention' involved in gathering food, looking after animals and making things, all of which allow the mind to keep a weather eye out for danger – a state of relaxed alertness close to what Buddhists would call kinetic meditation or mindfulness.

Other research by Roger Ulrich, the pioneer of evidence-based healthcare design, suggests that our responses to nature, and in particular the ability to be calmed and reassured by particular natural settings and views, are located in a much older, deeper part of the brain – the limbic system that generates our survival reflexes. Evolution, he suggests, would have favoured those early humans whose physiological reaction to certain natural features enabled them to recover swiftly from stressful, energy-burning fight-or-flight responses and encouraged them to remain in areas of safety and food.

The environment Ulrich identifies as providing this restorative sense of calm and security involves leafy plants and greenery, still or slow-moving water, spatial openness, free-standing trees and unthreatening wildlife – all features that produce the best recovery responses in modern-day stress tests. It is the landscape associated with E. O. Wilson's Biophilia Hypothesis and that the Kaplans, too, identify as making us feel most at ease. Evolutionary biologists Gordon Orians and Judi Heerwagen claim that this is the ghost of the savannah in our heads, harking back to our ancestry as hunter-gatherers in Africa. It is the environment we subconsciously mimic in our urban parks and gardens; that we cherish in old master paintings; that we idealize as Arcadia; that Humphry Repton, unwittingly working to the blueprint of his DNA, recreated for his clients. But it is also the landscape emerging with no human effort in the Southern Block at Knepp. It is open wood pasture – the scene that greeted early humans when they arrived in Europe, a continent thronging with gigantic herds of grazing animals, just like Africa; the ecosystem we continued to sustain with our royal hunting 'forests' and marginal 'wastes' of the grazing commons until the end of the Middle Ages not only because it provided us with the richest resources but because it was where we felt instinctively at home.

Over the past few years as rewilding has gained recognition it has drawn opposition from the champions of 'cultural land-scapes' who see untrammelled nature as a force that might obliterate our historical past. But it is worth considering what kind of landscape and what kind of culture they are talking about here. The natural features defended as our inalienable British heritage are almost always Victorian – the Highland deer-scapes of Landseer, the stone-walled crofts of the wool boom, the hedges and fields of the Enclosure Acts, grouse moors, canalized rivers, even mature forestry plantations. But there is another cultural landscape we might do better to evoke – the one eclipsed by the era of the industrial revolution, its loss lamented by the likes of John Clare and Gerard Manley Hopkins even as the transformation was under way. If medieval wood pasture – our true 'forest' – is the baseline, rewilding is far from vandalistic. It restores to us a richer, deeper country-side that accompanied us for thousands of years.

And it is this deeper nature which holds the key to our future, not only in terms of mental and psychological health but in services vital to our long-term prosperity and survival – like the protection of watersheds, water and air decontamination, flood mitigation, soil restoration, the provision of pollinating insects, the safeguarding of biological diversity and carbon sequestration. As the UK begins to divorce itself from European regulations and reconsider the costs of farming subsidies, there are big choices to be made. One of them will be how far to encourage environmental protection. Historically, UK policy does not have a good track record. It took EU legislation to clean up the rivers, beaches and bathing waters of 'the Dirty Man of Europe'. The EU changed our approaches to sewage treatment and releases of nitrates. It was the EU's air-quality framework directive that reduced our emissions of sulphur dioxide and nitrous oxide, and that, in 2015, fined the UK government for continuing to fail air-pollution standards in London

and other major cities. In 2017 the environmental law organization ClientEarth took legal action against the UK government
for the third time after it still failed to deliver improvements to
air pollution. It was Natura 2000 and European habitats direc-
tives that obliged the UK government to provide protected
wildlife zones and encouraged the reintroduction of the beaver.
With the notable exception of climate-change legislation, the
UK has consistently failed to lead environmental policies in
Europe. While Germany, the Netherlands, Denmark, Sweden
and Finland – Europe's environmental pioneers – have consistently driven up standards and encouraged massive growth in
green business, the UK has tried to dilute the EU energy efficiency directive, lift the ban on imports of carbon-intensive oil
from tar-sands and for years tried to block the EU pesticide
ban protecting pollinating bees. In a recent reversal, welcomed
by environmentalists, Environment Secretary Michael Gove
declared the UK government would now be supporting the
EU's extended ban on the bee pesticides neonicotinoids, but it
remained stalwart in its opposition to a ban proposed by the EU
in 2017 on the herbicide glyphosate.

Leaving the EU, nevertheless, has the potential to free the
UK from Common Agricultural Policy farming subsidies and
the perverse incentives that wreak destruction on the environment. It is a chance to rethink how we look at the countryside
and what we want it to provide for us. It is a chance to look at
farming and conservation together, as partners, on the same side
of the coin.

So far in the post-Brexit debate, farming and conservation
have been pitted against each other, as if the two must battle it
out for resources. But as experience at Knepp and elsewhere has
demonstrated, farming and conservation need not – should not
– be at loggerheads. Giving over areas that are not on prime
agricultural land to nature – 'land sparing' in the jargon – is
farming's greatest ally. By halting and reversing land degradation, securing water resources and providing insects for crop
pollination, rewilding provides services vital to the long-term

sustainability of agriculture and food production. The complex mosaic of habitats stimulated by free-roaming grazing animals as we have seen on post-agricultural land at Knepp is not only remarkably easy to achieve. Compared with conventional conservation, it is manifestly inexpensive. It also provides much of what we need and what our landscape is currently lacking: biodiversity, resilience against climate change and extreme weather, and natural resources. And it can still produce high-quality food, like pasture-fed meat.

But no matter how important the public benefits, no farmer or landowner can be expected to turn their land over to nature out of altruism. It has to make financial sense. As one landowner put it to us, you can't be green if you're in the red. Yet, to our minds, being in the red should – or could – be an incentive to go green. We're constantly surprised how few landowners in a similar position to ours, on marginal land and with mounting debts, fail to make that leap. Partly, to be sure, it is lack of 'head space' – that valuable, creative thinking time one simply doesn't have in an embattled situation. There is also a fear of change and fear of the unknown: the perceived dangers associated with the idea of 'wildness'; the desire to preserve what is considered as traditional, rural countryside with an aesthetically pleasing, tightly ordered landscape; the notion of rewilding as land 'abandonment'. And there are fears about loss of control, particularly in regard to public access, sporting rights and the ability to control populations of certain species – like the beaver – that might conflict with a landowner's interests and income.

This fear of the intrusion of bureaucrats into private land-management decisions is hugely underestimated by policymakers and conservationists and often outweighs any sympathies for nature that a landowner or farmer might have. According to an unpublished report by Natural England, the rate of meadow loss (of the 3 per cent of meadows remaining since the Second World War) doubled after the EU announced its Meadow Protection Plan in 2014. With no prospect of proper compensation and with their land about to be taken out of their control in perpetuity, many farmers responded by ploughing up their meadows before the tighter rules could be introduced. The Countryside and Rights of Way, or CROW, Act of 2000, which maps areas of mountains, moors, heaths and downs as 'open country', had a similar negative impact. A neighbour of ours ploughed up one of the last remaining fragments of lowland heathland in Sussex – and another, some land on the South Downs – in order to avoid designation and the associated headaches and costs of open access.

Charlie and I have been lucky in that the government has, ultimately, supported our project as an open-ended experiment. So far, the civil service has imposed few restrictions on us, but one of our enduring fears is that Knepp could be designated as a Site of Special Scientific Interest – a protected area where we are bound by law to continue to provide a habitat for specific species, like nightingales or turtle doves. We could, in effect, become victims of our own success. It would be extremely difficult to guarantee numbers of nightingales on our land since, we now know, they favour transitional vegetation. Halting our emerging scrub, locking it in stasis, would probably – like most targeted conservation interventions – involve mechanical intervention, most likely at our own expense. We cannot be responsible, either, for factors affecting migrants like nightingales and turtle doves en route from Africa. But more than that, slapping specific conservation targets on Knepp would straitjacket the dynamism that has brought us such exciting and unexpected results so far and compromise the opportunities for other species yet to emerge from the project.

But as well as fears of conservation interference and increased bureaucracy, there are other powerful disincentives for farmers to let go. Reverting arable land to scrub or woodland halves its value. In our case we are part of a family tradition that does not consider the land a saleable asset. But it is impossible to predict the future. Situations may change and subsequent generations may feel differently. What rewilding has done, in effect, is halve the value of the land we hand on to the next generation. There are also tax advantages at stake: farmland is exempt from capital taxation through Agricultural Property Relief, farm diesel is exempt from fuel duty and farmers receive 100 per cent relief on business rates. No other industry receives this kind of preferential treatment.

There are, as we have discovered, financial positives for those willing to clamber out of the heffalump trap. At Knepp, in the prosperous south-east, we have been able to capitalize on our farm buildings. Previously they only cost us money to maintain. Now we have adapted them for light industrial use, storage and offices. These businesses employ 198 people, bringing jobs and vitality back into the countryside. This has, of course, involved initial conversion costs. But in the long term, alongside our developing tourism business, farm shop and organic 'Wild Range' meat production, it will provide another income stream that, we hope, will secure the viability of the project, irrespective of what becomes of subsidies.

Tourism is undoubtedly one of the big potential winners of rewilding. With increasing urbanization more and more people are seeking out nature in their spare time. Rural tourism is believed to be worth around £14 billion a year in England. In Wales, where 'wildlife-based activity' generates £1.9 billion, walking, on its own, contributes £500 million to the economy – £100 million more than subsidized farming revenues. Micro-adventures are the new buzz-word with wildlife-watching high on the agenda. In Scotland wildlife tourism alone generates more than £1 billion and supports over 7,000 jobs. Around 245,000 people a year take whale- and dolphin-watching tours. A single charismatic species can tip the scales. The first ospreys to breed again in Britain, in 1959, were at Loch Garten on Speyside – a site that has now been visited by more than 2 million people, sometimes 90,000 in a single summer. It is the most watched bird nest in history anywhere on the planet. The first ospreys to nest in the Lake District, at the height of the foot-and-mouth clampdown in 2001, pumped a much-needed

£1 million into the Cumbrian economy that year, and have continued to contribute every year since. Across the UK 290,000 people a year visit nine key osprey-watching sites, including on Rutland Water, generating £3.5 million for local economies. The white-tailed sea eagles, extinct in Britain since the first decade of the twentieth century, that colonized the Isle of Mull from reintroduction programmes in Scotland in 1985, now bring an estimated £5 million a year into the island's economy and support 110 full-time jobs. If we are ever brave enough in the UK to reintroduce predators like the lynx and the wolf, the rewards in terms of tourism would be higher still. In Finland, wildlife watchers increased 90 per cent between 2005 and 2008 when brown bear and wolverine were re-established. Already, the once controversial beaver reintroduction in Scotland is drawing lucrative business to hotels, restaurants and pubs, and now the same looks set for Devon. The young couple who own the farm at the headwaters of the River Otter where we watched the beavers being released now supplement their farming income renting out accommodation for beaver-watchers. At Knepp, in 2017, the fourth year of our new tourism operation, we took 1,300 visitors on wildlife safaris, hosted 2,500 people at our safari campsite and showed 800 people from special interest groups, NGOs and private individuals, including government ministers and civil servants, around the project.

But not all rewilded land will produce charismatic headline species that tourists will flock to see and it is in the nature of rewilding for habitats to shift and species to move. Incentivizing farmers and landowners to give land over to nature has to rely on ways that value that transition and acknowledge the public services that dynamic, self-willed natural processes provide. This involves changing the way we measure things like productivity, prosperity, sustainability, profit and loss – the business models that evolved at a time when nature's bounty seemed limitless. Payments for ecosystems services, natural capital accounting, pro-biodiversity business and biodiversity offsetting are all now being explored as ways in which the value of nature can be measured in tangible financial terms, providing cost–benefit analyses for the protection of such natural assets as soil, water, air, trees, vegetation, biodiversity and uplifting views.

But the subject is controversial. Some argue that putting a value on nature – something that most of us feel goes beyond the world of economics, that touches the very essence of what it is to be human, that existed before we came into being – is not only immoral but logistically impossible. High-minded conservationists insist that the monetarization of nature can only lead what we most want to protect into the lions' den of commercialism, into the vagaries and self-interest of the financial markets, to arbitrary pricing and trade-offs that replace nature with an impoverished ghost of itself. How can one put a price on beauty or pure air, on a sense of harmony and well-being? Should these things ever be tradeable? Would you buy or sell your children's or your parents' health?

But making the moral case for protecting nature for its own sake, because it is beautiful and important and we have no right to destroy it – the case campaigners have been making for half a century or more – has demonstrably failed. When nature is valued at nothing, when it is invisible in the economic system by which we live, that system invariably tosses it aside. Our story at Knepp mirrors the inexorable erosion of nature across Britain over the last seventy years. But Charlie and I were not wilful destroyers. We simply had no incentive to think about nature; no means by which to identify where nature is, how deep it goes, how broad its reach, what benefits it brings. We had no idea what we had on our doorstep, or what we could have if we changed our ways. Ours was the worst kind of nimbyism. Like most farmers we considered ourselves stewards of the land while, deep down, we felt that nature was not farming business. Nature was something that happened elsewhere, away from the hard-nosed economics of agriculture. We travelled the world to see wildlife. We campaigned to stop the felling of rainforests and the building of dams. Yet we were blind to what we were doing in our own back yard. Had intensive farming been profitable for us we would undoubtedly be doing it still.

The way forward must be to give credit where credit is due. We can calculate the costs of ignoring nature without reducing the overarching sense that nature is, ultimately, priceless; without eroding any of its mystery and enchantment. We can acknowledge the likely impossibility of ever knowing all it provides for us on this planet while still valuing the benefits that stare us in the face. Hospitals and health services already estimate how improvements in air quality and access to green spaces reduce the health bill. Councils and insurance companies calculate what re-naturalizing rivers and restoring watersheds and floodplains can save them in terms of flood-damage costs. Water utilities know what re-naturalizing uplands saves their companies in the costs of filtering silt, pesticides and artificial fertilizers out of the water supply. The Natural Capital committee has suggested that planting 250,000 hectares (965 square miles) of woodland close to urban centres in Britain would deliver a net economic benefit of nearly £550 million in recreation and carbon sequestration.

Now that Britain has a chance to rethink, we need to consider removing farming – and fisheries – subsidies altogether, as environmental ministers at the Economics of Ecosystems and Biodiversity initiative urged the EU back in 2007. We should certainly question a Basic Payment scheme which rewards people for doing nothing other than owning land. An independent-minded UK could lead the way in agricultural reform. It could charge farmers for pollution, just like any other industry, and reward them, instead, for environmental services provided for the public good.

Crucial would be a shift in focus from specific targeted outcomes to broader ecological processes – looking at how well, or how badly, land is functioning. Instead of measuring a single service, which in the past has always been food, success could be measured through multiple services. So a system that is good at producing food but bad at water management would score poorly; and a system that scores optimally for water storage, flood mitigation, wildlife, carbon sequestration, nutrient cycling, pollination and pollution amelioration would receive the most support.

Of specific concern to biologists is that by rewarding ecosystem services of purely human benefit, biodiversity could lose out. What economic system would ever put the long-term prospects of the water flea or the ant at the top? In the complex web of an ecosystem, the humblest creature may have an exponential impact. Often we can't tell which is a keystone species until it's gone. Mounting evidence, however, suggests that the system that is best at delivering multiple ecosystems services is also the most complex and biologically diverse. Indeed biodiversity itself might be a proxy measure for ecosystems services.

Thinking holistically like this, rebuilding systems with natural processes rather than setting end points, measuring function as much as outcome, could change our whole relationship with the land. While celebrating the advances of the technological age that have brought us more than enough food to feed the world from less land than ever, it could also encourage us to address the failures of 'masculine' science – the mindset that holds new technology as the answer to all our problems and any idea of returning to the older technologies of traditional systems, and of yielding to nature, as a backward step.

As we skirt the blackthorn thickets with an ear out for turtle doves Charlie and I count mixed blessings. The joy at hearing the bird here, and hearing it now, is counterbalanced by the sands of time charging down to that single pinprick of loss. The turtle dove is a reminder that Knepp is an island, only a tiny scrap of the carpet – powerless, on its own, to save a species on a trajectory to extinction. Even if the rich tapestry of a turtle's three-brood summer were to be restored across the whole of England tomorrow, it is almost certainly too late for this lovely bird in this country. Its numbers have most probably fallen below the critical mass needed for the population's long term survival. Its crooning is an evocation of shifting baselines, a fading pulse from the landscape of the Elizabethans, the latest in the line of disappearance.

Our footsteps often feel heavy. Rewilding Knepp has changed the way we look at the world and much of it is depressing. When we go for a walk with friends elsewhere in the countryside – the same walks we used to enjoy without thinking in the past – chances are what we notice most is the silence and the stillness. As the landscape flashes by on a train or motorway, we now know what isn't there. Compared with Knepp, most of Britain seems like a desert. It brings an aching sadness, a sense of loss and frustration articulated best by the great American conservationist Aldo Leopold almost a century ago: 'One of the penalties of an ecological education is that one lives alone in a world of wounds.'

And yet, that gentle *turr-turr*-ing tugging at the heartstrings is also a signal of repair, recovery and rebirth, the re-braiding of unravellings. When the voice of the turtle is gone from our land in – who knows – another handful of summers, there is hope for the country it leaves behind, signs that the world is turning a corner. When it flies back to Africa for the last time, it will fly over a continent of Europe that is being recolonized by beavers, wolves, wolverines, jackals and bears; it will trail in its wake ecological awakenings, a hunger for nature and hope for a wilder world.

Appendix

Knepp Wildland Advisory Board

Keith Alexander, independent ecologist and specialist on saproxylic beetles

Martin Boers, Livestock Partnership Veterinary Practice

Prof. Paul Buckland, Professor in Environmental Archaeology, Bournemouth University

Jill Butler, Conservation Advisor, Woodland Trust

Prof. Mick Crawley, Emeritus Professor of Plant Ecology, Imperial College London

Prof. Alastair Driver, former National Conservation Manager, Environment Agency

Jason Emrich, Manager, Knepp Castle Estate, and Regional Director, Savills

Alison Field, Area Director for London & the South-East, Forestry Commission

Prof. Rob Fuller, former Science Director, British Trust for Ornithology

Emma Goldberg, Senior Forestry and Woodland Specialist, Natural England

Paul Goriup, Director of Fieldfare International Ecological Development PLC and Chairman, NatureBureau Ltd.

Penny Green, Ecologist, Knepp Wildland, and former Manager, Sussex Biodiversity Record Centre

Ted Green, Founding Member of the Ancient Tree Forum, and former English Nature Conservation Consultant to the Crown Estate at Windsor

Theresa Greenaway, former Manager, Sussex Biodiversity Record Centre

Dr Matthew Heard, Principal Scientific Officer, Natural Environment Research Council

Kristoffer Hewitt, Senior Advisor, Biodiversity Sussex & Kent Area, Natural England

Neil Hulme, independent conservation advisor and former Chair, Butterfly Conservation (Sussex Branch)

Hans Kampf, Senior Policy Advisor on Ecosystems and the Environment to the Dutch Government

Jason Lavender, Co-Director, High Weald Area of Outstanding Natural Beauty

Prof. Sir John Lawton, former Chair of Making Space for Nature, and President, Yorkshire Wildlife Trust

Dr Alex Lord, Projects Manager, Permian Global Research Ltd

Dr Pascale Nicolet, Director of Policy and Implementation, Freshwater Habitats Trust

Matthew Oates, National Specialist on Nature, National Trust

Jim Seymour, South-East Regional Land Management Programme Manager, Natural England

Julian Smith, Trustee, Knepp Castle Estate

Dr Ken Smith, former Head of Aquatic Research, RSPB

Jonathan Spencer, Head of Planning and Environment, Forestry Commission

Jim Swanson, Grazing Animals Project

Dr Frans Vera, Dutch ecologist and author of *Grazing Ecology & Forest History*

Joep van de Vlasakker, Large Herbivore Foundation

Dr Tony Whitbread, CEO, Sussex Wildlife Trust

Sources

1. Meeting a Remarkable Man under a Remarkable Tree

Alexander, Keith, Butler, J. E., and Green, T. E. 'The value of different tree and shrub species to wildlife'. *British Wildlife*, vol. 18, no. 1, pp. 18–28 (October 2006)

Butler, J. E., Rose, F., and Green, T. E. 'Ancient trees, icons of our most important wooded landscapes in Europe'. In: Read, H. et al. (eds). *Tools for preserving woodland biodiversity*, pp. 28–31. Textbook 2. Nononex, programme September 2001, Leonardo da Vinci, Sweden

Green, Ted. 'The forgotten army – woodland fungi'. *British Wildlife*, vol. 4, no. 2, pp. 85–6 (December 1992)

Green, Ted. 'The importance of open-grown trees – from acorn to ancient'. *British Wildlife*, vol. 21, no. 5, pp. 334–8 (June 2010)

Simard, S. W. and Durall, D. M. 'Mycorrhizal networks: a review of their extent, function, and importance'. *Canadian Journal of Botany*, vol. 82, issue 8, pp. 1140–65 (2004)

2. At Odds with Everything

Zayed, Yago. 'Agriculture: historical statistics'. House of Commons Briefing Paper, no. 03339 (21 January 2016)

3. The Serengeti Effect

Harrabin, Roger. 'Wildflower meadow protection plan "backfires"'. *BBC News* (3 September 2014) http://www.bbc.co.uk/news/science-environment-29037804

Plantlife report, *Our Vanishing Flora*. (2012) http://www.plantlife.org.uk/application/files/7214/8234/1075/Jubilee_Our_Vanishing_flora.pdf

4. The Secret of Grazing Animals

Bakker, E. S., et al. 'Combining paleo-data and modern exclosure experiments to assess the impact of megafauna extinctions on woody vegetation'. *Proceedings of the National Academy of Sciences* 113(4), pp. 847–55 (2016) http://www.pnas.org/content/113/4/847.full.pdf

Bakker, E. S., Olff, H., Vandenberghe, C., De Maeyer, K., Smit, R., Gleichman, J. M., and Vera, F. W. M. 'Ecological anachronisms in the recruitment of temperate light-demanding tree species in wooded pastures'. *Journal of Applied Ecology* 41, pp. 571–82 (2004)

Birks, H. J. B. 'Mind the gap: how open were European primeval forests?' *Trends in Ecology & Evolution* 20(4), pp. 154–6 (May 2005) https://www.researchgate.net/publication/7080887_Mind_the_gap_How_open_were_European_primeval_forests

Bokdam, J. 'Nature Conservation and Grazing Management. Free-ranging cattle as driving force for cyclic vegetation succession'. Ph.D. thesis, Wageningen University, Wageningen, Netherlands (2003)

Bonenfant, C., Gailard, Jean-Michel, et al. 'Empirical evidence of density-dependence in populations of large herbivores'. *Advances in Ecological Research*, vol. 41, pp. 314–45 (2009)

Gill, R. 'The influence of large herbivores on tree recruitment and forest dynamics'. In Danell, K., et al. (eds). *Large Herbivore Ecology, Ecosystem Dynamics and Conservation*, pp. 170–202 (Cambridge University Press, 2006)

Grange, S., Duncan, P., et al. 'What limits the Serengeti zebra population?' *Oecologia* 149, pp. 523–32 (2004)

Green, Ted. 'Natural Origin of the Commons: People, animals and invisible biodiversity'. *Landscape Archaeology and Ecology*, vol. 8, pp. 57–62 (September 2010)

Harding, P. T. and Rose, F. *Pasture-woodlands in lowland Britain. A review of their importance for wildlife conservation* (Huntingdon: Natural Environment Research Council, Institute of Terrestrial Ecology, 1986)

Hodder, K. H., et al. 'Large herbivores in the wildwood and modern naturalistic grazing systems'. Natural England, report no. 648 (2005)

Hopcraft, J. G. C., Olff, H., and Sinclair, A. R. E. 'Herbivores, resources and risks: alternating regulation along primary environmental gradients in savannas'. *Trends in Ecology and Evolution*, vol. 25 no. 2, pp. 119–28 (February 2010)

Lindenmayer, D. (ed.). *Forest Pattern and Ecological Process: A Synthesis of 25 Years of Research* (Commonwealth Scientific and Industrial Research Organisation, 2009)

Macnab, John. 'Carrying capacity and related slippery shibboleths'. *Wildlife Society Bulletin*, vol. 13, no. 4, pp. 403–10 (Winter, 1985)

Mduma, S. A. R., Sinclair, A. R. E., and Hilborn, R. 'Food regulates the Serengeti wildebeest: a 40-year record'. *Journal of Animal Ecology* 68, pp. 1101–22 (1999)

Mech, D., Smith, D. W., Murphy, K. M., and MacNulty, D. R. 'Winter severity and wolf predation on a formerly wolf-free elk herd'. *Journal of Wildlife Management* 65, pp. 998–1003 (2001)

Mouissie, A. M. 'Seed dispersal by large herbivores – implications for the restoration of plant biodiversity'. Doctoral thesis, Community and Conservation Ecology Group of the University of Groningen, The Netherlands. (2004)

Ratnam, J., Bond, W., et al. 'When is a "forest" a savanna, and why does it matter?' *Global Ecology and Biogeography*, vol. 20, pp. 653–60 (2011)

Remmert, H. 'The mosaic-cycle concept of ecosystems – an overview'. In: Remmert, H. (ed.) *The Mosaic-Cycle Concept of Ecosystems*, pp. 11–21 (Springer, Berlin, 1991)

Smit, C. and Putman, R. 'Large herbivores as environmental engineers'. In: Putman, R., Appolonia, M., and Andersen, R. (eds). *Ungulate Management in Europe*, pp. 260–83 (Cambridge University Press, 2011)

Smit, C. and Ruifrok, J. L. 'From protégé to nurse plant: establishment of thorny shrubs in grazed temperate woodlands'. *Journal of Vegetation Science* 22, pp. 377–86 (2011)

Smit, C. and Vermijmeren, M. 'Tree–shrub associations in grazed woodlands: first rodents, then cattle'. *Plant Ecology* 212, pp. 483–93 (2011)

Sommer, R. S., Benecke, N., Lõngas, L., Nelle, O., and Schmölcke, U. 'Holocene survival of the wild horse in Europe: a matter of open landscape?'. *Journal of Quaternary Science* 26, pp. 805–12 (2011)

Tansley, A. G. 'The development of vegetation – a review of Clement's *Plant Succession*'. *Journal of Ecology* 4, pp. 198–204 (1916)

Tansley, A G. 'The classification of vegetation and the concept of development'. *Journal of Ecology* 8, pp. 118–49 (1920)

Van Vuure, C. 'On the origin of the Polish konik and its relation to Dutch nature management'. *Lutra*, vol. 57, no. 2, pp. 111–30 (Vereniging voor Zoogdierkunde en Zoogdierbescherming, Holland 2014)

Vera, F. W. M. 'Can't see the trees for the forest'. In: D. Rotherham (ed). *Trees, Forested Landscapes and Grazing Animals – a European perspective on woodlands and grazed treescapes*, ch. 6, p. 99–126 (Routledge, 2013)

Vera, F. W. M. 'The dynamic European forest'. *Arboricultural Journal*, vol. 26, pp. 179–211 (2002)

Vera, F. W. M. 'Large-scale nature development – the Oostvaardersplassen'. *British Wildlife* 29, pp. 29–36 (June 2009) http://diaplan.ku.dk/pdf/large-scale_nature_development_the_ Oostvaardersplassen.pdf

Vera, F. W. M. 'The shifting baseline syndrome in restoration ecology'. In: Hall, M. (ed.). *Restoration and History – the search for a usable environmental past*, pp. 98–110 (Routledge Studies in Modern History, 2010) http://media.longnow.org/ files/2/REVIVE/The%20Shifting%20Baseline%20Syndrome %20in%20Restoration%20Ecology_Frans%20Vera.pdf

Vera, F. W. M., Bakker, E., and Olff, H. 'The influence of large herbivores on tree recruitment and forest dynamics'. In: Danell, K., Duncan, P., Bergstrom, R., and Pastor, J. (eds). *Large Herbivore Ecology, Ecosystem Dynamics and Conservation*, pp. 203–31 (Cambridge University Press, 2006)

Vera, F. W. M., Bakker, E., and Olff, H. 'Large herbivores: missing partners of western European light-demanding tree and shrub species?' In: Danell, K., Duncan, P., Bergstrom, R. and Pastor, J. (eds). *Large Herbivore Ecology, Ecosystem Dynamics and Conservation* (Cambridge University Press, 2006) http://media. longnow.org/files/2/REVIVE/Vera_Large%20herbivores%20 missing%20partners%20light%20demanding%20tree%20 and%20shrub%20species.pdf

Watt, A. S. 'On the causes of failure of natural regeneration in British oakwoods'. *Journal of Ecology*, vol. 7, pp. 173–203 (1919)

Young, T. P. 'Natural die-offs of large mammals: implications for conservation'. *Conservation Biology*, vol. 8, no. 2, pp. 410–18 (June 1994)

5. A World of Wood Pasture

Alexander, K. N. A. 'The links between forest history and biodiversity: the invertebrate fauna of ancient pasture-woodlands in Britain and its conservation'. In: Kirby, K. J. and Watkins, C. (eds). *The Ecological History of European Forests*, pp. 73–80 (Wallingford: CAB International, 1998)

Alexander, K. N. A. 'What are veteran trees? Where are they found? Why are they important?' In: Read, H., Forfang, A. S., et al. (eds). *Tools for preserving woodland biodiversity*, pp. 28–31. Textbook 2. Nanonex programme (Leonardo da Vinci, Sweden, September 2001)

Alexander, K. N. A. 'What do saproxylic (wood-decay) beetles really want? Conservation should be based on practical observation rather than unstable theory'. *Trees Beyond the Wood: Conference Pproceedings*, pp. 33–46 (September 2012)

Alexander, K. N. A. 'Non-intervention v intervention – but balanced? I think not.' *British Ecological Society Bulletin*, vol. 45, pp. 36–7 (August 2014)

Alexander, K. N. A., Sticker, D., and Green, T. 'Rescuing veteran trees from canopy competition'. *Conservation Land Management*, pp. 12–16 (Spring 2011)

Allen, Michael J. and Gardiner, J. 'If you go down to the woods today; a re-evaluation of the chalkland postglacial woodland; implications for prehistoric communities.' In: Allen, Michael J., Sharples, Niall, and O'Connor, Terry (eds). *Land and People: papers in memory of John G. Evans*, pp. 49–66 (Prehistoric Society Research Paper no. 2, Oxbow Books, 2009)

Godwin, H. *The History of the British Flora*. 2nd edn. (on analysis of non-arboreal pollen, p. 9 and p. 27) (Cambridge University Press, 1975)

Godwin, H. 'Pollen analysis – an outline of the problems and potentialities of the method. Part 1. Technique and interpretation'. *New Phytologist*, vol. 33, pp. 278–305 (1934)

Godwin, H. 'Pollen analysis – an outline of the problems and potentialities of the method. Part 2. General applications of pollen analysis'. *New Phytologist*, vol. 33, pp. 325–58. (1934)

Peterken, George. 'Recognising wood-meadows in Britain?'. *British Wildlife*, vol. 28, no. 3, pp. 155–65 (February 2017)

Post, L. von. 'Forest tree pollen in South Swedish Peat Bog Deposits (Om skogstradspollen i sydsvenska torfmosselagerfolijder (foredragsreferat))'. *Foerhandlingar*, vol. 38, pp. 384–434 (Geologiska Foereningen in Stockholm, 1916). Translation by Margaret Bryan Davis and Knut Faegri with an introduction by Knut Faegri and Johs. Iversen. *Pollen et Spores*, 9, pp. 378–401. In: Real, L. A. and Brown, J. H. (eds). *Foundations of Ecology*, pp. 456–82. (Classic Papers with commentaries, University of Chicago Press, 1967)

Ranius, T., Eliasson, P., and Johansson, P. 'Large-scale occurrence patterns of red-listed lichens and fungi on old oaks are influenced both by current and historical habitat density'. *Biodiversity Conservation* 17, pp. 2371–81 (2008)

Rose, F. 'The epiphytes of oak'. In: Morris, M. G. and Perring, E. H. (eds). *The British Oak, Its History and Natural History*. pp. 250–73 (The Botanical Society of the British Isles, E. W. Classey, Berks., 1974)

Rose, F. 'Temperate forest management: its effects on bryophyte and lichen floras and habitats'. In: Bates, J. W. and Farmar, A. M. (eds). *Bryophytes and Lichens in a Changing Environment*, pp. 211–33 (Clarendon Press, Oxford, 1992)

Smith, D., Nayyar, K., et al. 'Can dung beetles from the palaeoecological and archaeological record indicate herd concentration and the identity of herbivores?' *Quaternary International*, vol 341, pp. 1–12 (2013)

*

'Europe's Wood Pastures – condemned to a slow death by the CAP? A test case for EU agriculture and biodiversity policy'. EU booklet. (October 2015) https://arboriremarcabili.ro/media/cms_page_media/2015/11/20/Europe's%20wood%20pastures%20-%20booklet_hTeCQKP.pdf

6. Wild ponies, pigs & longhorn cattle

Hewitt, John. 'The hidden evolutionary relationship between pigs and primates revealed by genome-wide study of transposable elements', Phys.org (September 23, 2015) https://phys.org/news/2015-09-hidden-evolutionary-relationship-pigs-primates.html

McKenzie, Steven. ' "Alarming trend" of decline among UK's dung beetles'. *BBC News* (17 November 2015) http://www.bbc.co.uk/news/uk-scotland-highlands-islands-34831400

Nelson, Bryan. 'Pigs and humans share more genetic similarities

than previously believed'. Mother Nature Network (28
September 2015) http://www.mnn.com/earth-matters/animals/
stories/pigs-and-humans-more-closely-related-thought-
according-genetic-analysis

Provenza, F. D., Meuret, M., and Gregorini, P. 'Our landscapes,
our livestock, ourselves: restoring broken linkages among
plants, herbivores, and humans with diets that nourish and
satiate.' *Appetite*, vol. 95, pp. 500–519 (August 2015)

*

'UK dung beetles could save cattle industry £367m annually –
bug farm boss' Wales online. (27 August 2015) http://www.
walesonline.co.uk/business/farming/uk-dung-beetles-could-
save-9940684

http://www.dungbeetlesdirect.com/Dung-Beetles/About-Dung-
Beetles.aspx

7. Creating a Mess

Andersson, C. and Frost, I. 'Growth of *Quercus robur* seedlings
after experimental grazing and cotyledon removal'. *Acta
Botanica Neerlandica*, vol. 45, pp. 85–94 (1996)

Ausubel, Jesse H. 'The return of nature – how technology liberates
the environment'. *Breakthrough Journal* (Spring 2015) https://
thebreakthrough.org/index.php/journal/past-issues/issue-5/
the-return-of-nature

Bossema, J. 'Jays and oaks: an eco-ethological study of a symbiosis'.
Ph.D. thesis, Rijksuniversiteit Groningen (also published in
Behaviour 70, pp. 1–117). (1979)

Bossema, J. 'Recovery of acorns in the European jay (*Garrulus g.
glandarius* L.)'. *Proceedings Koninklijke Nederlandse Akademie
van Wetenschappen Serie C, Biological and Medical Sciences*,
vol. 71, pp. 10–14 (1968)

Chettleburgh, M. R. 'Observations on the collection and burial of
acorns by jays in Hinault Forest'. *British Birds*, vol. 45, pp.
359–64 (1952)

Davis, Donald, et al. 'Changes in USDA Food Composition Data
for 43 Garden Crops, 1950 to 1999'. *Journal of the American
College of Nutrition*, vol. 23, no. 6, pp. 669–82 (December 2004)

Den Ouden, J., Jansen, P. A., and Smit, R. 'Jays, mice and oaks:
predation and dispersal of Quercus robur and Quercus petraea
in North-western Europe'. In: Forget, P. M., Lambert, J. E., et

al. (eds). *Seed Fate: Predation, Dispersal and Seedling Establishment*, ch. 13, pp. 223–39. (Centre for Agriculture & Bioscience International, Wallingford, 2005)

Folger, Tim. 'The next green revolution'. *National Geographic Magazine* (October 2014)

Gustavsson, J., Christel Cederberg, C., Sonesson, U., et al. 'Global food losses and food waste – extent, causes and prevention'. Food and Agriculture Organization of the United Nations, Rome (2011) http://www.fao.org/docrep/014/mb060e/mb060e00.pdf

Lambert, Chloe. 'Best before – is the way we produce and process food making it less nourishing?' *New Scientist*, 17 October 2015

Mayer, Anne-Marie. 'Historical changes in the mineral content of fruits and vegetables'. *British Food Journal*, vol. 99, no. 6, pp. 207–11 (July 1997)

Midgley, Olivia. 'Increasing yields and rewilding spared land could slash greenhouse gas emissions by 80 per cent'. *Farmers Guardian Insight News*, 4 January 2016 https://www.fginsight.com/news/increasing-yields-and-rewilding-spared-land-could-slash-ghg-emissions-by-80-per-cent-8913

Monbiot, George. 'The Hunger Games'. *Guardian*, 13 August 2012

Priestley, Sara. 'Food Waste'. House of Commons Briefing Paper, no. CBP07552 (8 April 2016)

Royte, Elizabeth. 'How "ugly" fruits and vegetables can help solve world hunger'. *National Geographic Magazine*, March 2016

Yi, Xianfeng, et al. 'Acorn cotyledons are larger than their seedlings' need: evidence from artificial cutting experiments.' *Scientific Reports* 5, Article number: 8112 (2015)

Zayed, Yago. 'Agriculture: historical statistics'. House of Commons Briefing Paper, no. 03339 (21 January 2016)

*

'Sustainable Food – a recipe for food security and environmental protection?' Science for Environment Policy In-depth Report, European Commission, Issue 8 (November 2013) http://ec.europa.eu/environment/integration/research/newsalert/pdf/sustainable_food_IR8_en.pdf

OECD-FAO Agricultural Outlook. Chapter 3 Biofuels. (2013) http://www.fao.org/fileadmin/templates/est/COMM_MARKETS_MONITORING/Oilcrops/Documents/OECD_Reports/OECD_2013_22_biofuels_proj.pdf

Transport & Environment. 'Biodiesel 80 per cent worse for climate

than fossil diesel'. (6 April 2016) https://www.
transportenvironment.org/news/biodiesel-80-worse-climate-
fossil-diesel

8. Living with the Yellow Peril

Harvey, Graham. 'Ragwort – the toxic weed spreading through our
countryside'. *Daily Mail* (5 August 2007). http://www.dailymail.
co.uk/news/article-473409/Ragwort-The-toxic-weed-spreading-
countryside.html

Pauly, D. 'Anecdotes and the shifting baseline syndrome of
fisheries'. *Trends in Ecology & Environment*, vol. 10, p. 430
(1995)

*

http://www.ragwortfacts.com/ragwort-myths.html

Buglife leaflet on ragwort: 'Ragwort – noxious weed or precious
wildflower?' https://www.buglife.org.uk/sites/default/files/
Ragwort.pdf

'British Horse Society Ragwort survey reveals disturbing new
figures on horse fatalities', *Equiworld Magazine*. http://www.
equiworld.net/0803/bhs01.htm

Plantlife and Butterfly Conservation joint publication: 'Ragwort
– friend or foe?' (June 2008) http://www.plantlife.org.uk/uk/
our-work/publications/ragwort-friend-or-foe

Natural England information note. 'Towards a ragwort management
strategy'. (June 2003) http://holtspurbottom.info/LinkedDocs/
RagwortENinformationnote20June03.pdf

DEFRA Code of Practice on How to Prevent the Spread of
Ragwort (July 2004) https://www.gov.uk/government/uploads/
system/uploads/attachment_data/file/525269/pb9840-cop-
ragwort-rev.pdf

Ragwort Control Act: Consultation on the draft Code of Practice
to Prevent the Spread of Ragwort, Response from Wildlife &
Countryside Link (June 2004) http://www.wcl.org.uk/docs/
Link_response_to_consultation_on_ragwort_control_09Jun04.
pdf

9. Painted Ladies and the Perfect Storm

Deinet, S., Ieronymidou, C., McRae, L., et al. 'Wildlife comeback in
Europe – the recovery of selected mammal and bird species'.
Final report to Rewilding Europe by ZSL, BirdLife

International and the European Bird Census Council.
Zoological Society of London (2013) https://www.zsl.org/sites/
default/files/media/2014–02/wildlife-comeback-in-europe-the-
recovery-of-selected-mammal-and-bird-species-2576.pdf

Nogués-Bravo, D., Simberloff, D., Rahbek, C., and Sanders, N. J.
'Rewilding is the new Pandora's box in conservation'. *Current
Biology*, vol. 6, issue 3, pp. R87–R91 (8 February 2016)

Odadi, W. O., Jain, M., et al. 'Facilitation between bovids and
equids on an African savanna'. *Evolutionary Ecology Research*,
vol. 13, pp. 237–52 (2011)

Soulé, M. and Noss, R. 'Rewilding and biodiversity'. *Wild Earth*,
pp. 1–11 (Fall 1998)

Van de Vlasakker, Joep. 'Bison Rewilding Plan 2014–2024 –
Rewilding Europe's contribution to the comeback of the
European bison'. A report by Rewilding Europe (2014)

10. Purple Emperors

Bartomeus, I., Vilà, M., and Steffan-Dewenter, I. 'Combined effects
of *Impatiens glandulifera* [Himalayan balsam] invasion and
landscape structure on native plant pollination.' *Journal of
Ecology*, vol. 98, pp. 440–50 (2010)

Hejda, M. and Pysek. P. 'What is the impact of *Impatiens
glandulifera* [Himalayan Balsam] on species diversity of invaded
riparian vegetation?' *Biological Conservation*, vol. 132, pp.
143–52 (2006)

Holdich, D. M., Palmer, M., and Sibley, P. J. 'The indigenous status
of *Austropotamobius pallipes* [Freshwater White-clawed
Crayfish] in Britain'. In *Crayfish Conservation in the British
Isles, Conference Proceedings*, British Waterways Offices, Leeds
(25 March 2009)

Hulme, P. E., and Bremner, E. T. 'Assessing the impact of *Impatiens
glandulifera* [Himalayan balsam] on riparian habitats'. *Journal
of Applied Ecology*, vol. 43, pp. 43–50 (2006)

12. Turtle Doves

Dunn, Jenny C., et al. 'Post-fledging habitat selection in a rapidly
declining farmland bird, the European Turtle Dove *Streptopelia
turtur*'. *Bird Conservation International*, vol. 27, issue 1, pp.
45–57 (March 2017) https://www.cambridge.org/core/journals/
bird-conservation-international/article/postfledging-habitat-

selection-in-a-rapidly-declining-farmland-bird-the-european-
turtle-dove-streptopelia-turtur/271558A78B788247C6EDCD8F
725476DF

*

Read more at: http://www.rspb.org.uk/community/ourwork/b/
biodiversity/archive/2016/04/20/tracking-turtle-dove-nestlings-
to-investigate-post-fledging-survival-and-habitat-selection.
aspx#Ii3uE53mOOilE2sI.99
Fact-sheet on the European turtle dove, Birdlife International.
http://www.birdlife.org/sites/default/files/attachments/
factsheet_-_european_turtle-dove_ci_1_1.pdf

13. Rewilding the River

Harribin, Roger. 'Back to nature flood schemes need "government
leadership" '. *BBC News* (16 January 2014) http://www.bbc.co.
uk/news/uk-politics-25752320
Lean, Geoffrey. 'UK flooding: How a Yorkshire town worked with
nature to stay dry'. *Independent* (2 January 2016)

*

'Flood defence spending in England'. House of Commons briefing,
standard note SN/SC/5755 (19 November 2014)
'Flooding in Focus – recommendations for more effective flood
management in England'. RSPB. (2014) https://www.rspb.org.
uk/Images/flooding-in-focus_tcm9–386202.pdf
'How rewilding reduces flood risk'. Rewilding Britain report.
(September 2016) http://www.rewildingbritain.org.uk/assets/
uploads/files/publications/Final-flood-report/Rewilding-Britain-
Flood-Report-Sep-6–16.pdf
'Working with natural processes to reduce flood risks'.
Environment Agency, DEFRA, Natural Resources Wales. (July
2014) http://evidence.environment-agency.gov.uk/FCERM/
Libraries/FCERM_Project_Documents/WWNP_framework.
sflb.ashx
'Slowing the flow at Pickering', Forest Research https://www.
forestry.gov.uk/fr/slowingtheflow and Institute of Civil
Engineers https://www.ice.org.uk/disciplines-and-resources/
case-studies/slowing-the-flow-at-pickering
'The Pontbren Project – a farmer-led approach to sustainable land
management in the uplands'. Research report by the Woodland

Trust (February 2013) http://www.woodlandtrust.org.uk/
mediafile/100263187/rr-wt-71014-pontbren-project-2014.pdf

14. Bringing back the Beaver

Coghlan, Andy. 'Should the UK bring back beavers to help manage
floods?' *New Scientist* (13 November 2015)

Collen, P., and Gibson, R. 'The general ecology of beavers as related
to their influence on stream ecosystems and riparian habitats,
and the subsequent effects on fish – a review'. *Reviews in Fish
Biology and Fisheries*, vol. 10, pp. 439–61 (2001)

Elliott, M., Blythe, C., et al. 'Beavers – Nature's Water Engineers. A
summary of initial findings from the Devon Beaver Projects'.
Devon Wildlife Trust (2017)

Gurnell, J., Gurnell, A. M., Demeritt, D., et al. *The feasibility and
acceptability of reintroducing the European beaver to England*
(Natural England commissioned report NECR002, 2009)

Halley, D. J., and Roseel, F. 'The beaver's re-conquest of Eurasia:
status, population development and management of a
conservation success'. *Mammal Review*, vol. 3, pp. 153–78
(2002)

Hood, G. A. 'Biodiversity and ecosystem restoration: beavers bring
back balance to an unsteady world'. Plenary, 6th International
Beaver Symposium, Ivanić Grad, Croatia (September 2012)

Hood, G. A. and Bayley, S. 'Beaver (*Castor canadensis*) mitigate the
effects of climate on the area of open water in boreal wetlands
in western Canada'. *Biological Conservation*, vol. 141, pp.
556–67 (2008)

Jones, S., Gow, D., Lloyd Jones, A., and Campbell-Palmer, R. 'The
battle for British beavers'. *British Wildlife*, vol. 24, no. 6, pp.
381–92 (August 2013)

Law, A., Gaywood, Martin J., Jones, Kevin C., Ramsay, P., and
Willby, Nigel, J. 'Using ecosystem engineers as tools in habitat
restoration and rewilding: beaver and wetlands'. *Science of the
Total Environment*, vol. 605–6, pp. 1021–30 (2017)

McLeish, Todd. 'Knocking down nitrogen'. *Northern Woodlands*
(Spring 2016)

Manning, A. D., Coles, B. J., et al. 'New evidence of late survival of
beaver in Britain'. *The Holocene*, vol. 24, issue 12, pp. 1849–55
(2014)

Nyssen, J., et al. 'Effect of beaver dams on the hydrology of small mountain streams – example from the Chevral in the Ourthe Orientale basin, Ardennes, Belgium'. *Journal of Hydrology*, vol. 402, issues 1–2, pp. 92–102 (13 May 2011)

Parker, H., and Rosell, F. 'Beaver management in Norway: a model for continental Europe?' *Lutra*, vol. 46, pp. 223–34 (2003)

Pope, Lawrence. 'Dam! Beavers have been busy sequestering carbon'. *New Scientist* (17 July 2013)

Robbins, Jim. 'Reversing course on beavers – the animals are being welcomed as a defence against climate change'. *New York Times* (27 October 2014)

Rosell, F., Bozser, O., Collen, P., and Parker, H. 'Ecological impact of beavers *Castor fiber* and *Castor canadensis* and their ability to modify ecosystems'. *Mammal Review*, vol. 35, pp. 248–76 (2005)

15. Pasture-fed

Allport, S. 'The Queen of fats: an author's quest to restore omega-3 to the western diet'. *Acres USA*, vol. 38, no. 4, pp. 56–62 (April 2008)

Arnott, G., Ferris, C., and O'Connell, N. 'A comparison of confinement and grazing systems for dairy cows – what does the science say?' *Agri-search* report (March 2015)

Daley, C. A., Abbott, A., et al. 'A review of fatty acid profiles and antioxidant content in grass-fed and grain-fed beef'. *Nutrition Journal*, vol. 9, issue 10 (2010)

Dhiman, T. R. 'Conjugated linoleic acid: a food for cancer prevention'. *Proceedings from the 2000 Intermountain Nutrition Conference*, pp. 103–21 (2000)

Dhiman, T. R., Anand, G. R., et al. 'Conjugated linoleic acid content of milk from cows fed different diets'. *Journal of Dairy Science*, vol. 82, issue 10, pp. 2146–56. (1999)

Kay, R. N. B. 'Seasonal variation of appetite in ruminants'. In Haresign, W., and Cole, D. J. A. *Recent Advances in Animal Nutrition*, ch. 11 (Butterworth-Heinemann, 1985)

Liddon, A. *Eating biodiversity: an investigation of the links between quality food production and biodiversity protection* (Economic and Social Research Council report, 20 August 2009)

Lüscher, A., Mueller-Harvey, I., et al. 'Potential of legume-based grassland-livestock systems in Europe'. *Grass and Forage Science*, vol. 69, issue 2, pp. 206–28 (June 2014)

McCracken, D. and Huband, S., 'European pastoralism: farming with nature'. European Forum for Nature Conservation and Pastoralism http://mp.mountaintrip.eu/uploads/media/project_leaflet/pastoral_plp.pdf

Ponnampalam, E. N, Mann, N. J, and Sinclair, A. J. 'Effect of feeding systems on omega-3 fatty acids, conjugated linoleic acid and trans fatty acids in Australian beef cuts: potential impact on human health'. *Asia Pacific Journal of Clinical Nutrition*, vol. 15, issue 1, pp. 21–9 (2006)

Renecker, Lyle Al and Samuel, W. M. 'Growth and seasonal weight changes as they relate to spring and autumn set points in mule deer'. *Canadian Journal of Zoology*, 69(3), pp. 744–7 (1991)

Salatin, Joel. 'Amazing grazing'. *Acres USA Magazine* (May 2007)

Sutton, C. and Dibb, S. 'Prime cuts – valuing the food we eat'. A discussion paper by the WWF-UK and the Food Ethics Council (2013)

Taubes, G. 'The soft science of dietary fat'. *Science*, vol. 291, pp. 2535–41 (2001)

Xue, B., Zhao, X. Q., and Zhang, Y. S. 'Seasonal changes in weight and body composition of yak grazing on alpine-meadow grassland in the Qinghai-Tibetan plateau of China'. *Journal of Animal Science*, vol. 83, no. 8, pp. 1908–13 (2005)

*

'Pasture for life – it can be done: the farm business case for feeding ruminants just on pasture'. Pasture for Life (January 2016) http://www.pastureforlife.org/media/2016/01/pfl-it-can-be-done-jan2016.pdf

'Pastoralism and the green economy – a natural nexus?' International Union of Nature and Natural Resources, United Nations Environment Programme report. (2014)

'The potential global impacts of adopting low-input and organic livestock production'. United Nations Food & Agriculture Organisation report. (27 March 2014)

'What's your beef?' National Trust report. https://animalwelfareapproved.us/wp-content/uploads/2012/05/067b-Whats-your-beef-full-report.pdf

16. Rewilding the Soil

Anderston, Bart. 'Soil food web – opening the lid of the black box'. *Energy Bulletin* (7 December 2006) http://www2.energybulletin. net/node/23428

Ball, A. S. and Pretty, J. N. 'Agricultural influences on carbon emissions and sequestration'. In: Powell, J., et al. (eds). *Proceedings of the UK Organic Research 2002 Conference*, pp. 247–50 (Organic Centre Wales, Institute of Rural Studies, University of Wales, Aberystwyth, 2002)

Barański, M., et al. 'Higher antioxidant and lower cadmium concentrations and lower incidence of pesticide residues in organically grown crops: a systematic literature review and meta-analyses'. *British Journal of Nutrition*, vol. 112, issue 5, pp. 794–811 (September 2014)

Bathurst, Bella. 'Kill the plough, save our soils'. *Newsweek* (6 June 2014)

Case, Philip. 'Only 100 harvests left in UK farm soils, scientists warn'. *Farmers Weekly* (21 October 2014)

Cole, J. 'The effect of pig rooting on earthworm abundance and species diversity in West Sussex, UK'. MSc thesis, Centre for Environmental Policy, Faculty of Natural Sciences, Imperial College London (11 September 2013)

Davis, D. R., Melvin, D., and Riordan, H. D. 'Changes in USDA Food Composition Data for 43 Garden Crops, 1950 to 1999'. *Journal of the American College of Nutrition*, vol. 23, issue 6, pp. 669–82 (2004)

Hickel, Jason. 'Our best shot at cooling the planet might be right under our feet'. *Guardian* (10 September 2016)

Khursheed, S., Simmons, C., and Jaber, F. 'Glomalin – a key to locking up soil carbon'. *Advances in Plants & Agriculture Research*, vol. 4, issue 1 (2016)

Lambert, Chloe. 'Is food really better from the farm gate than supermarket shelf?' *New Scientist* (14 October 2015)

Ling, L. L., et al. 'A new antibiotic kills pathogens without detectable resistance'. *Nature*, vol. 517, pp. 455–9 (January 2015)

Liu, X., Lyu, S., Sun, D., Bradshaw, C. J. A., and Zhou, S. 'Species decline under nitrogen fertilization increases community-level competence of fungal diseases'. *Proceedings of the Royal Society B*, vol. 284, issue 1847 (25 January 2017)

Luepromchai, E., Singer, A., Yang, C.-H., and Crowley, D. E.

'Interactions of earthworms with indigenous and bioaugmented PCB-degrading bacteria'. *Federation of European Microbiological Societies Microbiology Ecology*, vol. 41, issue 3, pp. 191–7 (2002)

Merryweather, James. 'Meet the glomales – the ecology of mycorrhiza'. *British Wildlife*, vol 12, no. 2, pp. 86–93 (December 2001)

Merryweather, James. 'Secrets of the soil'. *Resurgence & Ecologist*, issue 235 (March/April 2006)

Meyer, Anne-Marie. 'Historical changes in the mineral content of fruits and vegetables'. *British Food Journal*, vol. 99, no. 6, pp. 207–11 (July 1997)

Noel, S., Mikulcak, F., et al. ELD Initiative. (2015). 'Reaping economic and environmental benefits from sustainable land management'. Report for policy and decision makers, Economics of Land Degradation Initiative. (2015) http://www.eld-initiative.org/fileadmin/pdf/ELD-pm-report_05_web_300dpi.pdf

Schaechter, Moselio ('Elio'). 'Mycorrhizal fungi: the world's biggest drinking straws and largest unseen communication system'. Small Things Considered (a blog for sharing appreciation of the width and depth of microbes and microbial activities on this planet). (August 2013) http://schaechter.asmblog.org/schaechter/2013/08/mycorrhizal-fungi-the-worlds-biggest-drinking-straws-and-largest-unseen-communication-system.html

Sutton, M., et al. (eds). *The European Nitrogen Assessment – Sources, Effects and Policy Perspectives* (Cambridge University Press, 2011)

Van Groenigen, J. W., Lubbers I. M., et al. 'Earthworms increase plant production: a meta-analysis'. *Scientific Reports*, vol. 4, article no. 6365 (2014)

Woods-Segura, James. 'Rewilding – an investigation of its effects on earthworm abundance, diversity and their provision of soil ecosystem services'. MSc thesis, Centre for Environmental Policy, Faculty of Natural Sciences, Imperial College London. (September 2013)

Xavier, L. J. C. and Germida, J. J. 'Impact of human activities on mycorrhizae'. *Microbial Biosystems: New Frontiers. Proceedings of the 8th International Symposium on Microbial Ecology,*

Atlantic Canada Society for Microbial Ecology, Halifax, Canada, 1999

Zaller, J. G., Heigl, F., et al. 'Glyphosate herbicide affects belowground interactions between earthworms and symbiotic mycorrhizal fungi in a model ecosystem'. *Scientific Reports*, vol. 4, article no. 5634 (July 2014)

Zhang, W., Hendrix, P. F., et al. 'Earthworms facilitate carbon sequestration through unequal amplification of carbon stabilization compared with mineralization'. *Nature Communications*, vol. 4, article no. 2576 (2013)

*

Economics of Land Degradation Initiative report (September 2015) http://www.eld-initiative.org/fileadmin/pdf/ELD-pm-report_05_web_300dpi.pdf

'Glomalin: hiding place for a third of the world's stored soil carbon'. *Agricultural Research Magazine*, US Department of Agriculture (September 2002) https://agresearchmag.ars.usda.gov/2002/sep/soil

Restoring the climate through capture and storage of soil carbon through holistic planned grazing. Savory Institute (2013)

'Status of the World's Soil Resources'. Main report; Food and Agriculture Organization of the United Nations and Intergovernmental Technical Panel on Soils, Rome, Italy (2015) http://www.fao.org/3/a-i5199e.pdf

'UK soil degradation'. Postnote no. 265, Parliamentary Office of Science and Technology (July 2006) http://www.parliament.uk/documents/post/postpn265.pdf

www.soilfoodweb.com

17. The Value of Nature

Bird, W. 'Natural Thinking – investigating the links between the natural environment, biodiversity and mental health'. RSPB report (June 2007)

Chen, H., et al. 'Living near major roads and the incidence of dementia, Parkinson's disease, and multiple sclerosis: a population-based cohort study'. *The Lancet*, vol. 389, no. 10070, pp. 718–26 (18 February 2017)

Kaplan, S. 'The restorative effects of nature – toward an integrative framework'. *Journal of Environmental Psychology*, vol. 15, pp. 169–82 (1995)

Orians, G. H., and Heerwagen, J. H. 'Evolved responses to landscapes'. In: Barkow, J. H., Cosmides, L., and Tooby, J. (eds). *The Adapted Mind: Evolutionary Psychology and the Generation of Culture*, pp. 555–79 (Oxford University Press, 1993)

Pyle, R. M. 'The extinction of experience'. *Horticulture*, vol. 56, pp. 64–7 (1978)

Williams, A. G., Audsley, E., and Sandars, D. L. 'Determining the environmental burdens and resource use in the production of agricultural and horticultural commodities'. Main Report, DEFRA Research Project ISO 20 (Cranfield University, Bedford and DEFRA, 2006)

Taylor, R. C., et al. *Measuring holistic carbon footprints for lamb and beef farms in the Cambrian Mountains*. Countryside Council of Wales report (2010)

Ulrich, R., et al. 'Stress recovery during exposure to natural and urban environments'. *Journal of Environmental Psychology*, vol. 11, pp. 201–30 (1991)

Ulrich, R. S. 'Aesthetic and affective response to natural environment'. In: Altman, I., and Wohlwill, J. F. (eds). *Behaviour and the Natural Environment*, pp. 85–125 (Plenum, New York, 1983)

*

'Estimating local mortality burdens associated with particulate air pollution'. Public Health England report. (9 April 2014)

'The State of Natural Capital – protecting and improving natural capital for prosperity and wellbeing'. Natural Capital Committee report (2015) http://socialsciences.exeter.ac.uk/media/universityofexeter/collegeofsocialsciencesandinternationalstudies/leep/documents/2015_ncc-state-natural-capital-third-report.pdf

Bibliography

Blencowe, Michael and Neil Hulme. *The Butterflies of Sussex* (Pisces Publications, 2017)

Bosworth-Smith, R. *Bird Life & Bird Law* (John Murray, 1905)

Campbell-Palmer, Róisin, et al. *The Eurasian Beaver Handbook* (Pelagic Publishing, 2016)

Carroll, Sean B. *The Serengeti Rules – the quest to discover how life works and why it matters* (Princeton University Press, 2016)

Clements, Frederic E. *Plant Succession – an analysis of the development of vegetation* (The Carnegie Institute of Washington, 1916)

Coles, B. J. *Beavers in Britain's Past* (Oxbow Books, UK, 2006)

Collier, Eric. *Three Against the Wilderness* (Touch Wood Editions, 2007, first published 1959)

Crumley, Jim. *Nature's Architect – the beaver's return to our wild landscapes* (Saraband, 2015)

Cummins, John. *The Hound and the Hawk – the art of medieval hunting* (Weidenfeld & Nicolson, 1988)

Darwin, Charles. *The Formation of Vegetable Mould, through the action of earth worms, with observations on their habits* (John Murray, 1881)

Dent, Anthony. *Lost Beasts of Britain* (Harrap, 1974)

Gould, John. *Birds of Great Britain* (5 vols: n.p., 1862–73)

Goulson, Dave. *Bee Quest* (Jonathan Cape, 2017)

Grandin, Temple. *Livestock Handling & Transport* (4th edition, Centre for Agriculture and Biosciences International, 2014)

Grandin, Temple and Catherine Johnson. *Animals in Translation – the woman who thinks like a cow* (Bloomsbury, 2005)

Harvey, Graham. *The Carbon Fields – how our countryside can save Britain* (Grass Roots, UK, 2008)

Harvey, Graham. *The Forgiveness of Nature – the story of grass* (Jonathan Cape, 2001)

Helm, Dieter. *Natural Capital – valuing the planet* (Yale University Press, 2015)

Henderson, George. *The Farming Ladder* (Faber & Faber, 1943)

Hoskins, W. G. *The Making of the English Landscape* (Little Toller Books, 2013; first edn. Hodder & Stoughton, 1955)

Jefferies, R. *Nature Near London* (Chatto & Windus, 1883)

Juniper, Tony. *What Nature Does for Britain* (Profile Books, 2015)

Lawton, John. *Making Space for Nature – a review of England's wildlife sites and ecological network.* (Department for Environment, Food and Rural Affairs) (16 September 2010)

Leopold, Aldo. *A Sand County Almanac* (Oxford University Press, 1949)

Lovegrove, Roger. *Silent Fields – the long decline of a nation's wildlife* (Oxford University Press, 2007)

Mabey, Richard. *Weeds – how vagabond plants gate-crashed civilisation and changed the way we think about nature* (Profile Books, 2010)

Mabey, Richard. *Whistling in the Dark – in pursuit of the nightingale* (Sinclair Stevenson, 1993)

McCarthy, Michael. *The Moth Snowstorm* (John Murray, 2015)

McCarthy, Michael. *Say Goodbye to the Cuckoo* (John Murray, 2009).

Marris, Emma. *Rambunctious Garden – saving nature in a post-wild world* (Bloomsbury, 2011)

Monbiot, George. *Feral – searching for enchantment on the frontiers of rewilding* (Allen Lane, 2013)

Montgomery, David R. and Anne Biklé. *The Hidden Half of Nature – the microbial roots of life and health* (W. W. Norton, 2016)

Norton-Griffiths, M., and A. R. E. Sinclair. *Serengeti: Dynamics of an Ecosystem* (University of Chicago Press, 1979)

Oates, Matthew. *In Pursuit of Butterflies – a fifty-year affair* (Bloomsbury, 2015)

Ohlson, Kristin. *The Soil Will Save Us – how scientists, farmers and foodies are healing the soil to save the planet* (Rodale, 2014)

Quammen, David. *The Song of the Dodo – island biogeography in the age of extinctions* (Scribner, 1996)

Rackham, Oliver. *Ancient Woodland – its history, vegetation and uses in England* (Edward Arnold, London, 1980; and new edition Castlepoint Press, Kirkcudbrightshire, 2003)

Rackham, Oliver. *The History of the Countryside – the classic history of Britain's landscape, flora and fauna* (Phoenix, 2000)

Rackham, Oliver. *Woodlands* (The New Naturalist, Collins, 2006)

Robinson, Jo. *Pasture Perfect – the far-reaching benefits of choosing meat, eggs and dairy products from grass-fed animals* (Vashon Island Press, 2004)

Schwartz, Judith. *Cows Save the Planet – and other improbable ways of restoring soil to heal the earth* (Chelsea Green, 2013)

Stace, Clive A. and Michael J. Crawley. *Alien Plants* (The New Naturalist, William Collins, 2015)

Stapledon, Sir George. *The Way of the Land* (Faber & Faber, 1942)

Stewart, Amy. *The Earth Moved – on the remarkable achievements of earthworms* (Frances Lincoln, 2004)

Stolzenburg, William. *Where the Wild Things Were – life, death and ecological wreckage in a land of vanishing predators* (Bloomsbury, USA, 2008)

Tansley, A. G. *The British Islands and their Vegetation.* Vols 1 & 2 (Cambridge University Press, 3rd edn, 1953)

Tansley, A. G (ed.) *Types of British Vegetation* (Cambridge University Press, 1911)

Teicholz, Nina. *The Big Fat Surprise* (Scribe, 2014)

Thomas, Keith. *Man and the Natural World – changing attitudes in England 1500–1800* (Allen Lane, 1983)

Thompson, Ken. *Where Do Camels Belong? – the story and science of invasive species* (Profile Books, 2014)

Tubbs, C. R. *The New Forest – a natural history* (The New Naturalist, Collins. 1998)

Tudge, Colin. *The Secret Life of Trees* (Allen Lane, 2005)

Vera, F. W. M. *Grazing Ecology and Forest History* (CABI Publishing, 2000)

Walpole-Bond, John. *A History of Sussex Birds* (Witherby, 1938)

Wilson, Edward O. *Biophilia* (Harvard University Press, 1984)

Wilson, Edward O. *The Diversity of Life* (W. W. Norton, 1999)

Wilson, Edward O. *Half-Earth – our planet's fight for life* (Liveright Publishing, 2016)

Wohlleben, Peter. *The Hidden Life of Trees – what they feel, how they communicate* (Greystone Books, Canada, 2016)

Yalden, Derek. *The History of British Mammals* (Poyser Natural History, 1999)

Young, Rosamund. *The Secret Life of Cows* (Faber & Faber, 2017)

Acknowledgements

The Knepp rewilding project owes an enormous debt to two people who have been behind it from the very start. The first is Charlie's cousin, Julian Smith, trustee of Knepp Estate, who came on the first trip to the Oostvaardersplassen and immediately saw the potential for a naturalistic grazing project on the Sussex clay. He helped Charlie compose his initial 'Letter of Intent' to the government, and has been a source of moral support ever since.

The second is our Estate Manager, Jason Emrich, who took on Knepp just two weeks after the sale of all our farm machinery in 2000. We were already in the throes of restoring the Repton Park when he arrived but as far as he, or anyone else, knew, the rest of the land was destined to be contract-farmed. More conventional estate managers might have thrown up their hands in horror when the idea of rewilding was first mooted a year or so later, and come up with a thousand and one reasons why we shouldn't do it. But Jason is a man of enterprise and extraordinary imagination. His ability to think creatively has spurred the project on, time and again, when we'd thought all hope was lost. He is also a master at filling out forms which seem to have no application to our situation at all. But above all, he is an entrepreneur, and of the mind that just because no one else is doing it, doesn't mean we shouldn't give it a try. We are unbelievably lucky to have found a natural ally in him, and his intelligent presence underpins our story.

Another man who found himself almost accidentally rewilded is our stockman Pat Toe, originally a tree specialist. It was almost certainly to our advantage that he had no background in farming at all because he rose to the challenge of free-roaming cows and pigs unhampered by preconceived ideas and, perhaps, without fully understanding what he was letting himself in for. His patience with our free-willed animals, especially in the challenging scenario of the Southern Block, is matched only by his ingenuity in solving problems and his unfailing sense of humour. Craig Line, whose job at Knepp has also shifted to the wild side, is Pat's spare pair of hands and we are hugely grateful to him for rising to the challenge of animal husbandry and for building our miraculous Temple Grandin cattle-handling system. We are indebted, too, to our vet Maarten Boers who oversees the welfare of our unconventional livestock. Pat, Craig and Maarten's work, and that of the enormously practical and experienced Andy Meadows, in charge of the longhorn herd in the Northern Block, has been key to proving that a naturalistic grazing system like ours is not only doable and desirable, but profitable too.

We would also like to thank Chris Cook for trusting his herd of longhorns to us in the first place; Mark Bateman for overseeing the introduction of our Exmoor ponies; Dan Readfern for his work on the game side of the Estate; Jeremy Curling for taking up seventy miles of internal fencing and building perimeter fences and bridges; and the late, much-lamented Bob Lack, our farm foreman.

Other members of the Knepp team sustain the project in fundamental ways, even as it continues to morph in scope and scale. We are hugely grateful to Julie Alexander, Kirsty Haydon, Maureen Line, Anne McGrath, Yasmin Newman and Elizabeth Nightingale, for allowing themselves to be process-led and for their continued commitment to the project; to Paul and Amy Nightingale, our first safari and campsite managers (now running their own on-site carpentry and livery businesses), for getting Knepp Wildland Safaris off to a flying start; and Rachel Knott and Ryan Greaves, our present campsite managers, for masterfully taking over the controls and growing the business.

Much of the integrity of the project rests on the shoulders of Penny Green, our in-house ecologist, snatched from the bosom of the Sussex Wildlife Trust. We hope they've forgiven us for she is a gem. Up with the lark, and often still awake for the moths and nightingales, she steers our surveying and monitoring programmes, marshalling armies of experts and volunteers with humour and enthusiasm, and expertly pulling all their data and her own together. Having also launched the safari side of our tourism business, she now heads a team of seven supplementary safari guides – Tom Forward, Lucy Groves, Laurie Jackson, Rina Quinlan, Darren Rolfe, Mike Russell and Sophie Trice – and occasionally even the great Chris Corrigan, regional director of the RSPB, all impressive ecologists in their own right and now wonderful ambassadors for the project.

Penny builds on the work of Theresa Greenaway, one of our earliest Advisory Board members and orchestrator of our original baseline survey, annual reviews and a five-year repeat survey. Having such a well-designed monitoring system in place at an early stage was crucial to our credibility and continues to inform our ongoing survey work. We would urge anyone considering a project like this to set up a proper baseline study ahead of anything else.

I have described the inspiration of Ted Green and Frans Vera in the book but sadly there has been no room to acknowledge the invaluable contributions from the rest of our Advisory Board (their names are listed separately). Their guidance, enthusiasm and expert knowledge, given generously in the midst of busy lives, have shored us up from the very beginning and helped keep the whole show on the road. We are eternally grateful to them all. One person, however, needs to be singled out for his support at several critical junctures. Jim Seymour of Natural England stuck his neck out for us on more than one occasion, defending our position before the Minister of the Environment when issues like ragwort threatened to derail us.

I would especially like to thank the following for reading drafts of the book and giving such elucidating and often entertaining notes in the margins: Prof. Mick Crawley, Paul Goriup, Peter Marren, Dr Lisbet Rausing, Jonathan Spencer and Dr Tony Whitbread.

I'm also hugely grateful to Dr Keith Alexander, Prof. Richard Bardgett, Harry Bowell, Peter Burgess, Jill Butler, Prof. Alastair Driver, Mark Elliott, David Gollins, Derek Gow, Ted Green, Neil Hulme, Hans Kampf, Prof. Sir John Lawton, Leo Linnartz, John Malley, John Meadley, Tony Morris, Matthew Oates, Pat Toe, Joep van der Vlasakker and Dr Frans Vera for commenting on chapters or sections relating to their own expertise; and to Penelope Greenwood and Mark Burrell for sharing with me their memories of Knepp during and after the war. Numerous others – too numerous to mention by name - have kindly responded to queries and I would like to thank them all for taking the time to answer so fully. Whatever errors that remain are my own, or a result of my own interpretation or later additions to the text.

For general inspiration and moral support I would also like to thank our so-called Rewilding Group – a motley collection of environmentally interested friends who, for nearly a decade now, have ventured forth every year to a different area of rewilding in Europe. From the Camargue to the Chernobyl Exclusion Zone, these trips have been a huge source of encouragement and stimulation, as well as, invariably, tremendous fun. One does not 'live alone in a world of wounds', as Aldo Leopold said of an ecological education, if one can share experiences like these with likeminded people who are such positive forces for change.

A huge thank you to my agent David Godwin and his wife, Heather Godwin; to my publisher, Ravi Mirchandani, editor Ansa Khan Khattak, copy editor Nicholas Blake, and publicist Paul Martinovic.

And my final and biggest thanks to my husband, Charlie Burrell, whose vision this is. I count it the greatest good fortune to be continually astonished by him after thirty-five years and to have embarked with him on what has to be the greatest adventure of our lives.

Index

Aberdeen Angus cattle *see under* cattle,
    breeds of
Aberfoyle, Scotland 232
adder's tongue fern (*Ophioglossum
    vulgatum*) 271
ADHD 249, 297
Adur, river/valley
    canalization of 210, 212, 213–14, 216,
        221, 223
    flooding 209, 210
    as HLS target area 175–6
    Operation Turtle Dove 199
    origin of name 213
    potential for beavers 236
    re-naturalization of 221–3, 228, 271
aesthetics, as ecosystem service 288
Africa 65, 66, 67, 196, 198, 252
agricultural fertilizers *see* chemical
        fertilizers
Agricultural Property Relief 302
Agriculture Act, 1947 23
air quality 206, 294–5, 299–300
alder (*Alnus glutinosa*) 1, 78, 123, 127
Alexander, Dr Keith 86
algae 278
Alice Holt, Hampshire/Surrey border 176
alien species 169–72, 242
Allen, Dr Mike 87
Alps 154
Alzheimer's disease 249, 260, 295
American mink (*Neovison vison*) 231–2
amphibians 238 *see also* common lizard,
        common newt, common toad, great
        crested newt, natterjack toad
ancient woodland 3–4, 23, 79, 128, 129,
        176, 207

anecic earthworms 274, 283
anemone *see* wood anemone
angelica *see* wild angelica
Anthropocene era 153, 258
antibiotics, new 284
    effects on the soil 22
    use in intensive livestock farming 249
ants 112, 166, 278
apex predator trophic cascades 153–4, 204
apple *see* crab apple
Appleby, Cumbria 226
aquatic invertebrates 238
    fairy shrimp (*Chirocephalus
            diaphanus*) 113
    krill 248
aquatic plants 113
arable farming *see also* food production
        and chemical fertilizers
    cereal production 4, 38, 132, 134–5,
        251
    crop yields and earthworms 278–9, 282
    decrease in land usage 135
    and flooding 211
    grain consumption 132, 133, 134, 251
    at Knepp 36, 38, 39–40
    policies/subsidies 33, 95–6
    Second World War 17–19, 22–3
Arctic alpine plants 87
Arctic char (*Salvelinus alpinus*) 224
ARK Foundation 158
artificial fertilizers *see* chemical fertilizers
Arun, river 209, 232
ash (*Fraxinus excelsior*) 62, 78, 81, 82, 127,
        175, 204, 207, 208, 224
ash die-back (*Chalara*) 81, 208
Asia 252, 262

aspen (*Populus tremula*) 224, 265
Atlas Mountains, Morocco 162
Atlas of European Breeding Birds 192
attention deficit hyperactivity disorder
    (ADHD) 249, 297
aurochs (*Bos primigenius*) 61, 62, 63, 65–6,
    75, 88, 127, 128, 160
avermectins 22, 114, 115, 249, 271

bacteria
    and carcass decomposition 70, 74
    decline in populations of 5
    and soil 275, 277, 278–9, 281
badger (*Meles meles*) 26, 94, 126, 173, 204
Baerselman, Fred 59
Balharry, Dick 235
Balkans 154
Baltic States 154
bank vole (*Myodes glareolus*) 270
Bannerman, David Armitage 199
barbastelle bat (*Barbastella barbastellus*)
    8, 114, 169, 238
Barkham, Patrick 295
barn owl (*Tyto alba*) 120
Barnes, Simon 295
basil thyme (*Clinopodium acinos*) 158
Bateman, Mark (stable manager) 106
bats 6, 26, 44, 147, 168–9, 238 *see also*
    barbastelle, Bechstein's, common
    pipistrelle, Daubenten's, greater
    horseshoe, whiskered bat
Bavaria, Germany 240–2
'BB' *see* Watkins-Pitchford, Denys
bearded tit (*Panurus biarmicus*) 57
bears 62, 155, 308 *see also* brown bear,
    grizzly bear
beautiful china mark moth *see under*
    moths, species of
Beaver Advisory Committee for England
    (BACE) 237, 242, 243
beavers *see also individual species*
    attitudes towards 74, 234–5, 236,
        237–8, 241, 242, 243, 301
    BBC *Springwatch* 243–4
    Devon Wildlife Trust 237–9, 243–5
    earliest presence of 75, 127
    future plans 292
    Knapdale trial 236, 237
    population increases 155, 239–40, 265,
        300, 308
    Rewilding Britain 10

    role of 157, 229–30, 232–45
    and tourism 304
Bechstein's bat (*Myotis bechsteinii*) 8, 169
Bee Quest (Goulson) 273
beech (*Fagus sylvatica*) 58, 62, 78, 79, 80,
    82, 204
beefsteak fungus (*Fistulina hepatica*) 27
bees 6, 112, 142, 203
bees, species of
    Melitta europaea 273
    mining bees
    red bartsia bee (*Melitta tricincta*) 273
    ridge-cheeked furrow bee
        (*Lasioglossum puncticolle*) 273
    rough-backed blood bee (*Sphecodes
        scabricollis*) 273
    see also bumblebees, mining bees,
        solitary bees
beetles
    and deadwood 47, 203, 271
    earliest presence of 86
    population increases 113, 142, 238
    in soil 278
    see also carrion beetles, click beetles,
        clown beetles, dung beetles,
        ground beetles, saproxylic
        beetles, soldier beetles, steely
        blue beetle, tiger beetles, violet
        click beetle, water beetles
Bernwood Forest, Oxfordshire 176
biodiversity
    benefits to economy 206, 307
    biodiversity intactness index 7
    fossil pollen evidence 82–5
    grazing animals as drivers of 59, 60, 68,
        157, 159, 160, 261, 266, 301
    and nature management 64–5, 206
    offsetting 206, 304
    role of 5, 307
    UK Biodiversity Action Plan species 8,
        169, 170, 269
biofuels 134–5
biomass plantation trials, Knepp 283–4
Biophilia Hypothesis (Wilson) 296–7, 298
Biotechnology and Biological Sciences
    Research Council 285
birch 78, 123–4, 128, 175, 199, 224, 225,
    265
Bird Life & Bird Law (Bosworth-
    Smith) 194
Birdlife International 155

birds
impact of habitat on UK populations
4–5, 128, 147–8, 196, 203
at Knepp 44, 169, 175, 192, 202
and oak trees 26
Oostvaardersplassen 69
species isolation 202–3
see also individual species
bird's-foot trefoil (*Lotus corniculatus*) 44,
251
bird's nest orchid (*Neottia nidus-avis*) 285
Birds of Great Britain, The (Gould) 190,
191
birds of prey *see* raptors
Birds of Sussex (Walpole-Bond) 191
Birds of the British Isles (Bannerman) 199
Bisham Woods, Berkshire 80
bison (*Bison bonasus*) 61, 74, 127, 157–9,
160, 292
bison wallows 158
bittern (*Botaurus stellaris*) 6, 57, 147, 169
black bryony (*Tamus communis*) 143
black redstart (*Phoenicurus ochruros*) 125
black stork (*Ciconia nigra*) 268
black tern (*Chlidonias niger*) 268
blackthorn (*Prunus spinosa*) 1, 83, 119,
122, 123, 127, 128, 190, 272, 307
blowflies 74, 270
blue tit (*Cyanistes caeruleus*) 47, 173, 180,
207
bluebell (*Hyacinthoides non-scripta*) 20–1,
129
boar *see* wild boar
bog myrtle (*Myrica gale*) 84
bog pimpernel (*Anagallis tenella*) 238
bog trees 78
boletes 26
Boletus mendax 285
Bookham Common, Leatherhead, Surrey
176
Borders Forest Trust 235
Borkener Paradies, Germany 83
Bosworth-Smith, R. 194
Bournemouth University 151, 288
bovine grazing relationship with equines
159–60 *see also* cattle
box, common (*Buxus sempervirens*) 128
bracken (*Pteridium aquilinum*) 113, 125,
143
bracket fungi 27
Buglossoporus quercinus 27

Ganoderma resinaceum 27
Phellinus robustus 27
Bramber, Sussex 213
bramble 1, 48, 66, 82, 101, 119, 122, 123,
125, 127, 128, 175, 190, 191, 269, 296
brambling (*Fringilla montifringilla*) 265
Bredon Hill, Worcestershire 204
Breite Nature Reserve, Romania 79
Brexit, potential effects/options 156, 300
British Equestrian Veterinary Association
(BEVA) 140
British Horse Society 140
British Islands and Their Vegetation
(Tansley) 64
British Trust for Ornithology 148, 187,
188, 193
brittlegills 26
broad-leaved dock (*Rumex
obtusifolius*) 140
broadleaved woodland 80, 128, 169 *see
also individual tree species*
Brookhouse Scrapes 169
broom (*Cytisus scoparius*) 123
brown bear (*Ursus arctos*) 63, 155, 204,
304, 308
brown hairstreak butterfly (*Thecla
betulae*) 8, 272
brown hare (*Lepus europaeus*) 170
brownfield sites, value of 125
browsing animals 49, 63, 66, 69, 87, 89, 90,
99, 103, 113, 122, 125, 127, 128, 175,
179, 224, 252, 253, 292
see also grazing animals
bryophytes 271
BSE crisis 133
Buckland, Professor Paul 114, 151
Buckley, Tom 304
bugle (*Ajuga reptans*) 129
Buglife, The Invertebrate Conservation
Trust 125
Buglossoporus quercinus (bracket fungus)
27
bullfinch (*Pyrrhula pyrrhula*) 120, 125
bumblebees 44, 205 *see also* short-haired
bumblebee
burbot (*Lota lota*) 10, 147
Burrell, Anthony 93
Burrell, Sir Charles Merrik 14
Burrell, Charlie 1, 5, 9, 10, 13, 14, 29, 32,
33, 37, 38, 40, 41, 45, 57, 70, 71, 72,
75, 97, 98, 102, 110, 114, 122, 130,

Burrell, Charlie (*cont.*)
144, 146, 152, 157, 161, 166, 174,
175, 179, 182, 187, 217, 218, 222,
223, 234, 237, 244, 250, 252, 255,
289, 296, 302, 305, 307
Burrell, Mark 39
Burrell, Sir Merrik 17, 18, 19
Burrell, Nancy 207, 208
Burrell, Ned 255
Burrell, Sir Percy 216
Burrell, Sir Raymond 70
Burrell, Sir Walter 32, 216, 231
Burrell, Sir William 14
Burton, Dr John 35
bush crickets 271
bushgrass (*Calamagrostris epigejos*) 157
Butler, Jill 56, 157
butterflies
breeding patterns 164–5, 205
impact of habitat on UK populations 6,
128, 166, 238
at Knepp 162–6, 173, 177–8, 179–83,
271–2
migration and travel 44, 164–5, 203
Oostvaardersplassen 69
butterflies, species of
Camberwell beauty (*Nymphalis
antiopa*) 178
common blue (*Polyommatus icarus*)
44, 176
dark green fritillary (*Argynnis
aglaja*) 44, 272
Duke of Burgundy (*Hamearis
lucina*) 176
Essex skipper (*Thymelicus lineola*) 44,
176, 272
green-veined white (*Pieris napi*) 272
high brown fritillary (*Fabriciana
adippe*) 176
large blue (*Maculinea arion*) 6
marbled white (*Melanargia
galathea*) 44, 176, 272
marsh fritillary butterfly (*Euphydryas
aurinia*) 159–60, 176
meadow brown (*Maniola jurtina*) 44,
176
painted lady (*Vanessa cardui*) 162–5
pearl-bordered fritillary (*Boloria
euphrosyne*) 129, 176, 296
purple emperor (*Apatura iris*) 8, 129,
176–8, 179–83, 272, 292

purple hairstreak (*Neozephyrus
quercus*) 272
Queen of Spain fritillary (*Issoria
lathonia*) 178
ringlet (*Aphantopus hyperantus*) 44,
176
scarce tortoiseshell (*Nymphalis
xanthomelas*) 178
small copper (*Lycaena phlaeas*) 112
small heath (*Coenonympha
pamphilus*) 272
small skipper (*Thymelicus
sylvestris*) 44, 176, 272
small tortoiseshell (*Aglais urticae*) 176
walled brown (*Lasiommata
megera*) 272
white admiral (*Limenitis camilla*) 128,
296
white-letter hairstreak (*Satyrium
w-album*) 8
wood white (*Leptidea sinapis*) 129
Butterfly Conservation 163, 178
buzzard (*Buteo buteo*) 26, 68, 120, 168,
207, 230

calcium 70, 74, 279, 280, 281, 285
California, University of 287
Camargue horses *see under* horses/ponies,
breeds of
Camberwell beauty *see under* butterflies,
species of
Campbell-Palmer, Roisin 237, 244
Canada 154, 239–40, 282
canals 210, 212, 213–14, 216, 217, 299
canary-shouldered thorn moth *see under*
moths, species of
capercaillie (*Tetrao urogallus*) 265
Capps Bridge, Shipley 210
Car Dykes, Fens 212
Carbon Farmers of America 287
Carbon Fields (Harvey) 286
carbon sequestration
and beaver ponds 240
and biodiversity 206
as ecosystem service 288, 289, 299
at Knepp 10
Making Space for Nature report 206
and mycorrhizae 285–7
planting woodlands 306
carline thistle (*Carlina vulgaris*) 158
Carlisle, Cumbria 226

carp-farming at Knepp 218, 219
Carpathian Mountains 79, 103,154
carrion beetles 68, 70
carrion crow (*Corvus corone*) 55, 207
Caryll family 13, 14, 94
Castle Dairy ice-cream 37
castoreum 229–30
castration, of ponies 260–61
catastrophic shift 156–7
cats, domestic 204
cattle *see also* pasture-fed meat
    annual die-offs 69, 70
    beef industry 103, 115, 134, 251
    carcasses, disposal of 70, 73, 292
    cattle-grids 72
    Chillingham herd 253
    commons grazing 89
    creators of biodiversity 113
    dairy, at Knepp 34, 41, 55, 102
    dairy industry 33, 102,115,134, 251
    diet/eating behaviour 33, 63, 66–7, 140,
        159
    disturbance 113
    ear-tagging 253
    free-roaming at Knepp 98, 99–103,
        113, 175, 250
        neighbours' attitudes to 72, 130,
            137, 293
    grain-fed 247, 248–9, 251–2, 253
    grazing relationship with equines 159,
        255
    handling systems 255–6, 258–9
    meat sales, Knepp Wild Range 75, 246-
        7, 289
    natural behaviour 99–103, 254, 255
    Oostvaardersplassen 68, 69, 92
    regulations 73, 253–4
    slaughter of 292
    temperament and whorl
        placement 257–8
cattle, breeds of
    Aberdeen Angus 96, 246
    Charolais 99
    Friesian 33–4, 99, 100
    Galloway 224
    Heck (*Bos taurus*) 57, 65–6, 67, 69,
        72, 98
    Hereford 99
    Highland 66, 157
    Holstein 33–4, 99, 100
    old English longhorn 98–103, 117, 118,

137, 139, 175, 246–7, 250, 253–4,
            257–9, 292, 293
        Red Poll 33–4, 55, 99
        Spanish fighting bull 66, 98
        White Belgian 214
        White Park (*Bos taurus*) 66
cedar of Lebanon (*Cedrus libani*) 48, 167
centipedes *see under* soil biota
Centre for Ecology and Hydrology 288
cereal production 4, 18, 33, 34, 37, 38, 132,
        133 134–5, 141, 233, 251
chaffinch (*Fringilla coelebs*) 180
Chalara/ash dieback 81, 207
chalk grassland 18, 87
charities, funding of tree plantations 127
Charles, Prince of Wales 142
Charles II 25
Charlie Burrell's Castle Dairy ice-
        cream 37
Charlwood 49
Charolais cattle *see under* cattle, breeds of
chemical build-up in soil
        dichlorodiphenyltrichloroethane
            (DDT) 282
        organochlorides – dieldrin 282
        polychlorinated biphenyls
            (PCBs) 282
chemical fertilizers *see also individual types*
    dependency on 23, 24, 34, 279
        effect on biodiversity 3, 274–5, 279
        and human health 280, 281
        inefficiency of 279–80
        invention of 22
        at Knepp 34, 41, 45, 46, 96, 250
        and mycorrhizae 21–2
        pasture-fed meat 250
        pollution caused by 21, 46, 275,
            279–80, 306
chemicals, synthetic/dangerous – build-up
        in soil 282
cherry *see* wild cherry
chicken-of-the-woods (*Laetiporus
        sulphureus*) 27
chiffchaff (*Phylloscopus collybita*) 207
children, access to nature 293–4, 295, 297
China 221, 227, 262
Chinese water deer (*Hydropotes
        inermis*) 49, 267
Churchill, Winston 110
cinnabar moth *see under* moths, species of
cirl bunting (*Emberiza cirlus*) 125

CLA *see* Country Landowners
    Association
CLA (conjugated linoleic acid) 248, 249
Clare, John 137, 139, 185
clay soil
    and grazing animals 113
    as habitat 273
    impact of 40, 43, 76, 105
    land drainage 215–17, 219
    Sussex Weald 34–6
Clements, Frederic 64
click beetles (*Calambus bipustulatus*) 271
climate change
    and biodiversity 9, 10, 188, 203
    and carbon sequestration *see* carbon
        sequestration
    and flooding risk 211, 220
    and nightingales 188
    UK legislation 300
climax vegetation theory 61, 63, 64, 82
Clinton Devon Estates 244
closed-canopy theory 61–5, 77–91
closed-canopy woodland 125, 156, 265,
    266
clover 24, 44, 105
clown beetles 74
club-rush *see* common club-rush
Cnappe/Cnapp *see* old Knepp Castle
Cockermouth, Cumbria 226
cod 147
collared dove (*Streptopelia decaocto*) 196,
    207, 208
Colorado State University 240
Common Agricultural Policy (EU) 38,
    95, 300
    decoupling farm subsidies 95–6
    Environmental Stewardship
        Schemes 174–5
    farming subsidies 23–4, 32, 33, 299,
        300, 306
    Higher Level Stewardship 174, 175
common blue *see under* butterflies, species
    of
common club-rush (*Schoenoplectus
    lacustris*) 272
common cow-wheat (*Melampyrum
    pratense*) 129
common dog-violet (*Viola riviniana*) 129,
    296
common field grasshopper (*Chorthippus
    brunneus*) 44, 112, 166

common fleabane (*Pulicaria
    dysenterica*) 165, 252
common fumitory (*Fumaria officinalis*) 3,
    197, 251
common frog (*Rana temporaria*) 238, 271
common gorse (*Ulex europaeus*) 17, 124,
    199
common lizard (*Zootoca vivipara*) 112,
    166, 238
common magpie (*Pica pica*) 55, 207, 293
Common Market *see* European Union
    (EU)
common milkwort (*Polygala vulgaris*) 158
common newt (*Lissotriton vulgaris*) 271,
    293
common ragwort (*Senecio jacobaea*) 137,
    138–46, 149, 150, 165, 272
common shrew (*Sorex araneus*) 94, 270
common snipe (*Gallinago gallinago*) 167
common spotted orchid (*Dactylorhiza
    fuchsii*) 285
common toad (*Bufo bufo*) 68, 270
Composition of Foods, The 281
coniferous woodland 80, 218, 223–4
conjugated linoleic acid (CLA) 248, 249
connectivity *see* landscape connectivity
    and Living Landscapes
conservation interventions, potential
    negative effects 302
coppice, woodland 147, 187, 191, 192, 234,
    238, 245
coppicing 62, 64, 127–9, 188, 296
corn bunting (*Emberiza calandra*) 5
corn marigold (*Glebionis segetum*) 170
corncockle (*Agrostemma githago*) 170
corncrake (*Crex crex*) 147
cornflower (*Centaurea cyanus*) 147, 170
corridors for wildlife 153, 205–6
Corsican pine (*Pinus nigra*) 157
Cotta, Heinrich von 90
Country Landowners Association 148,
    193, 237
Countryside Rights of Way Act 2000
    302–3
Countryside Stewardship Scheme 39,
    93–5, 117–18, 162, 174, 250
cow-wheat *see* common cow-wheat
cows *see* cattle
crab apple (*Malus sylvestris*) 83, 89, 126
crab spiders 271
Crabro scutellatus (wasp) 273

Craft Fairs 110–11, 178
Crawley, Professor Mick 145
crayfish 170
creeping thistle (*Cirsium arvense*) 140,
    141, 161, 162, 163, 165–6
crested dog's tail (*Cynosurus cristatus*) 44
crop pollination 10, 206, 300
Crow map of Knepp Estate 94–5, 118
crows 55, 70, 168, 207 *see also individual*
    species
crucian carp (*Carassius carassius*) 218, 219
Cuckmere, river 209
cuckoo (*Cuculus canorus*) 2, 8, 143, 148,
    192
cuckoo pint (*Arum maculatum*) 143
culling, livestock 75, 103, 246, 258
culm grasslands 203, 238–9
Cumbria 303
curled dock (*Rumex crispus*) 140

daffodils 141, 143
dairy farming
    effects of milk quotas 34, 38, 41
    foot and mouth disease 42
    grain-based diet 33, 251
    at Knepp 33, 34, 37, 38, 39, 40, 41
    mastitis 102
    separation of mothers/calves 102
Dalmatian pelican (*Pelecanus crispus*) 10
dams 220
damselflies 238, 271
Dangerous Wild Animals Act 108
Danube, river 241
dark green fritillary *see under* butterflies,
    species of
Dartford warbler (*Sylvia undata*) 125
Dartmoor 159
Dartmoor Hill Pony Association 261
Dartmoor pony *see under* horses/ponies,
    breeds of
Darwin, Charles 276, 283
Daubenton's bat (*Myotis daubentonii*) 114
DDT 282
dead donkey fly 74
dead wood/trees 27, 46–7, 48, 86, 238,
    271, 273
decoupling subsidies, impact of 95–6
Dee, river 210
deer *see also* Chinese water deer, fallow,
    muntjac, Père David, red deer, roe,
    sambar, sika

annual die-offs 69
areas for 49, 90, 263
at Knepp 13, 16, 28, 48, 49, 50,
    51–5, 72, 75, 95, 99, 101, 117,
    118, 122, 130, 139, 175, 252,
    253, 263
debarking of trees 66
creators of biodiversity 66, 68, 70
diet/eating behaviour 26, 29, 66, 68,
    139, 158, 252, 263
disturbance 63, 66
disease 123
hunting and population
    management 28, 49, 50, 51,
    63, 88, 89, 263, 264, 266–7
lekking 180
neighbours' attitudes to 130, 263
Norway 264, 266
Scotland 263, 264, 266, 299
supplementary feeding 253
deer fences 49, 90, 93–4, 108–9, 118, 126,
    133, 175
deer parks 13, 16, 28, 29, 48–52, 55, 93–5,
    117, 118, 130
DEFRA
    and beavers 234, 237, 242–3
    Countryside Stewardship Scheme
        see Countryside Stewardship
        Scheme
    ecosystem services 288, 291
    Environmental Stewardship Scheme
        see Environmental Stewardship
        Scheme
    Higher Level Stewardship
        Scheme 174–5
    'grass-fed' livestock 249
    and Knepp rewilding 91, 95, 138, 144,
        234, 254, 288, 289
    Making Space for Nature 206–7
    naturalistic flood management 226, 288
    Nature Improvement Areas 206, 207
        Pickering, Yorkshire Dales 226
    and ragwort 139, 141, 145
Denman, Lady 18
Denmark 300
Derek Gow Consultancy 244
Devensian era 87, 88
devil's bit scabious (*Succisa pratensis*) 45
Devon 203, 206
Devon Wildlife Trust 237–8, 243, 244
Dial Post 18

die-offs, animals 68, 69, 157
Dig for Victory 17–18, 23
diversification, at Knepp 37, 38, 75,
    218–19, 292, 303–4
Dixton Wood, Gloucestershire 204
Dog-barking Wood 176
dog rose (*Rosa canina*) 1, 17, 83, 119, 124,
    128, 148, 175
dog violet (*Viola odorata*) 129, 296
Doggerland 75
dogs/dog walkers 101, 160, 172, 258,
    292–3
dogwood (*Cornus sanguinea*) 83, 123
dolphins 147, 303
domestic cat (*Felis catus*) 204, 293
domestic goat (*Capra aegagrus hircus*) 67,
    140, 203
Donovan, Isobel 192
dormouse (*Muscardinus avellanarius*) 7,
    8, 128, 204
dragonflies 238
    scarce chaser dragonfly (*Libellula
        fulva*) 271
drainage *see* land drainage
drainage ploughs 214–15, 216–17
drought, effects of 81, 139, 196
    land resistance to 227
ducks 26, 231, 238, 268 *see also* mandarin
    duck, scaup duck
Duke of Burgundy *see under* butterflies,
    species of
Duncan (Exmoor stallion) 106–8
dune landscapes 157–9
dung beetles 68, 114–15, 274
    Geotrupes mutator 271
dunnock (*Prunella modularis*) 112
dusky thorn moth *see under* moths, species
    of

E. coli 278
eagle owl (*Bubo bubo*) 10
early purple orchid (*Orchis mascula*) 285
earthworms 48, 238, 274–83
    anecic 274, 283
    coelomic fluid 277
    crop yields 278
    detoxification of soil 282
    endogeic 274
    epigeic 274
    see also individual species
East Germany 154

ecoducts *see* land bridges
ecological corridors 153, 205–6
Economic and Social Research
    Council 247
Economics of Ecosystems and Biodiversity
    initiative 306
Economics of Land Degradation
    Initiative 284
economics of rewilding 301
ecosystem services 151, 206, 288–90, 304,
    306–7
eco-tourism 289, 304
edge effect, and isolated habitats 204–5
edible dormouse (*Glis glis*) 170
Edinburgh Zoo 236, 237, 244
Edlin, Herbert 80
education, and nature 293
Edward II 28
Egypt 276
Egyptian goose (*Alopochen
    aegyptiaca*) 169
elder (*Sambucus nigra*) 66, 123, 143, 199
Elizabeth I 25
elk *see* Eurasian elk (*Alces alces*; known as
    'moose' in N. America)
Ellenberg, Heinz 64
elm trees 62, 78, 81, 82, 127, 128
    Dutch elm disease 81
    see also smooth-leaved elm, wych elm
emergent properties 182–3
empathy, and nature 293–4, 295
Emrich, Jason 174
enchytraeid worms *see under* soil biota
endangered species 6, 307
energy/fuel, as ecosystem service 288
English Nature, application for
    funding 72–7, 91–2, 93, 118 *see also*
    Natural England
Ennerdale Water, Lake District 224–6, 288
Environment Agency 211, 221–2, 226,
    227, 237
environmental awareness, and age 148–9
environmental protection, future of in
    UK 299–300
Environmental Stewardship Scheme 174–5
Environmental White Papers, *The Natural
    Choice (2011)* 206
ephemeral ponds 113
epiphytes 238
equines *see* horses/ponies
Equus Survival Trust 104

erosion, long shore drift 213
  soil *see* soil erosion
  streambed 234
Essex skipper *see under* butterflies, species
  of
Estonia 4
EU (European Union) *see* European
  Union (EU)
Eurasian elk (*Alces alces*) 10, 61, 62, 63, 75,
  94, 127, 155, 240, 255, 292
Europe
  beaver reintroduction programmes 240
  horsemeat consumption 262
  rewilding projects 154–5
  tree fodder for livestock 252
  see also individual countries
European beachgrass (*Ammophila
  arenaria*) 157
European beaver (*Castor fiber*) 61, 62, 63,
  73, 233, 240
European bison (*Bison bonasus*) 61, 62,
  65, 73
European Nitrogen Assessment 280
European Union (EU)
  agri-environment programme 39
  Brexit potential effects/options 156,
    299, 300
  Common Agricultural Policy 38, 95,
    300
  effects of subsidies 23–4, 32, 33, 299,
    300, 306
  Habitats Directive 156, 205, 300
  land management reforms 95–6
  legislation affecting UK environmental
    protection 299–300
  Meadow Protection Plan 301–2
  Natura 2000 300
  see also individual countries
Exeter, University of 239, 244
exotic species 169–72
extinction of experience, in childhood 294
extreme weather events 81, 209–11, 220,
  225, 227

facilitation grazing, equines and
  bovines 159
fairy shrimp (*Chirocephalus
  diaphanus*) 113
fallen branches/leaves, role of 47–8
fallow deer (*Dama dama*) 13, 48, 49–50,
  51–5, 58, 72, 158, 175, 267, 293

fallow land 19
farm animals
  disease risks 73
  forest grazing rights 89
  quality of lives 69–70, 102
farm buildings, income from 303
farm machinery 40–1, 214–15, 216–17
farming
  intensive 3, 109, 134, 274, 275, 280
  at Knepp 30, 32, 70, 96, 100, 167, 288,
    305
  rotational 22–4, 37–9, 131, 283, 287
  tax advantages 302-3
Farming and Wildlife Advisory
  Group 237
Farming Ladder, The (Henderson) 23
farming subsidies
  Basic Payment 95–6
  effects of 23–4, 32, 33, 299, 300, 306
farmland
  abandoned *see* land abandonment
  biodiversity of 64
  decline in birds 5, 120
  field enlargement 24, 36
fats, attitudes to 251
fatty acids 247–8, 249, 251 *see also*
  nutrition
Faulkner, Charlotte 261
Fens, East Anglia 220
Feral (Monbiot) 10
Fermyn Woods, Brigstock,
  Northamptonshire 176, 177, 181
ferns 224
fertilizers *see* chemical fertilizers
field enlargement 24, 36
field grasshopper *see* common field
  grasshopper
field maple (*Acer campestre*) 62, 127
field mouse *see* wood mouse
field mushroom (*Agaricus campestris*) 114
field/short-tailed vole (*Microtus
  agrestis*) 47, 230, 270
fieldfare (*Turdus pilaris*) 8, 112, 120, 166,
  167, 265
figure of eight moth *see under* moths,
  species of
financial costs, rewilding 301, 304–6
fingered cowlwort (*Colura
  calyptrifolia*) 238
Finland 154, 155, 300, 304
fire, as natural process 80

fish 147, 234, 241, 247, 248 *see also*
     individual species
fishing subsidies 23–4, 299, 300, 306
fleabane *see* common fleabane
flies 142
     dead donkey fly 74
     fly larvae 238
     hoverflies 44, 238
Floodgates 210
floods
     and biodiversity 81, 206
     cost to the UK economy 227
     defences 210, 211, 288
     levees 211
     natural management of 206, 223,
          224–8, 277, 299, 306
     Netherlands 220
     UK 209–11, 225–7
flora 6, 44–5, 64–5, 82
     alpine/Arctic 87
     aquatic 113, 240
     see also injurious weeds; *individual*
          species
fly agaric (*Amanita muscaria*) 285
folk tales, and forests 81–2
Food and Agriculture Organization of the
     United Nations 275
food production
     as fuel 134
     grain consumption 251
     nutrition *see* nutrition
     pasture-fed meat *see* pasture-fed meat
     and rewilding 130, 131, 288, 289
     Second World War 17–19, 22–3, 251
     see also arable farming
food waste 132–5
foot and mouth disease 42, 133
Foreman, Dave 153
Forest History and Grazing Ecology
     (Vera) 56, 76
Forestry Commission 150, 223, 226, 237,
     283–4
forests
     definition/origin of terms 88–90
     and folk tales 81–2
     and grazing animals 60–1, 63
     regeneration 61, 63, 89, 90, 123–4, 126
4 per 1000 initiative 288
Fowler, John 216
Fox, Sir Cyril 82
foxes 70, 73, 230 *see also* red fox

foxglove (*Digitalis purpurea*) 141, 143
France 3, 4, 83, 128, 240, 262, 288
fresh water
     as ecosystem service 288, 289
     ephemeral ponds 113
     flooding risk and climate change 220
     quality at Knepp 289
freshwater amphibians 205
Friends of the Earth 237
Friesian cattle *see under* cattle, breeds of
fringe vegetation 83, 84, 85
froghoppers 271
frogs *see* common frog, marsh frog
Frome, river 239, 288
fuel production, as ecosystem service 288
fumaric acid 251
fumitory *see* common fumitory
fungi
     and anthills 113
     decline in populations of 5, 6, 74
     dune landscapes 158
     and oak trees 26, 27–8
     see also mycorrhizae/mycorrhizal
          fungi; beefsteak fungus, boletes,
          bracket fungi, brittlegills,
          chicken-of-the-woods, field
          mushroom, fly agaric, milkcaps,
          parasols, truffles, zoned rosette
          fungus
fungicides 22, 34, 113
fungus weevils (*Platystomos albians*) 271

gadwall (*Anas strepera*) 167
Galloway cattle *see under* cattle, breeds of
Ganoderma resinaceum (bracket
     fungus) 27
garden warbler (*Sylvia bori*) 129
gatekeeper butterfly (*Pyronia
     tithonus*) 176
geese 56, 68, 268
     as keystone species 59, 60
     see also Canada, Egyptian, greylag,
          Himalayan bar-footed, pink-
          footed goose
Geotrupes mutator (violet dor beetle) 271
Germany 83, 154, 156, 221, 227, 240–2,
     300
ghost moth (*Hepialus humuli*) 272
glassy-winged sharpshooter (*Homalodisca
     vitripennis*) 282
glomalin 286–7

glow-worm (*Lampyris noctiluca*) 147, 173
glyphosate 45, 300
goat, *see* domestic goat
goat willow (*Salix caprea*) 178
Godwin, Sir Harry 84
Goldberg, Emma 151, 161
goldcrest (*Regulus regulus*) 218
golden jackal (*Canis aureus*) 308
gorse *see* common gorse
goshawk (*Accipiter gentilis*) 158
Gould, John 190, 191, 194, 199
Goulson, Dave 273, 295
Gove, Michael 300
Gow, Derek 229, 232, 234, 235, 237, 241, 243, 244, 245
grain consumption 132, 133, 134
grain-fed meat 248, 249, 250, 251–2
Grandin, Temple 256–9
grant-aid, as woodland funding 127
grass-fed meat, definition of 249
    see also pasture-fed meat
grass snake (*Natrix natrix*) 8, 68, 148, 173, 230, 270
grasses, native 3, 4, 44, 82–5, 94, 105, 113, 157, 158, 159, 173, 190, 196, 205, 249, 250, 261
    commercial 3, 250
grasshopper *see* common field grasshopper
grasshopper warbler (*Locustella naevia*) 238
grassland 42, 60, 65, 67, 77, 84, 85, 86, 87, 90, 113, 125, 196, 205, 247, 270, 287–8, 289
    see also chalk grassland *and* culm grassland
grazing animals
    annual die-offs 68, 69–70
    and catastrophic shift 157–9
    and coppicing 127
    dietary/eating differences between species 66
    food availability and herd size 67, 68
    natural population control 67, 68, 75
    in prevention of vegetation succession 60–3, 65, 79, 118, 265, 266
    role of at Knepp 48–9, 113, 114, 118, 175
    seasonality of grazing 68, 253
    see also browsing animals; Oostvaardersplassen; *individual species*

Grazing Animals Project 151
grazing ecology 56–71
grazing systems 18, 23, 24, 287
Great Arber Lake, Germany 241
great bustard (*Otis tarda*) 147
great crested newt (*Triturus cristatus*) 125, 271
Great Fen 288
great sallow *see* goat willow
great spotted woodpecker (*Dendrocopos major*) 26, 47, 238
great white egret (*Ardea alba*) 57
great white shark (*Carcharodon carcharias*) 147
greater butterfly orchid (*Platanthera chlorantha*) 285
greater horseshoe bat (*Rhinolophus ferrumequinum*) 6
Greater Thames Marshes 206
Greece 154, 195
green bridges *see* land bridges
Green, Edward 'Ted' 13, 15, 16, 17, 19, 20, 22, 24, 25, 26, 27, 28, 29, 31, 39, 46, 47, 48, 56, 78, 98, 122, 151, 157, 167, 285, 295
Green, Penny 202, 207, 222, 269
green sandpiper (*Tringa ochropus*) 8, 169, 222
green-veined white *see under* butterflies, species of
green woodpecker (*Picus viridis*) 112, 192
Greenaway, Frank 168
Greenaway, Theresa 150, 168
Greenstreet (droving road) 18
Greenwood, Penelope 19
grey heron (*Ardea cinerea*) 47, 57, 168, 223, 230, 238, 241
grey partridge (*Perdix perdix*) 5, 149
grey willow (*Salix cinerea* subsp. *oleifolia*) 178
greylag goose (*Anser anser*) 57, 59, 60, 98
grizzly bear (*Ursus arctos horribilis*) 154, 155
ground beetles 6, 68
ground ivy (*Glechoma hederacea*) 129
grouse *see* red grouse *and* willow grouse
Gulf of Mexico 279

Haber, Fritz 22
habitat isolation 202–3, 204–5
Habitats Directive (EU) 156, 205, 300

Halley, Duncan 264
Hammer dam 223
Hammer Pond 219, 269, 272, 285
hare, brown, or European (*Lepus
     europaeus*) 68, 170, 172
harvest mouse (*Micromys minutus*) 269
harvestmen 271
Harvey, Graham 286
hawkweeds 143
hawthorn (*Crataegus monogyna*) 1, 17,
     83, 119, 121, 122, 123, 124, 128, 148,
     175, 199, 200
haylage 46
haymaking, and biodiversity 64
hazel (*Corylus avellana*) 78, 82, 83–4, 85,
     86, 123, 127, 128, 148, 199, 224
heather (*Calluna vulgaris*) 224, 225, 226,
     265
heathlands 4, 64, 191
Heck, Lutz 65, 66
Heck cattle *see under* cattle, breeds of
hedgehog (*Erinaceus europaeus*) 7, 148,
     270
hedgerows 4, 24, 36, 119, 190, 193
Heerwagen, Judi 298
Henderson, George 23
Henfield 223
Henry III 28
herb-rich pasture 250, 251, 252
herbicides 21–2, 45, 143, 250
herbivores, large *see* large herbivores
herd mentality, and handling systems
     255–6
Hereford cattle *see under* cattle, breeds of
herons *see* grey heron
herring (*Clupea harengus*) 293
Hicks, Olivia 188–9, 190
Hidden Life of Trees (Wohlleben) 21
high brown fritillary *see under* butterflies,
     species of
Higher Level Stewardship (HLS) 174–5
Highland cattle *see under* cattle, breeds of
Himalayan balsam (*Impatiens
     glandulifera*) 170, 171
Himalayan bar-headed goose (*Anser
     indicus*) 169
hippopotamus (*Hippopotamus
     amphibius*) 128
HLS (Higher Level Stewardship) 174–5
hoary ragwort (*Jacobaea erucifolia*) 143
hobby (*Falco subbuteo*) 8

Hoffmann, Luc 255
holly (*Ilex aquifolium*) 25, 124, 127, 128,
     224
Holocene era 75, 82–7, 127
Holstein cattle *see under* cattle, breeds of
Home Farm *see* Knepp Home Farm
honeysuckle (*Lonicera periclymenum*)
     128
hornbeam (*Carpinus betulus*) 62, 78, 79,
     82, 128
hornworts 271
horrid ground weaver spider
     (*Nothophantes horridus*) 125
horses/ponies
     annual die-offs 69, 70
     attitudes to eating meat of 261–3
     castration 260–1
     and cattle 159
     conservation grazing 260
     diet 66
     interglacial period 127
     at Knepp 260–3, 291
     Kraansvlak 159
     laminitis 105, 106
     meat production 261–2, 263, 292
     Oostvaardersplassen 68
     poisonous plants 143 *see also* common
          ragwort
     selling 75
     supplementary feeding 253
     wild 62, 63, 103
horses/ponies, breeds of
     Camargue horse 255
     Dartmoor pony 261
     Exmoor pony 72, 103–8, 109, 137, 139,
          166, 175, 260–3, 292
     Hucul 103
     Konik 57, 66, 67, 98, 103, 159
     New Forest 260
     Norwegian Fjord 103
     Swedish Gotlandruss 103
     tarpan (*Equus ferus ferus*) 61, 62, 63,
          66, 88, 103, 160
hound's tongue (*Cynoglossum
     officinale*) 158
house martin (*Delichon urbica*) 47, 173
house sparrow (*Passer domesticus*) 8
hoverflies 44, 238
Hucul horses *see under* horses/ponies,
     breeds of
Hulme, Neil 163, 178, 179, 272

human health *see also* nutrition
  accessibility to nature 206, 294–9
  accumulation of chemicals in fatty
      tissues 282
  and consumption of grain-fed
      meat 249
  declining nutritional value of
      foods 280–1
  diseases and soil bacteria 278
  and soil health 215, 289
hummingbird hawkmoth *see under* moths,
  species of

ice-cream business 37, 38
Iceland 164
Imperial College London 16, 188, 192, 274
industrial revolution 4, 99, 216–17, 299
industrialized agriculture *see* farming,
  intensive
Ingham, Elaine 275, 279, 280
injurious weeds 138, 140–1, 142, 146, 165
  see also broad-leaved dock, common
  ragwort, creeping thistle, curled
  dock, spear thistle
inning *see* land restoration
insect parasites 143
insecticides *see* pesticides
insects
  and bats 114
  dune landscapes 158
  decline in UK populations 6, 120, 125,
      203
  migration 164
  and ragwort 142–3
  sound of 44, 175
  travelling methods 44
  see also aquatic invertebrates, bees,
      beetles, bush crickets, butterflies,
      damselflies, dragonflies, flies,
      froghoppers, fungus weevils,
      harvestmen, leafhoppers,
      mayflies, midges, moths, orb
      weavers, soil biota, spiders,
      termites, wasps
Intergovernmental Technical Panel on
  Soils (UN) 284
International Union for Conservation of
  Nature (IUCN) 3
invasive species 113, 139, 169–72, 242
Invertebrate Species and habitats
  Information System (ISIS) 86

invertebrates *see also* insects; *and
      individual species*
  aquatic 238
  and coppicing 128
  decline in populations of 6
  at Knepp 44, 111–12, 166, 169, 271
  and oak trees 26
  saproxylic 47, 48
ISIS (Invertebrate Species and habitats
  Information System) 86
Italian ryegrass (*Lolium multiflorum*) 4,
  16, 250
Italy 262, 282
IUCN (International Union for
  Conservation of Nature)
  see International Union for
  Conservation of Nature
ivy (*Hedera helix*) 143

jack snipe (*Lymnocryptes minimus*) 167
jackals *see* golden jackals
jackdaw (*Coloeus monedula*) 52, 207
Japan 282
jay (*Garrulus glandarius*) 26, 78, 79,
      120–2, 175, 176, 207
Jefferies, Richard 186
Jockey Copse 18
John, King of England 25, 28, 51, 213
John Muir Trust 235
Juniper, Tony 284
juniper (*Juniperus communis*) 123, 224–5,
  265
Jura, France 83

Kampf, Hans 97–8, 151, 219–20, 221,
  263
Kaplan, Rachel 297, 298
Kaplan, Stephen 297, 298
Kendal, Cumbria 226
Kent and Sussex Weald, The (2003) 129
kestrel (*Falco tinnunculus*) 26, 173, 230
Keswick, Cumbria 226
kinetic meditation 297
King John Oak, Woodend Park, Devon
  25
kingfisher (*Alcedo atthis*) 230, 238, 241,
  293
Kirby, Keith 76, 91–2, 93, 118, 161
Kirk Fell, Lake District 224
Knapdale, Argyll 236
knapweed (*Centaurea nigra*) 44

Knepp Castle (Nash/1809+) xiii, xv,
  14, 214 *see also* old Knepp Castle
  (twelfth century)
Knepp Home Farm 31–42, 124, 128, 169,
  214–17, 218–19
Knepp lake *see* Knepp Mill Pond
Knepp Mill 223
Knepp Mill Pond 14, 187, 218, 231, 234,
  245, 269
Knepp Oak 13–15, 78
Knepp park *see* Repton park
Knepp Wildland Safaris (campsite/safari
  business) 292, 304
Knepp Wildland project
  Advisory Board 150–2, 160–1, 309–10
  ecosystem services scoring 288–90
  future of 291–308
Knights Templar 213
Konik pony *see under* horses/ponies,
  breeds of
Kraansvlak, The Netherlands 157–9, 160
krill 248

Lack, Bob 41
lady's bedstraw (*Galium verum*) 44, 158
laggs *see* water meadows
Lake District 223, 224, 225, 303
lakes 83, 84
  at Knepp 74, 219, 263, 271
Lancet 294–5
land abandonment 130, 136, 148, 154–6,
  264, 301
land agents' conference 174
land bridges 94, 159, 292
land degradation 275, 284–5, 300–1
land drainage 212–17, 218–19, 233
  reclamation of marshes 213
Land Girls 18
Land Improvement and Drainage
  Acts 216
land restoration 8–11, 282, 288, 299, 300–1
  see also individual projects
land sparing 300–1
land values 302
landmark trees 25
landscape connectivity 151, 205, 206
  corridors for wildlife 153, 205–6
lapwing (*Vanellus vanellus*) 5, 8, 57, 147,
  204, 222–3
larch (*Larix decidua*) 224
large blue *see under* butterflies, species of

Large Herbivore Foundation 151, 220
large herbivores
  and catastrophic shift 157–9
  earliest presence of 61, 85
  impact of man on populations 62–3
  see also grazing animals;
    Oostvaardersplassen
large predators 62, 67, 69, 105, 152, 153,
  155-6, 204, 267, 304 *see also* brown
  bear, golden jackal, grizzly bear,
  lynx, wolf, wolverine
Lawton, Prof. Sir John 206–7
leafhoppers 271, 281
Lennart von Post, Ernst Jakob 82, 83–4
Leopold, Aldo 154, 308
lesser redpoll (*Carduelis cabaret*) 167, 238
lesser spotted woodpecker (*Dryobates
  minor*) 8, 26, 269
lesser water-parsnip (*Berula erecta*) 271
Lewes, Sussex 209–10
Lewes District Council 227
lichens
  and closed-canopy theory 88
  Ennerdale 224
  at Knepp 112–13
  Kraansvlak 158
  loss of habitat 5, 6, 203
  Norway 265
  and oak trees 26
light-demanding trees and shrubs 83,
  89, 121 *see also* aspen, birch,
  blackthorn, bramble, broom,
  common privet, crab apple, dog
  rose, gorse, hawthorn, hazel,
  juniper, oak, rowan, sallow, Scots
  pine, wild cherry, wild pear, wild
  privet
lime trees 62, 78, 82, 85, 127, 128
Line, Craig 255
Linnartz, Leo 158
linnet (*Linaria cannabina*) 5, 125, 192
little egret (*Egretta garzetta*) 8, 57, 169,
  222
little owl (*Athene noctua*) 115, 170, 173
Littlehampton, Kent 210
liverworts 87, 271
livestock
  accumulation of chemicals in fatty
    tissues 282
  castration 260–1
  and handling systems 255–7

loss to flooding 211
and methane production 250
regulations 253
slaughter of 292
stocking densities 246
supplementary feeding 253
tree fodder for 252
Livestock Handling and Transport
(Grandin) 258
Living Landscapes 55, 151, 205, 206, 267
Liza, river 225
lizard *see* common lizard, sand lizard,
slow-worm
lob worm (*Lumbricus terrestris*) 277
Loch Garten, Speyside 303
Loddon lily (*Leucojum aestivum*) 170
long-eared owl (*Asio otus*) 8, 268
long-tailed tit (*Aegithalos caudatus*) 218
longhorn cattle *see* old English Longhorn
cattle
Lord, Dr Alex 188
lowland heathland, decline in 4
lynx (*Lynx lynx*) 10, 62, 63, 152, 155, 204,
267, 304, 308

McCarthy, Mike 295
mackerel 247
macromoths, and ragwort 142
Madgeland Wood 176
magnesium 70, 279, 280, 281, 285
magpie (*Pica pica*) 55, 207, 293
maiden's blush moth *see under* moths,
species of
Maidment, John 40
Maidstone, Kent 210
*Making Space for Nature: a review
of England's Wildlife Sites and
Ecological Network* 206–7
Malaysia 276, 282
mallard (*Anas platyrhynchos*) 218, 222, 223
Malta 2
Mammal Society 204
mammoth *see* woolly mammoth
mandarin duck (*Aix galericulata*) 222
mantle vegetation 83, 84, 85
maple 78 *see also* field maple (*Acer
campestre*)
marbled white *see under* butterflies,
species of
Marlborough Downs 206
Marlpost Wood 176

Marren, Peter 295
marsh fritillary *see under* butterflies,
species of
marsh frog (*Pelophylax ridibundus*) 57
marsh harrier (*Circus aeruginosus*) 57, 68
marsh ragwort (*Jacobaea aquatica*) 143
marsh speedwell (*Veronica scutellata*) 271
marsh tit (*Poecile palustris*) 129, 238
marshland 59–60, 68, 125, 209, 213, 221,
233, 255, 263
mast years 120
mayflies 271
meadow brown *see under* butterflies,
species of
meadow pipit (*Anthus pratensis*) 120, 147
Meadow Protection Plan (EU) 301–2
meadows
biodiversity of 64
decline in 4, 301–2
negative effect of Meadow Protection
Plan 301–2
Northern Block, at Knepp 94
recovery of 123, 157–9
sourcing native seeds 44–5
support for 142
meadowsweet (*Filipendula ulmaria*) 129
meat sales, at Knepp 75, 303
medicinal properties of vegetation 123,
124, 230, 252
Medmerry, West Sussex 210
megafauna 61, 65, 127, 157, 220
Melitta europaea see under bees, species of
Mens Nature Reserve, Sussex 80, 114
mental health 206, 249, 295, 297
Meon, river 232
Merck's rhinoceros (*Stephanorhinus
kirchbergensis*) 128
Merrik Wood, Knepp 49
meta-populations, and habitat chains 205,
232
methane production 250–1
Mexico 262
mice 26, 68, 121 *see also* dormouse,
harvest mouse, wood mouse,
yellow-necked mouse
micromoths 142
Middle Block
biodiversity 270, 271–2
funding 174, 175
and grazing animals 253–4
location/scope 93, 117

midges 114
millipedes *see under* soil biota
milk quotas, effects of 34, 38, 41
milkcap mushrooms 26, 285
mindfulness 297
mining bees 158
Ministry of Agriculture, Fisheries and
    Food 140
mink *see* American mink
mirror carp (*Cyprinus carpio carpio*) 218
Mississippi, river 279
mistle thrush (*Turdus viscivorus*) 112
mixed-farming systems 23, 24, 37–9
mob grazing 287
mole ploughs 41, 216–17
molluscs, life cycle and habitat 205
Monbiot, George 10, 295
money spiders (*Trematocephalus
    cristatus*) 271
Montagu's harrier (*Circus pygargus*)
    268
monumental trees *see* landmark trees
moorhen (*Gallinula chloropus*) 223
moose *see* Eurasian elk
Morocco 162
mosquitoes 114
Moss, Charles 82
mosses
    and beavers 238
    and closed-canopy theory 87
    decline in populations of 6
    at Knepp 113, 271
    Kraansvlak 158
    Norway 265
moths
    decline in UK populations 6
    at Knepp 114, 166, 169, 272
    and ragwort 142, 143, 147
    see also macromoths
moths, species of
    beautiful china mark moth (*Nymphula
        nitidulata*) 272
    canary-shouldered thorn moth
        (*Ennomos alniaria*) 272
    cinnabar moth (*Tyria jacobaeae*) 142
    coxcomb prominent (*Ptilodon
        capucina*) 272
    dusky thorn moth (*Ennomos
        fuscantaria*) 272
    figure of eight moth (*Diloba
        caeruleocephala*) 272

hummingbird hawkmoth
    (*Macroglossum stellatarum*) 114
maiden's blush moth (*Cyclophora
    punctaria*) 272
rush wainscot moth (*Globia algae*) 272
waved black moth (*Parascotia
    fuliginaria*) 272
mud 34–6
Mull, Isle of 304
muntjac deer (*Muntiacus reevesi*) 49, 267
mycorrhizae/mycorrhizal fungi 20–2, 30,
    275, 281, 285, 286, 287, 290

names, origins 28, 50–1, 124, 128
narrow-nosed rhinoceros (*Stephanorhinus
    hemiotechus*) 128
Nash, John 14
National Farmers' Union 23, 134–5, 148,
    193, 237, 243
National Health Service 295
National Parks, UK 4, 207
National Parks, US 4, 154
National Trust 150, 176, 193, 223, 237
National Trust for Scotland 235
Natterer's bat (*Myotis nattereri*) 238
natterjack toad (*Epidalea calamita*) 125
Natura 2000 (EU) 300
natural capital 151, 304
natural capital accounting 304
Natural Capital Committee 306
Natural England
    Invertebrate Species and habitats
        Information System 86
    and Knepp Wildland project 151, 161,
        174–5
    meadow loss report 301
    Natural Thinking 295
    and nightingales at Knepp 193
    Operation Turtle Dove 199
    and ragwort 143
    Wild Ennerdale 223
Natural Environment Research
    Council 284
naturalistic grazing systems 77, 96, 253–4,
    287, 333
naturalistic livestock system *see* naturalistic
    grazing systems
nature, accessibility to and effect on
    health 293–6
nature conservation, disincentives for
    farmers 302–3

nature conservation, history of 63
Nature Improvement Areas 206, 207
nature reserves, in UK 4
necrophagous insects 74
neighbours, attitudes to project 98,
    129–31, 137, 193, 292
Netherlands 92, 94, 157–9, 220–1, 227,
    240, 300
nettle *see* stinging nettle
New Forest, Hampshire 83, 87, 124, 176
New Forest pony *see under* horses/ponies,
    breeds of
New Zealand 276
Newhaven, East Sussex 210
newts *see* common, great-crested *and*
    palmate newts
NFU *see* National Farmers' Union
NHS *see* National Health Service
nightingale (*Luscinia megarhynchos*) 2, 8,
    129, 184–93, 267, 292, 302
nightjar (*Caprimulgus europaeus*) 147, 269
nitrates 21–2, 45, 46, 239, 277, 279–80
nitrogen 26, 46, 70, 279
nitrogen-fixating crops 23, 46
non-native species 169–72
North American beaver (*Castor
    canadensis*) 233, 239–40
North Devon 206
Northern Block
    biodiversity 270, 271–2
    creeping thistle outbreak 162
    funding 174, 175
    and grazing animals 117–18, 122, 250,
        252, 253
    location/scope 93–4, 97
    wild daffodils 143
Norton-Griffiths, Michael 65
Norway 156, 264–6
Norwegian Fjord pony *see under* horses/
    ponies, breeds of
Norwegian Institute for Nature
    Research 264
Noss, Reed 153
NPK (nitrogen, phosphorus, potassium)
    see individual components
nuthatch (*Sitta europaea*) 26
nutrition
    conjugated linoleic acid (CLA) 248,
        249
    declining value in foods 280–1
    fatty acids 247–8, 249, 251

omega oils 247–8, 249, 260
pasture-fed meat 247–9

oak trees
    ageing process 15, 26–7, 46–7
    ancient 24–6, 27, 28, 46, 79, 89
    and biodiversity 26–7, 269, 271, 272
    bog trees 78
    and butterflies 180–1, 296
    and closed-canopy forests 77–80
    coppicing 127, 296
    earliest presence of 62, 82–3
    and fungi 20–2, 27–8
    growing requirements 26, 78–80, 121
    and jays 120–2, 175
    at Knepp 13–15, 17, 18, 46–7, 120, 122
    root systems 19–20
Oates, Matthew 150, 176, 177, 178, 179,
    180, 295
oceanic liverwort *see* fingered cowlwort
old English longhorn cattle *see under*
    cattle, breeds of
old Knepp Castle (twelfth century) *see also*
    Knepp Castle (Nash/1809+)
    deer park 50, 95, 117
    location/origin xiii, 28, 50–1, 116
    nearby water 210, 213, 214
omega oils 247–8, 249, 260
Oostvaardersplassen 56–71, 73, 74, 92, 152
open grasslands, existence in prehistoric
    times 84
open wood pasture *see* wood pasture
Operation Turtle Dove 199–201, 202, 207
orb weaver spiders 271
orchids 18, 88, 238, 285 *see also* bird's
    nest, common spotted, early purple,
    greater butterfly *and* southern
    marsh orchid
Orians, Gordon 298
osprey (*Pandion haliaetus*) 8, 292, 303
Otter, river 242–4, 304
otter (*Lutra lutra*) 6, 75, 155, 231
Ottery St Mary 243
Our Vanishing Flora (2012) report 6
Ouse, river 209, 210, 227
Ouse and Adur River Trust 222
over-grazing 139, 224, 225, 263, 264–5
over-production 132, 135
owls 26, 68, 230, 268 *see also* barn owl,
    little owl, long-eared owl, short-
    eared owl

ox-eye daisy (*Leucanthemum vulgare*) 44
Oxford University 282

Packham, Chris 295
painted lady *see under* butterflies, species
	of
palmate newt (*Lissotriton helveticus*) 270
palynology 61, 77–8, 82–5, 91
pannage 13, 89
parasites, natural control of 158
parasiticides 114, 115, 158 *see also*
	avermectins
parasol mushroom (*Macrolepiota
	procera*) 114
park restoration projects 39
Parliament Oak, Sherwood Forest 25
pasture-fed meat
	beef 33, 246–7, 248, 250, 251, 260
	definition 249–50
	horse 261–3
	and methane production 250–1
	nutrition 247–9
	pork 260
Pasture for Life accreditation 249–50
pasture lands, biodiversity of 64
Pauly, Daniel 147
PCB (polychlorinated biphenyl) 282
peafowl (*Pavo cristatus*) 172
pear *see* wild pear
pearl-bordered fritillary *see under*
	butterflies, species of
Pearson, John 215
Pearson's draining plough 214–15, 216
pedunculate oak (*Quercus robur*) 78, 121
penduline tit (*Remiz pendulinus*) 57
Penrith, Cumbria 226
Percy the Peacock 172
Père David deer 263
peregrine falcon (*Falco peregrinus*) 8, 269
perimeter fencing 49, 93–4, 108–9, 118,
	133, 175
permanent pasture
	acreage in UK 135
	reducing CO_2 levels 287
permeability indexes 203, 204
permissive footpaths 291
pesticides 21–22, 113, 271, 274–5, 281,
	300
Petworth estate, fallow deer 49, 52
pheasant (*Phasianus colchicus*) 26, 45, 170,
	207

Phellinus robustus (bracket fungus) 27,
	204
Philippines 282
phosphate 21, 26, 45, 46, 239, 277
phosphorus 70, 74, 279
physical health, in humans 206
Pickering, Yorkshire Dales 226, 239
pied flycatcher (*Ficedula hypoleuca*) 26
pigs *see also* Tamworth pigs *and* wild boar
	and annual and biennial weed
		species 201
	diet 133
	herd mentality 255
	at Knepp 109–10, 137, 138, 166, 182
	meat production 259–60
	and sallow 182
	slaughter of 292
	and visiting public 293
pine marten (*Martes martes*) 231
pine-woods 80, 159 *see also individual
	species*
pink-footed goose (*Anser
	brachyrhynchus*) 174
pipistrelle bat (*Pipistrellus pipistrellus*) 114,
	168
place names, origins 28, 50–1, 124, 128
plant communities, catastrophic shift 156
plant-growth hormones 34
Plant Succession (Clements) 64
Plantlife 142
plants *see* flora
Platystomos albians (weevil) 271
Pleasure Grounds 45, 54, 101
Pleistocene era 127–8
ploughing 3, 302
	action of wild boar and pigs 73, 201,
		259
	ancient meadows and pasture land 45,
		251, 302
	Dig for Victory campaign 18
	early agriculture 81
	effect on soil 274
	effect on trees 19, 20, 21, 24
ploughs 214–15, 216–17 *see also* mole
	ploughs
Plumpton, East Sussex 209
poaching 293
Podoscypha multizonata (zoned rosette
	fungus) 27, 204
Poland 154
polecat (*Mustela putorius*) 68, 231, 269

pollarding 25, 64, 252
pollen 61, 77–8, 82–5, 86, 91, 141, 143, 203, 273
pollinators 6, 171, 206, 273, 300 *see also individual species*
pollution levels
    and beavers 239
    UK performance 299–300
polychlorinated biphenyl (PCB) 282
Pondtail Farm 162
ponies *see* horses/ponies
Pontbren, Brecon Beacons 227
Poorter, Ernst 59
pop-up Knepps 283
poppy (*Papaver rhoeas*) 147, 170
population densities, effects of species isolation 202–3
Portugal 154
potassium 70, 279
Pound Farm 210
Pownall, Thomas 81
predators 2, 21, 32, 62, 143, 152, 153, 155–6, 189, 204, 207, 267, 270, 304 *see also* large predators *and* small predators
primal/primeval forest 61, 78, 81–2, 85
priority species *see* biodiversity, UK Biodiversity Action Plan species
privet *see* wild privet
Prostomis mandibularis (beetle) 86
Public Health England 294
public relations 150
public rights of way 110, 111, 137, 258, 291, 292
Pumlumon, Wales 288
purple emperor *see under* butterflies, species of
purple hairstreak *see under* butterflies, species of
purple moor grass (*Molinia caerulea*) 238
PWN (Dutch water company) 158
Pyrenees 154

quail (*Coturnix coturnix*) 5
Quammen, David 5
Queen of Spain fritillary *see under* butterflies, species of

rabbit (*Oryctolagus cuniculus*) 68, 122–3, 126, 139, 145, 157, 170, 172, 173, 190

Rackham, Oliver 77–8, 80, 88
Raeburn, John 23
ragged robin (*Lychnis flos-cuculi*) 44, 129
Ragwort Control Act, 2003 141
ragwort *see* common, hoary *and* marsh ragwort
rainbow trout (*Oncorhynchus mykiss*) 172, 241
raptors 171, 268 *see also* buzzard, goshawk, kestrel, owls, peregrine falcon, red kite, sparrowhawk, white-tailed eagle
Rare Breeds Survival Trust 99, 104, 109
rarity of species, and attitudes to 170
rats 70
raven (*Corvus corax*) 8, 167–8, 207
raw materials/fibre, as ecosystem service 288
Raymond, Sir Charles 14
Raymond, Sophia 14
recreation, as ecosystem service 288, 289
red-backed shrike (*Lanius collurio*) 125, 158, 269
red bartsia bee *see under* bees, species of
red clover (*Trifolium pratense*) 44
red deer (*Cervus elaphus*) 49, 57, 61, 63, 66, 67, 68, 70, 72, 127, 139, 263, 265, 266, 267
red fox (*Vulpes vulpes*) 47, 57, 68, 70, 94, 204, 269
red grouse (*Lagopus lagopus scotica*) 4, 224, 265, 299
red kite (*Milvus milvus*) 6, 8
Red Poll cattle *see under* cattle, breeds of
red-spotted bluethroat (*Luscinia svecica*) 265
red squirrel (*Sciurus vulgaris*) 224
redstart (*Phoenicurus phoenicurus*) 265
redundancies, at Knepp 40
redwing (*Turdus iliacus*) 120, 167
reed-beds 6, 60, 263
reed mace (*Typha latifolia*) 113, 218, 272
reed warbler (*Acrocephalus scirpaceus*) 57, 218
Reg (digger driver) 222
reindeer (*Rangifer tarandus*) 255
reptiles 44 *see also* grass snake
Repton, Humphry 17, 46, 298
Repton park
    Countryside Stewardship Scheme funding 39, 93

Repton park (*cont.*)
    deer 48–52, 55, 93–5, 117, 130
    injurious weeds 145, 162
    land drainage 212–17, 218–19, 233
    oak trees 13–15, 46–7, 78, 120, 122
    restoration area 49, 93–4, 97, 117
    Second World War 17–19
    wildflower meadows 45–6
rewilding
    attitudes to 9, 91, 92, 129–31, 137, 153,
        291, 292, 299, 301
    costs 301, 302
    definitions 152, 157, 160–1
    and ecosystems services 9, 10, 288, 289,
        300, 303
    effect on biodiversity 7, 182
    effect on landscape 119, 227, 299, 304
    in Europe 160
    in the US 154, 156
    tourism 303, 304
    UK government response to 91, 92,
        93, 118
    as programme of soil restoration 283,
        285
Rewilding Britain (charity) 10
Rewilding Europe 155
Rewilding Institute (US) 153
Rhode Island, University of 240
rhododendron (*Rhododendron
        ponticum*) 113, 170, 172
Richard II 28
ridge-cheeked furrow bee *see under* bees,
        species of
rights of way *see* public rights of way
ring-necked parakeet (*Psittacula
        krameri*) 171
ringlet *see under* butterflies, species of
River Adur Navigation Act 212
rivers 156–7, 221, 225–8 *see also* floods;
        *individual rivers, re-naturalization
        of*
roads, impact on wildlife 94
robin (*Erithacus rubecula*) 55, 112
roe deer (*Capreolus capreolus*) 49, 61, 63,
        66, 68, 70, 75, 88, 89, 94, 122, 152,
        265, 266, 267
Romania 79, 83, 240, 256
Romney Marsh 212
rook (*Corvus frugilegus*) 26, 52, 168, 207
Rookery 49
Room for the River project 221

rotational farming systems *see* farming,
        rotational systems
Rothamsted Research, Harpenden 164
rough-backed blood bee *see under* bees,
        species of
rowan (*Sorbus aucuparia*) 83, 224, 265
Royal Bank of Canada 227
Royal Saxon Academy of Forestry 90
Royal Society 287
RSPB
    and beavers 237
    decline in UK bird populations 4–5
    and Knepp Wildland project 193, 202
    Natural Thinking 295
    and red-backed shrikes 269
    and turtle doves 195, 196, 197, 199, 202
rural tourism 303–4
rush wainscot moth *see under* moths,
        species of
Rutland Water 303
ryegrass *see* Italian ryegrass

SACs (Special Areas of Conservation) 4
safaris 292
Sahel zone, Africa 196, 198
sainfoin (*Onobrychis viciifolia*) 23
St John's wort (*Hypericum
        perforatum*) 143
sallow 17, 100, 148–9, 175, 176, 177,
        178–9, 181, 182, 183, 208, 246, 285,
        292 *see also individual species*
salmonella 278
salmonids 221, 234, 241, 247, 248
sand, colonization of 158, 159
sand lizard (*Lacerta agilis*) 158
sand martin (*Riparia riparia*) 230
sand wasps 158
        Gorytes laticinctus 273
Sandom, Dr Chris 86
saplings
    as food source 66
    protective value of thorny scrub 79, 90,
        122, 124, 126–7, 175
saproxylic beetles 47, 86, 203
        Dryophthorus corticalis 86
        Prostomis manibularis 86
SARISA (Soil and Rhizosphere
        Interactions for Sustainable
        Agri-ecosystems) 285
Savernake Forest, Wiltshire 176
Savory, Alan 287

Scandinavia 136, 155
scarce chaser dragonfly (*Libellula fulva*) 271
scarce tortoiseshell *see under* butterflies, species of
scarlet pimpernel (*Anagallis arvensis*) 3
scaup duck (*Aythya marila*) 169
scavenging animals 73, 168, 197, 198, 292
Schwab, Gerhard 241, 242
Scotland 185, 230, 232, 235, 236, 241, 244, 263-6, 296, 303, 304
Scots pine (*Pinus sylvestris*) 48, 80, 224, 265
Scottish Beaver Trial 237, 244
Scottish Highlands 63, 235, 263, 264, 265, 266
Scottish National Heritage 235
Scottish Wildlife Trust 236
scrub *see also* thorny scrub
    decline in 3, 17
    and grazing animals 48, 252
    at Knepp 118, 120, 122-3, 126-7, 129, 148, 174-5, 270
    Norway 265
    returning to agricultural conditions 283-4
    and specific conservation targets 302
    and turtle doves 199
    value of 123-6
    Vera theory 77, 83, 86-7
sea trout (*Salmo trutta*) 223
Second World War 17-19, 22-3, 104
seed-bearing weeds, decline in 6
seeds
    sourcing native 44
    transportation of 158
Serengeti 65, 84
Serengeti: Dynamics of an Ecosystem (Norton-Griffiths/Sinclair) 65
sessile oak (*Quercus petraea*) 78, 121
set-aside 95-6, 119
setaceous Hebrew character moth (*Xestia c-nigrum*) 272
Severn, river 210
sewage treatment plants, and worms 278
Seymour, Jim 161
shade-tolerant trees 79-80, 85, 86
sharp-flowered rush (*Juncus acutiflorus*) 238
sheep
    collapse of, in Norway 264

effect as grazers 4, 67, 224, 225, 227, 264
farming 33, 211, 241, 251
foot and mouth disease 42
grain-based diet 33
herd mentality 255
Jacob 48, 55
    at Knepp 37, 48, 55, 293
    non-native to Western Europe 67
    as reason for large predator control 62, 155
    soil compaction caused by 227
shepherd's purse (*Capsella bursa-pastoris*) 251
shifting baseline syndrome 147-8, 191
Shipley Parish Council 130-1
Shipley village
    effects of Second World War 18-19
    and Knepp project 130-1
    location 93
    and ragwort 144
    and role of river 210, 213, 219, 223
shooting, unauthorized 293
Shoreham, Kent 210, 213
short-eared owl (*Asio flammeus*) 268
short-haired bumblebee (*Bombus subterraneus*) 6
short-tailed/field vole (*Microtus agrestis*) 47, 230, 270
shrew *see* common shrew
Shropshire 210
shrubs 82, 157 *see also individual species*
signal crayfish (*Pacifastacus leniusculus*) 170
sika deer (*Cervus nippon*) 49, 267
silver fir (*Abies alba*) 78
silver-washed fritillary (*Argynnis paphia*) 129, 296
Silwood Park, Imperial College 16
Simard, Suzanne 21
Simpson, Alf and Iris 168
Sinclair, Anthony 65, 84
Single Farm Payment *see* farming subsidies, Basic Payment
sitatunga antelope 263
Sites of Special Scientific Interest (SSSIs) 4, 125, 143, 170, 203-4, 302
sitka spruce (*Picea sitchensis*) 223
skunk bear *see* wolverine
skylark (*Alauda arvensi*) 5, 8, 57, 115, 116, 120, 147, 167, 223

Slovenia 83
slow-worm (*Anguis fragilis*) 8, 148, 270
small copper *see under* butterflies, species
    of
small heath *see under* butterflies, species of
small-leafed lime (*Tilia cordata*) 147
small mammals
    habitat 68, 123, 158, 203, 230, 269–70
    predators of 121, 123, 204
    see also bank vole, common shrew,
        dormouse, field vole, harvest
        mouse, rats, short-tailed vole,
        squirrels, water vole, water
        shrew, wood mouse, yellow-
        necked mouse
small predators 123, 269
    see also polecats, stoats, weasels, water
        shrew
small skipper *see under* butterflies, species
    of
small tortoiseshell *see under* butterflies,
    species of
Smeaton, John 27
smooth-leaved elm (*Ulmus minor*) 78
snails 87, 113, 238
snake's head fritillary (*Fritillaria
    meleagris*) 170
snares, unauthorized 293
snowdrop (*Galanthus nivalis*) 170
soil
    and carbon sequestration 287, 288, 289
    catastrophic shift 156
    and earthworms 274–7, 282, 283
    erosion 225, 275
    and glomalin 286–7
    at Knepp 34–6
    natural management of 222, 277
    role of soil biota/microbes 274–9, 281,
        284–5, 287
    Sustainable Development Goals
        (UN) 284
    topsoil depletion 275
    value of restoration 206, 227, 282, 283
soil biota/microbes, role of 274–9, 281,
        284–5, 287
    bacteria *see* bacteria
    centipedes and millipedes 278
    collembola, or springtails 278, 281
    earthworms *see* earthworms
    enchytraeid worms 278
    nematodes 275, 277, 278, 281

mites 277, 278, 281
    protozoa 275, 277, 278, 281
soil compaction 274
soil erosion, 225, 275; natural management
    of 222, 277
Soil Food Web 278
soil run-off 239
Soil Science Association of America 240
soil sterilization 45
soldier beetles 271
solitary bees 112, 142
solitary wasps 142
Somerset 127, 239
Song of the Dodo, The (Quammen) 5
song thrush (*Turdus philomelos*) 146, 192,
        193
songbirds 4, 5, 68, 240, 268 *see also
        individual species*
Soulé, Michael 153
South America 262, 279
South Downs 18, 206
Southern Block
    biodiversity 119–22, 167–9, 171, 176,
        179–80, 207–8, 269–75
    birds 184–5, 207–8
    butterflies 176, 177–81, 272
    funding 95, 174, 175
    fungi 285
    and grazing animals 119, 122–3, 175,
        252, 263
    location/scope 93, 118–19, 150
    neighbours'/visitors' attitudes to
        130–1, 293
    progress of 291, 298
southern marsh orchid (*Dactylorhiza
    praetermissa*) 285
Southwater 176
Spain 2, 154
Spanish fighting bull *see under* cattle,
    breeds of
sparrowhawk (*Accipiter nisus*) 8, 26, 47,
    68
spear thistle (*Cirsium vulgare*) 113, 140
Special Areas of Conservation (SACs) 4
Special Protection Areas (SPAs) 4
species isolation 202–3, 204–5
Spencer, Jonathan 150
sperm whale (*Physeter macrocephalus*) 147
sphagnum moss 224
spiders 238, 271, 278
    see also crab spiders, money spiders

horrid ground weaver spider
(*Nothophantes horridus*) 125
spindle (*Euonymus europaea*) 123, 143,
158
spoonbill (*Platalea leucorodia*) 57
spotted flycatcher (*Muscicapa striata*) 8,
147, 238
Spring Wood 49, 114, 127, 129, 296
Spring Wood Pond 219
Springwatch 243–4
spurges 129
squirrels 26, 121
see also red squirrel
SSSIs see Sites of Special Scientific Interest
standing water, pollution levels 289
Standish, Arthur 124
Stapledon, Sir George 22, 23
star moss (*Tortula ruralis*) 224
starling (*Sturnus vulgaris*) 173
starvation, as natural process 69
State of Nature reports 5–7
Status of World Soil Resources (UN) 275
steely blue beetle (*Korynetes caeruleu*)
271
sterilization, soil 45
Steyning 213
Sting in the Tail, A (Goulson) 273
stinging nettle (*Urtica dioica*) 100, 101,
172, 190
stoat (*Mustela erminea*) 68, 173, 269
stock dove (*Columba oenas*) 207
stocking densities, livestock 150
Stonehenge 87
stoneworts 113
storms, as natural process 81
straight-tusked elephant (*Palaeoloxodon*
antiquus) 128
Stroud Sustainable Drainage Project 239
subsidies, see farming subsidies
supplementary feeding 65, 75, 201, 253,
263
Sussex Biodiversity Record Centre 150
Sussex Flow Initiative 227
Sussex University 273
Sussex Weald
agriculture 129, 131
clay soil 34–6, 113, 215
iron industry 25
origins of name 89–90
wildflower meadows 45, 46
Sussex Wildlife Trust 98, 150, 205, 227

Sustainable Development Goals (UN)
284
swallow prominent moth (*Pheosia*
tremula) 272
Swallows Farm 93
swan mussel (*Anodonta cygnea*) 259
Swanson, Jim 151
Sweden 94, 154, 300
Swedish Gotlandruss pony see under
horses/ponies, breeds of
sweet chestnut (*Castanea sativa*) 127, 170
sweet vernal grass (*Anthoxanthum*
odoratum) 44
swift (*Apus apus*) 173
Switzerland 156, 240
sycamore (*Acer pseudoplatanus*) 78, 157,
158, 159

tagging livestock 100
tall herb fen vegetation 238
Tamworth pigs 108–11, 139, 175, 259–60
Tansley, Sir Arthur 64, 82
tansy (*Tanacetum vulgare*) 143
targeted conservation interventions, effects
of 302
tarpan see under horses/ponies, breeds of
taxation, and farming 302–3
Tayside 235, 236
TB testing 254
teal (*Anas crecca*) 218
Ted see Green, Edward 'Ted'
tenant farmers, at Knepp 33
Tenchford 210, 223
termites 278
Texas, University of 280–1
Thames, river 210
Thompson, Ken 172
thorny scrub see also scrub; wood pasture
and grazing animals 117, 123, 159
intolerance for 90, 126
at Knepp 119
at Kraansvlak 159
and land abandonment 61
and nightingales 190-1
and oak trees 79, 122, 124
as protection for saplings 79, 126
as protection for woodland 124
regulatory protection of 89
value of 124–7
Vera theory 84, 85, 89, 90, 117
as wind break 84, 85

3 Cs (Cores, Corridors and
    Carnivores) 153
tidal marshes, reclamation of 213
tiger beetles 158
timber trade 17–18, 90
toad *see* common toad
Toe, Patrick 255
Toll Rides Off-road Trust (TROT) 291
topsoil depletion 215, 275, 276
Tour du Valat, Camargue, France 254–5
tourism 303–4
Town Field 115
tree fodder 252
tree pollen 82–5
tree sparrow (*Passer montanus*) 5
treecreeper (*Certhia familiaris*) 26, 173,
    238
trees
    dead wood 27, 46–7, 48, 238, 271, 273
    disease 21, 81, 207
    earliest presence of 61–2, 82–3
    and industrialized agriculture 24
    natural protection for saplings 124,
        126–7
    regeneration 63, 80, 90, 126
    role of decay 46–7, 48
    as tree fodder 252
    see also individual species
Trematocephalus cristatus (spider) 271
Trent, river 210
Trichomonas gallinae (bird disease) 196,
    199
trophic cascades *see* apex predator trophic
    cascades
trout, migration 234
truffles 26
Tudor Vermin Acts 233
Tumbledown Lagg 115
tuna 147, 247
Tunbridge Wells, Kent 210
turtle dove (*Streptopelia turtur*) 1–3, 4, 5,
    6, 7, 148, 194–202, 207–8, 292, 307,
    308

Uckfield, Sussex 210
UK, potential effects of leaving EU 156,
    299, 300
UK Biodiversity Action Plan species 8,
    169, 170, 269
Ulrich, Roger 297
United Nations 132, 275, 284

United States 22, 153, 155, 233–4, 240,
    247, 257, 264, 278, 282
United Utilities 223
University of California 287
University of Exeter 239, 244
University of Rhode Island 240
University of Texas 280–1
US Agricultural Research Service 286

vaccinations, livestock 254–5
Vegetation Ecology of Central Europe
    (Ellenberg) 64
vegetation succession 60, 61, 63, 79, 118,
    175, 264, 265, 266
Vera, Frans 56, 58–60, 64, 69, 76, 77–91,
    117–18, 151, 157, 220
Vera theory 77–91
vermicompost 279, 282
Vermin Acts 233
Vermuyden, Cornelius 220
Vertical Looking Radars (VLRs) 164
Victorian era 212–17, 219, 299
violas 158
violet *see* common dog-violet
violet click beetle (*Limoniscus
    violaceus*) 203–4
viruses, role of soil biota/microbes 278
Vision for the Wildlife of Sussex, A
    (1996) 205
Vlasakker, Joep van der 103, 151
VLRs 164
vocabulary, of nature 293
volunteers, conservation reliance on 127

Wageningen University, Soil Biology
    group 278
Wainwright, Alfred 224
Walker, Alice 105
walled brown *see under* butterflies, species
    of
Walpole-Bond, John 191, 195
wapiti (*Cervus canadensis*, known as 'elk'
    in US) 240
wasps 142, 203
    Crabro scutellatus 273
    see also sand wasps
water *see also* floods *and* ephemeral ponds
    catastrophic shift 156, 157–8
    as ecosystem service 288, 289
    management of 220–1, 224–8
    pollution levels 239

purification 206, 221, 227, 239
storage 234, 306
understanding 220–1
water beetles, in ephemeral ponds 113
water crowfoot (*Ranunculus aquatilis*) 113
water meadows (laggs) 17, 167, 168, 178,
218, 219, 221, 263
as flood mitigation 221
at Knepp 114, 167, 168, 218, 219
and red deer 263
Second World War 17
water mint (*Mentha aquatica*) 238
water plants, decline in populations of 6
water shrew (*Neomys fodiens*) 269
water starwort (*Callitriche stagnalis*) 113
water violet (*Hottonia palustris*) 271
water vole (*Arvicola amphibious*) 7, 68,
230–2, 245
Watkins-Pitchford, Denys 'BB' 178
waved black moth *see under* moths, species
of
Weald Meadows Initiative 45, 46
weasel (*Mustela nivalis*) 68, 155, 269
Weeds Act, 1959 140
weeds, seed-bearing, decline in 6
weirs, removal of 221–2, 223
West Grinstead 18, 212
West Sussex County Times 137
Westonbirt Arboretum,
Gloucestershire 127
wet dune slacks/hollows 159
wetland 4, 174, 191, 221, 227, 254–5
see also beavers; Oostvaardersplassen
whales 303
Wharfe, river 210
wheat crops 18, 34
as fuel 134
at Knepp 36
price of 96
yields 135
wheatear (*Oenanthe oenanthe*) 112, 265
Where Do Camels Belong?
(Thompson) 172
whiskered bat (*Myotis mystacinus*) 168
Whitbread, Dr Tony 98, 150
Whitby, Dave 52
white admiral *see under* butterflies, species
of
White Belgian cattle *see under* cattle,
breeds of
white bryony (*Bryonia dioica*) 143

white-clawed crayfish (*Austropotamobius
pallipes*) 170
white hart 51
white-letter hairstreak *see under*
butterflies, species of
White Park cattle *see under* cattle, breeds
of
white poplar (*Populus alba*) 157, 158
white stork (*Ciconia ciconia*) 268, 292
white-tailed sea eagle (*Haliaeetus
albicilla*) 57–8, 70, 304
whitethroat (*Sylvia communis*) 192
Wicker, John 94
wigeon (*Anas penelope*) 218
wild angelica (*Angelica sylvestris*) 251
wild animals *see also individual species*
disease risks 73
and early 'forests' 89
quality of lives 69–70
wild apple *see* crab apple
wild boar (*Sus scrofa*) 13, 28, 29, 55, 61, 63,
73, 75, 88, 94, 108–9, 127, 155, 182,
201, 234, 265, 292
wild cherry (*Prunus avium*) 83, 89
wild daffodil (*Narcissus
pseudonarcissus*) 143
Wild Ennerdale 223–6, 288
wild horses 62, 63, 103
wild mouflon (*Ovis orientalis*) 67
wild pear (*Pyrus communis*) 83, 89
wild privet (*Ligustrum vulgare*) 83
Wild Purbeck 206
wild service tree (*Sorbus torminalis*) 126,
175
wild thyme (*Thymus serpyllum*) 113
Wild Wood Day 97
wildflower meadows *see* meadows
Wildlands Network, US 153
Wildlands Project, US *see* Wildlands
Network
Wildlife & Countryside Link 139, 141
Wildlife and Wetlands Trust 237
Wildlife Conservation Society 240
wildlife corridors 153, 205–6
wildlife tourism 292, 303–4
Wildlife Trusts
Devon 237–8, 243, 244
Living Landscapes 205
Nature Improvement Areas 207
Nightingale Workshop 193
Scottish 236

Wildlife Trusts (*cont.*)
  size of sites 203
  Sussex 98, 150, 205, 227
Willams, Bud 255
Williams, Eunice 255
willow grouse (*Lagopus lagopus*) 265
willow (*Salix* spp.) 58, 59, 68, 69, 123, 127,
    182, 230, 234, 238, 241, 245, 265
  see also individual species
willow tit (*Poecile montanus*) 125, 238
willow warbler (*Phylloscopus*
    trochilus) 125, 129
Wilson, E. O. 5, 29, 6–7, 298
Windsor Great Park 204
wisent (*Bison bonasus*) 61, 65 see also
    European bison (*Bison bonasus*)
Wohlleben, Peter 21
wolf (*Canis lupus*) 10, 62, 63, 74, 152, 155,
    156, 165, 204, 304, 308
wolverine (*Gulo gulo*) 62, 155, 304, 308
Wood, Andrew 174
wood anemone (*Anemone nemorosa*) 129
wood mouse, or long-tailed field mouse
    (*Apodemus sylvaticus*) 79, 270
wood pasture
  effects on pollen dispersal 84–5
  English Nature debate on 92
  and jays 121
  and hazel 83-4, 85
  in the Holocene era 87, 298
  at Knepp 50, 270, 298, 299
  and oak trees 79, 121
  in medieval times 50, 88, 90, 299
  in Romania 79, 83, 256
  and saproxylic beetles 86
  and thorny scrub 84, 85, 90
  Vera theory 79, 83–8, 98
wood pigeon (*Columba palumbus*) 26,
    207
wood white see under butterflies, species
    of
woodcock (*Scolopax rusticola*) 8, 167, 204,
    238, 267

Woodend Park, Devon 25
woodland, decline in 3–4
woodland fires, as natural process 80
Woodland Trust 56, 126, 227
woodlark (*Lullula arborea*) 8, 158, 167
woolly mammoth (*Mammuthus*
    primigenius) 74
Worcestershire 210
Workington, Cumbria 226
World Wildlife Fund 255
worm casts, value of 274, 278–9, 283
worms see earthworms *and individual*
    species
Wren, Gill 283
wren (*Troglodytes troglodytes*) 112
Wright, Sara 286
wych elm (*Ulmus glabra*) 78, 123
Wye, river 275

Y2Y see Yukon to Yellowstone
    Conservation Initiative
Yasmin (PA to Charlie) 255
yellow archangel (*Lamium*
    galeobdolon) 129
yellow iris (*Iris pseudacorus*) 272
yellow loosestrife (*Lysimachia*
    vulgaris) 273
yellow-necked mouse (*Apodemus*
    flavicollis) 270
yellowhammer (*Emberiza citrinella*) 5, 8,
    120, 192
Yellowstone National Park 154
yew (*Taxus baccata*) 143, 172, 173
Yorkshire 210
Yukon to Yellowstone Conservation
    Initiative (Y2Y) 154

zander (*Sander lucioperca*) 241
zero-grazing, effects of Common Market
    policies 33
zoned rosette fungus (*Podoscypha*
    multizonata) 27
Zoological Society of London 155